Psychology
and Theology
In Western Thought
1672-1965
A Historical and Annotated Bibliography

Bibliographies
in the
History of Psychology and Psychiatry
A Series

Robert H. Wozniak, General Editor

Psychology and Theology

In Western Thought

1672-1965

A Historical and Annotated Bibliography

Hendrika Vande Kemp

In collaboration with H. Newton Malony

KRAUS INTERNATIONAL PUBLICATIONS
Millwood, New York
A Division of Kraus-Thomson Organization Limited

First printing 1984

Printed in the United States of America

Portions of the following entries are taken from *Encounter with Books: A Guide to Christian Reading*, ed. by Harish D. Merchant. Second printing, November 1971. Intervarsity Press, Downers Grove, Illinois 60615: numbers 6, 196, 335, 350, 354, 386, 389, 392, 456, 543, 548, 586, 635, 782, 798, 805, 808, 819, 828, 852, 859, 881, 882, 883, 909, 916, 918, 919, 920, 930, 947, 971.

Library of Congress Cataloging in Publication Data
Vande Kemp, Hendrika.
    Psychology and theology in Western thought, 1672–1965.
    (Bibliographies in the history of psychology and
psychiatry)
    Includes index.
    1. Psychology, Religious—Bibliography. 2. Psychology
and religion—Bibliography. I. Malony, H. Newton.
II. Title.   III. Series.
Z7204.R4V36 1984 [BL53]   016.2'001'9   82-49045
ISBN 0-527-92779-1

To
Hendrik and Petronella Vande Kemp
and their descendants

Contents

Contents

Preface

The integration of psychology and theology has become an explicit area of interest for many psychologists in recent years. In fact, psychotheological integration has developed a professional identity of its own, alongside pastoral psychology and the psychology of religion. As a witness to this special identity, several journals have arisen devoted specifically to psychology and theology: the *Journal of Religion and Health* (1961), the *Journal of Psychology and Theology* (1973), the *Journal of Christian Counseling* (1977), the *Journal of Psychology and Judaism* (1977), and the *Journal of Psychology and Christianity* (1982; formerly the *CAPS Bulletin*). Special training institutions have arisen as well, beginning with the founding of the Graduate School of Psychology at Fuller Theological Seminary in the early 1960s and the Rosemead Graduate School at Biola College (now Biola University) in the 1970s. These were followed by the Psychological Studies Institute in Atlanta and various smaller groups in the late 1970s. A growing literature, representing most of the major Protestant and Catholic publishing houses, and several in the Jewish tradition, focuses on both theoretical-conceptual and practical aspects of this integration.

Several earlier bibliographies have referenced aspects of this literature. Most relevant among them are William W. Meissner's *Annotated Bibliography in Religion and Psychology* (The Academy of Religion and Mental Health, 1961); Donald Capps, Lewis Rambo, and Paul Ransohoff's *Psychology of Religion: A Guide to Information Sources* (Gale Research Company, 1976); and Benjamin Beit-Hallahmi's *Psychoanalysis and Religion: A Bibliography* (Norwood Editions, 1978). Meissner's bibliography was based on *Psychological Abstracts* and thus limited primarily to journal articles published since the late 1920s. The Capps, Rambo, and Ransohoff bibliography relied on essentially the same sources, starting with the time period at which Meissner finished and supplementing his work in several areas. Beit-Hallahmi's bibliography is limited to psychoanalysis and religion. The present work differs from the above in several ways. First, it focuses on book-length publications, monographs, and pamphlets, including no periodical articles

Preface

except those included in the annotations on major integrative journals. Second, it accesses the literature in a different manner, not relying on *Psychological Abstracts* at all. Third, the scope is expanded to include a number of specifically theological categories which are not relevant to the psychology of religion but are of considerable import for the task of conceptual-theoretical integration.

Psychology and Theology in Western Thought is intended as a historical bibliography, covering the time span from the late seventeenth century to 1965. The cutoff was made at 1965 because the later 1960s and the 1970s saw a massive increase in the number of books dealing with some aspect of psychotheological integration, and ample information on these more recent titles can easily be found in current published references. This Bibliography is meant to provide information on earlier, less accessible sources on psychotheological integration.

In addition, the Bibliography covers religion from a Western perspective, treating psychology in its relation to Judeo-Christian traditions. Eastern religions differ from those in the West in that theology, psychology, and philosophy are generally treated as indivisible parts of the same whole. Since Eastern religion does not distinguish between psychology and theology, the integration of the two fields has not been an issue. In contrast, Western works on Eastern religion have made this distinction; however, the majority of such titles were produced after 1965. Since it is Western thought that has emphasized disciplinary distinctions and has thus forced the issue of integration, the decision was made to focus primarily on Western thought.

The work began on our own campus at Fuller Theological Seminary. An initial card catalog search led us to nearly half of the volumes included in the bibliography. We next reviewed the indexes and bibliographies in these volumes searching for titles not held in our library. Our personal libraries, including many titles not held by the seminary library, were then added to the file. An additional source for titles was provided by antique book dealers whose catalogues list many old and reprint titles: John Gach Books, The Epistomologist, De Anima Books in Psychology, and University Microfilms International Psychology On-Demand Reprints. We also searched relevant sections of Baldwin's *Dictionary of Psychology and Philosophy*, and early issues of the *United States Catalogue of Books in Print* (prior to 1915), the *Cumulative Book Index*, and a catalogue of Union Seminary Library holdings. Lists generated in this manner were then matched with the Capps et al. bibliography, Beit-Hallahmi, and a short bibliography by G. Allison Stokes in the *Religious Studies Review*, and any previously omitted titles were added to the files. Incomplete references were supplemented with information from *The United States Catalogue of Books*, *The National Union Catalogue*, and the *British Museum General Catalogue of Printed Books*.

Book reviews provided a major source of material for annotations on books not available to us. Book review sections in older theological journals also led us to many titles not previously recognized in the literature. Initially we reviewed all the book reviews in the following journals to compile a working list of books: the *Journal for the Scientific Study of Religion*, the *Journal of the American Academy of Religion*, the *Journal of the American Scientific Affiliation*, the *Psychological Bulletin* (through 1938), *the American Journal of Psychology*, and the *Hibbert Journal*. When book reviews were needed to annotate unavailable books, the following journals were searched: *The American Journal of Theology*, *The American Journal of Religious Psychology*, the *Anglican Theological Review*, *The British Journal of Psychiatry*, *The British Journal of Medical Psychology*,

Preface

The Bulletin of the Menninger Clinic, Contemporary Psychology, The Ecclesiastical Review, The Expository Times, The Journal of Nervous and Mental Disease, The Journal of Religion, The Journal of Pastoral Care, Pastoral Psychology, The Personalist, The Reformed Church Review, and *Theology in Life.* The list of periodicals and serials was completed by consulting the *Union List of Serials* and the *British Union List of Serials.*

Annotations are organized according to a system developed by the first author, including both psychological and theological categories. Within each section, entries are arranged in chronological order. Included in each entry, when available, are last and first name of author(s), original foreign-language title and publication data, English title, translator, city of publication, publisher, date of publication, and number of pages. For works published both in the United States and Great Britain or the United States and Canada, alternate titles and publication data are provided wherever these were available. For edited works, the names of all contributing authors are included. Annotations are intended to provide both a psychological and theological orientation, and strong identifications with particular "schools" or traditions are identified whenever possible.

Acknowledgments

Many individuals have contributed to this bibliography in a significant way. We are especially grateful to Robert Wozniak, whose invitation to contribute to this series of bibliographies was a primary source of motivation. We are also grateful to J. Harold Ellens, who unknowingly challenged us to prove him wrong when, at the 1981 John G. Finch Symposium, he said "much of the really creative and definitive material on the intersection of theology and psychology has been published since 1977." Hal has also challenged us through his dedicated leadership in the Christian Association for Psychological Studies. A significant theoretical contribution was made by Richard A. Muller, whose expertise as a church historian first led us to the personalist philosophers and their very significant contribution to the historical base for integration. Richard joined us and several students for a historical seminar on integration. We want to thank R. Timothy Kearney and Karen G. Morgan for the annotations written in the context of this course, and Richard Sanders for his review of the Union Seminary holdings. We also wish to thank Paul W. Pruyser for his history of psychiatry and religion at the Menninger Foundation (entry number 1026), which was written especially for this Bibliography. Helen Poixotto, Thomas Mann, and Adele R. Chwalek, of the Catholic University of America, provided us with information on the *Studies in Psychology and Psychiatry*, and the history of psychology at the Catholic University. Merle R. Jordan, of Boston University's Danielsen Institute for Pastoral Counseling, first made us aware of *The Journal of Psychotherapy as a Religious Process*. Eva Burczyk, of the Yale University Library, and Elizabeth Swayne, of the Boston University Library, both provided photocopies of sections of this journal that made annotations possible. Harry B. Adams, of the Yale Divinity School screened the Lyman Beecher Lecture series for relevant contributions. Jim Dittes provided information on the Dwight Harrington Terry Lectures. William McGuire, of the Princeton University Press, provided similar information on the Bollingen Foundation and the Bollingen Series. Linda Walker, Robert J. Carlson, and William T. Wright, of Prairie View Hospital, and Theodore M. Johnson, of Philhaven Hospital, provided infor-

Acknowledgments

mation on the various hospitals associated with the Mennonite Mental Health Services. Gordon R. Kieft responded to our inquiries about Bethesda Outpatient and Counseling Services, and Arthur R. Van Tuinen answered similar questions about Pine Rest Christian Hospital and Rehabilitation Services. Herman J. Williams and John H. Peatling provided us with exhaustive information on the Union College Character Research Project. Christine Erdmann of the Whittier College Library and Albert W. Fowler of the Friends Historical Library of Swarthmore College provided photocopies of portions of *Inward Light* that aided in our annotations. Helen Douglas, of the Institute of Formative Spirituality at Duquesne University, provided information on *Envoy*. Janice Denyer of the Metropolitan Toronto Library Board provided photocopies of contents of the very rare *Journal of Psychosophy*. David M. Wulff of Wheaton College suggested several translated German sources. Paul Ford of Fuller Theological Seminary provided both moral support and inspiration, and guidance to some important sources in the Catholic literature. Bruce Abbott, of McAllister Library, spent many hours at the computer terminal aiding us in our final efforts to locate books through interlibrary loan and filling in missing bibliographic information. Others who patiently answered questions and responded to inquiries were Colin Brown and Geoffrey Bromiley of Fuller Theological Seminary; Reuven P. Bulka; Seward Hiltner; Marion Holena Levine of the Francis A. Countway Library of Medicine; Roger Stewart of the University of Southern California; Anita J. Faatz of the Otto Rank Association; Oscar Burdick of the Charles Holbrook Library at the Pacific School of Religion; and Stanley Clarke Wyllie of the Dayton and Montgomery County Public Library. The facilities at The Huntington Memorial Library, the Libraries of the University of California at Los Angeles and the Occidental College Library were also extremely helpful to us.

We are especially grateful to those who assisted in the "nitty-gritty" details of the bibliographer's task. Bertha Jacklitch searched the card catalog and library shelves for missing dates, page numbers, and complete names. She also patiently handled all the pains of the word-processing system. Donna Viselli assisted her in the typing task and proofreading of the manuscript. Janice Holton De Block cross-checked the references against entries in the *United States Catalogue*, *The National Union Catalogue*, and *The British Museum General Catalogue*. Mary McLeod Stoddard spent many hours in local libraries, tracing information on authors. We also wish to thank Virginia Staudt Sexton for her history of The American Catholic Psychological Association (entry number 1024), and Kathy De Raud of McAllister Library for her help at the computer terminal. Finally, Anne Coughlin and Theresa Thompson aided in the task of indexing.

PART ONE

Historical and Philosophical Bases for Integration

Major Reference Works

This section includes dictionaries, encyclopedias, and bibliographies of relevance to the integration of psychology and theology. These reference works were selected for their unusual scope and diversity, and do not constitute an exhaustive list of such works. However, they will lead the reader to the major sources necessary for beginning inquiry in this interdisciplinary endeavor.

[1901] **1. Baldwin, James Mark, ed.**

     Dictionary of Philosophy and Psychology. Including Many of the Principal Conceptions of Ethics, Logic, Aesthetics, Philosophy of Religion, Mental Pathology, Anthropology, Biology, Neurology, Physiology, Economics, Political and Social Philosophy, Philology, Physical Science and Education and giving a Terminology in English, French, German, and Italian. 3 Vols. in 4. New York: Macmillan Co., 1901–1905, 644+892+ 1192 pp. Reprint. Gloucester: Peter Smith, 1949–1957.

     An invaluable reference work, including contributions from nearly sixty philosophers and psychologists. Volumes I and II constitute the dictionary, and contain many entries relevant to psychology and theology. Volume III, Parts I and II, compiled by Benjamin Rand, features many relevant bibliographies including the history of philosophy, the philosophy of religion, and psychology. In addition to founding *Psychological Review* (1894), Baldwin wrote influential works on mental development, social and moral development, genetic logic, and genetic epistemology.

[1929] **2. Price, Harry, comp.**

     Short-Title Catalogue of Works on Psychical Research, Spiritualism, Magic, Psychology, Legerdemain, and other Methods of Deception,

3

Charlatanism, Witchcraft, and Technical Works for the Scientific Investigation of Alleged Abnormal Phenomena, from circa 1450 A.D. to 1929. London: The National Laboratory of Psychical Research, 1929, pp. 67–422.

[1932] **3. Murchison, Carl Allanmore, and Harden, Luberta, eds.**
The Psychological Register. Vol. 3. Worcester, Mass.: Clark University Press, 1932, xi+1269 pp.
  Murchison attempts to provide biographies of all living psychologists, including members of the American Psychological Association as well as psychologists in thirty-two foreign countries.

[1955] **4. Ferm, Vergilius Ture Anselm.**
A Dictionary of Pastoral Psychology. New York: Philosophical Library, 1955, xi+336 pp.
  A major dictionary of psychological terminology for the pastoral counselor, including nine pages on psychology of religion, and three pages on religion and mental health.

[1958] **5. Klausner, Samuel Z., ed.**
Preliminary annotated Bibliography and Directory of Workers in the Field of Religion and Psychiatry. New York: Columbia University, Bureau of Applied Social Research, 1958, n.p.
  There are 1,155 entries arranged alphabetically by author, including biographical information about the authors when available. The focus is on theoretical relations between religion and psychiatry and the role relations of ministers and psychiatrists. Psychology of religion is not included.

[1961] **6. Meissner, William W.**
Annotated Bibliography in Religion and Psychology. New York: Academy of Religion and Mental Health, 1961, xi+235 pp.
  This listing includes 2,905 annotated entries up to 1960, primarily journal articles, gleaned from 350 reviews or collections which are also cited.

[1962] **7. Little, Lawrence Calvin.**
Researches in Personality, Character and Religious Education: A Bibliography of American Doctoral Dissertations, 1855–1959, with an Index prepared by Helen-Jean Moore. Pittsburgh: University of Pittsburgh Press, 1962, iv+215 pp.
  Over 6,300 dissertations listed in alphabetical order by author.

[1964] **8. Freeman, Ruth St. John, and Freeman, Harrop Arthur.**
Counseling, A Bibliography (with Annotations). New York: Scarecrow Press, 1964, 986 pp.
  The 213-page "Religion" section of this bibliography includes more than eighteen hundred books and articles from the period 1950–1964.

[1965]   **9. *Menges, Robert J., and Dittes, James E.***

Psychological Studies of Clergymen: Abstracts of Research. London, New York: Nelson, 1965, 202 pp.

Contains abstracts of more than seven hundred books, articles, and dissertations. The authors demonstrated that the studies were related in terms of similarities of problems studied, research design and techniques, and conclusions, bringing unity and identity to a previously unorganized field.

Historical Works

Here are included histories of psychology which have a general philosophical orientation, as well as other selected historical works which are of relevance to the integration of psychology and theology.

[1818] **10. Heinroth, Johann Christian.**

Lehrbuch der Storungen des Seelenlebens. 1818. ENGLISH: *Textbook of Disturbances of Mental Life.* Translated by J. Schomorarak. 2 vols. Baltimore, Md.: Johns Hopkins University Press, 1975.

Heinroth in many ways anticipated the dynamic psychology of Freud, using such terms as id (es), ego (ich), and conscience (uber-uns). However, Heinroth, a Lutheran, views his whole psychology in a Christian context with strong religious overtones, and declares that selfishness (rather than Freud's later narcissism) is the key to all pathology.

[1848] **11. Hickock, Laurens Perseus.**

Rational Psychology; Or, the Subjective Idea and the Objective Law of All Intelligence. Schenectady: G. Y. Van Debogert, 1848. Reprint. Delmar, N.Y.: Scholars's Facsimiles & Reprints, 1973, xix+717 pp.

According to Hickock, ". . . in this science, i.e., rational psychology, we pass from the facts of experience wholly out beyond it, and seek for the *rationale* of experience itself in the necessary and universal principles which must be conditional for all facts of a possible experience." As Roback observes, Hickock used his psychology as the foundation for an ontology which is hinted at in the last twenty pages of the book, which deal with "the facts of a comprehending reason which come within the compass of an absolute personality." While Aaron Roback in his history textbook denounces this section of the book as an apologetic for natural theology, it offers rich insight into the psychology-theology relationship of the nineteenth century.

[1854]   **12. Hickock, Laurens Perseus.**
Empirical Psychology; Or, the Human Mind as Given in Consciousness. For the Use of Colleges and Academies. New York and Chicago: Ivison, Blakeman, Taylor & Company, 1854, xii+400 pp.

Hickock, who was president of Union College, adopts the German distinction between rational and empirical psychology, and is critical of the British empiricists and Scottish realists. He distinguishes between the psychology of man and the psychology of angels, as based on the difference between pure and incarnate spirit.

[1869]   **13. Hartmann, Eduard von.**
Philosophie des Unbewussten. Versuch einer Weltanschauung. Berlin: C. Duncker, 1869, iv+678 pp. ENGLISH: *Philosophy of the Unconscious: Speculative Results according to the Inductive Method of Physical Science.* 3 vols. Translated by William Chatterton Coupland. London: Trubner & Co., 1884. New York: Macmillan Co., 1884.

The culmination of German romantic philosophy. Expanding on the work of Carl Gustav Carus, von Hartmann describes three layers of the unconscious, documenting his theories with a wealth of illustrative and supporting materials. He considers religion as volitional illusion.

[1871]   **14. Munsell, Oliver Spencer.**
Psychology; Or, the Science of the Mind. New York: Appleton and Company, 1871, xxxvi+320 pp.

[1883]   **15. Britten, Emma Hardinge.**
Nineteenth Century Miracles; Or, Spirits and Their Work in Every Country of the Earth. A Complete Historical Compendium of the Great Movement Known as "Modern Spiritualism." Manchester, N.Y.: W. Britten, 1883, vi+556 pp.

Britten's work is characterized by the same meticulous scholarship and detail as Henri Ellenberger's *Discovery of the Unconscious*, and serves as a valuable companion to the latter. Britten focuses on more than twenty countries and includes lists of members of various societies for psychical research, the founders of journals, and other valuable information. Unfortunately, the book is not indexed.

[1883]   **16. Harris, Samuel.**
The Philosophical Basis of Theism: An Examination of the Personality of Man to Ascertain His Capacity to Know and Serve God, and the Validity of the Principles Underlying the Defence of Theism. New York: Charles Scribner's Sons, 1883, xxii+564 pp.

Extensive considerations of both philosophical psychology and epistemology, and their bearing on the possibility of knowledge of God.
Harris was a systematic theologian at Yale.

[1887]   **17.** *Janet, Paul Alexandre René, and Séailles, Gabriel.*
Histoire de la philosophie, les problemes et les écoles. Paris: Libraire Ch.
Delagrave, 1887, iii+391 pp. ENGLISH: *A History of the Problems of*
Philosophy. 2 vols. Translated by Ada Monahan. Edited by Henry Jones.
London and New York: Macmillan & Co., 1902, xxviii+389 pp., xiii+
375 pp.

[1896]   **18.** *White, Andrew Dickson.*
A History of the Warfare of Science with Theology in Christendom.
2 vols. New York: D. Appleton and Company, 1896, xxiii+415 pp.,
xiii+474 pp. London: Macmillan & Co., 1896.

White was president and professor of history at Cornell. Of special
interest are the sections in Volume 2 labeled "from miracles to medicine" (dealing with pastoral medicine), "from fetich (sic) to hygiene,"
"from 'demoniacal possession' to insanity," and "from diabolism to hysteria."

[1897]   **19.** *Mercier, Desiré Felicien Francois Joseph.*
Le origines de la psychologie contemporaine. Louvain: Institut Superi-
eur de Philosophie, 1897, xii+486 pp. ENGLISH: *The Origins of Contem-*
porary Psychology. Translated by W. H. Mitchell from the second French
ed. New York: P. J. Kenedy & Sons, 1918, xii+351 pp.

A history of psychology from a Scholastic perspective. Cardinal
Mercier, who was at this time the Archbishop of Maldines, critiques
Cartesianism and its sequelae, and surveys the neo-Thomistic movement,
demonstrating that only upon the conception of man's nature as maintained by a sane Scholasticism is it possible to create a consistent psychology taking adequate account of the soul.

[1911]   **20.** *Cutten, George Barton.*
Three Thousand Years of Mental Healing. New York: Charles
Scribner's Sons, 1911, viii+318 pp.

This volume is one of several historical accounts of religious phenomena written by Cutten. Other books of his deal with glossolalia and the
physiological basis of faith, a position later embraced by Leuba, among
others. In this volume Cutten tries to set Christian Science within the
context of pre-Christian as well as Christian healing. His history is accurate, although his opinions are definitely antisupernatural and prosugges-
tion.

[1911]   **21. Dessoir, Max.**

Abriss einer Geschichte der Psychologie. Heidelberg: Carl Winter's Universitätsbuchhandlung, 1911, xi+272 pp. ENGLISH: *Outlines of the History of Psychology.* Translated by Donald Fisher. New York: Macmillan Co., 1912, xxix+278 pp.

A philosophically oriented history with major emphasis on the soul, by a well-known German psychologist.

[1912]   **22. Brett, George Sydney.**

A History of Psychology. 3 vols. Vol. 1. *Ancient and Patristic.* Vol. 2. *Mediaeval and Early Modern Period.* Vol. 3. *Modern Psychology.* xx+388 pp., London: George Allen & Unwin, 1912–1921, xx+388 pp., 394 pp., 322 pp. Edited and abridged by R. S. Peters. London: George Allen & Unwin, 1953, 742 pp.

Brett was affiliated with the University of Toronto from 1908 through 1944, serving as head of the department and later as dean of the graduate school. R. S. Peters was affiliated with Birkbeck College of the University of London. The first history of psychology written in English, Brett's was very much in the philosophical tradition and includes much of the theological tradition as well. Brett uses the term "psychosophy" to refer to those views of the soul which are allied to theology, especially in discussing the Arabian tradition.

[1916]   **23. Wyss, Dieter.**

Die tiefenpsychologischen Schulen von den Anfangen bis zur Gegenwart; Entwicklung, Probleme, Krisen. Gottingen: Vandenhoeck & Ruprecht, 1916, 412 pp+illus. ENGLISH: Depth Psychology: A Critical History, Development, Problems, Crises. Translated by Gerald Onn. London: George Allen & Unwin; New York: W. W. Norton, 1966, 568 pp.

A thorough history of depth psychology, including a lengthy discussion of Freudian psychoanalysis and the influence of Johann F. Herbart, Gustav Theodor Fechner, Josef Breuer, and Theodor H. Meynert. Succeeding sections include the Freudian School (Karl Abraham, Sandor Ferenczi, Otto Fenichel), the British School (Edward Glover, Ernest Jones, Anna Freud, Melanie Klein), the New York Group (Heinz Hartmann, Ernst Kris, R. Loewenstein, René Spitz, Phyllis Greenacre, Erik H. Erikson, Theodore Reik, Wilhelm Reich, Paul Federn, Franz Alexander), the Neo-Freudians (Alfred Adler, Karen Horney, Erich Fromm, Harry Stack Sullivan, Harald Schultz-Hencke, Thomas French, Sandor Rado, Abram Kardiner, Jane Pearce, Saul Newton, Ernest G. Schachtel), and philosophically-oriented schools (Carl Gustav Jung, Otto Rank, Ludwig Binswanger, Martin Buber, Max Ferdinand Scheler, Karl Lowith, E. Michel, P. Christian, Viktor Von Weiszacker, Henry Ey). He concludes with a critique.

[1927]   **24. Roback, Abraham Aaron.**

The Psychology of Character with a Survey of Temperament. London: Kegan Paul, Trench, Trubner & Co.; New York: Harcourt Brace & Co.,

1927, xxiv+595 pp. 2 rev. ed., New York: Harcourt, Brace & Co., 1928, xxiv+605 pp.

Roback devotes 450 pages of his book to a historical survey, and the remainder to his own constructive statement. He regards character as "An enduring psychophysical disposition to inhibit impulses in accordance with a regulative principle."

[1929]   **25. *Müller-Freienfels, Richard.***

Die Hauptrichtungen der gegenwärtigen Psychologie. Leipzig: Quelle & Meyer, 1929. ENGLISH: *The Evolution of Modern Psychology.* Translated by W. Béran Wolfe. New Haven: Yale University Press, 1935, xxiii+ 513 pp.

Müller-Freienfels regards consciousness as a totality of the knowing faculties. Of major interest is the section on "The psychology with 'soul' " which includes discussion of Theodore Lipp's psychology of the "I," L. William Stern's personalism, and Eduard Spranger's cultural scientific psychology.

[1932]   **26. *Vogel, Claude Lawrence, ed.***

Psychology and the Franciscan School: A Symposium of Essays. Milwaukee: Bruce Publishing Co., 1932, 168 pp.

Nine papers presented at the annual Franciscan educational conference. The lead essay, on the psychology of Duns Scotus and modernity, is by Father Longpre, and covers the tradition from Hales to Scotus. Other essays include a discussion of present-day phases of psychoanalysis and the guidance of souls. The book is of historical as well as practical interest.

[1934]   **27. *Reilly, George Cajetan.***

The Psychology of Saint Albert the Great Compared with that of St. Thomas. Washington, D.C.: Catholic University of America, 1934, x+95 pp.

While these thinkers are similar in doctrine, Albert's psychology anticipates the modern scientific tradition while that of Thomas Aquinas represents the speculative approach.

[1935]   **28. *Zilboorg, Gregory.***

The Medical Man and the Witch During the Renaissance. Baltimore: The Johns Hopkins Press, 1935, x+215 pp.

A historical treatment covering (1) the *Malleus Maleficorum,* (2) medicine and the witch in the sixteenth century, and (3) the contributions of Johann Weyer.

[1937]   **29. *Deutsch, Albert.***

The Mentally Ill in America: A History of Their Care and Treatment from Colonial Times. Garden City, N.Y.: Doubleday, Doran & Company, 1937, xvii+530 pp.

Deutsch actually begins his history with a discussion of "prophets, demons and witches," demonstrating that "at first, healing art was inextricably bound up with religion, and in truth served only as an adjunct of the latter." Of special interest is the chapter on moral treatment, focusing on the work of Philippe Pinel, William Tuke, and others following in this tradition.

[1939] **30. Fay, Jay Wharton.**

American Psychology before William James. New Brunswick, N.J.: Rutgers University Press, 1939, x+240 pp.

Fay begins his study with a reconstruction of the Puritan mind, its Calvinistic theology and Scholastic Platonism. Scholars included in review are Samuel Johnson, William Brattle, Jonathan Edwards, Thomas Clap, Johann Daniel Gros, John Witherspoon, Samuel Stanhope Smith, Levi Hedge, Benjamin Rush, Frederick Beasley, Asa Burton, Thomas C. Upham, Friederich August Rauch, Samuel Simon Schmucker, Asa Mahan, Laurens P. Hickock, Francis Wayland, Joseph Haven, James Rush, Noah Porter, John Dewey, James McCosh, Borden P. Bowne, and David Jayne Hill.

[1941] **31. Zilboorg, Gregory, with Henry, George W.**

A History of Medical Psychology. New York: W. W. Norton & Company, 1941, 606 pp. +illus.

An extensive history, with information about early journals, sophisticated discussions of linguistic usage, and valuable discussions of religious influences. The history reflects an antireligious bias not evident in Zilboorg's later works in psychology and religion. One of the most valuable histories available.

[1945] **32. Brennan, Robert Edward.**

History of Psychology from the Standpoint of a Thomist. New York: Macmillan Co., 1945, xvi+277 pp.

Contrasts an empirical with an ontological psychology (i.e., philosophy with science). Brennan retells the history of psychology as a reaction to the philosophic tradition of Aristotle and a desire to reduce behavior to positivistic dimensions. Introduction is by Jacques Maritain.

[1947] **33. Kemp, Charles F.**

Physicians of the Soul: A History of Pastoral Counseling. New York, London and Toronto: Macmillan Co., 1947, xiv+314 pp.

A broad overview including psychology of religion, pastoral psychology, mental hygiene, and related movements, with an emphasis on the Protestant tradition. Points out that the great preachers in the Reformation tradition were all great pastors as well, thus writing a new type of church history.

[1950] **34. Entralgo, Pedro L.**

Introduccion historica al estudio de la patologia psicosomatica. Madrid: Paz Montalvo, 1950, 152 pp. ENGLISH: *Mind and Body, Psychosomatic Pathology; A Short History of the Evolution of Medical Thought.* Translated by Aurelio M. Espinosa, Jr. London: Harvill, 1956, 150 pp. New York: P. J. Kenedy & Sons, n.d.

The dust jacket states that "Entralgo shows that medical treatment . . . has always been concerned with the mind as well as the body . . . with . . . person as well as with . . . illness. He traces this attitude . . . throughout the early Christian period down to the present day." The foreword is by E. B. Strauss.

[1952] **35. *Roback, Abraham Aaron.***
History of American Psychology. New York: Library Publishers, 1952, xiv+426 pp.

Roback's intent in the writing of this volume was to "bridge the gulf between the pre-experimental and experimental epochs, and to fill in the gaps, to some extent, in both the too brief and the deliberately circumscribed histories of psychology." Scholars discussed at length in his review include Samuel Johnson, Jonathan Edwards, William Brattle, John Witherspoon, Samuel Stanhope Smith, Benjamin Rush, Frederick Beasley, Asa Burton, Thomas C. Upham, Friedrich Augustus Rauch, Samuel Simon Schmucker, Laurens Perseus Hickock, Asa Mahan, Francis Wayland, Mark Hopkins, Noah Porter, D. Howland Hamilton, Edward J. Hamilton, Borden Parker Bowne, James McCosh, John Clark Murray, John Dewey, George Trumbull Ladd, Henry Philip Tappan, Daniel Denison Whedon, Rowland Gibson Hazard, William James, G. Stanley Hall, James Mark Baldwin, James McKeen Cattell, Edward Bradford Titchener, Hugo Münsterberg, Charles H. Judd, James Rowland Angell, John Broadus Watson, Morton Prince, William McDougall, R. S. Woodworth, Kurt Lewin, Edward Chace Tolman, Leonard Thompson Troland, Gordon W. Allport, Henry A. Murray, Ernest R. Hilgard, Sigmund Freud, Alfred Adler, Otto Rank, Wilhelm Stekel, Theodor Reik, Wilhelm Reich, Christian von Ehrenfels, Kurt Koffka, Wolfgang Köhler, Max Wertheimer, Alfred Korzybski, Thomas Aquinas, Johann Daniel Gros, Edward Aloysius Pace, Thomas Verner Moore, Robert Edward Brennan, J.S.A. Bois, and Noel Mailloux. While there is much valuable material here for the scholar in psychology and theology, Roback's antitheological bias must be kept in mind. He coins the term "theognostic" to describe ". . . the quality which many philosophers of a theological cast of mind presume to possess, of being able to tell the world all the plans and designs of God as if they were peeping through the keyholes of heaven . . . Almost all conservative theologians are theognosticians."

[1954] **36. *Bromberg, Walter.***
Man Above Humanity: A History of Psychotherapy. Philadelphia: Lippincott, 1954, xiii+342 pp+illus. Rev. eds. under the titles *The Mind of Man* (1958) and *From Shaman to Psychotherapist: A History of the Treatment of Mental Illness*. Chicago: H. Regnery, 1975, vii+360 pp.

A history of mental healing beginning with early witchcraft and magic and ending with twentieth-century developments.

[1954] **37. Misiak, Henryk, and Staudt [Sexton], Virginia M.**
Catholics in Psychology: A Historical Survey. New York, Toronto and London: McGraw-Hill Book Company, 1954, xv+309 pp.+illus.

A comprehensive overview of Catholics in the history of psychology. Early German contributors included Franz Brentano, Carl Stumpf, August Messer, Karl Marbe, and Johannes Müller. Major contributors in the twentieth century are Desiré Felicien François, Joseph Mercier, Edward Aloysius Pace, Joseph Fröbes, Albert Edward Michotte, Johannes Lindworsky, Agostino Gemelli, Eric Wasmann, Émile Peillaube, Kazimierz Twardowski, Thomas Verner Moore, Hilda Gertrude Marley, and the Louvain scholars Armand Thiéry, Arthur Fauville, Raymond Buyse, René Dellaert, Étienne De Greeff, Jozef Nuttin, and Gerard de Montpellier. Biographical material is also provided on the following Catholic psychologists: Jean Frans Fransen, Joseph Maréchal, Roland Dalbiez, Maryse Choisy, Charles Blondel, Jean Lhermitte, Maurice Verdun, Jules De La Vaissière, Jean Henri Fabre, Arnaud d'Agnel, Robert D. Sinety, J. DeTonquédec, Antonin Eymieu, Siegfried Behn, Max Ettlinger, Otto Willmann, Alexander Willwoll, W. Lankes, J. Leicester King, James J. A. Van Ginneken, F.J.J. Buytendijk, Franciscus M.J.A. Roels, Siebertus Rombouts, J.P.W. Ellerbeck, Michael Maher, Peter J. R. Dempsey, Feruccio Banissoni, Mario Ponzo, Maria Montessori, Mieczyslaw Dybowski, Kazimierz Dworak, Joseph Pastuszka, Piotr Chojnacki, Paul Siwek, Juan Luis Vives, Manuel Barbado Vieja, José Germain, Frans Van Cauwelaert, Marc P. De Munnynck, Charles Baudouin, John Chrysostom, Raphael McCarthy, Rudolph Allers, Walter G. Summers, Robert Brennan, Noel Mailloux, and Roger Philip. Also includes information on organizations and periodicals in the area of integration.

[1956] **38. Van den Berg, Jan Hendrik.**
Metabletica; of, leer der verauderingen, beginselen van een historische psychologie. Nijkerk: G. F. Callenback, 1956, 225 pp.+illus. ENGLISH: *The Changing Nature of Man: Introduction to a Historical Psychology, Metabletica.* Translated by H. F. Croes. New York: W. W. Norton, 1961, 252 pp.

Proposes the theory that human nature changes and that life during different ages is essentially different. Van den Berg suggests that the history of psychology should be a study of the "psychologies" which have characterized different ages.

[1961] **39. Roback, Abraham Aaron.**
History of Psychology and Psychiatry. New York: Philosophical Library, 1961, xiii+422 pp.+illus.

In this concise overview, Roback offers thumbnail sketches of many psychologists not treated in other histories. Of special interest is the section on demonism.

14

[1963]   **40. *Braceland, Francis James, and Stock, Michael.***
Modern Psychiatry, a Handbook for Believers. Garden City, N.Y.: Doubleday, 1963, 346 pp.

A historical survey, emphasizing therapy more than theory. The interaction of psychiatry and religion is also briefly treated. The handbook is not reflective of the most recent efforts in pastoral counseling or the field of integration.

[1963]   **41. *Hunter, Richard A.***
Three Hundred Years of Psychiatry 1535—1860. A History Presented in Selected English Texts. London, New York, and Toronto: Oxford University Press, 1963, xxvi+1107 pp.

Hunter has collected more than three hundred excerpts from the psychiatric literature, each excerpt supplemented with the author's name, dates of birth and death, qualifications, and main offices. References to religion are indexed under religion and insanity, religious experience (and epilepsy), religious instruction of lunatics, religious melancholy, and religious scruples.

[1963]   **42. *Kantor, Jacob Robert.***
The Scientific Evolution of Psychology. 2 vols., Chicago: Principia Press, 1963, xxii+387 pp, xxi+427 pp.+illus.

Because of its breadth, this is a valuable historical source. However, the author's bias must be kept in mind. Kantor states that he "began his historical studies with the conviction that the evolution of scientific psychology should be treated without the thralldom of transcendental assumptions and has found no basis for altering his opinion." Of special interest is the section on "the naturalization of soul" in Volume two.

[1963]   **43. *Watson, Robert Irving.***
The Great Psychologists: from Aristotle to Freud. Philadelphia: Lippincott, 1963, 572 pp.

Watson, writing in the tradition of Brett rather than that of Boring, provides a very readable overview of the historical philosophers and theologians in the history of psychology. Chapters on the Patristic and Scholastic traditions are included. Watson later edited the *Journal of the History of the Behavioral Sciences*.

The Mind-Body Relationship

The relationship between mind and body, between unextended, thinking substance and extended unthinking substance, between the material and the nonmaterial, between the spiritual and the corporeal, has intrigued philosophers for centuries. All metaphysics, epistemologies, and anthropologies reflect a solution—explicit or implicit—to this problem. In this section, which is by no means exhaustive, are included some of the most integrative sources. Further discussion of the mind-body relationship may be found in many of the philosophically oriented histories of psychology, in books on the soul, and in the Christian and biblical psychologies.

[1845]   **44. Mahan, Asa.**
      A System of Intellectual Philosophy. New York: Saxton & Miles, 1845, xiv+330 pp.
      In this excellent overview of mental philosophy, with an emphasis on faculty psychology, Mahan rejects materialism, ideal dualism (Kant), subjective idealism, pantheism (Schelling), pure idealism (Hegel), modern transcendentalism, and eclecticism (Cousin) for Scottish Realism. He also discusses the realities of matter and spirit and supports the immortality of the soul.

[1854]   **45. Brodie, Benjamin Collins.**
      Psychological Inquiries: In a Series of Essays, Intended to Illustrate the Mutual Relations of the Physical Organization and the Mental Faculties. London: Longman, Green and Longmans, 1854, viii+264 pp. Also under the title *Mind and Matter: or Physiological Inquiries. In a Series of*

17

Essays, Intended to Illustrate the Mutual Relations of the Physical Organization and the Mental Faculties. New York: G. P. Putman & Co., 1857, viii+279 pp.

These are essays in the form of dialogues suggesting that human mental faculties are physiologically based and dependent on natural evolution for their superiority over the animals. This predates Darwin but anticipates him.

[1858]   **46. Jones, Thomas Wharton.**
A Catechism of the Physiology and Philosophy of Body, Sense and Mind. London: n.p., 1858.

[1864]   **47. Brittan, Samuel Byron.**
Man and His Relations: Illustrating the Influence of the Mind on the Body: the Relations of the Faculties to the Organs, and to the Elements, Objects and Phenomena of the External World. New York: W. A. Townsend, 1864, xiv+578 pp.

Brittan, a physician who used the pseudonym, "a dweller in the temple," also authored several works on spiritualism.

[1870]   **48. Maudsley, Henry.**
Body and Mind: An Inquiry into Their Connection and Mutual Influence, Specially in Reference to Mental Disorders. Being the Gulstonian Lecture for 1870. London: Macmillan & Co., 1870, x+189 pp. Enl. ed., London: Macmillan & Co., 1873, xii+342 pp.

Maudsley, Fellow of the Royal College of Physicians and Professor of Medical Jurisprudence in University College, London, was a leading proponent of materialism. This book is based on the Gulstonian Lectures delivered to the Royal College of Physicians in 1870, with two psychological articles added in the enlarged edition. Maudsley offers an exposition of the physiology of mind, delineates the features of some forms of mental "degeneracy" focusing on the operation of physiological causes, and offers a general survey of "mind pathologies" and relevant research. Finally, he delineates his philosophical orientation opposing metaphysical psychology as a hindrance to physiological inquiry and proposes a doctrine of "spontaneous generation" to replace the Theory of Vitality.

[1871]   **49. McCosh, James.**
Christianity and Positivism: A Series of Lectures to the Times on Natural Theology and Apologetics, [Delivered in New York, Jan. 16 to March 20, 1871, on the "Ely Foundation" of the Union Theological Seminary.] New York: R. Carter & Brothers, 1871, vii+369 pp. Cambridge: John Wilson, 1871, 369 pp.

McCosh, President of Princeton Seminary, focused his second series of lectures on Christianity and Mental Science, including proofs of the existence of mind, ideas on what the mind reveals to us, and a definition of substance as that which has being, potency, and permanence. McCosh, who is known in theological circles for the rapprochement of theology and evolutionary theory, criticizes the progress of free thought in America as well as the various proponents of materialism. His voluminous intellectual output included a psychological series which embraced the emotions, the motive powers, and cognition. This trilogy of books, widely used in American universities in the late nineteenth century included *Emotions* (1880), and *Motive Powers*, and *Cognitive Powers* (1886). McCosh also authored an undated pamphlet for the American Tract Society entitled *The Imagination: Its Uses and Abuses.*

[1872] **50. *Tuke, Daniel Hack.***
Illustrations of the Influence of the Mind upon the Body in Health and Disease, Designed to Elucidate the Action of the Imagination. London: J. & A. Churchill, 1872, xvi+444 pp.

A physician who edited the *Journal of Mental Science* and was president of the Medico-Psychological Association in England, Tuke attempted to present the psychophysical principles of the mind-body problem found by modern physiology. First published as a series of articles in the *Journal*, 1870–1872, these essays propose an interactionist theory.

[1873] **51. *Bain, Alexander.***
Mind and Body: the Theories of Their Relation. London: Henry S. King & Co., 1873, 196 pp.+adv. New York: Appleton & Co., 1873, 196 pp.

Bain, a major proponent of psychophysical parallelism, here clearly articulates his position on "concomitant variation." Bodily and mental events are coincident and correlated, but neither is the cause of the other.

[1874] **52. *Lewes, George Henry.***
Problems of Life and Mind. First Series: The Foundations of a Creed. . . . 2 vols. London: Trubner, 1874–1875. Reissued as *Problems of Life and Mind.* 2 vols. Boston: Houghton, Mifflin, 1891. Third Series: Vol. 1. *The Study of Psychology; Its Object, Scope, and Method.* Vol. 2. *Mind as a Function of the Organism. The Sphere of Sense and Logic of Feeling. The Sphere of Intellect and Logic of Signs.* London: Trübner, 1879. Boston: Houghton, Osgood, 1879–1880.

Psychology is defined as "the analysis and classification of the *Sentient functions and faculties*, revealed to observation and induction, complete by the reduction of them to their *conditions of existence*, biological and social." Includes critiques of Auguste Comte, J. S. Mill, Herbert Spencer, and Kant. Lewes was a member of London's literary and scientific circles, and he produced works in the fields of marine biology, physiology, psychology, history of philosophy, and metaphysics.

[1878]   **53. Romanes, George John.**
"Physicus" A Candid Examination of Theism. Boston: Houghton, Osgood & Company, 1878, xviii+197 pp. London: Trubner, 1878, xviii+ 197 pp. The English & Foreign Philosophical Library, Volume 9.

This pseudonymously published work meticulously examined a variety of theistic arguments, arriving at complete agnosticism. Especially interesting to psychologists for its analysis of John Locke, J. S. Mill, William Paley, and materialism.

[1888]   **54. Caird, John.**
Mind and Matter: A Sermon Preached Before the British Medical Association, on Tuesday, Aug. 7, 1888. Glasgow: J. Maclehose & Sons, 1888, 27 pp.

Caird authored numerous works in the philosophy of religion.

[1889]   **55. Wythe, Joseph Henry.**
The Physiology of the Soul. New York: Hunt & Eaton; Cincinnati: Cranston & Stowe, 1889, 332 pp.

A treatise on the mind-body problem.

[1903]   **56. Strong, Charles Augustus.**
Why the Mind Has a Body. New York: Macmillan Co.; London: Macmillan & Co., 1903, x+355 pp.+adv.

A professor of Psychology at Columbia at the turn of the century, Strong attempts to solve the mind-body problem via a panpsychism proposal. He suggests that his proposition solves the problem of both parallelism and interactionism. He affirms the reality of the body alongside the efficiency of the mind. He was heavily dependent on William James and George Frederick Stout.

[1911]   **57. McDougall, William.**
Body and Mind: A History and a Defense of Animism. New York: Macmillan Co., 1911, xix+384 pp. London: Methuen & Co., 1911, xix+384 pp.+adv.

The history of the mind-body problem contained in this work constitutes more than 100 pages and was hailed by A. A. Roback as "the most extensive discussion of the mind-body problem to this day." McDougall mentioned twenty or more "solutions" to the problem, including interactionism, occasionalism, psychophysical parallelism, the double aspect hypothesis, epiphenomenalism, the identity hypothesis, materialism, and idealism.

[1914]   **58. Driesch, Hans Adolf Eduard.**
The Problem of Individuality: A Course of Lectures Delivered before the University of London in October 1913. London: Macmillan & Co., 1914, ix+84 pp.+advs.

Proofs offered in defense of vitalism and a discussion of the problem of monism. Driesch was Professor of Philosophy at Heidelberg and later at Leipzig.

[1916]   **59. *Driesch, Hans Adolf Eduard.***

Leib und Seele; eine Prüfung des psycho-physischen Grundprobleme. Leipzig: E. Reinecke, 1916, vi+108 pp. 2 ed. under the title *Leib und Seele; eine Untersuchung über das psychophysische Grundproblem.* Leipzig: E. Reinecke, 1920, viii+114 pp. ENGLISH: *Mind and Body: a Criticism of Psychophysical Parallelism.* Translated by Theodore Besterman. New York: Dial Press; London: Methuen & Co., 1927, 191 pp.

Driesch attacks mechanism and parallelism in the same vein as Borden T. Bowne. He asserts that one can examine only physical reactions, never psychical or mental ones, and only by reasoning from experience. All psychological affirmations are based on analogy. Driesch represents the vitalist position.

[1917]   **60. *Streeter, Burnett Hillman, ed.***

Immortality: an Essay in Discovery Coordinating Scientific, Psychical, and Biblical Research. London: Macmillan & Co., 1917, xiv+380 pp. +adv.

Includes chapters by Streeter, A. Clutton-Brock, C. W. Emmet, and J. A. Hadfield. Hadfield's psychological contribution asserts that the main problem in psychology is the relation between body and mind. He states his thesis thus: that the tendency of the mind towards independence and autonomy suggests the possibility of its becoming entirely liberated from the body, and continuing to exist in a disembodied state.

[1922]   **61. *Pratt, James Bissett.***

Matter and Spirit: A Study of Mind and Body in Their Relation to the Spiritual Life. New York: Macmillan Co., 1922, ix+232 pp.

Reviews four basic contemporary positions vis-à-vis the mind-body relationship: (1) parallelism, represented by Paulsen (2) materialism, represented by Howard C. Warren, C. A. Strong, R. W. Sellars, and W. P. Montague (3) interactionism, represented by George Trumbull Ladd, Wilhelm Wundt, and Carl Stumpf (4) denial of the problem, represented by B. H. Bode, Bernard Bosanquet, R.F.A. Hoernle, John Broadus Watson, E. P. Frost, E. A. Singer. In response to the question, "what interacts with matter?" Pratt rejects the answers "consciousness" and "material substance" in favor of "self or personality," relying on William McDougall's exposition. Pratt's position is one of absolute theistic personalism in the tradition of Bosanquet and F. H. Bradley. The Nathaniel W. Taylor lectures, Yale Divinity School, 1922.

[1923]   **62. *Bosanquet, Bernard.***

Three Chapters on the Nature of Mind, by the Late Bernard Bosanquet. Edited by Helen Bosanquet. London: Macmillan & Co., 1923, vii+ 159 pp.

Looks at mind from the perspective of the biographer and novelist, as regarded in the theories of Franz Brentano and Alexius Meinong, and in the philosophy of Bertrand Russell.

[1924] **63. *Crowson, E. H.***

The Function of Spirit in Matter. Boston: Stratford Company, 1924, 131 pp.

This book is reviewed in *The Personalist* by Wilbur H. Long. Matter and Spirit are regarded as two ontological categories, with the former being an eternally generated mode of the latter. Matter is the medium by which Spirit expresses and realizes itself.

[1925] **64. *Laird, John.***

Our Minds and Their Bodies. London: Oxford University Press, H. Milford, 1925, 122 pp.

This is a survey volume detailing common sense, scientific and philosophical evidence for dualism (or the opposite: monism). The author affirms the reality of mind without asserting its materiality.

[1925] **65. *Morgan, Conway Lloyd.***

Life, Mind, and Spirit. Being the Second Course of the Gifford Lectures Delivered in the University of St. Andrews in the year 1923 under the General Title of Emergent Evolution. New York: H. Holt & Co., 1925, xix+316 pp. London: Williams & Norgate, 1926, xix+316 pp.

Morgan, Professor Emeritus at Bristol, claims there is no disjunctive antithesis between evolutionary progress and Divine Purpose. Other areas considered are the nature of mind, pleasure and pain, action and thought, self and other, behavior, and God's Purpose.

[1926] **66. *Troland, Leonard Thompson.***

The Mystery of Mind. New York: D. Van Nostrand Company, 1926, xi+253 pp.

This work argues the case for idealism, and for the unreality of matter as such. However, this is in the context of a sophisticated general psychology which includes discussions of nerve action and physiological psychology as well as the action of the subconscious and superconscious mind. Troland was on the faculty at Harvard and served as president of the Optical Society of America.

[1927] **67. *Santayana, George.***

The Realm of Essence. Book First of Realms of Being. New York: Scribners, 1927, xxiii+183 pp. London: Constable, 1928, xxiii+183 pp.

This is the first of four volumes on being by Santayana. Essence is defined as the proper nature of appearances. Santayana warns against psychologism, the tendency to describe the mind apart from the body and to make psychology merely literary.

[1928]   **68. Scheler, Max Ferdinand.**
Die Stellung des Menschen im Kosmos. Darmstadt: O. Reichl, 1928, 114 pp. ENGLISH: *Man's Place in Nature*. Translated by Hans Meyerhoff. Boston: Beacon Press, 1961, xxxv+105 pp.
Scheler was second only to Husserl in launching the phenomenological movement. He taught philosophy at the University of Munich until 1910 and at the University of Cologne. This book, a fragmentary draft for a work which was never written, is Scheler's last work and represents the final phase of his philosophical world view. It is an "orthodox phenomenological analysis of love, hate, sympathy, pity, and so on which includes a running criticism of metaphysical and naturalistic theories of the emotions (including Freud's)." He puts forward a strict organismic monism or psychophysical parallelism and makes a break with orthodox theism in his concept of the "self-deification" of man, though he views "life" and spirit as complementary.

[1929]   **69. Morgan, Conway Lloyd.**
Mind at the Crossways. London: Williams & Norgate, 1929, xi+275 pp.
Here, Morgan sets forth the principle of relational interpretation as a substitute for classical conceptions of causality.

[1930]   **70. Hart, Charles Aloysius.**
The Thomistic Concept of Mental Faculty. Washington: Catholic University of America, 1930, 142 pp.
Hart's thesis for the Catholic University of America deals with the mind-body problem and related issues.

[1930]   **71. Santayana, George.**
The Realm of Matter. Book Second of Realms of Being. New York: Scribners; London: Constable, 1930, xv+209 pp.
Santayana defines matter as the region and method of power.

[1931]   **72. Stout, George Frederick.**
Mind and Matter. The First of Two Volumes Based on the Gifford Lectures Delivered in the University of Edinburgh in 1919 and 1921. Cambridge: University Press, 1931, xiv+325 pp.
Stout reviews animism (teleological and aesthetic), interactionism, parallelism, and materialism, with an extensive critique of the latter. Criticism is also leveled at sensational realism, monadism, and subjectivism. The author defends the commonsense view of an embodied self. Stout was a leader in the British development of functionalism, and is famous for his doctrine of conation, the fact and experience of striving.

[1932]   **73. Myers, Charles Samuel.**
The Absurdity of Any Mind—Body Relation. London: Oxford University Press, H. Milford, 1932, 27 pp.

Formerly editor (and founder) of the *British Journal of Psychology* (1911–1924), Myers served as Lecturer in Experimental Psychology at Cambridge from 1909 to 1922, when he became director of the National Institute of Industrial Psychology, of which he was co-founder. The lecture was delivered on 19 May 1932 at University College, London, as the second Leonard Trelawney Hobhouse Trust Lecture. Myers asserts that "throughout life, directive activity, together with the associated, characteristic, mechanical activities, is synonymous with mental activity. The activities of what we artificially separate as living matter and mind are identical, each comprising the same directive and peculiar mechanical activities. There can be no mind-body *relation* in the presence of this *identity*. The only distinction that can be drawn is one between the living individual and individual objects of the lifeless universe." In the personalist tradition, he ends with a discussion of self-activity (conation) and of modifications of that self-activity (affects).

[1934]   **74. Mayer, Fred Sidney.**
Why Two Worlds? The Relation of Physical to Spiritual Realities. Philadelphia: J. B. Lippincott Company, 1934, 272 pp. Reprint. New York: AMS Press, 1972, 272 pp.
   Exploration of the mind-body problem from the perspective of the New Jerusalem Church. Distinguishes among factual, ethical, and spiritual truths.

[1937]   **75. Santayana, George.**
The Realm of Truth. Book Third of Realms of Being. London: Constable & Co., 1937, xiv+142 pp; New York: Scribners, 1938, xiv+142 pp.
   Santayana defines truth as the total history and destiny of matter and spirit, or the enormously complex essence they exemplify by existing.

[1940]   **76. Santayana, George.**
The Realm of Spirit. Book Fourth of Realms of Being. New York: Scribners, 1940, xiii+302 pp.
   Spirit is defined as the witness or moral sensibility that is subject to the double assault of material events and dramatic illusions.

[1948]   **77. Leon, Philip.**
Body, Mind and Spirit. London: Student Christian Movement Press, 1948, 128 pp.
   Leon, professor at University College, Leicester, was active in the Oxford Group Way. His book purports to be written for the "non-philosophic" reader, and attempts to advance a mind-body theory. He contrasts the world's twin foundations: "the miracles of science" and "the science of miracles." Both Materialism and Mentalism-Idealism are examined as species of phenomenalism and are contrasted with his "philosophy of miracle," constituted in the exercise of power over nature by holy men. Mental illness is then examined as the self-limitation of the spirit.

[1951] **78. *Onian, Richard Broxton.***

*The Origins of European Thought about the Body, the Mind, the
Soul, the World, Time and Fate: New Interpretations of Greek, Roman
and Kindred Evidence also of Some Basic Jewish and Christian Beliefs.*
Cambridge: University Press, 1951, xvii+547 pp.

Evidencing fine classical scholarship, the author treats (1) the mind
and the body, (2) the immortal soul and the body, and (3) fate and time.
Onian was Hildred Carlisle Professor of Latin at London University. His
work includes Greek etymology as well.

[1952] **79. *Stout, George Frederick.***

*God and Nature. The Second of Two Volumes based on the Gifford
Lectures delivered in The University of Edinburgh in 1919 and 1921.*
Edited by A. K. Stout. Cambridge: University Press, 1952, liv+339 pp.

This volume continues the argument begun in *Mind and Matter*. It
includes a detailed exposition and criticism of pluralism as set forth by
Bertrand Russell.

[1956] **80. *Peursem, Cornelis Anthonie Van.***

Lichaam-Ziel-Geest: De mens als orientatie vanuit zijn wereld. Utrecht:
Erven J. Bijleveld, 1956, 166 pp. ENGLISH: *Body, Soul, Spirit: A Survey
of the Body-Mind Problem.* Translated by Hubert H. Hoskins, London:
Oxford University Press, 1966, vii+213 pp.

Reviews the positions of Plato, Aristotle, Aquinas, René Descartes,
L. Feuerbach, A. Gehlen, H. Plessner, J. P. Sartre, M. Merleau-Ponty,
L. Wittgenstein, G. Ryle, and S. Hampshire, as well as the primitive and
archaic period and the biblical views. In conclusion, body and mind are
regarded as unity, becoming separated-articulated in the process of self-
objectivization.

[1957] **81. *Meyer, Arthur Ernest***

*Mind, Matter and Morals: The Impact of the Revolutionary New Find-
ings in Neurophysiology and Psychology Upon the Problems of Religion,
Ethics, and Human Behavior.* New York: American Press, 1957, 192 pp.

The Philosophy
of Personalism

The philosophy of personalism is an essential presupposition for models of integration emphasizing relational theology and interpersonal theories of psychology. Ralph Tyler Flewelling, in Dagobert D. Runes's *Dictionary of Philosophy*, defines personalism as "any philosophy which considers personality the supreme value and the key to the meaning of reality." The term was first used in 1863 by Bronson Alcott for "the doctrine that the ultimate reality of the world is a Divine Person who sustains the universe by a continuous act of creative will." In America, theistic personalism was first given form by Borden Parker Bowne. Flewelling includes the following distinctions: monadism (Gottfried Wilhelm von Leibnitz), teleological personalism (R. H. Lotze), theistic personalism (Rudolf Eucken), phenomenological personalism (William Stern), subjective idealism (George Berkeley, A. C. Frazer, T. H. Green, Edward Caird, James Ward), singularism (A.J.B. Balfour, J. Cook Wilson, William Ritchie Sorley), monadistic personalism (H. Wildon Carr), humanistic personalism (F.C.S. Schiller), atheistic personalism (J.M.E. McTaggart), theistic personalism (Borden Parker Bowne, George Trumbull Ladd, John Wright Buckham), personal idealism or absolutistic personalism (Mary Whiton Calkins), personal realism (G. A. Wilson, H. A. Youtz, Ralph Tyler Flewelling, James Bissett Pratt). Other personalist philosophers included Edgar Sheffield Brightman and Albert Cornelius Knudson. Personalist tendencies were also evident in William Ernest Hocking, Josiah Royce, Henri Bergson, and Rudolf Otto. Beginning in 1920 Flewelling edited the journal *The Personalist* (*see* entry no. 1036).

[1894] **82. Illingworth, John Richardson.**
Personality Human and Divine. New York and London: Macmillan & Co. 1894, xv+274 pp.

27

These were the Bampton Divinity Lectures at Oxford University in 1894. Illingworth asserts that human personality is predominantly spiritual and that this dimension of the person reveals God. This is an early statement of the personalist perspective wherein the highest ethical and idealistic capabilities of individuals are held to be the best evidence available for demonstrating theism.

[1897]   **83. Bosanquet, Bernard.**
Psychology of the Moral Self. London: Macmillan & Co., 1897, vii+ 132 pp. New York: Macmillan Co., 1897, viii+132 pp.
Bosanquet's psychology relies on William James, Hugo Münsterberg, James Sully, and George Frederick Stout.

[1899]   **84. Ward, James.**
Naturalism and Agnosticism: The Gifford Lectures Delivered Before the University of Aberdeen 1896−1898. 2 vols. London: Adam and Charles Black, 1899. New York: Macmillan, 1899. 2 ed., revised. 2 vols. London: Adam and Charles Black, 1903, xv+333 pp., xiii+301 pp.
These volumes comprise both the 1896−97 and the 1897−98 Gifford Lectures. Ward notes how the presuppositions of science made idealism ill-conceivable and suggests that the naturalistic view of the world, although in error, has no room for God. He regards agnosticism as skeptical and naturalism as dogmatic, and suggests that the basis of theism is idealism, which includes purpose and the transempirical. Ward was the founder of the Cambridge laboratory and a philosopher in the tradition of act psychology and personalism.

[1909]   **85. Buckham, John Wright.**
Personality and the Christian Ideal: a Discussion of Personality in the Light of Christianity. Boston and New York: Pilgrim Press, 1909, xvi+ 263 pp.
Personality imposes an eternal order upon the natural order of individualism. Selfhood is realized in acts of personalizing (as opposed to depersonalizing). Consciousness of self increases with consciousness of God.

[1912]   **86. Bosanquet, Bernard.**
The Principle of Individuality and Value; The Gifford Lectures for 1911, delivered in Edinburgh University. London: Macmillan & Co., 1912, xxxvii+409 pp. +adv.
Bosanquet argues for interaction of body and mind. The appearance of consciousness does not preclude continuity of organic regulation, but opens up new apprehensions of the whole. Bosanquet characterized personalism in the form of Absolute Idealism.

[1913] **87. Bosanquet, Bernard.**
The Value and Destiny of the Individual; The Gifford Lectures for 1912, delivered in Edinburgh University. London: Macmillan & Co., 1913, xxxii+331 pp.

Further lectures on personalism. Bosanquet includes soul-making, the will, good and evil, and the religious consciousness.

[1914] **88. Ladd, George Trumbull.**
What Can I Know? An Inquiry into Truth, Its Nature, the Means of Its Attainment, and Its Relations to Practical Life. New York and London: Longmans, Green & Co., 1914, vi+2+311 pp.+adv.

The great American textbook writer in psychology here explores problems of epistemology, steering a middle road between credulity and skepticism. The first book in a series of four.

[1915] **89. Ladd, George Trumbull.**
What Ought I to Do? An Inquiry into the Nature and Kinds of Virtue and into the Sanctions, Aims and Values of the Moral Life. New York and London: Longmans, Green & Co., 1915, vii+3+311 pp.+adv.

Ladd traces the origins and development of responsibility. The significance and value of the intention of being good and of doing one's duty are discussed, and followed by a brief defense of the supreme worth of moral ideals in the evolution of personal life. Maxims for settling cases of conscience are included, as well as a chapter on morality and religion.

[1915] **90. Ladd, George Trumbull.**
What May I Hope? An Inquiry into the Sources and Reasonableness of the Hopes of Humanity, Especially the Social and Religious. New York and London: Longmans, Green & Co., 1915, xv+1+310 pp.+adv.

Ladd explores the nature and sources of hope, its limitations, assurance, and practical uses. He also discusses scientific, political, and social hopes. There are separate chapters on hope of immortality, moral perfection, and a divine kingdom.

[1916] **91. Merrington, Ernest Northcroft.**
The Problem of Personality. A Critical and Constructive Study in the Light of Recent Thought. London: Macmillan & Co., 1916, x+229 pp.

A Lecturer at the University of Sydney, Merrington reviews the views of William James, F. H. Bradley, Josiah Royce, George H. Howison, F.C.S. Schiller, Hastings Rashdall, and Andrew Seth Pringle-Pattison. God is regarded as the ideal and perfect personality.

[1917] **92. Oman, John Wood.**
Grace and Personality. Cambridge: Cambridge University Press, 1917, xiii+295 pp. New York: Macmillan Co., 1925, 318 pp.

Oman translates the theological conception of faith into terms of the relationship of man to a "gracious personality," thus offering a theological interpretation of grace in personalistic terms.

[1918]   **93. *Calkins, Mary Whiton.***

The Good Man and the Good: an Introduction to Ethics. New York: Macmillan Co., 1918, xx+219 pp.+adv.

Representing the personalist perspective, Calkins points to two similarities between religion and morality: (1) the good man and the lover of God are both conscious of their personal object and (2) the moral, like religious consciousness, is a "private" experience involving the realization of the person's own unique, individual relation to the personal object. Calkins completed doctoral studies under William James at Harvard and served as president of the American Psychological Association in 1905.

[1918]   **94. *Ladd, George Trumbull.***

The Secret of Personality. The Problem of Man's Personal Life as Viewed in the Light of an Hypothesis of Man's Religious Faith. New York and London: Longmans, Green & Co., 1918, ix+1+287 pp.+adv.

A. A. Roback states that in this book, " . . . religion, philosophy, and psychology are all interwoven to produce a personalistic pattern on a voluntaristic principle. The will, which, in modern psychology has been rejected as an element, was to Ladd the cornerstone of his psychology." Ladd's theological training was at Andover Newton Theological Seminary, and he published a number of articles in the *Andover Review.*

[1919]   **95. *Streeter, Burnett Hillman, ed.***

The Spirit; God and His Relation to Man Considered from the Standpoint of Philosophy, Psychology and Art. London: Macmillan & Co., 1919, xii+381 pp.+adv.

Includes chapters by J. Arthur Hadfield (on the psychology of power), C. W. Emmet (on the psychology of grace and the psychology of inspiration), C.A.A. Scott, Andrew Seth Pringle-Pattison, Lily Dougall, A. Clutton-Brock, and Burnett Hillman Streeter.

[1920]   **96. *Radhakrishnan, Sarvepalli.***

The Reign of Religion in Contemporary Philosophy. London and Toronto: Macmillan & Co., 1920, xii+463 pp.

Radhakrishnan reviews Gottfried Wilhelm von Leibnitz's monadism, James Ward's personalism, Henri Bergson's absolute idealism, the philosophies of William James, Rudolf Eucken, and Bertrand Russell, the personal idealism of F.C.S. Schiller, G. H. Howison, Hastings Rashdall, and A. J. Balfour.

[1921]   **97. *Heath, Arthur George.***

The Moral and Social Significance of the Conception of Personality. Oxford: Clarendon Press, 1921, vii+159 pp.

Heath was a Fellow of New College, Oxford. The reviewer in *The Personalist* states that Heath argues for the personalist position. Heath regards the personality as a continuous self, conscious that it is a unity of diverse states, with phases extending over a period of time, and contrasted with the world itself. Moral goodness in its most characteristic form demands personality. The highest goodness is the personal goodness of finite personalities. The divergence between personal development and social duty is a genuine fact.

[1922]   **98.** *Hoernlé, Reinhold Friedrich Alfred.*

Matter, Life, Mind, and God: Five Lectures on Contemporary Tendencies of Thought. New York: Harcourt, Brace & Co., 1922, xiii+ 215 pp. London: Methuen, 1923, xiii+215 pp.

Hoernlé critiques the personalism of S. Alexander, B. Bosanquet, William Ernest Hocking, William James, Andrew Seth Pringle-Pattison, C.C.J. Webb, James Ward, Hastings Rashdall as well as the psychologies of James Bissett Pratt and George Malcolm Stratton. Behaviorism offers us deliverance from body-soul dualism. Religion and the existence of God can be discussed only from an experiential, insider's perspective.

[1923]   **99.** *Buckham, John Wright.*

Personality and Psychology; An Analysis for Practical Use. New York: George H. Doran, 1923, xv+202 pp.

Buckham's book is reviewed in *The Personalist* by Wilbur H. Long. He asserts that the self is *not* completely revealed by biology and anthropology and cannot be defined adequately in terms of impersonal habits and impulses. The key to personality is found not in control *by* instincts but in control *of* the instincts. The self consists in ethical personality.

[1924]   **100.** *Hoernlé, Reinhold Friedrich Alfred.*

Idealism as a Philosophical Doctrine. London: Hodder & Stoughton, 1924, xi+189 pp. Expanded in *Idealism as a Philosophy.* New York: George H. Doran, 1927, xx+330 pp.

Hoernlé was previously an assistant professor of philosophy at Harvard, and at the time of this writing was professor of philosophy at the University of Witwatersrand, Johannesburg, South Africa. Here, he distinguishes among spiritual pluralism (exemplified by George Berkeley and James Ward), spiritual monism (exemplified by A. Schopenhauer and Henri Bergson), critical idealism (exemplified by Immanuel Kant), and absolute idealism (exemplified by G.W.F. Hegel, F. H. Bradley, and Bernard Bosanquet). Excellent bibliography.

[1924]   **101.** *Muirhead, John Henry, ed.*

Contemporary British Philosophy: Personal Statements. 1 and 2 ser. London: George Allen & Unwin, 1924 and 1925; New York: Macmillan Co., 1924 and 1925, 432 pp., 365 pp.

Especially relevant for integration are the essays by Bernard Bosanquet, H. Wildon Carr, Reinhold Friedrich Alfred Hoernlé, Dean Inge, J.
Ellis McTaggart, F.C.S. Schiller, A. E. Taylor, James Ward, and Clement J. C. Webb.

[1924] **102. Pierce, Edgar.**

The Philosophy of Character. Cambridge: Harvard University Press,
1924, xi+435 pp. +illus.

Wilbur H. Long, in his review in *The Personalist*, describes this book
as "a metaphysics of personality." It offers an introduction to purposive
psychology in the tradition of William McDougall, Henri Bergson, and
F.C.S. Schiller, and is very similar to the psychology of William Stern.
Pierce offers a philosophy of personalism involving "semipluralistic panpsychism or monadism" combined with a doctrine of synthesis or integration.

[1926] **103. Bishop, William Samuel.**

The Theology of Personality. New York: Longmans, Green & Co., 1926,
ix+231 pp.

W. Bertrand Stevens, in his review in *The Personalist*, describes the
author's perspective as Anglican, but deeply informed by Catholicism and
Protestantism.

[1926] **104. Valentine, Cyril Henry.**

Modern Psychology and the Validity of Christian Experience. London:
Society for Promoting Christian Knowledge, 1926, xix+236 pp. New York
and Toronto: Macmillan Co., 1926, xix+236 pp.

Valentine espouses a philosophy of personalism, especially that of
F. H. Bradley and Andrew Seth Pringle-Pattison. A fully developed personality is necessary for the knowledge of God. In a sophisticated attempt
at integration, Valentine parallels the following doctrines of the church
and theories of psychology: doctrine of man and theory of the unconscious; sin and complexes and repression; salvation and integration and
adaptation; God and reality; Christ and transference and identification;
and Holy Spirit and the supraliminal.

[1927] **105. Knudson, Albert Cornelius.**

The Philosophy of Personalism. A Study in the Metaphysics of Religion.
New York: Abingdon Press, 1927, 438 pp.

A definitive critique and summary of personalism, "that form of
idealism which gives equal recognition to both the pluralistic and monistic
aspects of experience and which finds in the conscious unity, identity and
free activity of personality the key to the nature of reality and the solution
of the ultimate problems of philosophy." The historic roots of theistic
personalism include the spiritual individualism and activism of Leibnitz,
the immaterialism of Berkeley, the epistemology and ethical conception
of personality of Kant, and a general formulation by Lotze. The modern

conceptualization was by Borden Parker Bowne of Boston University. An atheistic version was articulated by J.M.E. McTaggart and a pantheistic version by William Stern. Among theistic versions the most popular was neo-Hegelian absolutism, which was advocated by F. H. Bradley, Bernard Bosanquet, Edward Caird, Josiah Royce, Henry Jones, Alfred Edward Taylor, William Ernest Hocking, and Mary Whiton Calkins. Relativistic theism was advocated by Charles Renouvier and William James, teleological theism by George H. Howison, Wilhelm Vatke, and H. Wildon Carr. "Typical" theistic personalism was advocated by A. C. Fraser, James Ward, A. J. Balfour, Andrew Seth Pringle-Pattison, J. Cook Wilson, Hastings Rashdall, William Ritchie Sorley, C.C.J. Webb, Rudolf Eucken, George Trumbull Ladd, and Borden Parker Bowne.

[1928] **106. *Hocking, William Ernest.***

The Self, its Body and Freedom. New Haven: Yale University Press; London: Oxford University Press, H. Milford, 1928, ix+178 pp.

Mind is distinct from body in being space-free, time-free, and concerned with meanings rather than facts. This is why behaviorism is inadequate. The body is required by the mind as part of its being, and thus the most valid position on the body-mind question is that of spiritual monism. Hocking rejects the determinism of natural science and claims that "I am never merely the last term of any series which I observe." Originally presented as the Dwight Harrington Terry Lectures at Yale University.

[1930] **107. *Vaughan, Richard Miner.***

The Significance of Personality. New York: Macmillan Co., 1930, viii+302 pp.

A review in *The Personalist* ascribes to Vaughan a twofold aim: (1) to explain the historic problems of Christianity so as to reveal the deep reason in the doctrinal positions taken by the church, and (2) to throw more light on these historical and more recent questions. Personalism is applied to an understanding of (1) the nature of God, (2) Jesus, and (3) the Trinity.

[1931] **108. *Crutcher, Roberta.***

Personality and Reason. London: Favil Press, 1931, ix+178 pp.

A review in *The Personalist* states Crutcher's position as follows: "Personality is to be conceived as an activity unanalyzable except for purposes of study, containing within itself the source of its activity." Her position is regarded as deviating from the predominating views of personalism. She regards the Trinity as "a means of maintaining personality in a supreme being who is able to transcend and yet provide ground for cosmic activity." She also affirms the personality of God, but in an unorthodox fashion. The preface is by H. Wildon Carr.

[1934] **109. *Turner, John Evan.***
Essentials in the Development of Religion: A Philosophic and Psychological Study. New York: Macmillan Co., London: George Allen & Unwin, 1934, 308 pp.

In the tradition of personalism, Turner examines man as a moral self and related issues of moral experience, criteria of good, good and evil. He also includes a discussion of the divine personality.

[1935] **110. *Stern, William Louis.***
Allgemeine Psychologie auf personalistischen Grundlage. The Hague: M. Nijhoff, 1935, xxviii+831 pp. +illus. ENGLISH: *General Psychology from the Personalistic Standpoint.* Translated by Howard Davis Spoerl. New York: Macmillan Co., 1938, xxii+589 pp. +illus.

This is the last of Stern's books on "critical personalism" in the tradition of Eduard Spranger and Wilhelm Dilthey. Every mental function is centered in a person, who becomes the object of psychological study. Stern's psychology dissociated itself from mere analyses of consciousness and from introspective systems. He replaces the spirit/matter dualism with that of person/thing, which becomes the basis for his entire metaphysical system: the entire world can be regarded, metaphorically, "from above" and "from below." The human personality is self-determining, purposive, and meaningful. It also subordinates itself to the suprapersonal, relating to other persons and humanity. Personality and environment are "convergently" related to each other. The life of personality presents itself in two aspects: the physical is expression while the psychic is impression; both are forms of the same experience. A student of Hermann Ebbinghaus, Stern thoroughly mastered the fields of child psychology and differential psychology. He was Professor of Psychology at Hamburg.

[1936] **111. *Buckham, John Wright.***
Christianity and Personality. New York: Round Table Press, 1936, xi+ 192 pp.

Buckham presents a theistic personalism, and regards freedom as a necessary element in personality. God is the object of experience through beauty, duty, prayer, and Christ.

[1936] **112. *Mounier, Emmanuel.***
Manifeste au service du personnalisme. Paris: F. Aubier, 1936, 242 pp. ENGLISH: *A Personalist Manifesto.* Translated by Monks of St. John's Abbey. New York and London: Longmans, Green & Co., 1938, xxii+298 pp.

Mounier was a leader in the French personalist movement and edited its journal, *Esprit.* He defines personalism as "any doctrine or civilization that affirms the primacy of the human person over material necessities and over the whole complex of implements man needs for the development of his person."

[1937] **113. Pratt, James Bissett.**

Personal Realism. New York: Macmillan Co., 1937, xi+387 pp.

Pratt aims "to defend both Realism and the actuality of the individual." Includes extensive discussion of realistic epistemology, the problem of knowledge, and "the metaphysical consequences which seem to follow naturally, if not with absolute logical necessity, from the position maintained by Critical (or Dualistic) Realism." Of special interest are chapters on "The unavoidability of the mind–body problem," "Consciousness, knowledge, and the self," "The nature of the self," and "The will and its freedom."

[1938] **114. Bertocci, Peter Anthony.**

The Empirical Argument for God in Late British Thought. Cambridge: Harvard University Press, 1938, xv+311 pp.

Examines arguments in the personalist tradition under the following chapter headings: James Martineau's revolt against sense-bound empiricism (discusses the psychology of conscience); conflict of the empirical and nonempirical in Andrew Seth Pringle-Pattison's theism (including the nature of self); halting empiricism in James Ward's theistic monadism (personalism and panpsychism); William R. Sorley's moral argument for God; and Frederick Tennant's teleological argument (including self and the soul).

[1940] **115. Aubrey, Edwin Ewart.**

Man's Search for Himself. Nashville: Cokesbury Press, 1940, 222 pp.

The Cole Lectures at Vanderbilt University in 1940, by a professor of Christian Theology and Ethics at the University of Chicago. Topics addressed include the solitariness of man, the person in community, the search for integration, and the search for freedom. Aubrey concludes that (1) we live in a dynamic world; (2) every life is a unique bottleneck of time; (3) these unique beings are bound together and find their individual fullness only in fellowship; (4) this fellowship is not attainable by rational communication; (5) men therefore ought to love one another; (6) no better embodiment of love in a dynamic world is to be found than in Jesus Christ; and (7) the universe is one and all its parts are continuous with one another.

[1946] **116. Mounier, Emmanuel.**

Traité du caractere. Paris: Editions du seuil, 1946, 795 pp. ENGLISH: *The Character of Man.* Translated by Cynthia Rowland. London: Rocklift, 1956, 341 pp.

Written by a French personalist philosopher–psychologist, this is a study of the human character with emphasis on the self.

[1951] **117. McKenzie, John Grant.**

Nervous Disorders and Religion: a Study of Souls in the Making. London: George Allen & Unwin, 1951, 183 pp.

McKenzie, who was at this time Professor of Social Science and Psychology at Aberdeen, originally presented these ideas as the 1947 Tate Lectures. He describes his psychology as personalist: the integrating principle of the dynamic organization is the self or subject with its own dynamic tendency toward a self-conscious harmonious individual or whole. He rejects the Freudian psychology espoused in his earlier works.

[1952] **118. Caruso, Igor A.**

Psychoanalyse und Synthese der Existenz; Beziehungen zwischen psychologischer Analyse und Daseinswerten. Vienna: Herder, 1952, 239 pp.+illus. ENGLISH: *Existential Psychology: from Analysis to Synthesis.* Translated by Eva Krapf. New York: Herder & Herder; London: Darton, Longman & Todd, 1964, xx+227 pp.+illus.

Caruso outlines a personalistic psychology which takes account of both man's conditioned and determined aspects and his freedom and responsibility. Psychotherapy must be more than purely psychological and more than logo-therapeutic. Relies not only on Sigmund Freud, C. G. Jung, and Alfred Adler, but also on the psychologies of Piaget and Wolfgang Köhler, the spiritual psychologies of Karl Jaspers, Paul Tournier, and Viktor E. Frankl, the existentialism of Jean Paul Sartre and Simone de Beauvoir, and the writings of Emmanuel Mounier and C. Baudouin.

[1952] **119. Flewelling, Ralph Tyler.**

The Person or the Significance of Man. Los Angeles: The Ward Ritchie Press, 1952, xii+339 pp.

This work is a response to requests for reissuing of the author's *Creative Personality*, and summarizes the philosophy of personalism. A sophisticated discussion including epistemology and other basic issues in philosophy of science. Excellent glossary.

[1957] **120. Campbell, Charles Arthur.**

On Selfhood and Godhood; the Gifford Lectures Delivered at the University of Saint Andrews during sessions 1953–1954 and 1954–1955. Revised and expanded. London: George Allen & Unwin; New York: Macmillan Co., 1957, xxxvi+436 pp.+adv.

A philosophical-theological discussion of the relation of selfhood to personhood, the relation of body to mind, the structure and function of the mind, free will and morality.

[1957] **121. Johnson, Paul Emanuel.**

Personality and Religion. New York: Abingdon Press, 1957, 297 pp.+illus.

Reviews the personality theories of Freud (infancy), Kurt Lewin (childhood), Harry Stack Sullivan (adolescence), and Gordon Allport (maturity) and develops his theory of "dynamic interpersonalism" which is contrasted with the personalism of Borden P. Bowne and Edgar S. Brightman and the personalistic psychology of William Stern and Gordon Allport. The tension between psychology and religion centers in the tension between heroic independence and creative dependence as a response to the human condition of loneliness.

PART TWO

Biblical and Theological
Bases for Integration

Concerning the Soul

The soul has a central place in nearly all discussions concerning the integration of theology and psychology. Since "psychology" literally denotes the study of the mind, or soul, it was originally one of three divisions of "pneumatology," the study of spiritual beings. Psychology concerned itself with the human soul, natural theology with the soul of God, and angelography and demonology with other spiritual beings. In this section are included a number of classical theological works on the human soul, critiques which assert that we now have a "psychology without a soul," and later psychologies which emphasize the soul and the spiritual component of the person. While there are no comprehensive sources prior to 1965 which deal with the evolution of the term "psychology," a fairly complete history may be derived from later sources.*

[1672] **122. Willis, Thomas.**

De anima brutorum quae hominis vitalis ac sensitiva est, exercitationes duae. Prior physiologica ejusdem naturam, partes, potentias & affectiones tradit; altera pathologica morbos qui ipsam & sedem ejus primariam, nempe cerebrum & nervosum genus afficiumt, explicat, eorumque

---

*The major sources are as follows:
1. Lapointé, François H. "Origin and Evolution of the Term Psychology." *American Psychologist* 25 (1970): 640–646.
2. Lapointé, François H. "Who Originated the Term 'Psychology'?" *Journal of the History of the Behavioral Sciences* 6, no. 3 (1972): 328–335.
3. Vande Kemp, H. "Origin and Evolution of the Term 'Psychology': addenda."*American Psychologist* 35 (1980): 774.

therapeias instituit . . . Studio Thomae Willis. Londini: Typis E. F. Impensis Ric. Davis, 1672. (45) + 400 + (16) pp. London: Wells & Robertson Scott, 1672, 565 pp. ENGLISH: *Two discourses concerning the soul of brutes, which is that of the vital and sensitive of man. The first physiological, shewing the nature, parts, powers and affections of the same. The other is pathological, which unfolds the diseases which affect it and its primary seat; to wit, the brain and nervous stock, and treats of their cures: with copper cuts.* Translated by S. Pordage. London: Thomas Dring, 1683, 246 pp. Reprint. Gainesville: Scholars' Facsimiles & Reprints, 1971, 234 pp.

A textbook of neuroanatomy (with illustrations) and pathology which focuses on both organic and functional disorders and their treatment. The soul is regarded as neither incorporeal nor immortal.

[1730] **123. Baxter, Andrew.**

An Enquiry into the Nature of the Human Soul, Wherein the Immateriality of the Soul is Evinced from the Principles of Reason and Philosophy. London: James Bettenham, 1730, 376 pp. Reprint. Louisville, Ky.: Lost Cause Press, 1961, 376 pp.

[1802] **124. Drew, Samuel.**

An Essay on the Immateriality and Immortality of the Human Soul, Founded Solely on Physical and Rational Principles. St. Austell: Edmund Hennal, 1802, xx+268 pp. Later editions under the title *An Original Essay.* . . . Bristol: Richard Edwards . . . . 1803, 306 pp. Baltimore: A. Neal, 1810, 210 pp.

Writing against the background of growing materialism and the proposition that there was no substance apart from the physical in human beings, Drew wrote a polemic attesting to rational and physical proof for the soul. The arguments were deductive yet convincing enough to evoke much reaction from scholars. He attempted to avoid biblical authority and to prove the soul's reality on secular grounds.

[1836] **125. Fechner, Gustav Theodor.**

Das Buchlein vom Leben nach dem Tode. Dresden: Ch. F. Grimmersche, 1836, 50 pp. ENGLISH: *On Life After Death.* Translated by Hugo Wernekke. London: Sampson, Low, Marston, Searle, & Rivington, 1882, 95 pp. Also under the title *The Little Book of Life After Death.* Translated by Mary C. Wadsworth, Boston: Little, Brown & Company, 1904, xxvii+ 108 pp. Reprint. New York: Pantheon Books, 1943, pp. 21–90.

Originally published under Fechner's penname, Dr. Mises, the second edition bore Fechner's name and omitted several controversial passages. The booklet went into twenty different editions in three languages. Fechner asserts that one lives on earth three times: before birth in continual sleep, during life in alternating waking and sleeping states, and after death in a continual waking state. He states that his panpsychism was influenced by J.G.F. Billroth. Later editions of the Wernekke translation contain the material deleted in the 1866 edition. The Wadsworth translation included an introduction by William James. In the Pantheon reprinting additional translations by Eugene Jolas are included, featuring selections from *Zend-Avesta* and *Über Die Seelenfrage*.

[1838] **126. *Feuchtersleben, Ernst Freiherr Von.***

Zur Diatetik der Seele. Wien: Armbruster, 1838, xiv+150 pp. ENGLISH: *The Dietetics of the Soul*. London: J. Churchill, 1852, ix+202 pp. Translated by Henry Aime Ouvry. New York: C. S. Francis & Co., 1854.

The German original of this classic went into more than 30 editions, and includes chapters on the mind-body relationship as well as on mental and physical hygiene.

[1842] **127. *Schmucker, Samuel Simon.***

Psychology, or, Elements of a New System of Mental Philosophy on the Basis on Consciousness and Common Sense. Designed for Colleges and Academies. New York: Harper & Brothers, 1842, xxii+227 pp.

Schmucker, a Lutheran clergyman trained at Princeton University and the University of Pennsylvania, regards mental philosophy as the science which discusses the properties of the human soul. A. A. Roback states in *History of American Psychology* that "Schmucker enjoyed the respect of his contemporaries, and in spite of the small compass of his textbook it was popular in academies and colleges, perhaps for that reason as well as for its rippling style and its religious atmosphere." Schmucker taught at Gettysburg Seminary and was affiliated with the Evangelical Lutheran Church.

[1845] **128. *Bush, George.***

The Soul: An Enquiry into Scripture Psychology. New York: Redfield, 1845, 141 pp.

A Christian anthropology from a Swedenborgian perspective.

[1847] **129. *Moore, George.***

The Power of the Soul over the Body, Considered in Relation to Health and Morals. New York: Harper & Brothers, 1847 and 1852, vi+270 pp.+advs.

This book was written when Mesmerism was in vogue. It was intended to be a sober, rational, yet positive statement on the reality of the soul (defined as the thinking, willing, and acting part of the human being). It includes essays originally designed to be talks to young men. This is the most popular work of this English physician.

[1849] **130. *Newman, Francis William.***

The Soul, Her Sorrows and Her Aspirations: An Essay Towards the Natural History of the Soul, as the True Basis of Theology. London: John Chapman; Boston: Little, Brown & Co., 1849, xii+222 pp.+advs.

In discussing the functions and relations of the soul, Newman calls for a return to spiritualism rather than religiosity.

[1885]   **131. *Hecker, Isaac Thomas.***

Questions of the Soul. New York: Appleton & Co., 1855, 294 pp. Reprint. New York: Arno Press, 1978, 294 pp.

Hecker, a Paulist heavily involved with the Brook Farm movement in the 1840s, here sought to introduce persons whose minds were needful of religion to such a religious experience. He did not seek to defend the church, but to appeal to human need. He appealed to Protestantism to affirm Catholicism. He went beyond the Transcendentalists, who affirmed the goodness of the person, to assert their spiritual needs.

[1859]   **132. *Alger, William Rounseville.***

A Critical History of the Doctrine of a Future Life. With a Complete Bibliography of the Subject. Philadelphia: Childs & Peterson, 1859, [77] pp. 4 ed. New York: W. J. Widdleton, 1861, x+914 pp.

A comprehensive overview of both Christian and non-Christian theories concerning the soul, with a bibliography of more than five thousand items. Probably the most valuable resource in this area.

[1868]   **133. *Porter, Noah.***

The Human Intellect with an Introduction upon Psychology and the Soul. New York: C. Scribner's & Company, 1868, xxvii+673 pp.

In the Scottish tradition, Porter mapped out the territory of cognitive psychology, covering questions of sense perception, imagination, memory, and reasoning, as well as a theory of knowledge. Roback characterizes Porter as a staunch intuitionist, an interactionist, and theistic philosopher who uses the argument from design in "writing a psychology for the glorification of God." Psychology is a legitimate and necessary discipline, studying the soul, that part of the person which animates life and lies between body and spirit. Porter assumed the presidency of Yale in 1871.

[1872]   **134. *Paine, Martyn.***

Physiology of the Soul and Instinct as Distinguished from Materialism; with supplementary Demonstrations of the Divine Communication of the Narratives of Creation and the Flood. New York: Harper & Brothers, 1872, xiv+707 pp.

A. A. Roback summarizes this volume as follows: "The work as a whole is a crusade against materialism, in any of its forms, and an extended tirade against the doctrine of evolution, which was then gaining ground, as well as an attempted vindication of the biblical account of creation, miracles, etc., on a fundamentalist basis. Paine throughout the volume piles Ossa on Pelion to prove that modern scientists who deny the existence of a soul, or who see no difference between the mind of man and that of the ape or lower animals, except in degree, are perverse in their reasoning. He rakes up scores of arguments and illustrations to sustain his position, so that in a sense, this *omnium gatherum* may serve as an anthology of scientific opinion on many vital points during the middle of the nineteenth century." (*History of American Psychology*, pp. 82–83).

[1873] **135. *Ives, Charles Linnaeus.***

The Bible Doctrine of the Soul, an Answer to the Question: Is the Popular Conception of the Soul that of Holy Scriptures? New Haven: Judd & White, 1873, 119 pp. Rev. ed., *The Bible Doctrine of the Soul; or, Man's Nature and Destiny as Revealed.* Philadelphia: Claxton, Remsen & Haffelfinger, 1878, x+334 pp.

Ives seeks to refute the claims of Universalism, Romanism, Spiritism, Swedenborgianism, and popular conceptions of the soul that view it as exclusively human, immaterial, and immortal. Using biblical material to support his views, he asserts that all animals have souls, that the human soul is material and mortal, that the biblical soul has a resurrection, that the wicked are destined for eternal death, and that an intermediate state occurs between mortal and immortal life. He examines passages he judges incorrectly used to support the notion of a disembodied state, explores the nature of angel souls (both good and evil), and the doctrines of immortality in the Old and New Testaments. Ives was Professor of Theory and Practice of Medicine at Yale.

[1874] **136. *Gillett, Ezra Hall.***

God in Human Thought; or,Natural Theology Traced in Literature, Ancient and Modern, to the Time of Bishop Butler; With a Closing Chapter on the Moral System, and an English Bibliography, from Spenser to Butler. Vol. 2. New York: Scribner, Armstrong & Co., 1874, 417–834 pp. +adv.

Most valuable for the 33-page bibliography, which includes writings on the soul by Thomas Morton, Sir John Davies, Edward Kellett, Kenelm Digby, Edward Herbert, Edward Reynolds, Jacob Behmen, Thomas Hobbes, Seth Ward, Henry More, Henry Woolner, H. Hills, William Bates, Charles Blount, Rene Des Cartes, Richard Baxter, George Rust, R. Bentley, Henry Layton, Timothy Manlove, J. S. William Coward, Matthew Hole, John Turner, John Broughton, William Assheton, W. Coward, John Turner, F. Gregory, William Sherlock, Richard Burthogge, Henry Dodwell, Edmund Chishull, S. Clarke, D. Whitby, Thomas Milles, John Norris, Benjamin Hampton, Richard Fiddes, Joseph Hallett, Isaac Watts, S. Colliber, Dean Sherlock, John Jackson, and Samuel Colliber.

[1882] **137. *Hartmann, Karl Robert Eduard von.***

Die Religion des Geistes. Berlin: C. Duncker, 1882, xii+328 pp. ENGLISH: *The Religion of the Future.* Translated by Ernest Dare. London: W. Stewart & Co., 1886, 119 pp.

[1890] **138. *Rohde, Erwin.***

Psyche: Seelenkult und Unterblichkeitsglaube der Griechen. Freiburg: Mohr, 1890, 711 pp. ENGLISH: *Psyche: The Cult of Souls and Belief in Immortality among the Greeks.* Translated by W. B. Hillis. London: Kegan Paul; New York: Harcourt, 1925, xiv+626 pp. +adv.

A history of the soul in Greek literature from Homer through the post-Platonic period. Of special interest is the appended discussion of split personality, including the disintegration of consciousness and reduplication of personality.

[1893] **139. *Müller, Friedrich Max.***

Theosophy: or, Psychological Religion; the Gifford Lectures Delivered Before the University of Glasgow in 1892. London and New York: Longmans, Green & Co., 1893, xxiii+585 pp.

The Gifford lectures for 1892, followed two series on the physical and anthropological aspects of religion. Müller defines psychological religion as the attempt to discover the true relation between the soul and God. The true relation between human and divine soul should be as clear as the most perfect logical syllogism. According to Müller, "Christianity represents a synthesis of Semitic and Aryan thought which forms its real strength and its power of satisfying not only the requirements of the heart, but likewise the postulates of reason."

[1897] **140. *Dresser, Horatio Willis.***

In Search of a Soul: A Series of Essays in Interpretation of the Highest Nature of Man. Boston: Ellis; London and New York: G. P. Putnam's Sons, 1897, 273 pp.

This is an apology for the spiritual reality of persons and an argument against materialism. These were speeches delivered at various times in the Boston area. The content is in the idealist tradition of the New England Thoreauist.

[1898] **141. *Driscoll, John Thomas.***

Christian Philosophy: a Treatise on the Human Soul. 2 ed. New York: Benziger Brothers, 1898, xvi+269 pp. Albany: J. B. Lyon, printer, 1898, xiii+269 pp.

Driscoll defines psychology as "the philosophy of the soul of man, of the soul as the principle and source of sensitive and especially of intellectual operations." While the principles set forth are those of scholastic philosophy, especially those of St. Thomas Aquinas, Driscoll offers a broad overview of the history of the soul drawing on both theological/philosophical sources and the contributions of the "new psychology" of the late nineteenth century. Topics treated include the substantiality of the soul (transcendental, phenomenal, agnostic, materialistic, and scholastic views), materialism, the simplicity of the soul, positivism, the spirituality of the soul, pantheism, soul and body, brain and thought, the origin of the soul (theories of emanation, traducianism, manifestation, evolution, and creation), immortality, and personality. Driscoll's treatise offers a valuable history of philosophical psychology.

[1898] **142. *James, William.***

Human Immortality: Two Supposed Objections to the Doctrine. Boston and New York: Houghton, Mifflin and Company, 1898, ix+70 pp.

From the Ingersoll Lectures for 1898. James here refutes some of his own arguments against immortality first presented in *The Principles of Psychology*. He asserts, first, that "even though our soul's life (as here below it is revealed to us) may be in literal strictness the function of a brain that perishes, yet it is not at all impossible, but on the contrary quite possible, that the life may still continue when the brain itself is dead." Here he defends the transmission theory against the production theory. He then clears away, with a theistic and pantheistic solution, the "stumbling block" arising from "the incredible number of beings which, with our modern imagination, we must believe to be immortal, if immortality be true."

[1900] **143. *Penn-Lewis, Jessie.***
> *Soul and Spirit: a Glimpse into Bible Psychology, Together with Papers on "Soul Force" Versus "Spirit Force" from the Overcomer.* Leicester: The Overcomer Book Room, 1900, 81 pp. Fort Washington, Penn.: The Christian Literature Crusade, n.d.
>
> Penn-Lewis argues for the tripartite nature of persons in the context of a detailed exploration of the implications of the spirit-soul distinction for the sanctification process. She asserts that "The 'spiritual' man, therefore, is one in whom, through the dividing of soul and spirit by the Word of God, the *spirit has been freed* from the entanglement of the 'soul,'. . . and joined to the Lord in union of essence—spirit with spirit—*one* spirit—so that the soul and body may serve as vehicles for the expression of the will, and life, and love of the Lord Himself through the believer." In describing the tripartite nature, she states "that the 'soul' is the seat of the self-consciousness (the personality, the will, the intellect), and stands between the spirit—the seat of the God-consciousness; and the body—the seat of the sense, or world-consciousness."

[1902] **144. *Bradford, Amory Howe.***
> *The Ascent of the Soul.* New York: The Outlook Co., 1902, xi+319 pp. Also under the title *The Growth of the Soul.* Cambridge: Melrose, 1903, 319 pp.
>
> Consists of a series of edifying sermons on the following topics: the awakening of the soul, first steps and hindrances in its upward life, reawakening, the place of Jesus Christ, nature and culture, and questions concerning death as the end.

[1904] **145. *Waller, George.***
> *The Biblical View of the Soul.* London and New York: Longmans, Green & Co., 1904, xiv+170 pp.

[1905] **146. *Carus, Paul.***
> *The Soul of Man: An Investigation of the Facts of Physiological and Experimental Psychology.* 3 ed. Chicago: Open Court Publishing Company, 1905, xviii+482 pp; London: Kegan Paul, Trench, Trubner, 1905, xviii+482 pp.

Carus served as editor of *The Open Court* (an early journal devoted to the science-religion relationship) and *The Monist* (devoted to the philosophy of science). He also wrote on Eastern religions, mythology, ethics, and natural theology.

[1905] **147. *Münsterberg, Hugo.***

The Eternal Life. Boston and New York: Houghton, Mifflin and Company, 1905, 72 pp.+advs.

Münsterberg asserts that eternal life cannot logically mean a mere extension of time, so that it must be different in a quantitative manner in relation to the present life. His solution is found in attitudes of the will: "a will can never strive for more space and time, but only for more significance and value and satisfaction."

[1909] **148. *Crawley, Alfred Ernest.***

The Idea of the Soul. London: A & C Black, 1909, viii+307 pp.

Essentially a textbook of psychology, with practical examples in psychology and roots in comparative religion. The author was a social anthropologist and folklorist.

[1911] **149. *Buck, Jirah Dewey.***

New Atavar and the Destiny of the Soul: The Findings of Natural Science Reduced to Practical Studies in Psychology. Cincinnati: The Robert Clark Co., 1911, xxiv+226 pp.

Buck wrote numerous works on free-masonry and theosophy.

[1911] **150. *Steven, George.***

The Psychology of the Christian Soul. New York and London: Hodder & Stoughton, 1911, viii+304 pp.

Steven, presenting his ideas originally as the 1911 Cunningham Lectures, regards psychology of religion as "only the explaining of the way in which the deeper things of life work within the human mind." He is guided by three major principles of education: enlightenment of the mind, freedom of the soul to serve, and unifying of the soul. His discussion of the subconscious begins with Herbart and traces the apperceptive tradition through hypnotism and psychic studies. Steven relies on Leuba, Starbuck, Hall, George Albert Coe, and George Bissett Pratt, as well as the philosophy of personalism. He summarizes the positions of Pelagianism, Augustinianism, and Semi-Pelagianism, rejecting these alternatives for a view which permits the personality of Christ to impress human personality.

[1912] **151. *Gruender, Hubert.***

Psychology without a Soul; A Criticism. St. Louis: B. Herder, 1912, xviii+245 pp.+adv.

Father Gruender's treatise constitutes an apologetic for Scholastic philosophy and an argument against the materialism and positivism of

Structuralism and early Functionalism, exemplified primarily by Titchener and James. Gruender argues for the soul's substantiality, simplicity, spirituality, and immortality.

[1914] **152. Davis, Thomas Kirby.**
Mind and Spirit: A Study in Psychology. Boston: Sherman, French & Co., 1914, 115 pp.
    Primarily an overview of orthodox views on the soul.

[1916] **153. Saunders, Kenneth James.**
Adventures of the Christian Soul: Being Chapters in the Psychology of Religion. Cambridge: University Press, 1916, xii+145 pp.
    Introduced by the Dean of St. Paul's, Saunders presents psychology of religion from a Christian and developmental perspective, in a reliable and readable style.

[1917] **154. Hadfield, James Arthur, ed.**
Immortality: An Essay in Discovery Coordinating Scientific, Psychical and Biblical Research. London: Macmillan & Co., 1917, xvi+388 pp.
    Essays by Burnett H. Streeter; A. Clutton-Brock and C. W. Emmett; Lily Dougall; and J. A. Hadfield.

[1919] **155. Marshall, Henry Rutgers.**
Mind and Conduct: Morse Lectures Delivered at Union Theological Seminary in 1919. New York: Charles Scribner's Sons, 1919, ix+236 pp.
    Marshall's book is reviewed by R. M. Wenley in the *Anglican Theological Review*. Marshall covers many of the categories of the traditional faculty psychology and looks at the metaphysical problems of psychology from a common-sense perspective. He provides a serious discussion of the psychological factors in experience and gives a detailed analysis of the collision between vitalism and mechanism.

[1920] **156. Rashdall, Hastings.**
King's College Lectures on Immortality. Edited by Walter Robert Matthews. London: University of London Press, 1920, viii+248 pp.
    A collection of five essays by J. F. Bethune-Baker (The religious value of the idea of a future life), A. Caldecott (The argument from emotions), Hastings Rashdall (The Moral argument for personal immortality), W. Brown (Immortality in the light of modern psychology), and H. Maurice Relton (The Christian contribution to the conception of eternal life).

[1924] **157. Laird, John.**
The Idea of the Soul. London and Toronto: Hodder & Stoughton, 1924, viii+192 pp. New York: George H. Doran, 1925, viii+191 pp.
    Laird includes a survey of the doctrine of the "self" from Democritus

to Lotze. This is followed by a discussion of selfhood from biological, physiological, and metaphysical perspectives. The final chapter is on immortality. Laird focuses on the continuity involved in the sense of self, and attempts to refute the impersonalism of John Dewey.

[1926]   **158. *Driesch, Hans Adolf Eduard.***

Grundprobleme der Psychologie: ihre Krisis in der Gegenwart. Leipzig: E. Reinicke, 1926, ix+249 pp. ENGLISH: *The Crisis in Psychology.* Princeton: Princeton University Press, 1926, xvi+275 pp.

R. T. Flewelling, in his review in *The Personalist*, describes this volume as valuable for personalism. Driesch discusses the soul as necessary to a scientific outlook on psychological facts and asserts that psychology cannot ignore metaphysical assumptions without suicidal results. The soul is needed as a concept of order and has a "whole-making causality". Driesch regards "soul" and "mind" as concepts superior to "consciousness" or its contents.

[1927]   **159. *Müller-Freienfels Richard.***

Geheimnisse der Seele. Munich: Delphin, 1927, 349 pp. ENGLISH: *Mysteries of the Soul.* Translated by Bernard Miall. London: George Allen & Unwin, 1929, 348 pp. New York: A. A. Knopf, 1929.

A philosophic treatment of the phenomenon called "soul" which is heavily informed by the psychological and psychical research of the early twentieth century. Includes chapters on metaphysics, evolution, mental development, and social psychology. Of particular interest are the chapters on the unique effect of the American thrust on these matters and the psychology of religion.

[1930]   **160. *Rank, Otto.***

Seelenglaube und Psychologie; eine prinzipielle Untersuchung über Ursprung, Entwicklung und Wesen des Seelischen. Leipzig: F. Deuticke, 1930, 193 pp. ENGLISH: *Psychology and the Soul.* Translated by William D. Turner. Philadelphia: University of Pennsylvania Press, 1950; New York: A. S. Barnes, 1961, viii+195 pp.

Rank emphasizes the importance of the spiritual and the impossibility of escaping human yearning for immortality. Psychology grew out of such spiritual belief and seeks to preserve the ideology of immortality while no longer believing in the soul to which it owes its existence. The immortal was located first in the body, then the collective soul, then procreative sexuality, and finally in the collective works of the individual. The localization of the soul changed accordingly during the animistic, sexual, and psychological eras. Rank states that "therapy works only as long as it can sustain man's ancient illusory belief in the soul and only when it can offer him a soul without psychology." Freud's psychology is criticized for its denial of this spiritual issue.

[1931] **161. *Crawshaw, William H.***

The Indispensable Soul. New York: Macmillan Co., 1931, 315 pp.

Rejects the behavioristic psychologies which have cast out the soul, and argues for its necessity in the scientific enterprise. Mind is different from nature in that it can restore order it has destroyed and can even restore itself. While matter involves questions of causality, life and mind involve ends and purposes. Spiritual continuity can only be found through an oversoul. Crawshaw offers an overview of general psychology while using traditional categories related to the soul. An excellent example of theoretical integration.

[1932] **162. *Holman, Charles Thomas.***

The Cure of Souls, A Sociopsychological Approach. Chicago: University of Chicago Press, 1932, xv+331 pp.

Holman here considers the following issues: what ails sick souls?; the case work method in the cure of souls; psychiatry and the cure of souls; the function of religion in the cure of souls; and spiritual therapeutics. The book is reviewed by William A. Cameron in the *Journal of Religion*.

[1935] **163. *Ikin, Alice Graham.***

Religion and Psychotherapy: A Plea for Cooperation. London: Student Christian Movement Press, 1935, 139 pp.

The reviewer in *The Expository Times* regards Ikin's volume as "eminently wise on how the pastor should deal with spiritual problems."

[1936] **164. *Sheldon, William Herbert.***

Psychology and the Promethean Will: A Constructive Study of the Acute Common Problem of Education, Medicine, and Religion. New York: Harper & Brothers, 1936, x+265 pp.

Sheldon, well known for his later writings on somatotypes, coins the phrase "animectomy complex," the fear of loss of soul, which is aggravated by psychology's banishing of the soul. The crucial problem of today lies in the area pertaining to purposive orientation in time. Psychoanalysis is regarded as a highly specialized technique for dealing radically with desperate religious problems.

[1946] **165. *Frankl, Viktor Emil.***

Ärtzliche Seelsorge. Vienna: Franz Deuticke, 1946, 192 pp. ENGLISH: The Doctor and the Soul: an Introduction to Logotherapy. Translated by Richard Winston and Clara Winston. New York: Knopf, 1955, xxi+279 pp.

An exposition of the basis principles of logotherapy, Frankl's version of existential psychotherapy.

[1947] **166. *Hirsch, Woolf.***

Rabbinic Psychology: Beliefs about the Soul in Rabbinic Literature of the Talmudic Period. London: Edward Goldston, 1947, 291 pp.; Reprint. New York: Arno Press, 1973, 291 pp.

This book is an introduction to the major themes of rabbinic theology—the concept of the soul, its preexistence and its afterlife.

[1950] **167. Bookstaber, Philip David.**

The Idea of the Development of the Soul in Medieval Jewish Philosophy. Philadelphia: Maurice Jacobs, 1950, 104 pp.

A summary, with footnoted illustrations, of the ideas of Isaac Ben Solomon Israeli, Saadia Ben Joseph Al-Fayyumi, Bachya Ben Joseph Ibn Pakuda, Solomon Ibn Gabirol, Joseph Ibn Zadik, Judah Halevi, Abraham Ibn Daud, and Moses Maimonides.

[1950] **168. Strasser, Stephan.**

Het Zielsbegrip in de Metaphysische en in de Empirische Psychologie. Leuven: Hoger Instituut voor Wijsbegeerte, 1950, xiii+221 pp. ENGLISH: *The Soul in Metaphysical and Empirical Psychology.* Translated by Henry T. Koren. Pittsburgh: Duquesne University Press, 1957, 275 pp.

Strasser's treatment of the soul follows the Thomistic tradition. A German translation appeared in 1955.

[1951] **169. Sherrill, Lewis Joseph.**

The Struggle of the Soul. New York: Macmillan Co., 1951, vii+155 pp.

A scholarly account relying on theological and psychological theory, with each developmental stage clearly demarcated and summarized. Sherrill discusses which factors help the person to reach out in the pilgrimage and which do not.

[1956] **170. Owen, Derwyn Randolph Grier.**

Body and Soul; A Study on the Christian View of Man. Philadelphia: Westminster Press, 1956, 239 pp.

A valuable contribution to the history of syncretism. Owen examines the religious view of man, the biblical view (Hebraic), the psychosomatic, and that of "scientism." His own perspective relies on the theologies of H. Wheeler Robinson and J.A.T. Robinson.

[1960] **171. White, Victor.**

Soul and Psyche: An Enquiry into the Relationship of Psychotherapy and Religion. New York: Harper & Brothers, 1960, 312 pp.

First presented as the Edward Cadbury Lectures at the University of Birmingham from 1958 to 1959. The guiding assumption is the identity of the "soul" of religion and the "psyche" of psychology, which implies the identity of health and holiness, sanity and sanctity. White's perspective is essentially an exposition of Jungian psychology and analysis, but his commitment is that of a Catholic Christian.

[1964] **172. Bennett, John Godolphin.**

A Spiritual Psychology. London: Hodder & Stoughton, 1964, 256 pp.

Bennett's writings are primarily in the area of Buddhism.

173. *Drakeford, John W.*

Psychology in Search of a Soul. Nashville: Broadman Press, 1964, 301 pp.

A conceptual, historical, and empirical overview of the psychology of religious movements with a special emphasis on religion and personality. In this excellent synthesis, Drakeford encourages psychology to open itself to the insights of religion with the hope that its soul may be restored.

174. *Cobb, John B.*

A Christian Natural Theology. Based on the Thought of Alfred North Whitehead. Philadelphia: Westminster Press, 1965, 288 pp.

Cobb, a Methodist minister, dedicated this book to Charles Hartshorne. Chapters 2 and 3 focus on Whitehead's view of the human soul and human responsibility, and are thus of relevance for the formulation of an integrated anthropology and personality theory. Cobb concludes that "we can conceive of the soul occupying generally the region of the brain, receiving the causal efficacy of every portion of the brain at once, and experiencing its own synthesis of all these influences in its own unified subjective immediacy."

Biblical and Christian Psychologies

When the term "psychology" was first naturalized into the English language, its meaning was ambiguous. As Lapointé (1970) points out, "the term psychology was about to become anything but the 'study of the soul' " (p. 645; cited on p. 41 of this book). When physiological psychologists and moral philosophers began using the term, Christian anthropologists and theologians began to qualify their works with the label "Christian psychology," since they were still concerned with the human soul in the context of a more general study of spiritual beings. Most orthodox Christian psychologies conceived of man as consisting of only two distinct parts, body and soul, a view technically called *dichotomy*. Alternatively, others conceived of man as consisting of body, soul, and spirit, a view designated as *trichotomy* and originating in Greek philosophy. In this section are included some of these early nineteenth-century Christian psychologies as well as later relevant works in the tradition of Christian anthropology.

[1837] **175. M'Cormac, Henry.**

The Philosophy of Human Nature, in its Physical, Intellectual, and Moral Relations; with an Attempt to Demonstrate the Order of Providence in the Three-fold Constitution of our Being. London: Longman, Rees, Orme, Brown, Green & Longman, 1837, x+564 pp.

A general psychology in the tradition of the mental and moral philosophers is offered by M'Cormac, who explores the laws of sensation in depth, along with the laws of the mind. The moral order receives the greatest emphasis, as stated by the author in his introduction: "A brief outline of the physical condition of man has been given, while the necessity of elevating it, in order to secure the general advancement, has been urged. But more especially, the supremacy of the moral law—the connexion which we thereby maintain with the Deity and with another form of existence, and the not to be evaded obligation under which we labour to obey it, have been set forth. This has been shown to be the corner-stone of human excellence; that, before which, mere intellect sinks into insignificance, and without which, talent, rank, or power, is an idle dream."

[1840] **176. *Rauch, Friedrich August.***

Psychology; or, A View of the Human Soul: Including Anthropology. New York: M. W. Dodd, 1840, 388 pp.

This is the second English title using the word "psychology". Rauch was *extraordinarius* at Heidelberg, but opposition led him to come to the United States, where he became president of Marshall College in 1836, after serving as professor in biblical literature at the German Reformed Theological Seminary in New York. Psychology and theology are connected by their common subject, which is man. Rauch united German and American mental philosophies, relying on John Locke, Dugald Stewart, Thomas Reid, Thomas Brown, K. Rosenkranz, Carl Gustav Carus, Carl Daub, E. Stiedenroth, Snabedissen, C. A. von Eschenmayer, Johann Christian August Heinroth, Georg W. F. Hegel, Immanuel Kant, Edmund J. Wirth, Steffens, J. F. Herbart, and von Hartman. Rauch's discussion of the personality prefigures the later philosophy of personalism: personality unites soul and body, and is complete only when we are conscious of God and our relation to him. He classifies religions into three groups: those of desire (Buddhism); of imagination (Brahmism, Persian, Egyptian, and Greek); and of understanding or cool reflection (Roman). These are opposed to the true religion of Christianity, in which the activity of God touches the heart of man.

[1843] **177. *Beck, Johann Tobias.***

Umriss der biblischen Seelenlehre. Stuttgard: Belser, 1843, xvi+135 pp. ENGLISH: *Outlines of Biblical Psychology.* Translated from third enlarged and corrected German edition. Edinburgh: T & T Clark, 1877, xvi+ 170 pp.+adv.

Beck was Professor of Theology at Basel and later at Tübingen. Beck takes a classic trichotomic position, and explores the life of the human soul *(Nephesh)* in relation to spirit *(Ruach)* and heart *(Leb)*.

[1855] **178. *Delitzsch, Franz Julius.***

System der biblischen Psychologie. Leipzig: Dorffling und Franke, 1855, viii+438 pp. ENGLISH: *A System of Biblical Psychology.* Translated by Robert Ernest Wallis. Edinburgh: T & T Clark, 1867, xvi+585 pp. Reprint. Grand Rapids: Baker Book House, 1966, xvi+585 pp.

Delitzsch was Professor of Philosophy and Theology at Erlangen and later Professor of Theology at Leipzig. In 1886 he founded the "Judaica Institute" in Leipzig. Biblical psychology is defined as "a scientific representation of the doctrine of Scripture on the psychical constitution of man as it was created, and the ways in which this constitution has been affected by sin and redemption." Delitzsch's position is essentially trichotomic. The first chapter offers an excellent historical overview of previous biblical psychologies.

[1874] **179. *Sutherland, George.***

Christian Psychology: a new Exhibition of the Capacities and Faculties of the Human Spirit, Investigated and Illustrated from the Christian Standpoint. Sidney: William Maddock; Melbourne: George Robinson; Adelaide: W. C. Rigby; Dunedin, N.Z.: H. Wise; Brisbane: Watson and Co.; Hobart Town: Walsh and Son, 1874, 450 pp.

Sutherland illustrates the intimate connection between theology and psychology and treats the following issues: intellectual capacity, emotional susceptibility, executive power, normal faculty, and habitudes. The work is poorly indexed.

[1874] **180. *Woodward, Thomas Best.***

A Treatise on the Nature of Man, Regarded as Triune; With an Outline of a Philosophy of Life. London: Hodder & Stoughton, 1874, 277 pp.

[1879] **181. *Laidlaw, John.***

The Bible Doctrine of Man. The 7th Series of the Cunningham Lectures. Edinburgh: T & T Clark, 1879, 379 pp.

Laidlaw was Professor of Theology at New College, Edinburgh. The book is most valuable for its overview of trichotomic anthropologies and various tripartite theories.

[1879] **182. *Mead, Charles M.***

The Soul Here and Hereafter: A Biblical Study. Boston: Congregational Publishing Society, 1879, xv+462 pp.

Mead, professor at Andover Theological Seminary, offers a critique of C. L. Ives' "Bible Doctrine of the Soul," White's "Life in Christ," J. Pettingell's "Theological Trilemma," and J. B. Heard's book on the "Tripartite nature of man." Mead accepts at least a modified version of trichotomy.

[1896] **183. *Hurst, John Fletcher.***

Literature of Theology: A Classified Bibliography of Theological and General Religious Literature. New York: Hunt & Eaton; Cincinnati: Crantson & Curts, 1896, xv+757 pp.

Of relevance are pp. 173–4, "Psychology of the Bible," where the biblical psychologies of Johann Tobias Beck, Franz Delitzsch, and Charles L. Ives are cited.

[1900?] **184. *Chambers, Oswald.***

Biblical Psychology: A Series of Preliminary Studies. 2 ed. London: Simpkin Marshall, n.d., viii+269 pp.

In a series of lectures first delivered at London's Bible Training College, Chambers presents a trichotomic position. Powers of the soul are described for the "unregenerate nature" and contrasted with their counterparts "in those who are born again of the Spirit of God." William James is the psychological model, though not explicitly acknowledged.

[1910] 185. *Warner, Horace Emory.*

The Psychology of the Christian Life: A Contribution to the Scientific Study of Christian Experience and Character. New York and Chicago: Fleming H. Revell Co., 1910, 401 pp.

Warner uses the following definition: "Christian psychology is the study of the soul in its exhibition of the phenomena of the Christian life. It is the systematic, scientific knowledge of psychical activities involved in Christian experience and their coordination in conduct and character. It is the exploration of the entire field of interrelated phenomena appearing in the life of the Christian. It is the classification of all the facts thus discoverable in their correlated order. It is the formulation of the evident laws of the spiritual, experimental action developed under the Gospel of Jesus Christ."

[1911] 186. *Robinson, Henry Wheeler.*

The Christian Doctrine of Man. Edinburgh: T & T Clark, 1911, x+ 365 pp.

Robinson was Tutor in Rawdon College and Senior Kennicott Scholar at the University of Oxford. He surveys the main problems of Christian anthropology from the most modern psychological and historical viewpoints.

[1912] 187. *Fletcher, M. Scott.*

The Psychology of the New Testament. 2 ed. London and New York: Hodder & Stoughton, 1912, xii+332 pp.

Biblical psychology is defined as the description and explanation which the Scriptures give of the mental and spiritual constitution of man. Its description of the mind focuses on the ethical and religious, and tends to be theocentric in nature. Fletcher organizes his material in chapters relating to flesh, heart, soul, and spirit, and offers an overview of the biblical psychologies of Johann Tobias Beck, Roos, Olshausen, Franz Julius Delitzsch, J. B. Heard, and Ellicott. Biblical psychology counters trends toward materialism, absolute idealism, and pragmatism.

[1913] 188. *House, Elwin Lincoln.*

The Psychology of Orthodoxy. New York and Chicago: Fleming H. Revell Co., 1913, 265 pp. +advs.

A Christian psychology for the lay reader. Christian psychology is defined as the science of the mind and spirit. House holds the trichotomist view of Franz Julius Delitzsch and Ellicott, and is critical of New Thought and Christian Science, defending the Church of Christ.

[1913] **189. McCrossan, Charles Wesley.**
The Mind Science of Christ Jesus: A Treatise on Christian Psychology Showing the Power of Suggestion and Revealing the Secrets of Mental and Spiritual Healing. Santa Cruz: The Sentinel Publishing Company, 1913, 202 pp. +adv.

A Christian anthropology written primarily as a critique of Christian Science. McCrossan draws a parallel between the mind of man, containing realms of conscious, subconscious, and superconscious, and the mind of God, which includes the realms of the Son, the Father, and the Holy Spirit (the Mother God). He claims that "Christian Science can heal no disease which cannot be healed by mentality alone; that is by suggestion and autosuggestion."

[1914] **190. Stalker, James.**
Christian Psychology. New York and London: Hodder & Stoughton, 1914, 281 pp. +adv.

Stalker, an Aberdeen theologian, first presented these lectures at Union, Richmond, and Auburn theological seminaries, and acknowledged his indebtedness to William James and William Hamilton. The work is an elementary introduction to psychology, from an evangelical, trichotomic perspective differentiating among body, soul, and spirit.

[1923] **191. Bishop, William Samuel.**
Spirit and Personality, An Essay in Theological Interpretation. New York: Longmans, Green & Co., 1923, xi+188 pp.

Written from an Anglican perspective, a comparison and a contrast of the biblical views of Paul and James are central to the book's anthropology and personality theory.

[1924] **192. Norlie, Olaf M.**
An Elementary Christian Psychology: A General Psychology from a Christian Viewpoint. Minneapolis: Augsburg Publishing House, 1924, 270 pp.

This text was commissioned by the Board of Elementary Education of the Norwegian Lutheran Church in America. Norlie sets forth a dichotomic Christian psychology, equating soul with spirit, ghost, heart, and mind. He discusses the body-soul relationship from the perspectives of idealism, materialism, double aspect theory, parallelism, incarcerationism, and interactionism. Faith and conscience have both been neglected by psychology. Norlie's discussion of "natural and renewed states" offers an excellent psychology of conversion. The unity of body and soul is seen in continuity, identity, personality, and character. The valuable literature review includes English, Danish, Norwegian, Swedish, and German sources.

[1928] 193. *Keyser, Leander Sylvester.*

A *Handbook of Christian Psychology*. Burlington, Iowa: The Lutheran Literary Board, 1928, 169 pp.

A late version of the "biblical psychologies," Keyser's offers a dichotomic view. Excellent annotated bibliography.

[1940] 193. *Garrison, Winfred Ernest, ed.*

Faith of the Free. Chicago: Willett, Clark & Co., 1940, 276 pp.

This Festschrift for Edward Scribner Ames includes writings by Van Meter Ames, William Clayton Bower, Marguerite Harmon Bro, and others. "Free" in the title refers to the Chicago emphasis on trusting the spirit embedded in human beings to find that which is of deepest value. Personalism, as understood by this group of thinkers, was anti-institutional. The contributors to the volume were all members at one time of the University Church of Disciples of Christ, of which Ames was the pastor from 1900 to 1940.

[1952] 195. *Cross, Hildreth Marie.*

An Introduction to Psychology: An Evangelical Approach. Grand Rapids: Zondervan Publishing House, 1952, 464 pp.

The author's definition of psychology "includes the study of behavior, the consideration of all mental phenomena and *the investigation of the spiritual interests of the individual*," and specifies that the environment must include the supernatural as well as the natural. Her summary outlines the dynamic Christian personality.

[1955] 196. *Witherington, Henry Carl.*

Psychology of Religion: A Christian Interpretation. Grand Rapids: W. B. Eerdmans Publishing Co., 1955, 344 pp.

Witherington limits his focus to the Christian religion and illustrates his examples with biblical material. His anthropology is trichotomic, distinguishing between spirit and soul. Unusual aspects of his treatment include religion and semantics, prophetic concepts in religion, psychology and revivals.

Psychology and Biblical Studies

The psychology of religion influenced exegetical efforts from the turn of the century. In this section are included attempts at new understandings of major biblical characters, the psychology of prophecy, the psychology of miracles, the psychology of inspiration and revelation, and psychological implications for exegesis and hermeneutics.

[1873] **197. Boudreaux, Florentin J.**

God our Father. Baltimore: John Murphy & Co.; New York: Catholic Publications Society, 1873, 216 pp. London: Burns & Oates, 1878, vi+116 pp. Reprint. Chicago: Loyola University Press, 1962, 216 pp.

Boudreaux, a Jesuit, examines the paternal relation of the deity to humankind in an effort to counteract the prevailing images of God as tyrant and other images that produce a morbid spirituality centered on fear.

[1906] **198. Kaplan, Jacob Hyman.**

"Psychology of Prophecy: a Study of the Prophetic Mind as Manifested by the Ancient Hebrew Prophets." *American Journal of Religious Psychology and Education* (1906): 169–203. Also in book form. Philadelphia: J. H. Greenstone, 1908, xii+148 pp.

Kaplan deals with premonition, revelation, dream, vision, audition, ecstacy, and inspiration, and focuses on the prophetical call, the moment when each prophet became conscious of the call of God. He distinguishes between eastern and western attitudes to God, the former emphasizing immediacy and the latter secondary causes. Psychology is expected to establish (rather than deny) the prophetic experience.

[1907] **199. Raymond, George Lansing.**

Th Psychology of Inspiration: An Attempt to Distinguish Religious from Scientific Truth and to Harmonize Christianity with Modern Thought. New York: Funk & Wagnall's, 1907, xix+340 pp.

An early treatise addressing claims concerning the inerrancy-infallibility of scripture. Arguing that scriptural truth should be regarded as suggestive rather than literal, Raymond considers "the nature and influence upon thought and action of what is termed inspired or revealed truth." Includes enumeration of students and graduates of Presbyterian seminaries in 1895 and 1907 as increased evidence of credulity created by modern science.

[1910] **200. Joyce, Gilbert Cunningham.**

The Inspiration of Prophecy: An Essay in the Psychology of Revelation. London and New York: Oxford University Press, H. Frowde, 1910, 195 pp.

Lectures delivered to the Society of Sacred Study in the Dioceses of St. Asaph and Bangor. With an awareness of current work in psychology of religion, the author explores criteria for true and false modes of inspiration, focusing on biblical data.

[1922] **201. Micklem, Edward Romilly.**

Miracles and the New Psychology: A Study in the Healing Miracles of the New Testament. London: Oxford University Press, H. Milford; New York: Oxford University Press, 1922, 143 pp.

The reviewer in *The Personalist* describes Micklem as a devout believer who disagrees with Freud and offers a critique of the Freudian position on religion. Micklem regards most (though not all) biblical miracles as ". . . such as would naturally fall under the control of psychotherapy as practiced by a great character with a profound faith in God speaking to a people traditionally and intellectually prepared."

[1923] **202. Jefferson, Charles Edward.**

The Character of Paul. New York: Macmillan Co., 1923, viii+381 pp.

Jefferson, pastor of the Broadway Tabernacle in New York City, here presents a series of proposed sermons on Paul similar to his earlier study of Jesus (entry number 233). While Jefferson uses no sources from the psychological literature, his stated intent is definitely a study of Paul's personality: "I am not concerned just now with his ideas but with his disposition, not with his doctrines but with his habitual moods, not with his system of thought but with his character."

[1924] **203. Nicole, Albert.**

Judas the Betrayer: A Psychological Study of Judas Iscariot. 1924. Translated from the French. Grand Rapids: Baker Book House, 1957, 81 pp.

Nicole held pastorates in France, Germany and Switzerland before becoming a traveling minister of the Free Church, with residence in Lausanne. He examines the psychology of Judas in three phases: (1) as the gospels describe him prior to the Last Supper; (2) the tragic struggle which took place between Jesus and his rebellious disciple at the Last Supper; and (3) the end of the tragedy after the Last Supper. Nicole asserts that Judas was *not* a "devil" when Christ chose him, and that he became one because of two specific vulnerabilities: (1) Judas, a Judean under Roman rule, was from the beginning a more ardent patriot than believer, cherishing the idea that Christ might re-establish the kingdom of Israel and make him one of its trustees; (2) Judas hoped to derive financial benefit from his position, a hope thwarted in Christ's interactions with the rich young ruler, Zaccheus, and Mary Magdelene. In the latter situation Judas was able "to use a religious varnish to hide his true feelings, and give selfish interest the appearance of virtue." Nicole regards the accounts of the betrayal in Matthew and Luke as complementary: "One shows the ulterior motives for this sinister proceeding, while the other shows us the inward forces at work acting directly on the will of the traitor until they finish by conquering it entirely."

[1924] **204. *Povah, John Walter.***

The New Psychology and the Bible; A Lecture Delivered at a Vacation School for Old Testament Study, at King's College Hostel, September 1924. London: Longmans, Green & Co., 1924, 32 pp.

Focusing primarily on the Old Testament, Povah analyzes the experiences of Hosea and the Suffering Servant in detail. He examines the psychological insight of the prophets, relying primarily on Freud and Jung.

[1925] **205. *Povah, John Walter.***

The New Psychology and the Hebrew Prophets. London and New York: Longmans, Green & Co., 1925, xiv+207 pp.

A history of prophecy demonstrating its shifting relation to the unconscious. Povah seeks to make sense of the experience of the prophets in terms of psychic development (cathexis, repression, defense). Evidences respect for biblical criticism as well as psychoanalytic theory.

[1926] **206. *Micklem, Nathaniel.***

Prophecy and Eschatology. London: George Allen & Unwin 1926, 248 pp.

An initial lengthy chapter on psychology and prophecy is followed by psychological studies of Elijah, Amos, Hosea, Isaiah, Jeremiah, and Ezekiel. Published by the Selly Oak Colleges Central Council for Publications.

[1926] **207.** *Povah, John Walter.*
The Old Testament and Modern Problems in Psychology. London and New York: Longmans, Green & Co., 1926, vii+151 pp.

According to the reviewer in the *Anglican Theological Review*, Povah is widely read in psychology and has long been a painstaking student of the Bible. However, in this book many chapters include no psychology at all.

[1929] **208.** *Wheeler, Robert Fulton.*
A Study in the Psychology of the Spirit. Boston: R. G. Badger, 1929, 250 pp.

[1930] **209.** *Vaughan, Richard M.*
The Significance of Personality. New York: Macmillan Co., 1930, 302 pp.

The reviewer in *The Personalist* ascribes to Vaughan a twofold aim: (1) to explain the historic problems of Christianity so as to reveal the deep reason in the doctrinal positions taken by the church and (2) to throw more light on these historical and more recent questions. Personalism is applied to an understanding of (1) the nature of God, (2) Jesus, and (3) the Trinity.

[1940] **210.** *Churchill, Winston.*
The Uncharted Way: the Psychology of the Gospel Doctrine. Philadelphia: Dorrance and Company, 1940, 266 pp.

An examination of the roots of religion, individualism, science, human conduct, and human hope, through the examination of the Old Testament prophets and the parables of Jesus. The reviewer in *Time* states that "the essence of the prophets' perception was a form of creative, evolutionary energy, through which an individual might free himself from fear, desire, moral death. This form of energy is described in the gospels . . . by the word *Agape*: non-possessive rather than possessive love. This was and is, he believes, perhaps as actual a force as electricity."

[1940] **211.** *Frayn, Reginald Scott.*
Revelation and the Unconscious. London: Epworth Press, 1940, 230 pp.

A Ph.D. dissertation for the University of London. Revelation is the impact of God upon individual personalities. Christian leaders were personalities whose whole consciousness was "integrated." The perfect revealer was Jesus Christ, who was perfectly "integrated." Frayn also analyzes the significance of prophets. His work is in the tradition of Freud and Jung, but rejects the notion of the "superconscious."

[1942] **212.** *Hughes, Thomas Hywel.*
Psychology and Religious Truth. London: George Allen & Unwin, 1942, 160 pp.

Hughes presented this material in lectures at Bangor University College in 1941. He regards psychology as "handmaid of the gospel." Psychology may help us to understand how God's grace saves.

[1947] **213. *Künkel, Fritz.***

Creation Continues, A Psychological Interpretation of the First Gospel. New York: C. Scribner's Sons, 1947, xiv+317 pp. 2 ed., edited by Elizabeth Künkel and Ruth Spafford Morris. Waco, Tex.: Word Books, 1973.

Religion and psychology have in common their concern with the origins of consciousness. Matthew ". . . teaches step by step the inner experiences of the average disciple, and this means he shows us our own way from the first encounter with Jesus up to the final integration of the spirit of Christ." Künkel's analysis of Matthew's gospel focuses upon the crossroads between old and new (Chapters 14–18) as exemplified by the Gate (1–4, vs. 26–28), the Chart (5–7, vs. 24–25), and the Way (8–13, vs. 19–23). He relies on the biblical commentaries of Eiselen-Lewis-Downey, Gerald Heard, Stanley Jones, G. C. Morgan, T. H. Robinson, H. B. Sharman, Burnett Hillman Streeter, Ernest Tittle, and T. Wilkens.

[1948] **214. *Hulme, William Edward.***

The Psychology of Religious Prophecy. Madison, Wis. Published by the Microcard Foundation for the American Theological Library Association, 1948 and 1959, vi+305 pp.

Originally a doctoral dissertation at Boston University.

[1948] **215. *Kluger, Rivkah Scharf.***

Die Gestalt des Satans im Alten Testament. Zurich: Rascher, 1948, 148 pp. ENGLISH: *Satan in the Old Testament.* Translated by Hildegard Nagel. Evanston, Ill. Northwestern University Press, 1967, xvii+173 pp.

A volume in the series Studies in Jungian Thought, edited by James Hillman. Was originally Part 3 of Jung's *Symbolik des Geistes,* but is not included in editions of his complete works.

[1951] **216. *Gerber, Israel Joshua.***

The Psychology of the Suffering Mind. New York: Jonathan David Co., 1951, 202 pp.

According to Drakeford, Gerber examines the experiences of Job in light of psychological theory; tries to diagnose Job's difficulties; and discusses techniques of his friends as they tried to counsel him.

[1951] **217. *Wolff, Werner.***

Changing Concepts of the Bible: a Psychological Analysis of its Words, Symbols, and Beliefs. New York: Hermitage House, 1951, 463 pp. +illus.

Wolff attempts to retranslate the biblical mythology contained in Genesis 1:1–2:4 into modern concepts through a detailed study of the text itself, comparable texts from other religious traditions, and the process of cultural development. His eighteen chapters include fourteen which explore key concepts in Hebrew thought via the method outlined above, and four which outline the problem and present an overview of the solution, including a proposed "new translation of the story of the world's creation." Extensive bibliography in multiple languages.

[1952] **218. Jung, Carl Gustav.**

Antwort auf Hiob. Zürich: Rascher, 1952, 169 pp. ENGLISH: *Answer to Job. The Problem of Evil: Its Psychological and Religious Origins.* Translated by R.F.C. Hull. London: Routledge & Kegan Paul, 1954, xviii+ 194 pp. Princeton: Princeton University Press, 1958, xvii+194 pp.

In this most controversial Jungian treatise, the author applies the concept of the *enantiodromia* to the individuation of God himself. The first phase takes place in Yahweh's struggle with Job. In guilt he recognizes that he has treated mankind unjustly, and the sacrifice of Christ appears as a reparation. Through the work of the Spirit of Truth another reconciliation of opposites is necessitated, this one symbolized in the Revelation of St. John.

[1953] **219. Allen, Charles Livingstone.**

God's Psychiatry: the Twenty-Third Psalm, the Ten Commandments, the Lord's Prayer, the Beatitudes. Westwood, N.J.: Fleming H. Revell Co., 1953, 159 pp.

Allen defines psychiatry as the healing of the mind and soul and examines the biblical passages for guidelines on mental hygiene. Respectively, they tell us how to think of God, God's rules for living, how to talk to God, and what are the keys to the kingdom. Allen was pastor of Grace Methodist Church in Atlanta.

[1954] **220. Wellisch, Erich.**

Isaac and Oedipus: a Study in Biblical Psychology of the Sacrifice of Isaac, the Akedah. London: Routledge & Kegan Paul, 1954, xi+131 pp.

The Akedah Motif is seen as the biblical solution to the compromise resolution of the Oedipal Complex. Its main features are "the struggle between two apparently equal good principles; the search for a solution; and phenomena which can best be interpreted by the assumption of the interference by an external moral power."

[1956] **221. Klein, Walter Conrad.**

The Psychological Pattern of Old Testament Prophecy. Evanston, Ill. Seabury-Western Theological Seminary, 1956, 95 pp.

Psychology is defined as an "effort of the mind as subject to understand itself as object." Klein reviews psychoanalytic interpretations of prophecy by John Walter Povah, A. Allwohn, E. C. Broome, Theodor Reik, Oscar Pfister, Karen Horney, Alfred Adler, C. G. Jung and J. B. Rhine. An adequate psychology must be wholistic, purposive, and transcendent.

[1959] **222. Carter, Gerald Emmett.**
Psychology and the Cross. Milwaukee: Bruce, 1959, xiv+135 pp.
Emphasizes the Catholic view of atonement.

[1959] **223. Cox, David.**
Jung and St. Paul: a Study of the Doctrine of Justification by Faith and its Relation to the Concept of Individuation. New York: Association Press, 1959, 358 pp. London: Longmans, Green & Co.,1959, xiv+358 pp.
At the end of this scholarly treatise, Cox articulates the clear and hidden parallels between justification and individuation. The essential differences lie in the fact that justification precedes all advance toward a full life while individuation crowns such an advance. Thus, Christianity offers Christ from the beginning and the Christian way is easier than the analytic quest.

[1959] **224. Dewar, Lindsay.**
The Holy Spirit and Modern Thought: an Inquiry into the Historical, Theological, and Psychological Aspects of the Christian Doctrine of the Holy Spirit. London: A. R. Mawbray, 1959, 216 pp. New York: Harper, 1960, 224 pp.
Dewar seeks to correct two fundamental errors in the way the modern church thinks about the Holy Spirit: forgetting that He is at work at a natural level in all people as well as in a supernatural level with Christians, and tending to think unconsciously of the Spirit as an "it" and hence not taking trinitarian theology seriously enough. He brings psychological insights developed in his practice as a psychiatrist to his discussion, but only after tracing the development of pneumatology of the Church.

[1960] **225. Reik, Theodor.**
The Creation of Woman: a Psychoanalytic Inquiry into the Myth of Eve. New York: George Braziller, 1960, viii+159 pp.
Reik begins with the problem of the two creation narratives in Genesis and the need for reconciliation. He reconstructs the primal tradition from which the biblical narrative evolved. Through his archeological psychoanalysis he determines that Eve's creation saga presents itself as a distorted and displaced part of the initiation ceremony, especially the rebirth of the novice and the choice of consort.

[1961] **226. Reik, Theodor.**
The Temptation. New York: George Braziller, 1961, 256 pp.
The story of Abraham and Isaac is reinterpreted in terms of initiation rites.

[1961] **227. Ross, William Gordon.**
Companion of Eternity. New York: Abingdon Press, 1961, 239 pp.
Ross articulates epistemological issues for the scientist, linguist, and theologian in the study of person and personality.

2. BIBLICAL AND THEOLOGICAL BASES

[1963] **228. *Henderson, Joseph L., and Oakes, Maud.***
The Wisdom of the Serpent: The Myths of Death, Rebirth and Resurrection. New York: George Braziller, 1963, xxiv+262 pp.+illus.

A Jungian approach to myths concerned with the theme of death. In the Christian tradition, includes the ritual of baptism, the valley of dry bones (Ezekiel), the Revelation of St. John, I Kings 17, and John's gospel.

[1965] **229. *Barkman, Paul Friesen.***
Man in Conflict. Grand Rapids: Zondervan Publishing House, 1965, 189 pp.

Barkman lays the groundwork for a biblical psychology, which he defines as an "attempt to ferret out the exact psychological meaning of each book of the Bible, each idea, and even each statement." Here he applies the psychoanalytic theory of neuroses to the Epistle of James.

Psychologies of Jesus

The personality of Jesus was of special interest to both psychologists of religion and theologians who acquired psychological knowledge. While the psychology of Jesus does not differ in any major ways from the psychology of other Biblical characters, works on this topic are numerous enough to warrant their inclusion in a separate section for easy access and comparison.

[1893] **230. Bradford, Amory Howe.**
> *Heredity and Christian Problems*. New York: n.p., 1893, 291 pp. New York and London: Macmillan & Co., 1895, xiv+281 pp.
>
> Of relevance is the chapter on Christ. Bradford demonstrates that Christ could not be explained by the operation of the laws of heredity and environment. He reflects something more than the life and nature of the Jewish race, and the environing circumstances under which he lived, would have made him. The additional dimension is the dimension of personality.

[1897] **231. Forrest, David William.**
> *The Christ of History and of Experience, Being the Kerr Lectures for 1897*. Edinburgh: T. & T. Clark, 1897, xx+479 pp.
>
> The third of the Kerr lecturers, Forrest was a young clergyman in the United Presbyterian Church of Scotland. A major issue of interest is Forrest's discussion of the fatherhood of God in the Synoptics and John.

[1907] **232. Hitchcock, Albert Wellman.**
> *The Psychology of Jesus: a Study of the Development of His Self-Consciousness*. Boston: Pilgrim Press, 1907, xvii+279 pp.

Hitchcock, pastor of Central Church Worcester, was inspired to write this book by Baldensperger's *Das Selbstbewusstsein Jesu*, and describes the task as "a scientific use of the imagination in reconstructing a man's soul and formulating his inner life from even a few fixed facts." The introduction is by G. S. Hall.

[1908] **233. Jefferson, Charles Edward.**
The Character of Jesus. New York: T. Y. Crowell & Company, 1908, viii+353 pp.

Here are reprinted twenty-six discourses delivered by Jefferson to his congregation in the Broadway Tabernacle of New York City. He includes in his definition of Jesus's character "the sum of the qualities by which Jesus is distinguished from other men . . . the sum total of his characteristics, his moral traits, the features of his mind and heart and soul." The book provides an in-depth description of the personality of Christ.

[1909] **234. Wright, Emily Dudley.**
The Psychology of Christ. New York: Cochrane Publishing Company, 1909, 105 pp.

In her author's preface, Wright states that "it is my purpose in this little volume to present a Science of the Soul, from the light of psychic phenomena." Affiliated with the Froebel Institute in Lansdowne, Pennsylvania, Wright aligns herself strongly with the rationalist tradition. Her topics include the will, conscience, soul, spirit, mind (or source), and wisdom. She asserts that "to be a student of Psychology is to know self, and to know self is to be a psychic. The one example of a known self, a psychic, is Christ, the true and perfect Psychic. . . . To apply psychology is truly to apply Christ; to apply His life principles to our lives in the fullest activity, to live in all the currents that make physical, moral, intellectual, mental, spiritual life *one* life. . . ." Wright defines love as "self-diremption—the outpouring of all that is highest, strongest, purest, and best that the self has ever found—absolute flight of the self from the self."

[1913] **235. Schweitzer, Albert.**
Die psychiatrische Beurteilung Jesu. Darstellung und Kritik. Tubingen: J.C.B. Mohr, P. Siebeck, 1913, vii+46 pp. ENGLISH: *The Psychiatric Study of Jesus: Exposition and Criticism*. Translated by Charles R. Joy. Boston: Beacon Press, 1948, 81 pp.

Originally Schweitzer's thesis for the doctor of medicine degree, he details the current theories of psychopathology and compares them with the findings of higher criticism of the Bible. Refuting the works of George Lomer (=George de Loosten), Charles Binet-Sangle, William Hirsch, and Emil Rasmussen, who classified Jesus as a psychopathological prophet of the paranoid type, he interprets Jesus' paranoia as understandable in light of his culture.

[1917] **236. Hall, Granville Stanley.**
Jesus, the Christ, in the Light of Psychology. 2 vols. New York: Appleton & Co., 1917, xxx+740 pp; Garden City: Doubleday, Page & Co., 1917, 650 pp.

In this work, perhaps his greatest, Hall applies the principles of psychoanalysis to the Christian faith and calls psychology to task for its inattention to the spiritual side of life. Love and service are seen as the two basic precepts of deity from within the man-soul, the collective racial unconscious. Miracles are regarded as "the baby talk" of the Christian faith, and the incarnation involved the death of the old, objective God-out-there and his resorption and internalization in the person. The Christian faith was part of a vital evolutionary process in which the ideal self is embodied in the individual soul.

[1917] **237. Robertson, James Alexander.**
The Spiritual Pilgrimage of Jesus; the Bruce Lectures, 1917. London: T & T Clark & Co., 1917, 287 pp. Boston: Pilgrim Press, 1921, 287 pp.

W. Bertrand Stevens' review in *The Personalist* states that Robertson uses "the psychological method" to gain insight into the self-consciousness of Jesus. His discussion includes the God-consciousness of Jesus, his divine vocation, and the cross in his experience.

[1920] **238. Berguer, George.**
Quelques traits de la vie de Jesus, au point de vue psychologique et psychoanalytique. Geneva: Edition Atar, 1920, cviii+267 pp. ENGLISH: *Some Aspects of the Life of Jesus: From the Psychological and Psycho-Analytic Point of View.* Translated by Eleanor Stimson Brooks and Van Wyck Brooks. New York: Harcourt, Brace & Co., 1923, viii+332 pp.

Berguer first delivered these ideas as lectures at the University of Geneva in 1917 and 1919. He adopts Coe's methodology which distinguishes between structure and function. The structural perspective approaches Christ's life from the angle of resemblances to our own; the functional examines his particular aims and dynamics. Excellent footnotes for psychoanalytic sources. Includes a chronological bibliography of "lives of Jesus" from 1800 to 1918. Berguer authored an earlier study on Christ in 1896, as well as several other books in the psychology of religion.

[1922] **239. Bundy, Walter Ernest.**
The Psychic Health of Jesus. New York: Macmillan Co., 1922, xviii+299 pp.

According to the review by James Main Dixon in *The Personalist*, Bundy discusses the positions of six German writers who deal with the question of the psychic health of Jesus in a "very drastic and unspiritual way." The major question addressed by Bundy is, "Was Christ a paranoiac or mentally diseased?"

71

2. BIBLICAL AND THEOLOGICAL BASES

[1925] **240. Bond, Jesse Hickman.**

Industrial Influence on the Psychology of Jesus. A Study of the Origin, Processes and Results of Psychological Conflict in His Ethical Struggle. Boston: R. G. Gorman, 1925, 155 pp.

Analyzes the life of Jesus through a socio-psychological model in which Jesus is seen as relating himself to God through his experience as the son of a skilled workman. Thereafter his self-consciousness was interpreted as a function of a reexamination of the prophets and a yearning for the triumph of ethical ideals. The messianic hope was an ethical hope for the nation and the parables are psychological means by which to realize these goals.

[1931] **241. Fromm, Erich.**

Die Entwicklung des Christus Dogmas; eine psychoanalytische Studie zur sozialpsychologischen Funktion der Religion. Vienna: Internationaler psychoanalytischer Verlag. 1931, 71 pp. ENGLISH: *The Dogma of Christ and Other Essays on Religion, Psychology and Culture.* Translated by James Luther Adams. London: Routledge & Kegan Paul; New York: Holt, Rinehart & Winston, 1963, x+212 pp.

Incorporating a critique of Theodor Reik, Fromm's aim is "to understand dogma on the basis of a study of people, not people on the basis of a study of dogma." Fromm traces the development of Christology through the Council of Nicea. Other essays include an analysis of the Old Testament's prophetic concept of peace.

[1933] **242. Dunlap, Knight, and Gill, Robert Sutherland.**

The Dramatic Personality of Jesus. Baltimore: The Williams & Wilkins Company, 1933, vi+186+3 pp.

By treating the *dramatic* personality of Jesus, the authors bracket the question of his existence as historical fact. They emphasize that Jesus' personality has been *credential* as well as dramatic: one "which has not been subjected to the rigors of logical criticism and which therefore is not restricted as to the features it can involve, however contradictory or inconsistent the sum total may be." The authors search for a "sound" personality who is also naturalistic, stripped of the conventionalization of tradition. An original treatment which does not rely on previous "psychologies of Jesus."

[1934] **243. Day, Albert Edward.**

Jesus and Human Personality. New York and Cincinnati: Abingdon Press, 1934, 269 pp.

The Lyman Beecher Lectures for 1934. Day explores the contribution preaching can make to personality, addressing the questions (1) what is the nature of personality? and (2) have we in Jesus an answer to the demands of personality? Includes a wide-ranging bibliography.

[1937] **244. Lang, Lewis Wyatt.**
Christ's Psychology of the Kingdom: A Study in Modern Psychology of the System of Jesus in the Gospels. London: Group Publications, 1937, vi+200 pp.

Lang's book was published under the auspices of the London Clinic of Religious Psychology. He presents selected gospel materials which are analyzed to demonstrate the soundness of Jesus's psychology, and adds collateral material from modern biographies to support this assertion. He applies modern psychoanalytic concepts including the personality, pleasure, and reality principles, self-value, and primary and secondary psychodormas (these latter terms coined by the author). W. E. Bundy, reviewing this book in the *Journal of Religion,* feels that the author has insufficient knowledge of biblical criticism.

[1948] **245. Deane, Wallace.**
The Personality of Jesus. London: Epworth Press, 1948, viii+182 pp.

A devotional rather than scientific work with quasi-psychological headings such as "reactional," "emotional," and "volitional." A. E. Barnett, in his review in the *Journal of Pastoral Care,* considers the work as very similar to Charles Edward Jefferson's *The Character of Jesus* (entry number 233).

[1949] **246. Beyer, Maximilian.**
Christ. New York: Philosophical Library, 1949, ix+284 pp.

Spelling out the details of the Beyer Re-Education Method, the author offers an exposition of a method of healing found in the work of Christ; the method bases healing on the removal of the consciousness of guilt.

[1953] **247. Reich, Wilhelm.**
Wilhelm Reich Biographical Material; a History of the Discovery of the Live Energy, the Emotional Plague of Mankind. Vol. 1 *The Murder of Christ.* Rangeley, Maine; Orgone Institute Press, 1953, 227 pp. Also under the title *The Murder of Christ: the Emotional Plague of Mankind.* New York: Farrar, Strauss, & Giroux/Noonday Press, 1953, 228 pp. Also under the title *The Murder of Christ.* New York: Simon & Schuster/Touchstone Books, 1953, 228 pp. London: Souvenir Press, 1975, 12+227 pp.

In this seminal work, Reich explores the nature of human cruelty by examining the story of Christ's death and its lesson for modern man. The Simon & Schuster edition includes an appendix in which Reich applies this lesson to the American social scene in the period from 1940 to 1952. This is an essential source for understanding the intellectual growth of Reich's thinking.

[1965]   **248. Leslie, Robert C.**

Jesus and Logotherapy: the Ministry of Jesus as Interpreted through the Psychotherapy of Viktor Frankl. New York and Nashville: Abingdon Press, 1965, 143 pp.

The system of logotherapy sheds new light on the following biblical incidents and characters: the Temptation of Jesus, Zaccheus, The Rich Young Ruler, the Samaritan Woman, the paralyzed youth, Simon the Pharisee, Peter, Mary and Martha, the Bethesda invalid, the Gerasene demoniac, and Jesus as Servant.

PART THREE

The Psychology of Religion

Psychology of Religion— General

The books in this chapter provide an overview of the psychological study of religion. The earlier works include the "classics" of such authors as James H. Leuba, George Albert Coe, Elwood Worcester, George Malcolm Stratton, Eduard Spranger, James Bissett Pratt, Robert H. Thouless, Edmund S. Conklin, and Paul E. Johnson, as well as similar works by lesser-known authors. These books include a variety of topics in the psychology of religion, so that they are not easily classified elsewhere. The later works in this chapter were written after the first major period of interest in the psychology of religion had passed and emphasis on more practical applications had launched the pastoral counseling movement. Specific works on pastoral counseling, as well as works integrating psychology and theology, are included in later chapters.

[1826] **249. Reed, Sampson.**
Observations on the Growth of the Mind. Boston: Cummings, Hilliard & Co., 1826, 44 pp. rev. ed., *Observations on the Growth of the Mind; With Remarks on some other Subjects.* Boston: Clapp, 1838, vii + 192 pp. Reprint. Gainesville: Scholars' Facsimiles & Reprints, 1970, viii + 192 pp.

Reed, the son of a Unitarian clergyman, attended Harvard Divinity School and later became a druggist. His "observations" attempt to establish a basis for church doctrine through the metaphysical structure of the universe and the ways in which this structure is disclosed in natural laws. Active in the Swedenborgian church, he helped found the *New Jerusalem Magazine* in 1827, contributing the eight essays in this volume which include a discussion of miracles and the problem of hereditary evil.

[1847]   **250. Bush, George.**
Mesmer and Swedenborg; or, the Relation of the Developments of Mesmerism to the Doctrines and Disclosures of Swedenborg. New York: J. Allen, 1847, x+2+13+288 pp.

Bush was a minister and Swedenborgian scholar.

[1855]   **251. Alliott, Richard.**
Psychology and Theology; or, Psychology Applied to the Investigation of Questions Relating to Religion, Natural Theology, and Revelation. London: Jackson and Walford, 1855, xi+352 pp.

Alliott, Professor of Theology and Mental Philosophy at Western College/Plymouth, first presented these ideas as The Congregational Lecture for 1854. He asks two questions relating to religion: "one, whether religion is the offspring of a distinct mental faculty; and the other, whether the will (which must have to do with its production) be a self-determining power." In the realm of natural theology, he asks "what is our idea of God, how this idea is gained, and what proof we have of the objective reality of his existence?" In reference to Christianity, he asks "whether supernatural communications from God are possible; whether such communications are necessarily restricted, either as to their subject-matter or the mode in which they may be made; what evidence will suffice to prove that a supernatural communication is from God, and therefore authoritative; and whether we have such evidence of the Divine origin of Christianity?" Finally, he asks "whether, on the supposition that Christianity is of God, the New Testament gives us a fallible or an infallible representation of it; and whether, if infallible, is it necessarily without any admixture of what is merely human?" This work is within the tradition of mental philosophy or mental science.

[1876]   **252. Brinton, Daniel Garrison.**
The Religious Sentiment, its Source and Aim; A Contribution to the Science and Philosophy of Religion. New York: Holt & Co., 1876, iv+284 pp.

As a philosopher, Brinton, a physician, attempts to inquire what in the mind of man gave birth to religion. He bases his conclusions on inductive reasoning gleaned from a study of American Indians. He sees religion as the rational expression of inbred capacities parallel to physical expressions of inborn capacities in the body.

[1888]   **253. Ward, Duren James Henderson.**
How Religion Arises: A Psychological Study. Boston: George H. Ellis, 1888, 74 pp.

This short book is based on Ward's doctoral dissertation at The University of Leipzig. The major content is a summary of philosophical theories focusing on will, emotions, and thought as origins of religion. Ward asserts that these three faculties are sequentially involved: the religious thought gives rise to feelings and volitions which give rise to motives and incentives. In contrast to the James-Lange theory of emotion, Ward asserts that "an act of knowledge precedes every emotion, and is its substance." Regarding the origins of religion, Ward states that "not until the self became conscious of itself as over against what it supposed to be another Self in nature,—seen in a single object or in the totality of a universe,—and had conceived of some personal relationship between the two, can religion be said to have begun."

[1896]   **254. Leuba, James Henry.**

Studies in the Psychology of Religious Phenomena: The Religious Motive, Conversion, Facts, and Doctrines. Worcester, Mass: J. H. Orpha, 1896, 385 pp.

Leuba's dissertation at Clark University under G. S. Hall.

[1897.]   **255. Joly, Henri.**

Psychologie des saints. Paris: V. Lecoffre, 1897, ix+201 pp. ENGLISH: *The Psychology of the Saints.* Translated by George Tyrell. London: Duckworth, & Co., New York: Benziger Brothers, 1898, xv+184 pp.

Joly was formerly Professor at the Sorbonne and at the College of France. This book serves as a general introduction to a series, edited by Joly, of books devoted to specific saints.

[1897]   **256. Sabatier, Auguste.**

Esquisse d'une Philosophie de la Religion d'apres la Psychologie et l'Histoire. Paris: Fischbacher, 1897, xiv+415 pp. ENGLISH: *Outlines of a Philosophy of Religion Based on Psychology and History.* New York: James Pott & Company, 1897, 348 pp.

Sabatier was a Huguenot connected with the Protestant Faculties of Theology at Strasburg and Paris. Religion is regarded as arising out of the conflict of self-consciousness and world-consciousness. He explores the psychological origin and nature of religion, religion and revelation, miracle and inspiration, and religious development of humanity. This exploration is followed by a section on the origins, essence, and historical forms of Christianity, and a critical theory of religious knowledge.

[1899]   **257. Hudson, Thomson Jay.**

The Divine Pedigree of Man; Or, the Testimony of Evolution and Psychology to the Fatherhood of God. Chicago: A. C. McClurg & Co., 1899, xxviii+379 pp.

Man's remotest ancestor, the"moneron," exhibits an essentially godlike quality of mind. The "moneron" shows a mind with divine traits. Since man is descended from the "moneron," his pedigree is divine.

[1899]   **258. Sabatier, Auguste.**

Les religions d'autorité et la religion de l'esprit. Paris: Fischbacher, 1899, xii+570 pp. ENGLISH: *Religions of Authority and Religion of the Spirit.* Translated by Louise Seymour Houghton. New York: McClure, Phillips and Co., 1903, 410 pp.

Sabatier, representing the French school of symbolo-fideism, applies the historical and psychological method to his analysis of religions. The book is divided into three sections. The first explores Roman Catholic systems of dogma and ecclesiastical organization. The second section examines older Protestantism, which is similar in form to Roman Catholicism. These two systems represent religions of authority which look to an external standard and measure of religion (the Church and the Scripture, respectively). In the third section, Sabatier examines the religious consciousness of Jesus and the apostolic conception of inspiration. These concepts represent religions of the Spirit, which hold to a moral, autonomous authority. Church history is regarded as the history of psychological evolution.

[1900] **259. *Coe, George Albert.***
The Spiritual Life: Studies in the Science of Religion. New York: Eaton and Mains; Cincinnati: Curts & Jennings, 1900, 279 pp.

Examining seventy-seven subjects, Coe uses both the questionnaire and hypnotic method to study phemonena of religious awakening, adolescent difficulties, religious dynamics, and divine healing and spirituality. In his comments on the religious nurture of youth, Coe advocates playing down the conflict and stress in order to nourish more fruitful religious development. A classic in the field.

[1902] **260. *Everett, Charles Carroll.***
The Psychological Elements of Religious Faith. Edited by Edward Hale. New York: Macmillan Co., 1902, xxii+215 pp. London: Macmillan & Co., 1902, xiii+215 pp.

Introduces Schleiermacher's system. Based on notes from thirty years of lectures.

[1903] **261. *Hoffman, Frank Sargent.***
Psychology and Common Life; A Survey of the Present Results of Psychical Research with Special Reference to their Bearings upon the Interests of Everyday Life. New York, London: G. P. Putnam's, 1903, viii+286 pp.

Hoffman offers a general psychology which emphasizes psychic processes rather than the "new" physiological psychology. Topics discussed include the brain, attention, memory, hallucinations, sleep, hypnotism, and mental diseases. Most relevant for integrative purposes is his skeptical overview of psychic research and healing movements. He discusses in detail the work of Phineas Parkhurst Quimby, Mary Baker Eddy, and their followers, and judges the Mental Science movement to be far more scientific than Christian Science. He also analyzes the work of the "faith-curists," emphasizing A. B. Simpson of New York City and John Alexander Dowie, who ran a "divine healing home" in Chicago. Finally he criticizes the theory of a secondary self (subliminal self, unconscious), finding it even less acceptable than a theory of the influence of the

General

"departed dead": "For it would be an appeal to beings having minds and motives like our own and therefore knowable, not a wholly mysterious entity of whose modes of action we can never have any direct knowledge."

[1903] **262. MacDonald, Greville.**
The Religious Sense in its Scientific Aspect. New York: A. C. Armstrong & Son, 1903, vi+243 pp. London: Hodder & Stoughton, 1903, xvi+ 243 pp.
Describes religions of service, of renunciation, and of freedom.

[1905] **263. King, Irving.**
The Differentiation of the Religious Consciousness. Lancaster, Pa.: Macmillan Co., 1905, 72 pp.
King's Ph.D. thesis from the University of Chicago.

[1906] **264. Case, Carl Delos.**
The Masculine in Religion. Philadelphia: American Baptist Publication Society, 1906, 120 pp.
Case was pastor of the Hanson Place Baptist Church in Brooklyn, New York. Here, he addresses the feminine note in modern society, evidences of a feminine Christianity, the mental sexual differences, the modern versus the Biblical religious type, some presuppositions of sex in religion, men and the church, men and the lodge, men and business, and the manliness of Christ.

[1908] **265. Cutten, George Barton.**
The Psychological Phenomena of Christianity. New York: C.Scribner's Sons, 1908, xviii+497 pp.
Cutten, a Baptist minister, explores the following phenomena in detail: the religious faculty, mysticism, ecstacy, glossolalia, visions, dreams, stigmatization, witchcraft, demoniacal possession, monasticism and asceticism, religious epidemics, contagious phenomena, revivals, faith cure, Christian Science, miracles, conversion, age, sex, intellect, knowledge, imagination, inspiration, will, emotions, worship, prayer, sexuality, denominationalism, immortality, and preaching.

[1908] **266. Worcester, Elwood.**
The Living Word. New York: Moffat, Yard, & Company, 1908, xvii+ 351 pp. London: Hodder & Stoughton, 1909, xi+280 pp.
Infused with the inspiration of Gustav Theodor Fechner and the poet Friedrich Ruckert, Worcester expands on the three motives of faith in God (traditional, practical, and rational), on good and evil, on angels, and on life after death.

[1909] **267. Galloway, George.**
The Principles of Religious Development: A Psychological and Philosophical Study. London: Macmillan & Co., 1909, xx+363 pp.

Galloway, a philosopher at the University of St. Andrews, focuses first on the idea of development and its application to history, including the histories of religion. He asserts that the origins of religion must be connected to the whole mind rather than one of its functions, and explores the three classic functions of feeling, thinking, and willing as they relate to religion. Final problems of religious development include the nature of evil, immortality, and the relation of religious development to the idea of God.

[1909] **268. *Jordan, Humfrey Robertson.***

Blaise Pascal: A Study in Religious Psychology. London: Williams & Norgate, 1909, ix+264 pp.

Jordan provides a detailed biography of Pascal as a basis for his psychological understanding of Pascal's philosophy of religion. Jordan then examines Pascal's early devotional instinct and bigotry, his mental anxiety subsequent to the death of his father, his hatred of casuistry, his perplexity at the impotence of human reasoning, and his acknowledgment of the important role of the imagination and emotion. Jordan concludes that Pascal ultimately turned to his instinct after "failing to find any guidance in reason. . . . he proclaims that in this he is justified—that for most men some assumption about the nature of existence must be made—and that there is on this matter no other guide than instinct—so that each man must go where he feels himself led."

[1909] **269. *Leuba, James Henry.***

The Psychological Origin and the Nature of Religion. London: A. Constable & Company, Ltd., 1909, 95 pp. Chicago: Open Court Publishing Co., 1912, 94 pp.

Leuba differentiates among mechanical behavior, which involves no reference to personal beings; coercitive behavior, or magic; and anthropopathic behavior. He discusses the origins of ideas of ghosts, nature-beings and gods, who represent unseen personal beings; magic and religion; and the original emotion of primitive religious life. The belief in a superior power integrates will, intellect, and emotions, which cannot be separated in a reductionistic manner.

[1910] **270. *Henke, Frederick Goodrich.***

A Study in the Psychology of Ritualism. Chicago: University of Chicago Press, 1910, vii+96 pp.

The author's Ph.D. dissertation at the University of Chicago. Henke's major thesis is "that the type of reaction designated as ritualism is always social, that it is performed to mediate practical control, and that it has a natural history in accordance with well-known psychological laws." He also asserts that "the ceremony is in no wise imposed from without by some higher power. The thus-saith-the-Lord of the mystical experience of the great leader, prophet, or apostle, at the base of the ceremony, is at most no more than an excellent indication of the interlocutory nature of consciousness or of the sudden incursion of material from the fringe into the focus of attention." Henke's discussion includes the general characteristics of ritualism, its development, the place of attention in primitive ceremony, the psychology of supernaturalism in the ritual, the relation between ritual development and social consciousness, and the survival of the ceremony. As an illustration of ritual development, Henke examines the rituals of the Semites and the emergence of the Eucharist.

[1911] **271. *Stratton, George Malcolm.***
Psychology of the Religious Life. London: George Allen & Co. 1911, xii+376 pp.

Stratton's volume, the work of an experimental psychologist, assumes that all religion results from efforts to find final resolution to inner self conflicts and outer tension. This is an early attempt to apply dynamic psychology, evolutionary processes, and pragmatic philosophy to religious cognition and experience.

[1912] **272. *Leuba, James Henry.***
A Psychological Study of Religion: Its Origin, Function, and Future. New York: Macmillan Co., 1912, xiv+371 pp.

Leuba's volume is an example of thorough-going reductionism of religion to psychology. He states "the Gods are inductions from experience" and "religious experience belongs entirely to psychology." Proposes religion to be a rational behavior to which persons refer when mechanical and magical behavior fails. Leuba was a part of the Clark school of religious psychology and dedicated this book to G. Stanley Hall, Clark's president and his early teacher.

[1912] **273. *McComas, Henry Clay.***
The Psychology of Religious Sects: A Comparison of Types. New York and Chicago: Fleming H. Revell Co., 1912, 235 pp. Reprint. New York: AMS Press, 1973, 235 pp.

McComas develops a typology based on action-oriented, experiential and intellectual approaches to religion which correspond with the respective emphases of childhood, adolescence, and adulthood. Eighteen religious groups are analyzed by these categories. He states that "Every group of worshippers has been drawn together by influences which may be explained naturally." Roback names McComas, along with James, Starbuck, Leuba, and Stratton as early leaders in religious psychology.

[1913] **274. *Waterhouse, Eric Strickland.***
The Psychology of the Christian Life. London: C. H. Kelly, 1913, viii+ 119 pp.

In this book, designed for "the intelligent general reader," Waterhouse summarizes the early psychology of religion and contributes the results of his own informal interviews. Topics include psychology and religion, primitive religion, the religion of childhood and youth, conversion, types of religious experience, mysticism (visions and revelations), the psychology of prayer, the social aspect of religion (fellowship and doctrine), religious education, and Christian life in the twentieth century.

[1914]   **275. Spranger, Eduard.**
Lebensformen. Festschrift fur Alois Riehl von Freunden und Schülern zu seinem siebzigsten Geburtstage dargebracht. Halle: A. S., 1914, pp. 413–522. Rev. and enl. *Lebensformen; geisteswissenschaftliche Psychologie und Ethik der Persönlichkeit. 2., völlig neue bearb. und erweiterte Aufl.* Halle: M. Niemeyer, 1921, x+403 pp. ENGLISH: *Types of Men: The Psychology and Ethics of Personality.* Translated from the 5th German edition by Paul J. W. Pigors. Halle: M. Niemeyer, 1928, xii+402 pp.

According to the Harvard College Books in Psychology, "the most important book representing the Geisteswissenschaften." Succeeding Dilthey in the latter's chair at the University of Berlin, Spranger defined not only Weltanschauungen, but also Lebensformen, or "types of men," which included the theoretic, the economic, the esthetic, the social, the political, and the religious—which form the basis for the Allport–Vernon–Lindzey Study of Values.

[1915]   **276. Graves, Lucien Chase.**
The Natural Order of Spirit; A Psychic Study and Experience. Boston: Sherman, French & Co., 1915, v+365 pp.

Graves was affiliated with the American Society for Psychical Research, and supports his defense of spiritism with a series of studies conducted with Mrs. Chenoweth, a medium. His testimony to spiritual foundations includes summaries of the Hebraic and Pauline views and discussion of a variety of contemporary perspectives.

[1916]   **277. Coe, George Albert.**
The Psychology of Religion. Chicago: University of Chicago Press, 1916, xvii+365 pp.

A Professor at Northwestern Union Theological Seminary and Columbia Teacher's College, Coe was a leader in the "scientific study of religion." The psychology of religion is examined in the context of functional psychology, which is first and foremost a psychology of personal self-realization. Religious experience can be regarded as a psychic complex which needs to be viewed in its elements, or as an aspect of the valuational phase of experience. Includes both alphabetical and topical bibliographies.

[1916]   **278. Heisey, Paul Harold.**
Psychological Studies in Lutheranism. Burlington, Iowa: The German Literary Board, 1916, 143 pp.

In his psychological analysis of Lutheranism, the author relies on the classic works of Edward Scribner Ames, George Albert Coe, George Barton Cutten, William Ernest Hocking, G. Stanley Hall, James Henry

Leuba, Henry Clay McComas, Edwin Diller Starbuck, and Horace Emory Warner. Excellent overview of classics in Chapter 1.

[1916] **279. *Leuba, James Henry.***

The Belief in God and Immortality: A Psychological, Anthropological and Statistical Study. Boston: Sherman, French & Co., 1916, xvii+340 pp. + illus.

In his theoretical discussion, Leuba deals with the origin, nature, and function of the belief in immortality. As stated in the introduction, Leuba shows "that two quite different conceptions of personal immortality have been successively elaborated; and that the modern conception is not a growth from the primary belief, but an independent creation, differing radically from it in point of origin, in nature, and in function. Whereas the primary belief was forced upon men irrespective of their wishes as an unavoidable interpretation of certain patent facts (chiefly the apparition of deceased persons in dreams and in visions), the modern belief was born of a desire for the realization of ideals." Leuba further presents statistical data pertinent to the belief in a personal God and in personal immortality, indicating that many actually abhor the idea of immortality or are indifferent to it. The desire for immortality finds its main support in "the yearnings of the heart for the maintenance of bonds of love and friendship, and the desire to think highly of oneself and the Universe."

[1917] **280. *Boirac, Emile.***

L'avenir des sciences psychiques. Paris: Félix Alcan, 1917, 4+300+2 pp. ENGLISH: *The Psychology of the Future*. Translated by W. de Kerlor. New York: Frederick A. Stokes Company, 1918, 331 pp.

Boirac, the late Rector of the Academy of Dijon, explores the "forces" of suggestability, hypnotizability, magnetizability, and power of telepathy. These belong to the superconscious rather than the subconscious, and represent "spiritoidal" rather than spiritistic influence. Boirac suggests laws for their scientific study.

[1917] **281. *Wells, Wesley Raymond.***

A Behavioristic Study of Religious Values. Cambridge: Harvard University Press, 1917, xi+255 pp.

In this doctoral dissertation for Harvard University, Wells applies the behaviorism of Edwin Bissell Holt and John Broadus Watson to the study of values. Wells first discusses language as a form of behavior: using Holt, he states that "a word becomes the stimulus that releases response to the denotation of the word—to the object to which the word refers." Using Watson's definition of speech as a "system of 'conditioned reflexes,' " Wells states that "words become functional in habit systems so far as they become 'substitutable for the stimulus which originally initiated an act.' " Wells then defines value "in terms of specific response." Religious values are defined "by reference to the objects to which they attach, i.e., to the supernatural objects of belief, to the acts of worship that such beliefs lead to, and also to the beliefs themselves taken as forms of incipient behavior." Ideal values are those attached to unreal objects. Wells examines the instrumental values of religious belief in the course of racial evolution, and explicitly assumes a recapitulation theory of individual religious development. Thus, he asserts that "a program of religious education based upon the theory of recapitulation prescribes a re-living of the successive ancestral stages of religion by the developing individual." Wells also applies the Freudian formula, "emphasizing the value of religion as a form of sublimation, or substitution of the sex energy." Finally, he discusses the pragmatic fallacy, which asserts "that all beliefs which are valuable must *ipso facto* be true," and the fallacy of false attribution, "which occurs in the views of many writers on religion who err in interpreting the 'inner' religious experiences as revelations of outer reality in cases where the experiences are merely forms of emotionalism." He concludes that "a philosophy of religion which is built upon the science of value as a basis possesses in itself more value than a philosophy of religion which is concerned primarily with the question of truth." Wells provides an excellent review of the literature, relying on major writings from the philosophy of personalism (Bernard Bosanquet, Reinhold Friedrich Alfred Hoernlé, William Ernest Hocking, Andrew Seth Pringle-Pattison, William Ralph Inge, and Arthur James Balfour), the Gifford Lectures in natural theology (Friedrich Max Müller, Edward Caird, Josiah Royce, and William James), comparative religion, the psychology of religion, and the act psychologies of Christian von Ehrenfels and Alexius Meinong.

[1919] **282. Anderson, James Burns.**
   Applied Religious-Psychology. Boston: R. G. Badger, 1919, 83 pp.

[1919] **283. Reik, Theodor.**
   Probleme der Religionspsychologie. Leipzig and Vienna: Internationaler psychoanalytischer Verlag, 1919, xxiv+311 pp. 2 ed., and Das Ritual, psychoanalytische Studien. Leipzig: Internationaler Psychoanalytischer Verlag, 1928, 330 pp. ENGLISH: The Ritual: Psychoanalytic Studies. Translated by Bryan Douglas. New York: W. W. Norton, 1931, 367 pp. London: L. Virginia Woolf at the Hogarth Press and the Institute of Psychoanalysis. Also under the title The Psychological Problems of Religion. New York: Farrar, Strauss, & Co., 1946.
   Reik focuses on the understanding of Jewish rites and ceremonies.

[1920] **284. Pratt, James Bissett.**
   The Religious Consciousness: A Psychological Study. New York: Macmillan Co., 1920, viii+488 pp.
   Written by one of the early seminal thinkers in the psychology of religion, this volume defines religion as a "serious and social attitude" toward the ultimate and distinguishes this from knowing, feeling, and

willing. In discussing the whole range of religious phenomena, Pratt distinguishes religion (attitude) from theology (doctrine or belief). He states that "religion is not so much theology as life; it is to be lived rather than reasoned about."

[1921] **285. Pym, Thomas Wentworth.**
Psychology and the Christian Life. London: Student Christian Movement, 1921, xii+137 pp. New York: George H. Doran, 1922, xii+175 pp.

The author wrote this book as an attempt to summarize the teachings of psychology as they enlightened and informed Christianity. He takes the position that psychology is organized common sense and that Christianity can profit greatly from understanding how faith and trust work in human beings. He discusses faith and suggestion, sin, the character of Jesus, and psychoanalysis. The book is a survey rather than an exhaustive summary of the applications of psychology to Christianity. The bibliography lists few books.

[1921] **286. Wobbermin, Georg.**
Systematische Theologie nach religions-psychologischer Methode. Das Wesen der Religion. ENGLISH: *The nature of religion.* Leipzig: J. C. Hinrichs, 1921–1922, viii+498 pp. Translated by Theophil Menzel and Daniel Sommer Robinson. New York: Thomas Y. Crowell Company, 1933, xvi+379 pp.

Wobbermin succeeded Ernst Troeltsch at Heidelberg and later held the chair of systematic theology at Göttingen. After translating into German William James's *Varieties of Religious Experience,* he continued to develop the "religio-psychological" or "James–Schleiermacher" method. Of most interest are Wobbermin's critiques of James Leuba's psychology of religion and his discussion of the Freudian theory, as well as his overview of the work of Schleiermacher.

[1922] **287. Ericksen, Ephraim Edward.**
The Psychological and Ethical Aspects of Mormon Group Life. A Dissertation. Chicago: University of Chicago Press, 1922, x+101 pp. Reprint. Salt Lake City: University of Utah Press, 1975, xxii+101 pp.

A dissertation in the tradition of Chicago functionalism, completed under the direction of Edward Scribner Ames, George Herbert Mead, and James H. Tufts. The emphasis is on the social base of individual personality, and the meaning of religion is found in "spiritual values."

[1923] **288. Bruce, William Straton.**
The Psychology of Christian Life and Behavior. Edinburgh: T & T Clark, 1923, viii+335 pp. +adv.

Relying on William James, George Albert Coe, James Henry Leuba, Edward Scribner Ames, Thomas Wentworth Pym, William Ralph Inge, and James Bissett Pratt, the unique aspect of Bruce's psychology of religion is the inclusion of a chapter on industrial psychology.

[1923] **289. *Stratton, George Malcolm.***

Anger: Its Religious and Moral Significance. New York: Macmillan Co., London: George Allen & Unwin, 1923, x+277 pp.

Using religious texts as his data base, Stratton distinguishes among three kinds of religion: (1) Irate and martial religions (Judaism, Zoroastroism, Islam), (2) Unangry religions (Taoism, Vishnuism, Buddhism, Jainism), and (3) Religions of anger-supported love (Confucianism, Christianity). Relying on a post-Darwinian model of emotions, anger is regarded as an achievement in mental progress. The role of anger in the origins of religion is also examined, and Stratton offers "rules for the fighting mood," fifteen principles for handling anger in the service of good will.

[1923] **290. *Thouless, Robert Henry.***

An Introduction to the Psychology of Religion. Cambridge: Cambridge University Press, 1923, 286 pp. rev. ed., London: Cambridge University Press, 1971, viii+152 pp.

With an emphasis on the British tradition, this small volume represents a "classic" in the Jamesian approach to the psychology of religion. The 1971 revision recognizes the later empirical tradition without a need to incorporate it.

[1924] **291. *Selbie, William Boothby.***

The Psychology of Religion. Oxford: Clarendon Press, 1924, xii+310 pp.

This book is the first in a series on religion for theological students. It attempts to cover American as well as continental writings in an overview of the field, critiques the understanding of religion in the new psychology (i.e., psychoanalysis), and suggests psychology may be valuable, although limited.

[1925] **292. *Matthews, Walter Robert.***

The Psychological Approach to Religion. New York and London: Longmans, Green & Co., 1925, 3+73 pp.

Originally prepared by the Liverpool Diocesan Board of Divinity Publications in 1924.

[1925] **293. *Pym, Thomas Wentworth.***

More Psychology and the Christian Life. London: Student Christian Movement Press; New York: George H. Doran, 1925, x+178, pp.

Pym includes a discussion of the use and misuse of the imagination and the relation of faith and autosuggestion. He opposes the self-sacrifice of Christianity with the self-expression of the new psychology.

[1926] **294. *Hickman, Franklin Simpson.***

Introduction to the Psychology of Religion. New York: Abingdon Press, 1926, 558 pp.

Hickman published numerous volumes on Christian education through Abingdon. Here he includes the following topics: origin and methods of the psychology of religion; religion and the religious mind; structure of the religious experience; racial roots of religious tendencies; the personal factor in religious experience; the genesis of religious experience; normal growth in religious experience; the experience of conversion; the struggle against sin; religion as conduct control; the nature and function of worship; prayer as the essence of worship; the intermediation element in worship; the tendency to believe; the belief of God; and the belief in inspiration. Each chapter includes questions for further study and discussion and selected references.

[1927] **295. *Elliott, Harrison Sacket.***

The Bearing of Psychology upon Religion. New York: Association Press, 1927, 77 pp.

Elliott was professor of Religious Education and Psychology at Union Theological Seminary. He discusses (1) the findings of psychology regarding human nature; (2) the effect of science upon religious conceptions; and (3) the contribution of psychology to the experience of God. Elliott asserts that religion must not break psychological law, but use it. God is regarded as the Universe Personality.

[1927] **296. *Flower, John Cyril.***

An Approach to the Psychology of Religion. New York: Harcourt, Brace & Co.; London: Kegan Paul, Trench, Trubner & Co., 1927, 248 pp.

This Ph.D. dissertation for Cambridge originally bore the title "The Bearing of Recent Developments of Psychological Study upon Religion." Flower includes a discussion of the peyote cult of the Winnebago Indians, the religion of George Fox, and the psychopathology of religion.

[1927] **297. *Jordan, George Jefferis.***

A Short Psychology of Religion. New York: Harper & Brothers; London: J. Cape, 1927, 160 pp.

Jordan's book is reviewed in *The Personalist* by Wilbur H. Long, who commends the author for including sections on the psychology of sin, worship, and corporate religion, which are not included in typical psychology of religion texts. Jordan attacks the psychological fallacy in the following statement: "The truth is that psychology has not the power to destroy or build by its own weapons. Other questions have to be considered and the Christian has the right to ask that the psychologist shall show some sign of having really faced the significance of the spiritual experience of two thousand years."

[1927] **298. *Josey, Charles Conant.***

The Psychology of Religion. New York: Macmillan Co., 1927, xi+362 pp.

This is a sympathetic, yet scientific, treatise on religion by a university psychology professor. Intended to be an introduction, it ends up being an exhaustive treatment of many topics. It was written at a time when the psychology of religion was about to go on the wane in academic programs, but reflects no antireligious bias. Includes adequate sections on religious development.

[1927] **299.** *Kupky, Oskar.*

Jugendliche-Psychologie: ihre Hauptproblemen. Leipzig: Durr'schen Buchhandlung, 1927, 2+122 pp. ENGLISH: *The Religious Development of Adolescents, Based upon Their Literary Productions.* Translated by William Clark Trow. New York: Macmillan Co., 1928, vii+138 pp.

This is a study within the tradition of the Clark School of Religious Psychology, namely, via the use of empirical self-report. Based on content analysis of adolescent diaries, this volume includes reports embedded in psychological theories of development proposed by G. Stanley Hall. It was conducted in Germany.

[1927] **300.** *Sankey-Jones, Nancy Eleanor.*

Bibliography of Theodore Schroeder on the Psychology of Religion (with her *One Who is Different*). Cos Cob, Conn.: the author, 1927. Revised as *Bibliography of Theodore Schroeder on the Psychology of Religion and the Erotogenic Interpretation of Mysticism.* Cos Cob, Conn.: the author, 1934, 22 pp. +adv.

According to the author's introduction, "A hundred and sixty periodicals in six languages, have published Theodore Schroeder's psychological, philosophical, religious, medical, sociological and legal essays. . . ." Schroeder's analyses of religious phenomena covered a range of topics including sexual determinants in Mormon theology; religion and sensualism as connected by clergy; revivals and virtue; the erotogenesis of religion; the prophet Matthias; adolescence and religion; the sadomasochistic conflict of the Saint of Wildisbuch; the differential essence of religion; the psychogenetics of androcratic evolution in religious cultures; incest in Mormonism; proxies in Mormon polygamy; the pantheistic mysticism of certain "negroes"; matricide and maryolatry; revivals, sex, and the holy ghost; "divinity" in semen; why priests do not marry; bundling and spirituality; Christian Science and sex; Shaker celibacy and salacity; prenatal psychisms and mystical pantheism; phallic worship; psychological analysis of the Bishop Brown heresy case; the French prophets and John Lacey; religious humanism; manufacturing the "experience of God"; witchcraft and the erotic life. In 1922 Schroeder proposed an Institute of Religious Psychology "working with complete detachment from interest in religion's welfare."

[1928] **301.** *Frommel, Gaston.*

The Psychology of Christian Faith, Being Selections from the Writings of the Late G. Frommel. Edited by J. Vernon Bartlet. Translated by J. Macartney Wilson. London: Student Christian Movement Press, 1928, xxiii+194 pp.

Bartlet, a professor at Mansfield College, edits a collection of writings which present Frommel's approach to religion, his doctrine and faith, and his treatment of the Inner Life. Also included are Frommel's sketches of his teachers, Alexander Vinet and Cesar Malan.

[1928] **302. *Giloteaux, Paulin.***

Saint Teresa of the Child Jesus: Her Supernatural Character. Translated by William Reany. New York: Herder, 1928, xxiv+224 pp. Also published under the title *Psychology of Saint Teresa of the Child Jesus*. London: A. Ouseley, 1928, xxiv+224 pp.

An examination of the personality of Saint Teresa by a French Catholic writer.

[1928] **303. *Pitts, John.***

Psychology and Religion. London: The Kingsgate Press, 1928, 112 pp. New York: Revell, 1930, 112 pp.

Pitts states his Christian commitment and the limitations of psychology in his preface: "After all, Psychology may *explain* the mental laws to which religious experiences conform, but it does not *create* these experiences; it may set forth the psychological aspects of religion, but it can pronounce no judgment on the question of the ultimate truth of religion." His topics include definitions of psychology and religion, the psychological approach to religion, the psychological origin of religion, the psychological basis of religion, and the psychological factors in religion.

[1928] **304. *Uren, Albert Rudolph.***

Recent Religious Psychology: A Study in the Psychology of Religion: Being a Critical Exposition of the Methods and Results of Representative Investigators of the Psychological Phenomena of Religion. New York: C. Scribner's Sons; London: Simpkin, Marshall, Hamilton, Kent & Co.; Edinburgh: T & T Clark, 1928, xi+280 pp.

Uren's book is an attempt to provide pastors and students with a summary of the contributions of seven figures in the psychology of religion: William James, Edwin Diller Starbuck, George Albert Coe, James Bissett Pratt, Edward Scribner Ames, George Malcolm Stratton, and James Henry Leuba.

[1929] **305. *Ames, Edward Scribner.***

Religion. New York: Henry Holt & Co., 1929, vi+324 pp.

Ames articulates the position known as Instrumentalism, in which social interest produces sacredness, and God is reality idealized. He contrasts this position on God with the orthodox position of transcendent and absolute theism, and with contemporary humanism.

[1929] **306. *Conklin, Edmund Smith.***

The Psychology of Religious Adjustment. New York: Macmillan Co., 1929, xiv+340 pp.

A classic "psychology of religion." Conklin asserts that psychology is "without a soul" in that it is no longer philosophical. Psychology of religion is empirical. Rational psychology concerns itself with relating the data of empirical psychology to the problems of the soul. Conklin also distinguishes between the metaphysical self (the soul or spirit) and the empirical self which one knows and experiences. He rejects the pseudopsychologies of mysticism and psychic studies. Thus, he presents a psychology of religion which is clearly aware of its limits, which include neither ethics nor ontology.

[1929] **307.** *Dresser, Horatio Willis.*
Outlines of the Psychology of Religion. New York: Thomas Y. Crowell Company, 1929, xiii+451 pp.

Written in the spirit of William James, this volume attempts to be empirical and descriptive at the same time that it affirms the essence of religion to be inner experience and the question of the reality of the divine problematical. Dresser considers theology to be undergoing a reconstruction. He studied under Josiah Royce.

[1929] **308.** *Thurstone, Louis Leon, and Chave, Ernest John.*
The Measurement of Attitude: a Psychophysical Method and Some Experiments with a Scale for Measuring Attitudes toward the Church. Chicago and London: University of Chicago Press, 1929, xii+97 pp.

One of the earliest methodological treatises by Thurstone, the research sample includes undergraduate, graduate, and divinity students at Chicago, faculty members, and members of the Chicago Forum. Data are analyzed by groups, by sex, and by major religious affiliation (Roman Catholic, Protestant, Jewish).

[1930] **309.** *Grensted, Lawrence William.*
Psychology and God: A Study of the Implications of Recent Psychology for Religious Belief and Practice. London and New York: Longmans, Green & Co., 1930, xi+257 pp.

The 1930 Bampton Lectures in theology delivered by an Oxford professor. He affirms the essence of human inner experience as central to relating psychological and theological understandings. "Christian theism" is the phrase used to refer to a theological position which depends more on the insights gained from Jesus' teachings and life than from traditional dogma. Psychology is compatible with these views because of its emphasis on personality development.

[1930] **310.** *Waterhouse, Eric Strickland.*
Psychology and Religion: A Series of Broadcast Talks. London: Elkins Matthews & Marrot, 1930, xxiii+232 pp. New York: R. R. Smith, 1931, xxii+232 pp.

Waterhouse, who was Professor of Psychology and Philosophy at Richmond College (a school of divinity in the University of London/Surrey), presented these radio talks to an audience "unacquainted with psychology." He avoids the danger of psychologism by asserting that psychology is a descriptive science: "It just describes what it finds, but it cannot say in any final sense whether it is good or bad. That is the work of ethics. Nor whether it is true or false; that is the work of metaphysics." Waterhouse discusses the following topics: the beginnings and ends of religion; children's religious perceptions; unconscious experience; the value of imagination; belief, overbelief, and unbelief; reasoning, feeling, and action; the soul astray; conversion and its value; prayer; fellowship in religion; the religion of body and soul; the mystic way; the dream world and the waking world; character and its constituents; conscience and conflict; the roots of fear and joy; faith and worship; and the mystery and mastery of mind.

[1931] **311. Aubrey, Edwin Ewart.**

Religion and the Next Generation. New York and London: Harper & Brothers, 1931, xi+188 pp.

Aubrey deals with the following topics: (1) how the individual gets his religion, (2) what religion means, (3) religious infantilism and religious maturity, (4) the skeptic's search for the meaning of God, (5) prayer as a means of religious adjustment, (6) what significance has Jesus? (7) where our religion comes from, and (8) what the intellectual can do with institutional religion. He reflects awareness of modern psychology.

[1931] **312. Sanders, Charles F.**

The Taproots of Religion and Its Fruitage. New York, London, Toronto: The Macmillan Company, 1931, viii+266 pp.

Sanders, Professor of Philosophy at Gettysburg College, presents an introduction to religion from a personalist perspective. His main thesis "is to show that the status of religion in human experience is just as factual as science; that mystic experience is just as real as sense experience; that the faith which produces mysticism requires the same ardent application of our best powers of thought and experiment as other types of experience; and that the results are just as certain and positive." He defines religion as "life motivated, inspired and dominated by the consciousness of God." Personality is defined as "being which formulates ideals and moves toward their realization." Sanders regards the mystic experience as the focus for religious research. The research method in this field is contemplation, and an assumption is made of a profound sense of objectivity which characterizes the mystic awakening. Reason checks the mystic/religious experience and organizes it, leading to faith and knowledge.

[1931] **313. Trout, David McCamel.**

Religious Behavior: An Introduction to the Psychological Study of Religion. New York: Macmillan Co., 1931, xiv+528 pp.

Written for the "serious student" this volume is an example of texts for teaching the psychology of religion written during the second quarter of the twentieth century. The author rejects both mechanistic materialism and mystical vitalism as bases for religion and calls for a more cautious observation of behavior without overtheorizing. Offers suggestions for the use of each chapter and for a concluding project undertaken by each student. A most useful survey of the psychology of religion during the first three decades of the century is included.

[1932] **314. Day, Clarence.**
God and My Father. New York: Alfred A. Knopf, 1932, 83 pp.
An analysis of the personalities of the author's parents as revealed by their attitudes toward religion.

[1932] **315. Dimond, Sydney George.**
The Psychology of Methodism. London: Epworth Press, 1932, 154 pp.
Dimond explores the religious experiences of John and Charles Wesley and George Whitefield and treats such themes as conversion and character, crowd psychology, rhythm and song, ethics, and perfection.

[1933] **316. Dewar, Lindsay.**
Imagination and Religion. London: P. Allen & Co., 1933, viii+167 pp.
Dewar first demonstrates the place and importance of imagination in daily life, then explains the ceremonial of Anglo-Catholicism and shows its value from a psychological point of view.

[1933] **317. Leuba, James Henry.**
God or Man? A Study of the Value of God to Man. New York: Henry Holt & Co., 1933, xii+338 pp.
One of the later books written by this early reductionistic and behavioristic psychologist. It takes a functionalist position and suggests the existence of God is of less concern than his accessibility and the uses to which man puts Him. Leuba sees his writing as psychology, not speculation. He sees the essence of religion as communion with the divine as opposed to magic which attempts to manipulate reality and to mechanics which attempts to coerce reality. He shows how religion can serve human values.

[1934] **318. Baker, Archibald Gillies.**
Christian Missions and a New World Culture. Chicago and New York: Willet, Clark & Co., 1934, xiii+322 pp.
Baker explores the psychology and sociology of cultural change, challenging the nature and legitimacy of traditional missionary methods.

[1934] **319. Jahnsen, Thorleif.**
Heart and Spirit: On the Activity of Mind in General and Religious Psychology. Oslo: Cammermeyers Boghandel, 1934, 278 pp.

[1935] **320. Lindworsky, Johannes.**
Psychologie der Aszese. Winke für eine psychologischrichtige Aszese. Freiburg: Herder, 1935. ENGLISH: The Psychology of Asceticism. Trans-

lated by Emil A. Heiring. London: Edwards, 1936, 4+95 pp. Baltimore: Carroll Press, 1950, 95 pp.

[1935] **321. Van Til, Cornelius.**

Psychology of Religion. Philadelphia: Westminster Theological Seminary, 1935, 138 pp.

A class syllabus offering an overview and critique of William James, G. Stanley Hall, James Henry Leuba, Edwin Diller Starbuck, and George Albert Coe. Constructively, Van Til regards religion as joyful submission to the inevitable, and as subjective and objective redemption, manifested in miracle, revelation, regeneration, and conversion.

[1937] **322. Pear, Thomas Hatherley.**

Religion and Contemporary Psychology. London: Oxford University Press, 1937, 51 pp.

Pear, Professor of Psychology at the University of Manchester, first presented these ideas as the Riddell Memorial Lectures before the University of Durham at Armstrong College, Newcastle-upon-Tyne, in November 1936. The three lecture topics are "the sense of reality," "conscience and moral behavior," and "personal relationships."

[1937] **323. Stolz, Karl Ruf.**

The Psychology of Religious Living. Nashville: Cokesbury Press, 1937, 375 pp.

This is an exhaustive volume that deals with every aspect of religion and considers basic presuppositions and methods in the psychology of religion. A dynamic and voluntaristic position in psychology is assumed, although no mention is made of Freud's analysis in *The Future of an Illusion.*

[1938] **324. Cattell, Raymond Bernard.**

Psychology and the Religious Quest: An Account of the Psychology of Religion and a Defence of Individualism. London and New York: Thomas Nelson & Sons, 1938, viii+195 pp.

This noted research psychologist here contrasts psychology's support of individualism with religion's "theopsyche," or group mind.

[1938] **325. Hollington, Richard Deming.**

Psychology Serving Religion; A Practical Guide to Life Adjustments. New York and Cincinnati: Abingdon Press, 1938, 248 pp.

This book was billed by the publishers as "the first attempt to relate genetic psychology to religion in a comprehensive and systematic way." Serving as a practical guide to life adjustment, it deals with normal adjustment, maladjustment, and readjustment. Hollington was Professor of Church Administration and Pastoral Care at Garrett Theological Institute.

[1938] **326. *Northridge, William Lovell.***
Health for Mind and Spirit. New York and Cincinnati: Abingdon Press, 1938, 200 pp. Also under the title *Psychology and Pastoral Practice.* London: Epworth Press, 1938, 184 pp. Reprint. Great Neck, New York: Pastoral Psychology Book Club, 1953, 160 pp.

Northridge considers conversion and the role of repression; adolescent religious experience and emotion; unconscious guilt; and a discussion of sin versus symptoms.

[1939] **327. *Mellone, Sydney Herbert.***
The Bearings of Psychology on Religion. Oxford: B. Blackwell, 1939, vii+255 pp.

Mellone presents here studies in the history and psychology of religion. He regards the Freudian theories as destructive and merely speculative rather than demonstrated. He focuses on ceremonial and traditional elements in religion.

[1940] **328. *Cutten, George Barton.***
Instincts and Religion. New York and London: Harper & Brothers, 1940, 154 pp.

Instincts, intelligence, morals, and religion are examined from an evolutionary theological perspective.

[1940] **329. *Wilde, Reginald William.***
Religion in the Light of Psychology. New York: Lindsey, 1940, ix+11, 72 pp.

A psychology of religion from a Catholic perspective.

[1942] **330. *Graeber, Isaque, and Britt, Steuart Henderson, eds.***
Jews in a Gentile World; The Problem of Anti-Semitism. New York: Macmillan Co., 1942, x+436 pp.+illus.

The roots of the Nazi conflict in World War II, ascribed by Hitler himself to "conflicting ideologies," are here examined from various perspectives, including the psychological.

[1943] **331. *Conklin, Edwin Grant.***
Man, Real and Ideal: Observations and Reflections on Man's Nature, Development, and Destiny. New York: Charles Scribner's Sons, 1943, xvii+247 pp.

Conklin, Professor of Biology at Princeton and President of the American Philosophical Society, presented the essence of these lectures at the Sharp Foundation of the Rice Institute. They were published in *Rice Institute Pamphlet*, Vol. 28, October 1941 under the title "What is man?." Conklin covers topics of evolution and eugenics, development and differentiation. He asserts that the only legitimate faith is grounded in fact, and advocates a humanistic religion.

[1944] **332.** *Allport, Gordon Willard.*

The Roots of Religion: A Dialogue between a Psychologist and His Student. Boston: Editorial Board Advent Papers, Church of the Advent, 1944, 36 pp. Advent papers no. 1. New York: National Council of the Protestant Episcopal Church, 1944, 30 pp.

Allport, who served on the editorial board of *The Advent Papers*, attacks the naturalistic view of religion represented by Sigmund Freud and James Leuba in a hypothetical conversation between a student and professor. Following William James, he asserts that the fruits of religion are more important than its roots, and its intent more important than its content. He regards the relation between religion and psychopathology (or "theopathic" conditions) as resulting from the need to find support in a broken world. Allport also defends the Christian religion as having the best solution to The Problem of Evil as well as a solution for The Problem of Good, which lies in the Incarnation. He claims that "The person who directs his attention to his religious quest usually finds therapy along the way—unexpectedly."

[1944] **333.** *Blakemore, William Barnett.*

Sociological Behaviorism and Religious Personality. Chicago: University of Chicago Press, 1944, 12 pp.

Blakemore's essay was part of a dissertation submitted to the faculty of the University of Chicago Divinity School in 1941. He briefly attempts to apply George Herbert Mead's sociological behaviorism to the understanding of prophetic behavior and the institutional church, and offers a tight review of its major concepts. The prophet is an individual who comes to "a realization that implicit in present trends there is either a personal or group catastrophe." The prophet may "take refuge in unintelligibility" so that his message "can neither be misconstrued into a support of the *status quo* nor is it accessible to defeat by the typical patterns of argument of that day. The message may be ignored, but it cannot be perverted." The church, as a consummatory community, threatens human personality at its deepest base, and must therefore take a critical attitude towards its structures. Iconoclasm, defined as opposition to any objectification of religious terms, has resulted whenever Judeo-Christian terminology became bound to a particular culture, or became reified. This short essay offers an excellent summary of the major premises of what later became known as "symbolic interactionism."

[1944] **334.** *Hopkins, Pryns.*

From Gods to Dictators: Psychology of Religions and Their Totalitarian Substitutes. Girard, Kans.: Haldeman–Julius Publications, 1944, 168 pp. + illus.

Actually a study in comparative religions with little psychological sophistication. Includes a chapter comparing the stages of a successful psychoanalysis with "therapeutic" religious practice.

[1945] **335. Johnson, Paul Emanuel.**
Psychology of Religion. New York and Nashville: Abingdon-Cokesbury Press, 1945, 288 pp.
Johnson's book was written as an explication of the purposive psychology exemplified by Henry A. Murray of Harvard. Thus, religious experience was defined as a "spontaneous process in time motivated by value goals." He attempts to relate the findings of the psychology of religion up to the 1940s with the personalism of Edgar Brightman and Henry N. Wieman.

[1946] **336. Dunlap, Knight.**
Religion: Its Function in Human Life, a Study of Religion from the Point of View of Psychology. New York: McGraw-Hill Book Company, 1946, xi+362 pp. Reprint. Westport, Conn.: Greenwood Press, 1970, xi+362 pp.
Dunlap's assertion is that "the primary requisite for the study of the psychology of religion is the application of the methods of group psychology." His scholarly treatise draws on the writings of L. F. Alfred Maury, W. Robertson Smith, J. A. McCullogh, James G. Frazer, Arthur B. Cook, and Salomon Reinach. It includes discussion of sin, religious symbolism, religion and the food supply, funerary praxes and rituals, initiation, and proselytism and conversion.

[1947] **337. Estabrooks, George Hoben.**
Spiritism. New York: E. P. Dutton & Co., 1947, 254 pp.
Spiritism is examined here by a psychologist and educator who claims to steer a middle road between the skepticism of Freud and the credulity of J. B. Rhine and J. Eisenbud.

[1951] **338. MacLeod, Robert Brodie.**
Religious Perspectives of College Teaching in Experimental Psychology. New Haven: Edward W. Hazan Foundation, 1951?, 24 pp.
MacLeod's later writings were in the area of historical-philosophical psychology. He chaired the psychology departments at Swarthmore College, McGill University, and Cornell University.

[1951] **339. Smith, Alson Jesse.**
Religion and the New Psychology. Garden City and New York: Doubleday, 1951, 192 pp.
Smith's emphasis is on the last three decades of research in parapsychology.

[1952] **340. Faraon, Michael J.**
The Metaphysical and Psychological Principles of Love. Dubuque, Iowa: Wm. C. Brown and Company, 1952, vi+94 pp.
This Catholic author examines love as it can be analyzed from a philosophical and psychological perspective, rather than exploring the

virtue of charity. He seeks to demonstrate that systematic philosophy is not divorced from real life.

[1952] **341. Grensted, Lawrence William.**

The Psychology of Religion. London and New York: Oxford University Press, 1952, 181 pp.

Grensted, professor of Philosophy of Religion at Oxford, states that psychology of religion should be "an account of those aspects of human behavior which are commonly regarded as religious and an attempt to see how they can be explained." At the same time, it must show why these elements have been set aside as sacred. He emphasizes individual and corporate aspects of religion and religious development, and includes a discussion of reality. Includes annotated bibliography.

[1952] **342. Kagan, Henry Enoch.**

Changing the Attitude of Christian toward Jew: A Psychological Approach through Religion. New York: Columbia University Press, 1952, xvi+155 pp.

Kagan conducted an experiment with 525 Methodist and Episcopal youths in summer camps, comparing indirect, direct, and focused-interview approaches to combatting anti-Semitism. The direct method proved most effective.

[1953] **343. Hartshorne, Charles, and Reese, William L., eds.**

Philosophers Speak of God. Chicago: University of Chicago Press; London: Cambridge University Press, 1953, xii+535 pp.

Psychologists included in this overview are Gustav T. Fechner (modern panentheism), William James and Christian von Ehrenfels (limited panentheism), Edward Scribner Ames, Raymond B. Cattell, and Henry Nelson Wieman (extreme temporalistic theism), and Sigmund Freud (motive torque or psychological skepticism).

[1954] **344. Allport, Gordon Willard.**

The Nature of Prejudice. Cambridge, Mass.: Addison-Wesley Publishing Co., 1954, xviii+537 pp. +illus.

A "classic" study indicating that religion is one of the most influential factors in building up and perpetuating prejudice. Here Allport discusses the "two kinds of religion" which led to the later development of the extrinsic—intrinsic dimension: "interiorized" and "institutionalized."

[1954] **345. Ikin, Alice Graham.**

Life, Faith, and Prayer. New York: Oxford University Press, 1954, 127 pp.

Here, Ikin deals with scientific thinking and religious experience; sex; the relationship of self to society; problems of youth, midlife, and old age; the nature of man (sin, evil, personal integration); prayer; and the relationship between medical and spiritual healing.

[1956]   346.   *Festinger, Leon, Riecken, Henry W., and*
         Schacter, Stanley.
         When Prophecy Fails. Minneapolis: University of Minnesota Press,
         1956, vii+256 pp.
              Reports the details of a modern apocalyptic movement which was
         studied by social scientists. Using the first author's cognitive dissonance
         theory, this work analyzes the experience and behavior of a group which
         predicted the end of the world via a flood on a certain date but whose
         predictions were disconfirmed. One of the best known of this type of
         social psychological researches on religious phenomena.

[1956]   347.   *Olt, Russell.*
         An Approach to the Psychology of Religion. Boston: Christopher Publish-
         ing House, 1956, 183 pp.
              A brief, introductory overview of the field by a professor at Anderson
         College. Excellent bibliography.

[1956]   348.   *Wright, J. Stafford.*
         *Man in the Process of Time: A Christian Assessment of the Powers
         and Functions of Human Personality.* Grand Rapids, Mich.: Eerdmans,
         1956, 190 pp.
              Wright was Principal of Tyndal Hall, Bristol, England. While writing
         from an orthodox theological perspective, Wright discusses such topics as
         mending in time and space, miracles, occultism, spiritualism, poltergeist,
         and the evidence of spiritualism and reincarnation, as well as traditional
         topics. The book has excellent bibliographic references, suggestions for
         further reading after each chapter, and subject and author indexes.

[1958]   349.   *Argyle, Michael.*
         Religious Behavior. London: Routledge & Kegan Paul, 1958, 196 pp.+
         illus. Glencoe: The Free Press, 1959, 196 pp.+illus. 2 ed., *The Social
         Psychology of Religion, with Benjamin Beit-Hallahmi.* London and Boston:
         Routledge & Kegan Paul, 1975, x+246 pp.+illus.

[1958]   350.   *Clark, Walter Houston.*
         *The Psychology of Religion: An Introduction to Religious Experi-
         ence and Behavior.* New York: Macmillan Co., 1958, xii+485 pp. +illus.
              A "classic" in the psychology of religion, this volume covers method-
         ological problems in the study of religion, the phenomena of religious
         growth and various aspects of religious life. Especially interesting is
         Clark's discussion of the prophet, priest, and intellectual (theologian) and
         the lengthy section of study aids.

[1958]   351.   *Oates, Wayne Edward.*
         What Psychology Says about Religion. New York: Association Press,
         1958, 128 pp.; London: Hodder & Stoughton, 1960, 96 pp.

Oates, a leader in the pastoral counseling field, here reviews basic writings in the psychology of religion for the Christian layperson. In his chapters he addresses contrasting views about religion, asking whether religion is bondage to idols or freedom for growth; childishness or a way to maturity; a sickness or a way to health; and an illusion or a way to reality. Finally he discusses religion as the search for ultimate meaning in life. A short annotated bibliography of recommended readings is included.

[1958]   **352. Vetter, George B.**

Magic and Religion, their Psychological Nature, Origin and Function. New York: Philosophical Library, 1958; London: Vision, 1959, 555 pp. + illus.

Includes a thorough review of theories of religious origins, including the psychological works of Sigmund Freud, C. G. Jung, Robert H. Thouless, Erich Fromm, William James, and W. T. Stace. The origin of religion may be regarded as a problem in the psychology of learning. There is a lengthy discussion (over ninety pages) of belief and faith, and a discussion of the priesthood. Religion is regarded as a tendency to accept solutions of problems or difficulties by *postulate,* a form of neurotic adjustment.

[1959]   **353. Laukes, Harold.**

The Castle and the Field: An Essay in the Psychology of Religion. London: George Allen and Unwin, 1959, 80 pp.

[1959]   **354. Strunk, Orlo Jr., ed.**

Readings in the Psychology of Religion. Nashville: Abingdon Press, 1959, 288 pp.

Contains brief selections from early pioneer investigations in the psychology of religion, many of which are generally unavailable. Also includes brief selections from later investigators and a survey of the development of research in this field. Contributors include Edward Scribner Ames, Gordon W. Allport, Anton T. Boisen, Richard Maurice Bucke, R. P. Casey, George A. Coe, Felix Cohen, Walter H. Clark, Sigmund Freud, W. Edgar Gregory, G. Stanley Hall, Frank S. Hickman, Seward Hiltner, Pryns Hopkins, William James, Paul E. Johnson, C. G. Jung, Oskar Kupky, James Henry Leuba, O. Hobart Mowrer, Gardner Murphy, Wayne E. Oates, Mortimer Ostow, Rudolf Otto, James Bissett Pratt, E. J. Price, Leon Salzman, Sante de Sanctis, E. L. Schaub, Ben-Ami Scharfstein, Edwin Diller Starbuck, Karl R. Stolz, Francis L. Strickland, Orlo Strunk, Robert T. Thouless, David M. Trout, Evelyn Underhill, Henry Nelson Wieman, and Regina Wescott-Wieman.

[1960]   **355. Guirdham, Arthur.**

Man: Divine or Social. London: V. Stuart, 1960, viii + 230 pp.

Describes the Cosmic and Herd-Personality Urges responsible for individuation and the self-surrender leading to identification with God.

[1960]   **356.** *May, Rollo, ed.*
Symbolism in Religion and Literature. New York: George Braziller, 1960, 253 pp.

Brings together essays by Paul Tillich, Amos Wilder, Kenneth Burke, Talcott Parsons, A. Richards, Werner Heisenberg, Nathan Scott, and Alfred North Whitehead on the nature of symbols. Some were previously published in *Daedelus.* Depicting the point of view that modern culture has lost its basic symbols, May and the other writers call for a recovery of importance of metaphors and analogies in effective living. Illustrated widely with examples from psychotherapy.

[1960]   **357.** *Swanson, Guy E.*
The Birth of the Gods. The Origins of Primitive Beliefs. Ann Arbor: University of Michigan Press, 1960, ix+260 pp.

Beginning with a Durkheimian perspective, the author reviews data on fifty societies representing fifty sections of the globe. The reviewer in *Contemporary Psychology* describes the book as "a study of cultural reaction to social control."

[1962]   **358.** *Masters, R. E. L.*
Eros and Evil: The Sexual Psychopathology of Witchcraft. New York: Julian Press, 1962, xviii+322 pp.

As described by R. G. Gassert in the *Bulletin of the Menninger Clinic,* Masters offers a "combination of science, folk-lore, pseudo-theology and personal bias." Masters discusses the influence of the *Solanaceae* (belladonna, mandragora, and the henbanes) on the witches of the fifteenth to seventeenth centuries.

[1962]   **359.** *Schneiders, A. A., and Centi, Paul J., eds.*
Selected Papers from the American Catholic Association Meetings of 1960 and 1961. New York: Fordham University Press, 1962, 166 pp.

The 1960 symposium focused on problems in the teaching of scientific psychology in the denominational colleges, and featured a comparison of the Jewish, Protestant, and Catholic perspectives by B. N. Levinson, John M. Vaihinger, and LeRoy A. Wanck, respectively. The 1961 symposium covered issues in the assessment of candidates to religious life. The motivation and ideal image of man in education and learning theory are studied through theoretical reflections and results of recent research.

[1962]   **360.** *Strunk, Orlo.*
Religion: A Psychological Interpretation. New York: Abingdon Press, 1962, 128 pp.

From the perspective of a modified field theory, Strunk asserts that successfully internalized "religious factors always lead to integration of personality, for they obtain, one way or another, self-adequacy for the individual."

General

[1963] **361.** *Spinks, George Stephens.*
Psychology and Religion: An Introduction to Contemporary Views.
Boston: Beacon Press; London: Methuen & Co., 1963, xv+221 pp.

Spinks, a past editor of the *Hibbert Journal* and lecturer in psychology and religion at Oxford, provides both historical and contemporary overviews with an extensive bibliography. He includes an appendix on the nature of the soul in various western cultures.

[1964] **362.** *Brantl, George, ed.*
The Religious Experience. 2 volumes. New York: Braziller, 1964, 1144 pp. Vol. 1. *The Image and the Idol: the God of Immanence.* Vol. 2. *Beyond the Gods: The God of Transcendence. In Place of God: From Nihilism to Affirmation. A Gift of Presence: The God of Dialogue.*

Along with selections from classic literature, these two volumes include writings from the following psychologists and religionists: Thomas Aquinas, John Henry Cardinal Newman, Max Weber, Talcott Parsons, Josiah Royce, John Stuart Mill, Jonathan Edwards, Ignatius Loyola, St. Bernard of Clairvaux, St. Francis of Assisi, J. Bronowski, William James, Herbert J. Muller, Aldous Huxley, Erik Erikson, John Calvin, Martin Luther, Simone Weil, St. Basil, William Law, St. Augustine, Moses Maimonides, Reinhold Niebuhr, Gabriel Vahanian, Paul Tillich, St. Teresa, Emanuel Swedenborg, William F. Lynch, Friedrich Nietzsche, Thomas Henry Huxley, Morris R. Cohen, W. K. Clifford, Ignace Lepp, Max Scheler, Thomas Merton, Søren Kierkegaard, Blaise Pascal, John Woolman, St. John of the Cross, Father Alfred Delp, Sarvepalli Radhakrishnan, Jean Mouroux, Gabriel Marcel, Martin Buber, Nicolas Berdyaev, Alisdair MacIntyre, John Wesley, George Fox, William Law, Emmanuel Cardinal Suhard, Rudolf Otto, Pierre Teilhard de Chardin, St. Patrick, Thomas Traherne. Selections for the four "books" illustrate the "via positiva," "the via negativa," the atheist and agnostic positions, and the movement of the Infinite toward the finite.

[1964] **363.** *Maslow, Abraham Harold.*
Religions, Values, and Peak Experiences. Columbus: Ohio State University Press, 1964, xx+123 pp.

Values previously upheld by the claims of supernatural religion must be established on a foundation of truth if they are to be upheld. Organized religions attempt to pass on the "peak" experiences of their founders. Such peak experiences can be studied scientifically and are universally available to all, whether theists, agnostics, or atheists. Part of the Kappa Delta Pi lecture series.

[1965] **364.** *Herr, Vincent V.*
Religious Psychology. Staten Island, N. Y.: Alba House, 1965, 277 pp.

Herr was chairman of the department of psychology of Loyola University, Chicago. He places himself in the German tradition begun by Karl Girgensohn and Werner Gruehn, and continued by the *Eranos* group in Switzerland, the *Lumen Vitae* group in Brussels, and by the Dominican Fathers Noel Mailloux and Salmon. He includes an overview of religious development, elements of religious maturity, conversion, and the means for growth.

[1965]   **365.** *Meissner, William W.*

Group Dynamics in the Religious Life. Notre Dame, Ind.: University of Notre Dame Press, 1965, xii+188 pp.

This Roman Catholic counselor and priest applies research findings in group dynamics to the special context of the religious community.

Religion and
Psychopathology

Books in this section explore the relationship between religion and mental illness. Included are such issues as the pathological motivations underlying religious belief, the religious contents of various pathologies, demon possession and exorcism, and the criteria for distinguishing healthy from unhealthy religion.

[1835] **366. Brigham, Amariah.**

            Observations on the Influence of Religion upon the Health and Physical Welfare of Mankind. Boston: Marsh, Capen & Lyon, 1835, xxiv+331 pp. Reprint. New York: Arno Press, 1973, 331 pp.

            Brigham, one of America's early psychiatrists, makes a plea for practical integration. Excesses of the religious sentiment are at the roots of insanity and much suicidal behavior, and constitute a perversion of Christianity as well. He writes, ". . . if clergymen and the conductors of religious newspapers, would but pay a little attention to the studies I have mentioned, they would not insult hereafter the understanding of their more intelligent hearers and readers, and delude the ignorant and credulous with such like circumstances, and attribute them to the special influence of the Almighty. On the contrary they would rebuke those who offered such for publication, and then such occurrences would cease."

[1853] **367. Cooke, William.**

            A Commentary of Medical and Moral Life; or Mind and the Emotions, Considered in Relation to Health, Disease, and Religion. Philadelphia: C. J. Price & Co., 1853, xvii+327 pp.

            The author, a physician, offers a strong apologetic for Christianity in the statement that "the tendency of the Christian religion is to exalt all those faculties of the mind, and all those moral feelings that elevate character and promote health, usefulness, and happiness; and to repress those exercises of mind, and those moral feelings, (or excesses or perversions of feeling,) which produce distress, defame the character, and impair health." Cooke concurs with the observation that religiosity may contribute to mental distress, but deals with this by describing a variety of character types predisposing to certain types of reactions. In addition to challenging "medical men" to be spiritual guides for their patients whenever no one else is available, he admonishes them to take an interest in Christianity for their own sakes.

[1886] **368.** *Maudsley, Henry.*

Natural Causes and Supernatural Seemings. London: Kegan Paul, Trench & Co., 1886, vii+368 pp. Reprint. London: Watts & Co., 1939, ix+149 pp.

The noted physician presents a skeptical psychology of religion, claiming there is no way to distinguish true communion with the supernatural from the various malformities of the mind.

[1906] **369.** *Morse, Josiah.*

Pathological Aspects of Religions. Worcester: Clark University Press, 1906, 264 pp. *American Journal of Religious Psychology and Education,* Monograph Supplement no. 1.

Based on a dissertation completed at Clark University, this work offers a collection of instances of the perversion of the religious instinct, such as mysticism, fetichism, ritualism, and emotionalism.

[1909] **370.** *Williams, Charles.*

Religion and Insanity. London: Ambrose Company, 1909, 117 pp.

[1918] **371.** *MacKay, William MacIntosh.*

The Disease and Remedy of Sin. London: Hodder & Stoughton, 1918; New York: George H. Doran, 1919, xii+308 pp.

MacKay was pastor of Sherbrooke Church, Glasgow, and trained in medicine as well as theology. He discusses sin from a medical standpoint, discussing its origin, growth, and remedies.

[1919] **372.** *Cohen, Chapman.*

Religion and Sex: Studies in the Pathology of Religious Development. London, Edinburgh, Boston: T. N. Foulis, 1919, xiv+287 pp.

Cohen asserts that "There is really no escape from the position that so far as religious 'facts' are part of mental life, religion becomes logically a department of psychology," thus challenging the claim of theologians that "the 'facts' of the religious life belong to a world of inner experience, to a state of spiritual development which brings the subject into touch with a super-sensuous world not open to the normal human being, and with which science, as ordinarily understood, is incompetent to deal." He also asserts that "It is the religious explanation that has, over and over again, been shown unreliable, the non-religious explanation that has been finally established." Topics treated in the book include science and the supernatural, the primitive mind and its environment, the religion of mental disease, sex and religion in primitive life, the influence of sexual and pathologic states on religious belief, the stream of tendency, conversion, religious epidemics, and the witch mania.

[1921] **373. Mackie, Alexander.**

The Gift of Tongues: A Study in Pathological Aspects of Christianity. New York: George H. Doran, 1921, xiv+275 pp.

A historical study covering the whole range of Christian history from the apostolic age to the present. The argument is that the "gift of tongues" is considered a mark of spirituality simply because of its unusual character, that it is the expression of a diseased mind, and that it is almost always associated with antimoral conduct.

[1924] **374. Martin, Everett Dean.**

The Mystery of Religion: A Study in Social Psychology. New York and London: Harper & Brothers, 1924, xii+391 pp.

Martin, director of the People's Institute, here presents a study of the hidden motives behind religious behavior which give rise to its sense of mystery and analyzes these motives in the light of the new psychology. Martin treats religion as a psychopathic phenomenon, showing the analogy between certain phases of religion and types of dreams and abnormal behavior. The reviewer in *The New Republic* states that Martin "avoids the unconscious obscurantism of the priest and the false perspective of the psychiatrist." He reflects a background in behaviorism and Freudian psychology.

[1936] **375. Boisen, Anton Theophilus.**

The Exploration of the Inner World: A Study of Mental Disorder and Religious Experience. Chicago and New York: Willet Clark and Company, 1936, xi+322 pp.

Written by the founder of the Clinical Pastoral Education movement, this book details Boisen's understanding of the relation of religious experience to mental illness. It details his own saga and builds upon his understanding of how he mastered his insanity and utilized religion in its process. He feels that both religion and insanity are attempts at personal reorganization and suggests ways in which ministers of religion may contribute to the treatment of the mentally ill.

[1942] **376. Wise, Carroll Alonzo.**

Religion in Illness and Health. New York and London: Harper & Brothers, 1942, xiv+279 pp.

Influenced heavily by Anton Boisen, Wise was the Protestant chaplain at Worcester State Hospital at the time he authored this book. Wise's psychoanalytic perspective emphasizes the role of symbolization in the religious life: "The symbolic structure of religion offers a form through which meaning, value, and purpose are formulated and organized, either negatively or positively . . . ." True religion leads to the solution of conflict on the basis of cooperation with the fundamental realities of the universe; false religion leads to the use of evasion and concealment and escape or rebellion as dominant trends. A classic in the area of pastoral counseling.

[1950] **377.** *Ackerman, Nathan Ward, and Jahoda, Marie.*

Anti-Semitism and Emotional Disorder: A Psychoanalytic Interpretation. New York: Harper, 1950, xiv+135 pp.

This is one of a series of volumes sponsored by the American Jewish Committee to explore prejudice during the holocaust of the 1940s. This book includes case analyses of disturbed prejudiced persons who had undergone intensive psychotherapy. The place of religion in their lives is considered. Nathan Ackerman later became known as "the grandfather of family therapy."

[1950] **378.** *Keenan, Alan.*

Neurosis and Sacraments. New York: Sheed & Ward, 1950, xi+163 pp.

From a Catholic perspective, Keenan explores the effects of neglecting our primary personal need for God, and declares that when energies are not channeled toward that Last End, neurosis may be the result. Keenan formulates that suicide constitutes the person's expression of the conviction that the Last End has been lost. The religious drive can be desublimated, so that the necessary is camouflaged by the convenient. Keenan suggests that the Sacrament of Penance makes possible the return to God, and that wisdom, understanding, knowledge, and counsel are gifts of the Spirit which support the mind. Fortitude, piety, and fear of the Lord are corresponding gifts which support the will. Guilt created by the violation of conscience, which is the mirror of Christ, can be escaped through confession.

[1951] **379.** *McCasland, Selby Vernon.*

By the Finger of God: Demon Possession and Exorcism in Early Christianity in the Light of Modern Views of Mental Illness. New York: Macmillan Co., 1951, xi+146 pp.

A careful exegesis of exorcism in the biblical world, with an emphasis on the shift in methodology ushered in by the era of Christianity, in which demons were cast out in the name of Christ, the Messiah. The phenomenon of possession itself is reinterpreted as a manifestation of abnormal personality. The author is careless in his use of psychological terminology.

[1952] **380.** *Froissart, Jacques, ed.*

Trouble et Lumière. Brussels: Desclée de Brouwer, [1952?]. ENGLISH: *Conflict and Light: Studies in Psychological Disturbance and Adjustment.* Translated by Pamela Carswell and Cecily Hastings. London and

New York: Sheed & Ward, 1952, viii+192 pp.; Paulton and London: Purnell & Sons.

Froissart, better known as Father Bruno De Jesus-Marie, here edits the work of contributors Charles Journet, Louis Beirnaert, Françoise Dolto, Philippe de la Trinite, Rudolf Allers, Paul Cossa, Charles Henri Nodet, Gustave Thibon, Charles Baudouin, Etiènne de Greef, Marcel de Corte, Pere Gabriel de Ste. Marie-Madeleine, and Lucien-Marie de Saint-Joseph.

[1955] **381.** *Boisen, Anton Theophilus.*

Religion in Crisis and Custom: a Sociological and Psychological Study. New York: Harper & Brothers, 1955, 271 pp. Reprint. Westport, Conn.: Greenwood Press, 1973, xv+271 pp.

An application to American Protestantism of the author's theory of the potential religious growth that can follow psychosis.

[1955] **382.** *Oates, Wayne Edward.*

Religious Factors in Mental Illness. New York: Association Press, 1955, 239 pp. London: George Allen & Unwin, 1957, 239 pp.

Oates summarizes various studies in psychopathology. For the emotionally ill, their religious convictions become symbols for which they are willing to lose everything. He discusses how to distinguish healthful from unhealthful religion and how to use religion in a positive, constructive manner. Religion does not make one ill, but one's use of it may aggravate illness.

[1957] **383.** *Leach, Max.*

Christianity and Mental Health. Dubuque, Iowa: W. C. Brown, 1957, 135 pp.

[1958] **384.** *Baker, Oren Huling.*

Human Nature under God; Or, Adventure of Personality. New York: Association Press, 1958, 316 pp.

Clearly dichotomic in his anthropology, Baker interprets the biblical story as an account of the emergence of personhood from selfhood, relying primarily on Freud and George Herbert Mead. Christian psychotherapy moves through seven stages: confession, repentance, forgiveness, obedience, insight, faith, and joy.

[1959] **385.** *Anderson, George Christian.*

Man's Right to be Human: to Have Emotions without Fear. New York: Morrow, 1959, 191 pp.

A very readable guide to sorting out the positive and negative influences of religious life. Distinguishes between the healing and saving of souls. Anderson was Director of the Academy of Religion and Mental Health.

[1960] **386. Boisen, Anton Theophilus.**
Out of the Depths: An Autobiographical Study of Mental Disorder and Religious Experience. New York: Harper, 1960, 216 pp.

Boisen's autobiography describes in depth his relationship with Alice Batchelder, which was the key variable in his mental health, his five psychotic episodes, and his understanding of the nature of religious and psychotic experiences as reconstructive. Includes a detailed history of the early years of clinical pastoral education from the perspective of its founder.

[1960] **387. Northridge, William Lovell.**
Disorders of the Emotional and Spiritual Life. London: Epworth Press, 1960, xi+130 pp. Great Neck, New York: Channel Press, 1961, 130 pp.

Northridge, a Methodist pastor, first presented his ideas in a series of "sermon-lectures" followed by discussions. He addresses the fact that most unhappy church members who consult the spiritual director suffer from problems arising out of emotional disturbances rather than intellectual difficulties about the Faith. A sensitive exploration of psychological disorders.

[1961] **388. Caro Baroja, Julio.**
Las brujas y su mundo; con varias ilus. Madrid: Revista de Occidente, S. A., 1961, 381 pp. ENGLISH: *The world of the witches.* Translated by O.N.V. Glendenning. London: Weidenfeld and Niconson, 1964; Chicago: University of Chicago Press, 1965, xiv+313 pp.

Baroja asserts that "Between what physically exists and what man imagines or has in the past imagined to exist, there lies a region in which the evidently real and the imaginary seem to overlap. As a result, people—not to mention other kinds of animal life—could be thought to have certain characteristics of an unnatural kind. Sorceresses and witches have existed in this region of *experience*. . . ." Carajo considers the "origins in classical antiquity of the ideas which enter the complex of witchcraft and the realignment of these ideas in the later Middle Ages." He then focuses on the sixteenth- and seventeenth-century crises of witchcraft, with a special focus on the Basque regions. The study closes "with a discussion of the impact of eighteenth-century rationalism, which eventually ousted the belief in witchcraft from its place in the collective unconscious, to survive only in the marginal circles of cranks and neurotics, and in isolated peasantries." Sensitive to psychological and theological issues, and an excellent source for Spanish-language works.

[1962] **389. Vaughan, Richard Patrick.**
Mental Illness and the Religious Life. Milwaukee: Bruce Publishing Company, 1962, ix+198 pp.

The author, a psychologist and Jesuit priest, seeks to create an informed attitude toward and a sympathetic, intelligent understanding of the mentally ill religious. Portions of the book were first published as articles in *Review for Religious.*

[1964] **390. Knight, James Allen.**
A Psychiatrist Looks at Religion and Health. New York: Abingdon
Press, 1964, 207 pp.

Knight, affiliated with the Religion and Psychiatry program at Union
Theological Seminary, considers the spiritual concerns of mental health,
existential anxiety, and the uses and misuses of religion. His original
contribution is a chapter on Freud and Calvin, who are compared in their
ascetic tendencies, work ethic, religion, concepts of God, man and life,
and their heretical stance.

[1964] **391. O'Doherty, Eamonn Feichin.**
Religion and Personality Problems. Staten Island: Alba House, 1964;
Dublin: Clonmore and Reynolds, 1965, 240 pp.

Thirteen essays by a Catholic scholar at University College, Dublin.
Topics include the Oedipus Complex; adolescence and spiritual formation; personality and immortality; freedom, responsibility and guilt; mental suffering; psychopathology and mysticism; taboo, ritual, and religion;
the emotional development of the ecclesiastical student.

[1964] **392. Rokeach, Milton.**
The Three Christs of Ypsilanti: A Narrative Study of Three Lost
Men. New York: Alfred A. Knopf, 1964, xii+336 pp+iv.

Three chronic psychotics, all claiming to be Jesus Christ, are brought
together by a social psychologist for daily encounters over a period of two
years. This poignant, bitter, moving real-life story describes how each
man renounced his own identity and sought to adopt the name that
symbolized the greatest and best of man. The use of religion to solve
profound human deprivation and conflict is beautifully illustrated.

[1964] **393. Thach, Harrel G.**
God Gets in the Way of a Sailor. New York: Exposition Press, 1964,
266 pp.

An autobiographical account by a minister who spent six months as a
mental patient. Thach's major assertion is that the unconverted thought
he was mentally ill, while he himself regards his "illness" as God's work in
his life.

[1964] **394. Siirala, Aarne.**
The Voice of Illness: A Study in Therapy and Prophecy. Philadelphia:
Fortress Press, 1964, x+214 pp.

Siirala regards illness as the distorted relation between the individual
and the social group, so that healing is a restitution of an integrated
relationship between them. His thesis is that man's actual experience of
the whole structure of life is revealed in the way he forms his words. Thus,
schizophrenia becomes the focus for his study of the relationship between
prophetic religion and illness.

Religious Experience, Mysticism, Conversion

Books in this section deal with that dimension of religiosity Charles Y. Glock termed the experiential, which "gives recognition to the fact that all religions have certain expectations, however imprecisely they may be stated, that the religious person will at one time or another achieve direct knowledge of ultimate reality or will experience religious emotion." Books on conversion are included here, since most of these focus on the conversion experience itself rather than on its results, which may involve the other dimensions of religiosity.

[1746] **395. Edwards, Jonathan.**

A Treatise Concerning Religious Affections in Three Parts; Part I. Concerning the Nature of the Affections, and their Importance in Religion. Part II. Shewing What are no Certain Signs that Religious Affections are Gracious, or that they are not. Part III. Shewing what are Distinguishing Signs of Truly Gracious and Holy Affections. Boston: S. Kneeland and T. Greer, 1746, vi+343 pp. London: T. Fields, 1762, xii+263 pp.

Considered by many historians the first psychological work in America, this became one of Edwards's most widely read treatises. Sidney E. Ahlstrom, in A Religious History of the American People, states that "It is a classic evangelical answer to the question, What is true religion? Edwards's thesis, directly stated, is that 'true religion, in great part, consists in holy affections.' The 'affections' to Edwards are not simply the emotions, passions, or even the 'will,' but more fundamentally, that which moves a person from neutrality or mere assent and inclines his heart to possess or reject something. Love, therefore, 'is not only one of the affections but it is the first and chief . . . and the fountain of all the affections.'" Edwards delineates the twelve signs of genuine piety and the rightly inclined heart. Holy affections are spiritual, supernatural, and divine.

[1881] **396. *Faunce, Daniel Worchester.***

The Christian Experience: An Inquiry into its Character and its Contents. Philadelphia: American Baptist Publication Society, 1881, 220 pp.

[1896] **397. *Recejac, Edourd.***

Essai sur les fondements de la connaissance mystique. Paris: Félix Alcan, 1896, 306 pp. ENGLISH: *Essay on the Bases of the Mystic Knowledge.* Translated by Sara Carr Upton. London: Kegan Paul, Trench, Trubner, and Co., 1899, xi+287 pp.

Evelyn Underhill recommends this as "an important study on the psychology of mysticism."

[1899] **398. *Starbuck, Edwin Diller.***

The Psychology of Religion: An Empirical Study of the Growth of Religious Consciousness. London: Walter Scott, 1899, xx+423 pp.+adv. New York: Charles Scribner's Sons, 1900, xx+423 pp.

Starbuck's classic study of conversion was published in the Contemporary Science Series (Volume 38), edited by Havelock Ellis, with a preface by William James. Starbuck concludes that in religious education we must adapt ourselves to the needs and conditions of the individual, and sensitize ourselves to the stages of religious development, fostering growth into the next stage without hastening it unduly. Guidelines for the religious stance of the child, youth, and adult are, respectively, "conform," "be thyself," and "lose thyself."

[1900] **399. *Granger, Frank Stephen.***

The Soul of a Christian: A Study in the Religious Experience. New York: Macmillan Co.; London: Methuen & Co., 1900, xi+303 pp.

An early psychological study of mysticism written by an Anglican scholar.

[1902] **400. *James, William.***

The Varieties of Religious Experience: A Study in Human Nature; Being the Gifford Lectures on Natural Religion Delivered at Edinburgh in 1901–1902. New York and London: Longmans, Green & Co., 1902, xii+534 pp.

This book has become such a well-known classic that it has been reprinted at least once during every decade except the 1940s. The volume contains the following lectures: I. Religion and Neurology; II. Circumscription of the Topic; III. The Reality of the Unseen; IV, V. The Religion of Healthy-Mindedness; VI, VII. The Sick Soul; VIII. The Divided Self and the Process of Its Unification; IX, X. Conversion; XII, XIII. Saintliness; XIV, XV. The Value of Saintliness; XVI, XVII. Mysticism; XVII. Philosophy; XIX. Other Characteristics; XX. Conclusions; and Postscript.

[1903] **401. *Koons, William George*.**
The Child's Religious Life: A Study of the Child's Religious Nature and the Best Methods for its Training and Development. New York: Eaton and Mains; Cincinnati: Jennings & Pye, 1903, xii+270 pp.
A treatise on the psychology of conversion.

[1903] **402. *Saudreau, Auguste*.**
L'état mystique; sa nature, ses phases, et les faits extraordinaires de la vie spirituelle. Paris: Vic & Amat, 1903, 260 pp. ENGLISH: *The Mystical State, its Nature and Phases.* From 2 ed. Translated by D. M. B. London: Burns, Dates and Washbourne, 1924, xvi+204 pp.
Saudreau presents a comprehensive overview of mysticism from the early church fathers through the early twentieth century. After providing definitions and establishing the historical background of mysticism, he discusses the sufficient elements of the mystical state, the mystical realization of the presence of God, the phases of the mystical state, the differences between mystical and nonmystical contemplation, the unitive way, and the differences between the ascetical and mystical states. In his psychological analysis of mysticism he focuses on the role of the understanding and will, the "inferior portion," and the "intermediate powers."

[1905] **403. *Davenport, Frederick Morgan*.**
Primitive Traits in Religious Revivals: A Study in Mental and Social Evolution. New York: Macmillan Co.; London: Macmillan & Co., 1905, xii+323 pp.
Davenport, a sociologist at Hamilton College, distinguishes impulsive self-surrender from deliberate self-devotion, and the passional from the rational response. Analysis includes the Ghost dances of North American Indians, the American Negro, the Scotch-Irish revivals in Kentucky (1800) and Ulster (1859), the New England revivals under Jonathan Edwards, and U.S. revivals under Nettleton, Finney, and Moody.

[1905] **404. *Ladd, George Trumbull*.**
The Philosophy of Religion; A Critical and Speculative Treatise of Man's Religious Experience and Development in the Light of Modern Science and Reflective Thinking. 2 vols. New York: Charles Scribner's Sons, 1905, xx+2+616 pp., xii+590 pp. London: Longmans, Green, & Co., 1906.
Includes a review of the data of religious experience.

[1907] **405. *Cutten, George Barton*.**
Psychology of Alcoholism. London, Felling-on-Tyne and New York: W. Scott Publishing Co., 1907, xvi+357 pp.
Most important about Cutten's contribution is the chapter on religious conversion as a cure. This is based on three reasons: (1) conversion

creates desire for reform; (2) it changes associations, permitting the person to enter new environments; and (3) it provides emotional substitutes for alcohol.

[1910] **406. Ames, Edward Scribner.**
The Psychology of Religious Experience. Boston and New York: Houghton Mifflin Company, 1910, xi+427 pp.

Functional psychology, whereby the mental life of persons was understood as the channel wherein the organism adjusted itself to the environment, was used as the basis for examining religion, defined as "consciousness of the highest social values." Ames attempts to build on James' pragmatism and to bring together studies on the history of religion, the dynamics of conversion and theology's attempt to reconstruct itself. Sees philosophy and theology as grounded in the psychology of religious experience. Ames was influenced by Harold Höffding.

[1911] **407. Cornelison, Isaac Amada.**
The Natural History of Religious Feeling: A Question of Miracles in the Soul. An Inductive Study. New York and London: G. P. Putnam's Sons, 1911, xvii+273 pp.

Considers natural causes of religious feelings, religious ecstacy, conversion, and practical consequences of the doctrine of conversion. Cornelison concludes that conversion is an effect produced by natural causes, not a miracle of the soul. Appendix includes numerous examples of historical conversion experiences.

[1911] **408. Hill, John Arthur.**
Religion and Modern Psychology. A Study of Present Tendencies, Particularly the Religious Implications of the Scientific Belief in Survival; With a Discussion of Mysticism. London: W. Rider and Son, 1911, vii+200 pp.

[1914] **409. Burr, Anna Robeson (Brown).**
Religious Confessions and Confessants with a Chapter on the History of Introspection. Boston and New York: Houghton Mifflin Co., 1914, vii+562 pp.

A thorough study of the mystical tradition, with religious experience defined as a type of psychological experience. The history of introspection is most valuable, and supports the author's thesis that "the first effect of all elementary or imperfect self-study is mysticism," which reinforces further introspection.

[1915] **410. Gill, Richard Hooker Keller.**
The Psychological Aspects of Christian Experience. Boston: Sherman, French & Co., 1915, 104 pp.

A clergyman discusses the following aspects of Christian experience: sin, awakening, penitence and repentance, conversion and regeneration, the development of Christian strength, apostasy, emotions of religious life, conscience, and illusions and hallucinations.

[1915] **411. Tuckwell, James Henry.**
Religion and Reality: A Study in the Philosophy of Mysticism. London: Methuen & Co.; New York: Dutton, 1915, ix+318 pp. Reprint. Port Washington, New York: Kennikat Press, 1971, ix+318 pp.

Tuckwell defines philosophical mysticism as "that whole attitude of mind towards religion which results from a discovery of its rational basis and justification where it reaches its highest development in the experience of the genuine mystic." The focus of the book is on the mystic experience as "perfect experience," or an experience of the Absolute.

[1916] **412. Carpenter, William Boyd.**
The Witness of Religious Experience. The Donnellan Lectures Delivered before the University of Dublin, 1914, and in Westminster Abbey, Lent, 1916. London: Williams & Norgate, 1916, 111 pp.

Carpenter was Bishop of Ripon from 1884 through 1911 and served as subdean and canon of Westminster Abbey. Here, he asserts the fact that man is a religious animal, and that religion is a force which cannot be ignored and which lays its claim on the whole person. Religious consciousness in its development leads to self-realization, to the conviction of our own personalities, which involves realizing that within us there is a meeting ground between us and God. Carpenter demonstrates that the religious consciousness of Christ was of a different character than that of St. Paul, who had to undergo the process of "unselfing" in the pursuit of self-surrender. Carpenter concludes that "The principle to which religious consciousness bears witness, and which it insists upon in settling any operation, is harmony with the divine through self-surrender."

[1917] **413. Barrow, George Alexander.**
The Validity of the Religious Experience, a Preliminary Study in the Philosophy of Religion. Boston: Sherman, French & Co., 1917, xi+247 pp.

Seven lectures delivered at Harvard. Topics include (1) the problem of a philosophy of religion, (2) religion real and unique, (3) the soul of religion, (4) the test of religion, (5) human and superhuman, (6) personality, and (7) a foundation for theology.

[1917] **414. Otto, Rudolf.**
Das Heilige. Über das Irrationale in der Idee des göttlichen und sein Verhältnis zum Rationalen. Breslau: Trewendt und Granier, 1917, vi+216 pp. ENGLISH: *The Idea of the Holy: An Inquiry into the Nonrational Factors in the Idea of the Divine and Its Relation to the Rational.* Translated by John W. Harvey. London and New York: Oxford University Press, H. Milford, 1923, xv+228 pp.

In this classic manuscript, Otto examines the nature of those elements in the religious experience which lie outside and beyond the scope of reason. Certain "moments" of religious feeling are always found to recur, and religious feeling leads to a genuine knowing of the deity. Here Otto introduces the category of the numinous, the specific nonrational religious apprehension and its object, at all its levels, from the first dim stirrings to the most exalted forms of spiritual experience. Missing in the English translation is Otto's commentary on relevant portions of Wilhelm Wundt's *Völkerpsychologie*.

[1917] **415. Rouse, Ruth, and Miller, H. Crichton.**

Christian Experience and Psychological Processes: With Special Reference to the Phenomenon of Autosuggestion. London: Student Christian Movement Press, 1917, vii+147 pp.

Rouse and Miller seek to found an argument on what they call "the unexplained residue" remaining in consciousness over and above that of which psychology can give an account.

[1920] **416. Annett, Edward Aldridge.**

Conversion in India: A Study in Religious Psychology. Madras: Christian Literature Society for India, 1920, xiii+195 pp.

Using the questionnaire as well as autobiographical accounts, Annett applies recent psychology of religion to a new culture. He finds that conversion in India is not as thorough and radical an experience as it is in the West, and that in its extreme form it is relatively rare.

[1920] **417. Howley, John F. Whittington.**

Psychology and Mystical Experience. St. Louis, Mo.: B. Herder Book Company; London: Kegan Paul, Trench, Trubner & Co., 1920, 281 pp.

These essays began as a survey of recent writing on the psychology of religious experience for the journal *Studies* in 1913. Howley affirms experiments as auxiliaries to the facts of consciousness which he perceives to be the mainstay of the psychology of religion. He defines religious experience as that of which we are aware and can give some account, and analyzes Catholic and Protestant experience in terms of conversion and introversion, respectively.

[1922] **418. Brown, William Adams.**

Imperialistic Religion and the Religion of Democracy, a Study in Social Psychology. London: Hodder & Stoughton, Ltd., 1922; New York: Charles Scribner's Sons, 1923, xiv+223 pp.

The Martha Upton Lectures in Religion, 1922. Brown categorizes varieties of Christian experience as imperialistic, democratic, or individualistic vis-à-vis their social perspective.

[1922] **419. Halliday, William Fearon.**

Psychology and Religious Experience. New York: Richard R. Smith, 1922, 320 pp.

A book in "pastoral psychology" focusing on personal problems.

[1923] **420. Mudge, Evlyn Leigh.**

The God-Experience; A Study in the Psychology of Religion. Cincinnati: Caxton Press, 1923, 88 pp.

A psychological study attempting to identify the sensory factors and organic reactions involved in the religious person's experience of God. Includes literary and autobiographical testimony.

[1924] **421. *De Sanctis, Sante.***
La conversione religiosa, Studio biopsicologica. Bologna: Zanichetti, 1924, 300 pp. ENGLISH: *Religious Conversion: A Bio-Psychological Study.* Translated by Helen Augur. London: Kegan Paul, Trench, Trubner, & Co.; New York: Harcourt, Brace & Co., 1927, 324 pp.
This volume, written by an agnostic physician and biopsychologist, attempts to examine "the recognition and the predictability of the occurrence of religious phenomena in individuals immune from either insanity or the neuropathic diseases," i.e., normal persons. Includes an interesting discussion of the VI International Congress of Psychology, 1909, Geneva, at which the psychology of religion was considered. Proposes a dynamic understanding of conversion and accepts the reports of religious experience.

[1924] **422. *Fisher, Robert Howie.***
Religious Experience. London: Hodder & Stoughton, 1924; New York: George H. Doran, 1925, x+319 pp.
The Baird Lectures for 1924, presented by the minister of St. Cuthbert's Parish, Edinburgh. Encyclopedic in its scope, the volume treats many issues in psychology of religion.

[1924] **423. *Marechal, Joseph.***
Études sur la psychologie des mystiques. 2 vols. Bruges etc: Beyaert, 1924–1937, ENGLISH: *Studies in the Psychology of the Mystics.* Translated by Algar Thorold. London: Burns, Oates and Washburne, 1927, 344 pp. Albany: Magi Books, 1964, v+344 pp.
Evelyn Underhill describes this book as "valuable."

[1924] **424. *Strickland, Francis Lorette.***
Psychology of Religious Experience: Studies in the Psychological Interpretation of Religious Faith. New York and Cincinnati: Abingdon Press, 1924, 320 pp.
Strickland was a philosopher of religion. His work is evaluated by Leander Sylvester Keyser as follows: "An informing work, but too naturalistic in explaining Christian experience. Fails to correlate Christian theology and Christian psychology; hence, not thoroughly evangelistic."

[1925] **425. *Leuba, James Henry.***
The Psychology of Religious Mysticism. New York: Harcourt, Brace & Co.; London: Kegan Paul, Trench, Trubner & Co., 1925, xii+336 pp.
This is a later volume among many written by Leuba, who published his studies of conversion two years before Starbuck's better-known book

and who was the most prolific of the Clark school's students. He examined the origin of the mystical religious experience in the tendencies of human nature and discussed theology as inductive elaborations of experience.

[1925] **426.** *Underwood, Alfred Clair.*
Conversion Christian and Non-Christian; A Comparative and Psychological Study. New York: Macmillan Co.; London: George Allen & Unwin, 1925, 283 pp.

An historical and psychological study of the experience of conversion in Christianity, Hinduism, early Buddhism, Mohammedanism, and the mystery religions of the Roman Empire. A final chapter deals with the relative merits of each.

[1926] **427.** *Cadman, Samuel Parkes.*
Imagination and Religion. New York: Macmillan Co., 1926, 208 pp.

The Cole Lectures, 1924. Imagination is regarded as a primary component of religious experience as well as biblical exegesis.

[1926] **428.** *Dimond, Sydney George.*
The Psychology of the Methodist Revival: An Empirical and Descriptive Study. London: Oxford University Press, H. Milford, 1926, xv+296 pp.

Dimond attempts to relate contemporary behavioristic and social psychology of the 1920s to an analysis of the Methodist revivals. This is one of the earlier attempts at psychohistory and is a very thorough study in the classical psychology of religion.

[1926] **429.** *Edward, Kenneth.*
Religious Experience: Its Nature and Truth. Edinburgh: T & T Clark, 1926, xi+248 pp.

Theology and psychology are related in that theology is the science of religious experience from the side of its objective reference while psychology is the science of the same experience from a subjective point of view. The most useful theology for integration is experiential, rather than traditional or speculative. Edward warns against the fallacy of psychologism, the claim that that which is an unnecessary hypothesis for psychology is an illusion. Similarly, he asserts that there is no necessary connection between suggestion and delusion, and that the amount of emotional investment doesn't affect the question of objective reality.

[1927] **430.** *Cutten, George Barton.*
Speaking with Tongues: Historically and Psychologically Considered. New Haven: Yale University Press; London: Oxford University Press, H. Milford, 1927, xii+193 pp.

Cutten, president of Colgate University and author of *Three Thousand Years of Mental Healing,* published this book under the auspices of the James Wesley Cooper Memorial Publication Fund. Psychological "explanations" included ecstasy, hysteria, catalepsy, personal disintegration or dissociation of consciousness, automatism, and hypnotism. In this first English book on the topic, Cutten relies on the previously published French volume on tongues by E. Lombard and the German treatise by E. Mosiman.

[1927] **431. Jones, Rufus Matthew.**
New Studies in Mystical Religion; the Ely Lectures Delivered at Union Theological Seminary, New York, 1927. New York: Macmillan Co., 1927, 205 pp.
Jones completed a volume on mysticism two decades earlier.

[1927] **432. Mahoney, Carl K.**
The Religious Mind: A Psychological Study of Religious Experience. New York: Macmillan Co., 1927, xxii+214 pp.
This book is described by Wilbur H. Long (in *The Personalist*) as written for the general reader. Mahoney, a Methodist minister who later became Professor of Psychology and Philosophy at Dakota Wesleyan University, follows the typology for religious minds first articulated by Norman E. Richardson of Northwestern University. This typology includes the traditionalist, the critical type, the mystic, the executive type, the dogmatic propagandist, the ritualist (aesthete), the ascetic, and the reformer. The book is a psychology of religion including an analysis of conscious and unconscious mentality, types of religious experience, religious motivation, historic expression of religious aspirations, religious belief and thinking, ethicized religion, conversion, growth in religious experience, religious education, the religious significance of recent psychology, and the achieved experience.

[1929] **433. Chandler, Arthur.**
Christian Religious Experience. New York and London: Longmans, Green & Co., 1929, vii+115 pp.
Religious experience constitutes an awareness of a relationship of the soul to God. Chandler here counters the subjectivity engendered by the new psychology. Chandler was Bishop of Bloemfontein.

[1929] **434. Clark, Elmer Talmage.**
The Psychology of Religious Awakening. New York: Macmillan Co., 1929, 170 pp.
Using a sample of 2,174 subjects, Clark compares religious awakenings of the 1920s to those studied by Starbuck a generation before.

[1929] **435. Strachan, Robert Harvey.**
The Authority of Christian Experience: A Study in the Basis of Religious Authority. London: Student Christian Movement Press, 1929; Nashville: Cokesbury Press, 1931, 255 pp.
Strachan asserts that the seat of authority in religion is the individual

Christian conscience, but he rejects the subjectivism usually associated with such an assertion. He refutes the view of religion as illusion. Also valuable is his discussion of science and religion. Lectures delivered under the Alexander Robertson trust at the University of Glasgow in February 1929.

[1931] **436. *Gardner, Percy.***

The Interpretation of Religious Experience. Nashville: Cokesbury Press, 1931, 231 pp.

Gardner focuses on a dynamic psychology influenced by William James and William McDougall. According to the *Journal of Religion* reviewer, he is rather casual and unscientific, especially in the realm of telepathy and hypnotism.

[1932] **437. *Hynek, R. W.***

Konnersreuth: A Medical and Psychological Study of the Case of Teresa Neumann. Translated by Lancelot C. Sheppard. London: Burns Oates & Washbourne, 1932, v+150 pp.

Hynek's psychological interpretations of the case of Teresa Neumann focus on the hypothesis of hysteria and the authenticity of her stigmata. The author concludes that these phenomena can be regarded as marks of true mysticism and the presence of supernatural intervention.

[1933] **438. *Graham, John William.***

Psychical Experiences of Quaker Ministers. London: Friends Historical Society, 1933, vi+40 pp.

Graham prepared these reports for his presidential address to the Friends Historical Society, and they were published posthumously as a supplement to the society's journal. About thirty anecdotes are included.

[1933] **439. *Hughes, Thomas Hywel.***

The New Psychology and Religious Experience. London: George Allen & Unwin, 1933, 332 pp.

Regarding the new psychology as a menace to Christianity, Hughes challenges the behaviorism of J. B. Watson, Edwin Bissell Holt, and James Henry Leuba and the psychoanalysis of Sigmund Freud and Carl G. Yung (sic). He explores the question of the reality of the religious object, and asserts that we cannot account for the persistence of the idea of God if it is only an illusion. Other topics treated include the consciousness of sin, conversion, the sense of peace and power, and the sense of divine presence.

[1935] **440. *Dewar, Lindsay.***

Man and God: An Essay in the Psychology and Philosophy of Religious Experience. London: Society for Promoting Christian Knowledge; New York: Macmillan Co., 1935, viii+244 pp.

The Page Lectures at Yale University, 1932, and Bible Lectures at the University of Leeds, 1933.

[1935] **441. Thomas, William Bryn.**
The Psychology of Conversion: With Special Reference to Saint Augus-tine. London: Allenson & Co., Ltd., 1935, 190 pp.

Thomas, the Vicar of Kemble in Gloucestershire, here attempts to "co-ordinate the researches made regarding this vastly complicated phe-nomenon and attempt a synthesis of all that, on close examination, ap-pears valid and valuable in such researches." His major chapters focus on conversion in religious psychology, Saint Augustine, and a psychological analysis of conversion. Thomas operates on an assumption stated by Archbishop Trench in 1857, that "we are in need of, and gradually being forced into, a theology based on psychology." His goal is to steer between the extremes of attributing conversion merely to divine agency on the one hand, and to "subconscious incubation" on the other.

[1937] **442. Bewkes, Eugene Garrett, Bixler, Julius Seelye, Calhoun, Robert Lowry, and Niebuhr, H. Richard, eds.**
The Nature of Religious Experience; Essays in Honor of Douglas Clyde MacIntosh. New York and London: Harper & Brothers, 1937, xiv+ 244 pp.

This volume contains essays on religious knowledge and experience in honor of Douglas Clyde MacIntosh by former students on his sixtieth birthday. Contributors are Eugene G. Bewkes, Vergilius Ferm, George F. Thomas, Reinhold Niebuhr, Cornelius Kruse, Filmer S. G. Northrup, and the editors. The content considers issues in the philosophy of reli-gion. Includes bibliography of MacIntosh who taught at Yale.

[1937] **443. England, Frederick Ernest.**
The Validity of Religious Experience. London: Nicholson & Watson, 1937, ix+288 pp. New York: Harper & Brothers; London: Nicholson & Watson, 1938, 288 pp.

England treats religious experience psychologically as a genuine branch of human experience whose validity is to be tested in the same manner as any other. He explores the genesis and content of religious experience.

[1937] **444. Hughes, Thomas Hywel.**
The Philosophic Basis of Mysticism. Edinburgh: T & T Clark, 1937, ix+436 pp.

Hughes includes four chapters on the psychology of mysticism, constituting a thorough review of the psychological literature.

[1937] **445. Jones, Wilfred Lawson.**
A Psychological Study of Religious Conversion. London: Epworth Press, E. C. Barton, 1937, 397 pp.

Jones's book is based on research conducted for his master's thesis at the University of Reading, and examines what he labels as "the human factors" in conversion. Data collection involved the initial use of questionnaires, followed by personal interviews and information gathered from friends. Gradual converts are compared to the nongradual, and both are examined in Christian versus non-Christian communities. Jones examines manifestations of conversion in behavior, poise, and attitude, as well as the psychological consequences of conversion. Religious conversion is also compared to other forms of awakening (aesthetic, intellectual, love), and discussed in terms of its social, physiological, and temperamental conditions. He carefully avoids the psychologist's fallacy in his statement that "It would be manifestly unfair to expect psychological investigation to provide arbitrament for theological or metaphysical controversies. Psychological facts, of themselves, can neither necessitate nor invalidate any particular theological or metaphysical proposition."

[1937] **446.** *Knudson, Albert Cornelius.*

The Validity of Religious Experience. Cincinnati: Abingdon Press, 1937, 237 pp.

Knudson originally presented these ideas in a series of lectures at Southern Methodist University in 1937. He argues that religion is structured in the human mind and thus that it has as much logical validity as has philosophy, morality, or art.

[1938] **447.** *Moore, John Morrison.*

Theories of Religious Experience with Special Reference to James, Otto, and Bergson. New York: Round Table Press, 1938, xi+253 pp.

This volume analyzes the nature of conscious religious experience and its relevance to the validity of theological assertions in William James, Rudolf Otto, and Henri Bergson. The method excludes genetic and pathological considerations. Moore notes that William James affirmed the essential role of experience in religion, Rudolf Otto insisted on its non-rational dimension and Henri Bergson related religion to basic striving. Provides a helpful critique of these authors.

[1941] **448.** *Sampson, Ashley.*

Psychologist Turns to God. New York: Dacre, 1941.

A Catholic psychologist's account of his conversion experience.

[1943] **449.** *Carle, Charles.*

Mysticism in Modern Psychology. Some Critical Remarks about Magical Trends in "Psychoanalysis" and "Psychodiagnostics." New York: Psycho-Sociological Press, 1943, 47 pp.

A critique of psychoanalysis in the name of psychosociology, but with little sophistication in terminology.

[1946] **450.** *Görres, Ida Friederike Coudenhove.*

Das verborgene Antlitz: eine Studie über Thérèse von Lisieux. Freiburg: Herder Verlag, 1946, xiii+525 pp. 8 ed. under the title Das

Senfkorn von Lisieux. ENGLISH: *The Hidden Face: A Study of St. Thérèse of Lisieux*. Translated by Richard Winston and Clara Winston. New York: Pantheon Books, 1959, 428 pp.

A sensitive exploration of the life of St. Thérèse, based on her notebooks that contain the recollections of her early life and her brief years at the convent, a letter that describes her spiritual experiences to her sister, and conversations that were recorded at her sickbed. Of interest to the psychologist of religion is Thérèse's early illness, which her physician diagnosed as St. Vitus' Dance, but which was probably of psychogenic origin after her perceived abandonment by her sister. Görres discusses this illness in response to the family's interpretation of it as an assault by the Evil One: "A crisis which produces a state of confusion and agitation in body and soul, which attacks simultaneously a person's alertness, confidence, presence of mind and powers of resistance, can at the same time—while the state of the disease remains unchanged—*also* mean a grave temptation, a diabolical invitation to discouragement in the face of life." Görres adds that this crisis "can lead to stifling inhibitions, to erroneous interpretations of the self, to lifelong hypochondria about one's 'weak sides'—all attitudes which may later on hinder radical, heroic commitment. And we may well assume—many events from the lives of saints seem to confirm this—that the demons discern a lofty vocation in a person much sooner than do human beings, and bring to bear their power against him."

[1948] **451.** *Muthumalai, Albert.*
The Psychology of Conversion. Trichinopoly: Indian Catholic Theological Society, 1948?, 38 pp.

This Indian Jesuit, a convert from Protestantism, here discusses the process of conversion as primarily a psychological one. Logic and intellect can assist this psychological process, but it cannot result from argument alone.

[1957] **452.** *Sargant, William Walters.*
Battle for the Mind: A Physiology of Conversion and Brain-washing. London, Heinemann, [1957,] 248 pp. Also published in United States as *Battle for the Mind: How Evangelists, Psychiatrists, Politicians and Medicine Men Can Change Your Beliefs and Behavior.* Garden City, N.Y.: Doubleday & Co., 1957, 263 pp.

Sargant, a psychiatrist, explores the stress and emotional collapse often associated with conversion and the reversal of belief. He focuses especially on the techniques of John Wesley.

[1959] **453.** *Ames, Edward Scribner.*
Beyond Theology: the Autobiography of Edward Scribner Ames. Edited by Van Meter Ames. Chicago: University of Chicago Press, 1959, xii+223 pp. +illus.

Ames describes his autobiography as "a somewhat intimate and informal account of my religious experience from childhood to the development of my later views." In the liberal tradition of psychology and religion, Ames was for forty years pastor at University Church of the Disciples of Christ.

[1959] **454. Brandon, Owen.**
The Battle for the Soul; Aspects of Religious Conversion. Philadelphia: Westminster Press, 1959; London: Hodder & Stoughton, 1960, 96 pp.

A study of conversion based on pastoral experience and the psychology of religion.

[1959] **455. Ferm, Robert O.**
The Psychology of Christian Conversion. Westwood, N.J.: Fleming H. Revell Co., 1959, 255 pp.

Ferm claims that Christianity alone brings about a complete moral and spiritual transformation which conforms to the biblical definition. He points out the limitations of psychology and demonstrates the uniqueness of Christian conversion. Historical overview includes views of William James, Edwin Diller Starbuck, George Albert Coe, Elmer T. Clark, James Henry Leuba, Edward Scribner Ames, Alfred Claire Underwood, James Grant McKenzie, Gordon W. Allport, Edmund W. Sinnott, Paul Johnson, and Sverre Norborg. He examines the "evangelical crises" in the lives of Jonathan Edwards, John Wesley, Paul Bunyan, Peter Cartwright, George Whitefield, Adoniram Judson, C. S. Spurgeon, and J. Hudson Taylor.

[1959] **456. Lloyd-Jones, David Martyn.**
Conversions: Psychological and Spiritual. Chicago and London: Inter-Varsity Press, 1959, 40 pp.

As indicated on the flyleaf of this book, the author offers "A vigorously written critique of the book *Battle for the Mind* in which the author, Dr. William Sargant, raises, on psychological grounds, important questions concerning the nature of Christian conversion." After summarizing Sargant's main thesis, Lloyd-Jones discusses some of its implications, focusing on Sargant's interpretation of Pentecost and on the conversions of St. Paul and John Wesley. In a concluding section, Lloyd-Jones urges Christians to take warning from Sargant's work, and reconsider their evangelistic methods. Lloyd-Jones first presented these ideas to Christian ministers, under the auspices of The Evangelical Alliance at High Leigh, Hoddeston, Hertfordshire.

[1964] **457. Kelsey, Morton T.**
Tongue-Speaking: An Experiment in Spiritual Experience. Garden City, New York: Doubleday & Co., 1964, xii+252 pp.

Examining the contemporary manifestations of glossolalia, Kelsey takes into account biblical, psychological, and pragmatic considerations. He writes from a Jungian perspective.

[1965] **458. *Dodds, Eric Robertson.***

Pagan and Christian in an Age of Anxiety: Some Aspects of Religious Experience from Marcus Aurelius to Constantine. Cambridge: Cambridge University Press, 1965, xii+144 pp.

The Wiles Lectures at Belfast, 1963. Dodds examines the gradual withdrawal of a sense of divinity from the material world and the corresponding devaluation of ordinary human experience, as well as such phenomena as world-hatred and asceticism, dreams and states of possession, and pagan and Christian mysticism.

[1965] **459. *Goodenough, Erwin Ramsdell.***

The Psychology of Religious Experience. New York: Basic Books, 1965, xiii+192 pp.

Goodenough devotes two chapters to the definition of religion and psychology, and their basic assumptions. A third, extensive chapter on "The divided self in Greco-Roman religion" is devoted to the issue of body-mind dualism. Types of religious experience discussed are legalism, supralegalism, orthodoxy, supraorthodoxy, aestheticism, symbolism and sacramentalism, the church, conversion, mysticism, and religion as search.

Psychology of Prayer and Worship

Books in this section focus on Charles Glock's ritualistic dimension of religiosity, encompassing "the specifically religious practices expected of religious adherents." The psychologies of prayer and preaching are most common in this category, but there are also some psychological examinations of other liturgical dimensions such as the sacraments and the general idea of worship.

[1901]   **460. Hylan, John Perham.**

Public Worship: A Study in the Psychology of Religion. Chicago: Open Court Publishing Co.; London: Kegan Paul, Trench, Trubner & Co., 1901, 94 pp.

Hylan's doctoral thesis under G. Stanley Hall at Clark University. He calls for a nonlaboratory return to psychology as the science of the soul, an endeavor which, while not including mathematical formulas, will nevertheless be scientifically rigorous. He suggests this demands a new method. It is a questionnaire study on the meaning and effect of worship.

[1909]   **461. Strong, Anna Louise.**

The Psychology of Prayer. Chicago: The University of Chicago Press, 1909, 122 pp.

Originally published as Strong's doctoral thesis under the title "A Consideration of Prayer from the Standpoint of Social Psychology." Strong used the pseudonym "Anise."

[1913]   **462. Stolz, Karl Ruf.**

Autosuggestion in Private Prayer: a Study in the Psychology of Prayer. Grand Forks, N.D.: 1913, 138 pp. Rev. ed. *The Psychology of Prayer.* New York and Cincinnati: Abingdon Press, 1923, 247 pp.

This is Stolz's thesis for the University of Iowa in 1911. Stolz, a professor at Wesley College in Grand Forks, North Dakota, seeks to modify the conclusions that prayer is purely subjective in its effects and that it is a miracle-working process not reducible to natural law. Autosuggestion is defined as "a self-imposed idea which tends to realize itself automatically. An autosuggestion involves three phases: (1) the introduction of an idea into the mind by the self, (2) faith in the realization of the idea, (3) the self-realization of the idea." Based on questionnaire responses, Stolz discusses the role of attention in prayer, faith in prayer, the answer to prayer, devotional prayer, and unanswered prayers. Private, petitionary prayers are of two sorts: those answered through the self and those answered through another self. He states the following "reasons" for unanswered prayer: (1) lack of scientific discrimination, leading to prayers for things outside the domain of personal influence; (2) overcomplex petitions which are beyond the person's organic vitality for realization; (3) temperamental disqualifications which make persons unable to receive a dramatic answer to prayer; (4) lack of perseverance; (5) negative autosuggestion, which fixes the mind on the things it wants to be rid of; (6) automatic prayers, receiving little attention; (7) prayer during periods of spiritual dryness; (8) praying without rest; (9) lack of faith; (10) failure to provide information to those others who might assist in the answering of prayer; (11) making directions too directly to others, making them resistive; (12) a generally unsettled mental attitude. While Stolz assumes that "Christianity and prayer stand or fall together," he does not deal with the philosophical-theological questions he raises. As a psychologist, he asserts that prayer has several typical results which give it survival value for the Christian: (1) the praying individual is likely to survive his unbelieving fellow in the struggle for physical existence; (2) prayer is a molder of character; (3) prayers may be, but are not necessarily, expressions of free choice and self-determination. Stolz concludes that the study points toward a God who reveals himself in law and order and in regularity, and that prayer does not change God's purpose—rather, true prayer leads to the construction of a personality at one with God. He avoids the error of psychologism with the caveat that "A study of the mental processes involved in prayer neither proves nor disproves the existence of God."

[1918]   **463. *Gardner, Charles Spurgeon.***
Psychology and Preaching. New York: Macmillan Co., 1918, 389 pp.
This is an attempt to apply faculty and functional psychology to worship and preaching. The chapters are built around psychological categories such as feeling, attention, mental images, habit, and action. Written by a seminary professor of homiletics.

[1918]   **464. *Heiler, Friedrich.***
Das Gebet; eine religionsgeschichtliche und religionspsychologische Untersuchung. Munich: E. Reinhardt, 1918, xv+476 pp. ENGLISH: *Prayer: A Study in the History and Psychology of Religion*. Translated by

Samuel McComb and J. Edgar Park, London and New York: Oxford University Press, 1932, 376 pp.

Heiler, professor of the History and Philosophy of Religion at Marburg University and leader of the German Evangelical–Ecumenical Union, acknowledged a strong debt to Nathan Söderblom, Karl Adam, and Friedrich von Hügel. His study includes an overview of primitive and ritual prayer, prayer in Greek religions and in philosophical thought, prayer in the experience of great religious personalities, prayer in mysticism and prophetic religion, personal prayer, prayer in public worship, and the essence of prayer. According to Heiler, "Prayer is the expression of a primitive impulse to a higher, richer, intenser life." A classic in the field, the work contains more than two thousand quotations.

[1924] **465. *Crichton-Miller, Hugh.***

The New Psychology and the Preacher. London: Jarrolds, 1924, 276+ 7 pp. New York: Thomas Seltzer, 1924, x+246 pp.

W. Bertrand Stevens reviewed this book in *The Personalist*, and described it as an application of the new psychology to religion in general rather than to preaching in particular. Miller wrote this book as the third in a series beginning with *The New Psychology and the Teacher* and *The New Psychology and the Parent*. He emphasizes religion's occupation with the individual's adjustment to suffering, and suggests that "a religious philosophy in regard to suffering must be equally applicable to mental and bodily pain."

[1924] **466. *Felix, Richard W.***

Some Principles of Psychology as Illustrated in the Sacramental System of the Church. Washington, D.C.: Catholic University of America, 1924, 91 pp.

Felix, a Benedictine, wrote this dissertation under the direction of Edward Aloysius Pace. Felix focuses his psychological analysis on the visible signs of the Sacraments, and describes three psychological laws: the law of appeal to the senses, the law of sign appeal, and the law of social significance. He differentiates among three kinds of signs: (1) commemorative signs, which are aids to the memory; (2) demonstrative signs, which involve one person bringing something to the attention of another; and (3) promissory signs, which involve a tangible token of the pledge to fulfill in the future something promised in the past or present. Felix concludes that the church "allows the natural promptings of the human heart full play. She speaks to that human heart in a human way. She ministers to that heart through a Sacramental System that meets at once all the needs of nature, and satisfies completely every sound principle of true psychology." Hence, Felix adds, "it is that of all religionists, the Catholic alone, does not have to leave his psychology outside the Church door when he would enter in. Only that which is Divine could be so human."

[1924]   **467. Northridge, William Lovell.**
Recent Psychology and Evangelistic Preaching. London: Epworth Press, 1924, 96 pp.

In this short book Northridge covers the topics of medical psychology; emotion, intellect, and will in religious experience; the unconscious; and evangelistic preaching; conviction, faith, and conversion as components of the evangelistic method; and the personal qualities of the evangelist. He asserts that "there is no complete psychology of evangelism; that psychological principles are not adequate to explain spiritual experience." He draws two distinctions in support of this assertion. The first is that between immediate and ultimate causes of religious experience. The second is between true and false evangelism. The true evangelist does not rely on the power of suggestion, and his work leads to remolding of the personality according to the Spirit of Jesus, altering the foundations of individual character and men's conception of values. Finally, Northridge asserts that "The ideals of Christlike tenderness, disinterested service, and self-sacrifice which are the marks of the true Christian, are not developed from within, except through a Power that is superhuman."

[1927]   **468. O'Brien, John Anthony.**
Modern Psychology and the Mass: A Study in the Psychology of Religion. New York: Paulist Press, 1927, 32 pp.

[1925]   **469. Hardman, Oscar, ed.**
Psychology and the Church (Essay on the Psychology of Public Worship). London: Macmillan & Co., 1925, xiv+296 pp. New York and Toronto: Macmillan Co., 1925, 203 pp.

Contributors are E. J. Bicknell, L. F. Browne, G. H. Dix, Lawrence W. Grensted, James Arthur Hadfield, C. E. Hudson, W. R. Matthews, H. M. Relton, and Carl F. Rogers. Includes overviews of current state of psychology of religion and specific essays on prayer, public worship, religious education, preaching, evangelism, edification, moral development, spiritual healing, sectarianism, and schism. An Anglican perspective.

[1930]   **470. Parry, Ernest.**
Sermon Psychology. London: Hunter & Longhurst, 1930, vii+96 pp.

An overview of psychological findings which can be of use to the preacher.

[1931]   **471. Hodge, Alexander James.**
Prayer and Its Psychology. London: Society for Promoting Christian Knowledge; New York: Macmillan Co., 1931, xxii+220 pp.

Doctoral thesis at the University of London. Hodge seeks to "furnish a contribution toward the vindication of the Christian gospel in terms of modern psychological thought," and examines the nature and evolution of prayer, psychological aspects of prayer, and philosophical considerations. Extensive bibliography in English.

[1931] **472. *Moore-Browne, Pleasance.***

The Psychology of Worship. London: Society for Promoting Christian Knowledge, 1931, 67 pp.

Moore-Browne first presented these ideas to a meeting of the North-West London Lay Group of the Anglican Evangelical Group Movement, in the context of its studies on worship. The book was recommended by both Lawrence W. Grensted and Vernon F. Storr, the Archdeacon of Westminster.

[1934] **473. *Carter, Frank Craven.***

Psychology and Sacraments. London: Williams & Norgate, 1934, 142 pp.

God is the great "Hetero-Suggestor" and the Sacraments are means by which he sends the stream of his grace into the human soul. Carter includes an exposition on the leading conclusions of the new psychology.

[1934] **474. *Meland, Bernard Eugene.***

Modern Man's Worship: A Search for Reality in Religion. New York and London: Harper & Brothers, 1934, xix+317 pp.

Meland first surveys and evaluates liturgical movements in America, Germany, and France, including both Protestantism and Catholicism. He then articulates his own philosophy of religion, which he terms mystical naturalism. Finally, he discusses the possible fruits of nature worship.

[1939] **475. *Hughes, Thomas Hywell.***

The Psychology of Preaching and Pastoral Work. London: George Allen & Unwin, 1939; New York: Macmillan Co., 1941, 266 pp.

A practical treatise by the author of numerous books on psychology of religion.

[1956] **476. *Lee, Roy Stuart.***

Psychology and Worship. New York: Philosophical Library, 1956, 110 pp.

The Burroughs Memorial Lectures at the University of Leeds, 1953. Lee explores the main psychological processes operating in worship. The aspiration after God is classified as an instinct, and other elements of Freudian psychology are included. However, Lee points out that psychology can only study the ideas of men about God and their behavior in connection with these ideas. Thus, the final claims of the psychoanalytic theory of religion are rejected.

[1956] **477. *Moore, Thomas Verner.***

The Life of Man with God. New York: Harcourt, Brace & Co., 1956, 402 pp.

Moore administered a questionnaire to two hundred housewives, teachers, monks, priests, and nuns. Based on this study, he reports on the prayer life of Roman Catholics. He includes a fifteen-page annotated bibliography on the spiritual life.

[1961] **478. *Jackson, Edgar Newman.***

A Psychology for Preaching. Great Neck, N.Y.: Channel Press, 1961, 192 pp.

Jackson operates on the assumption that the sermon must be more than monologue, meeting actual needs of individuals within the matrix of a worshipping congregation. In 1956 Jackson authored a related book entitled *How to Preach to People's Needs*.

Faith: Belief and Unbelief

Books here deal with the cognitive aspects of religion, including both the ideological and intellectual dimensions of religiosity defined by Charles Glock. Some of these works might be defined as "psychologies of conviction," others focus specifically on doubt and unbelief, and still others rally recent psychological findings in the defense of the faith. Probably of the greatest social significance have been those works examining the relationship between faith and authority-authoritarianism.

[1822] **479. Beasley, Frederick.**
A Search for Truth in the Science of Human Mind, Part First. Philadelphia: S. Potter & Company, 1822, viii+561 pp.
   Beasley, an Episcopalian clergyman, was provost at the University of Pennsylvania and a member of the Philosophical Society. His purpose in this manuscript is to correct the Scottish philosophers in their exposition of the British empiricists. Of special interest is his critique of Hume's position on miracles.

[1901] **480. Johnson, Elias Henry.**
The Religious Use of Imagination. New York and Boston: Silver, Burdett and Company, 1901, ix+227 pp.
   Johnson, professor at Crozer Theological Seminary, speaks of imagination used to bring into clear outline the implicit beliefs of the mind.

[1907] **481. Pratt, James Bissett.**
The Psychology of Religious Belief. New York: Macmillan Co., 1907, xii+327 pp.+adv. London: Macmillan & Co., 1907, xii+327 pp.

Pratt, professor at Williams College, defined belief as "the mental attitude of assent to the reality of a given object."He articulates a "recapitulation theory" of religious development moving from primitive credulity to intellectual and emotional belief. The affective element is regarded as the most fundamental. Pratt's study was based on the questionnaire method, in the tradition of G. Stanley Hall, and includes an extensive bibliography. The preface is by William James.

[1909] **482. *Costin, William Wilberforce.***

Introduction to the Genetic Treatment of Faith-Consciousness in the Individual. Baltimore: Williams & Wilkins Company, 1909, 47 pp.

The author's Ph.D. thesis at Johns Hopkins University.

[1909] **483. *Inge, William Ralph.***

Faith and Its Psychology. London: Duckworth & Co., 1909, 248 pp. New York: Charles Scribner's Sons, 1910, x+248 pp.

Inge, a well-known Cambridge theologian, first presented these ideas in lectures at the Passmore Edwards Settlement. He includes an etymological survey of faith and its cognates, doctrines of the early church, and comparison of Catholic and Protestant views. He examines as grounds of faith the infallible church, the infallible book, and the person of Christ, and also examines and critiques the ontological, cosmological, and teleological arguments for the existence of God. Inge responds to the psychologies of George Trumbull Ladd, Gustav Theodor Fechner, James Bissett Pratt, Edwin Diller Starbuck, and William James.

[1910] **484. *Lindsay, James.***

The Psychology of Belief. Edinburgh and London: William Blackwood & Sons, 1910, xi+71 pp.

Belief in its highest forms is a movement of our being so central and fundamental that its issue is life. It influences activity in every sphere of being.

[1911] **485. *Murray, David Ambrose.***

Christian Faith and the New Psychology: Evolution and Recent Science as Aids to Faith. New York and Chicago: Fleming H. Revell Co., 1911, 384 pp.

Murray served as Principal of the Osaka Theological Training School. In the first section on "God and Nature," he reviews the etiological, cosmological, and teleological arguments for the existence of God. In the second section on "Revelation," he argues that revelation follows naturally from proofs of God's existence, and discusses the relationship of science and revelation. In the final section on "Christology," Murray discusses miracles, prayer, atonement, and the meaning of Christ's death. He uses the theory of evolution to argue that the "First Cause" must have been an "agency similar to the spirit of man because the thing that it must have done is something that no other known agency in the universe is ever known to do, but it is precisely the thing which just one agency, namely the soul or life principle of man constantly does, and which is its specific nature to do." He further uses evidence from psychical studies to argue that revelations from God are most likely received when the mind is dominated by the "subconscious." He also argues for "Fellowship" on an evolutionary basis, asserting that "God must afford to men acts of a personal and individual nature." The evolution theory therefore itself demands that such acts be done, "for at every upward step the facilities for making that step possible have always been afforded, and it would therefore be 'a break in the uniformity of nature' if these things, the necessary facilities for this next most important step, were not also afforded." Finally, he uses the most recent understanding of dissociated states (multiple personality) to argue for the trinitarian nature of God, and uses love as an explanation for the nature of atonement.

[1915] **486. Ladd, George Trumbull.**
What Should I Believe? An Inquiry into the Nature, Grounds and Value of the Faiths of Science, Society, Morals and Religion. New York and London: Longmans, Green & Co., 1915, xiii+275 pp.+adv.
  Belief is distinguished from knowledge and mere opinion. Ladd attempts to distinguish those forms of belief that make claims upon the conscience, put the person under rational obligation, and offer the comfort and rewards of right belief. He also explores the faiths of morality and religion and "the will to believe."

[1917] **487. Forbes, Waldo Emerson.**
Cycles of Personal Belief. Boston and New York: Houghton Mifflin Company, 1917, v+148 pp.
  In this discussion of belief and doubt, Forbes discusses the phases of illusion, disillusion, and reillusion.

[1918] **488. Jastrow, Joseph.**
The Psychology of Conviction: A Study of Beliefs and Attitudes. Boston and New York: Houghton Mifflin Company, 1918, xix+387 pp.
  A collection of papers on beliefs and attitudes, exploring the interaction of our logical and psychological natures. Jastrow states that convictions are born of emotion and nurtured by conviction: "the greatest triumph of the human mind was the gradual removal of large areas of belief from the influence of the personal psychology of conviction." Essays include (1) the psychology of conviction; (2) belief and credulity; (3) the will to believe in the supernatural; (4) the case of Paladino; (5) the antecedents of the study of character and temperament; (6) fact and fable in animal psychology; (7) the democratic suspicion of education; (8) the psychology of indulgence: alcohol and tobacco; (9) the feminine mind; and (10) militarism and pacifism.

[1920] **489. Lewis, John.**

The Vital and Social Factors in Religious Belief: Being a Study of Religion as the Passion for Life Mediated by the Social Factor. Manchester: T. Griffiths & Co., 1920, 342 pp.

The reviewer in *The Personalist* describes this book as a major statement of the functionalist perspective. "The conception of God was brought into being in response to the demands of the passion of life," as regulated and controlled by an "idealising power that is akin to the inner spirit of the universe."

[1921] **490. Wells, Wesley Raymond.**

The Biological Foundations of Belief. Boston: Raymond J. Badger, 1921, ix+124 pp.

A collection of five essays previously published by the author.

[1921] **491. Wyckoff, Albert Clarke.**

Acute and Chronic Unbelief: Its Cause, Consequence and Cure. New York and Chicago: Fleming H. Revell Co., 1921, 218 pp+adv.

Wyckoff was professor of Psychology of Religion at the Biblical Seminary of New York and pastor in the Reformed Church. He discusses unbelief or sub-belief in both chronic and acute forms, taking James Henry Leuba as a prime example. Superbelief or misbelief is discussed with an examination of Christian Science, New Thought, Spiritism, and Theosophy, as well as various forms of mental healing. Wyckoff also authored a short pamphlet entitled "The unbelieving psychologists and the Christian faith," which was published by the Biblical Seminary in New York in 1916.

[1926] **492. Campbell, Charles Macfie.**

Delusion and Belief. Cambridge: Harvard University Press, 1926, 78 pp.

Campbell asserts the biological indispensability of belief, and illustrates this assertion with case studies, setting forth various situations which compel human beings to construct elaborate systematized delusions in order to give substantial fulfillment to their need for a certain belief object. Campbell was coauthor of a series of papers in honor of Morton Prince.

[1927] **493. Stekel, Wilhelm.**

Zwang und Zweifel für Ärzte und Mediziner dargestellt. Leipzig: Weidmann, 1927, 2 vols. ENGLISH: *Compulsion and Doubt.* 2 vols. Translated by Emil A. Gutheil, New York: Liveright Publishing Corp., 1949; London: Peter Nevill, 1950, vii+645 pp.

Stekel discusses the unconscious in compulsive neurosis, doubt, homosexuality and patricide, obsessive neuroses, schizophrenia and compulsion, and criminal impulses. Stekel asserts that persons need to be brought to face the causes of their problems to which they are blinding themselves. Thus, he advocates a form of responsibility therapy.

[1928] **494. Juergens, Sylvester Peter.**
Newman on the Psychology of Faith in the Individual. New York: Macmillan Co., 1928, xvii+288 pp.
In the *Journal of Religion*, W. H. Horton reviewed this book along with Gaston Frommel's, whose position is very similar to that of Juergens. Juergens argues that the appeal which Christian revelation makes to our faith comes not from its intellectual cogency but from its perfect correspondence with that which conscience has already told us and its perfect fulfilment of that longing after reconciliation which conscience itself has left unsatisfied. Horton asserts that Juergens is unsuccessful in his attempt to demonstrate that Cardinal Newman was not a Kantian.

[1934] **495. Hirning, Jacob Louis.**
The Psychology of Religious Certainty. Chicago: University of Chicago Press, 1934, 91 pp.
Hirning's doctoral dissertation.

[1935] **496. Monahan, William Beattie.**
The Psychology of St. Thomas Aquinas and Divine Revelation. Worcester and London: E. Baylis & Son, 1935?, viii+304 pp.
Monahan here addresses the Thomistic theory of knowledge.

[1936] **497. Lundholm, Helge.**
The Psychology of Belief. Durham, N. C.: Duke University Press, 1936, vii+245 pp.
Examines the genesis of belief, belief as a permanent mental quality controlling conduct, and belief as experience.

[1939] **498. Selbie, William Boothby.**
The Validity of Christian Belief. London: Nicholson and Watson, 1939, 170 pp.
Selbie was Principal Emeritus of Mansfield College. In this work he makes no distinction between natural and revealed religion, and feels that Karl Barth and Heinrich Emil Brunner go too far in making this distinction. Selbie asserts that God is found in the very impulse to search for him. The channels of revelation are the pursuit of truth, mystical consciousness, and the moral sense.

[1942] **499. Fromm, Erich.**
Escape from Freedom. New York: Holt, Rinehart & Winston, Inc., 1941, 257 pp. Also published as *The Fear of Freedom*. London: K. Paul, Trench, Trubner, 1942, xi+257 pp.
In the foreword, Fromm states that "it is the thesis of this book that modern man, freed from the bonds of pre-individualistic society, which simultaneously gave him security and limited him, had not gained freedom in the positive sense of the realization of his individual self; that is, the expression of his intellectual, emotional and sensuous potentialities. Freedom, though it has brought him independence and rationality, has

made him isolated and, thereby, anxious and powerless." Most interesting for purposes of integration is Fromm's discussion of "Freedom in the Age of the Reformation," which includes an analysis of the personalities of Martin Luther and John Calvin, and the role of authoritarianism in their lives and theologies.

[1946] **500.** *Sheed, F. J.*

Theology and Sanity. New York: Sheed & Ward, 1946, x+407 pp.

Deeply rooted in Scholastic theology, Sheed here aims to train the Catholic Intellect, the function or faculty of the soul whose work is "to know, to understand, to see: to see what? to see what's there." This is contrasted with Will, the faculty of the soul, whose "work is to love—and so to choose, to decide, to act." Concern with the Will is a concern for sanctity, concern with the Intellect is a concern for sanity. Sanity, the mastery of the Church's perspective on reality, is a prelude to sanctity.

[1949] **501.** *Rümke, Henricus Cornelius.*

Karakter en Aanleg in Verband met het Ongeloof. Amsterdam: W. ten Have, 1949, 105 pp. ENGLISH: *The Psychology of Unbelief: Character and Temperament in Relation to Unbelief.* Translated by M.H.C. Willems. London: Rockliff, 1952, 67 pp.

Rümke, Professor of Psychiatry at Utrecht, devotes this short book to describing the seven stages in religious experience-development which culminate in belief. He distinguishes unbelief from disbelief, as the former has the typical form of genuine belief. Unbelief is regarded as an interruption in development.

[1950] **502.** *Allport, Gordon Willard.*

The Individual and His Religion. New York: Collier-Macmillan,1950, xi+147 pp. London: Constable, 1951, xiv+163 pp.

This volume signaled a resurgence of interest in religion among main stream psychologists. Based on the 1947 Lowell lectures in which Allport discusses "the psychology, not . . . the psychopathology, of religion," this book assumes a rationalistic understanding of religion in which persons seek the meaning of life. Allport includes helpful discussions of the meaning of faith and the positive function of doubt, and religious maturity.

[1950] **503.** *Bartlett, Frederick Charles.*

Religion as Experience, Belief, and Action. London and New York: Oxford University Press, 1950, 39 pp.

The Riddell Memorial Lecture. Belief is regarded as a leap from unfinished data to conclusions regarded as complete. It is justified by its results and action rather than by verification. Bartlett was a social psychologist and experimentalist.

[1954]   **504. Ostow, Mortimer, and Scharfstein, Ben-Ami.**
The Need to Believe: The Psychology of Religion. New York: International-
al Universities Press, 1954, 162 pp.
   An excellent overview of the psychoanalytic perspective on religion,
with a sensitivity to the religious life and examples from the range of world
religions. The authors state that "neither the psychological character or
origin of a belief proves it true or false . . . proof or disproof is something
that psychiatry as such cannot undertake." However, a distinction can be
made between good and bad religion on the basis of psychoanalytic
principles.

[1954]   **505. Thouless, Robert Henry.**
*Authority and Freedom: Some Psychological Problems of Religious Be-
lief*. Greenwich, Conn.: Seabury Press, 1954, 124 pp.
   The Hulsean Lectures at Cambridge, 1952. Thouless examines three
major questions, which are answered affirmatively: (1) is there now a
decline in religious conviction? (2) is it possible for a reasonable modern
man to accept a religious system of thought? and (3) are there respects in
which religious ideas are presented to modern man which unnecessarily
increase his difficulty of acceptance?

[1960]   **506. Cantril, Albert Hadley, and Bumstead, Charles Heath.**
Reflections on the Human Venture. New York: New York University
Press, 1960, xvi+344 pp.
   Blending literature, philosophy, and psychology, the authors explore aspects of human nature including man's faith: when do we become
aware of the need for faith? What conditions help us to make it operation-
al?

[1960]   **507. King, Peter D.**
The Principle of Truth. New York: Philosophical Library, 1960, 110 pp.
   King regards the pursuit of truth as a health-producing force, and as a
basis for principles of behavior and ethics. King was the clinical director of
a mental hospital.

[1963]   **508. Barker, Charles Edward.**
Psychology's Impact on the Christian Faith. London: George Allen
& Unwin, 1963, 220 pp. +adv.
   Barker asserts that psychology challenges not truth or the place of
religion as such, but the concepts and dogmas of historic faith. He
addresses three phenomena common in Christian therapy clients: strong
obsessive-compulsive symptoms, masochism and sexual inhibitions, dis-
tortions and anxieties. In the second part of the book, he reassesses the
emphasis of Jesus' teaching in a number of areas.

[1964] **509.** *Goldman, Ronald J.*

Religious Thinking from Childhood to Adolescence. London: Routledge & Kegan Paul, 1964, xii+276 pp. +illus.

A study of the effect of levels of cognitive operation upon religious thinking. This work draws heavily on the theory of the Swiss psychologist, Jean Piaget.

[1966] **510.** *Goldbrunner, Josef, ed.*

Der Zukunftbezug in der Verkündigung. Munich: Kösel Verlag, 1964. ENGLISH: *The Dimension of Future in Our Faith*. Translated by Veronica Riedl. Notre Dame, Ind.: University of Notre Dame Press, 1966, 137 pp.

This is the fifth volume of "Writings on Catechetics" edited by Goldbrunner. The major questions addressed by the contributors are "What are the consequences of the promise of the future Kingdom of God in the Christian life?" and "How is this relation to the future realized, and how does the future dimension affect the Christian?" The authors seek a pastoral theology that makes the eschatological dimension relevant for the contemporary Catholic both in catechetics and homily. Contributors include Goldbrunner, Eugen Walter, Theodor Filthaut, Matthias Rinser, Alexander Sand, Josef Dreissen, Heinrich Spaemann, Ludwig Wolker, Karl Aloys Altmeyer, and Otto Betz.

PART FOUR

Psychology and Theology: The Practical Dimension

Spiritual Healing

Volumes included here stress the spiritual rather than psychological or physical methods of healing. Thus, these are influenced by the more traditional works in pastoral care while they also reflect an awareness of "the new psychology." Questions concerning the soul and the mind-body relationship often arise in this context, as does the more general relationship between religion and psychology-psychiatry and the question of a Christian personality theory.

[1884] **511. Evans, Warren Felt.**
The Primitive Mind-Cure. The Nature and Power of Faith; or, Elementary Lessons in Christian Philosophy and Transcendental Medicine. 5 ed. Boston: H. H. Carter & Karrick, 1884, x+215 pp.

   Evans was one of the more prominent writers in the last half of the nineteenth century who promoted spiritual healing. This is the fifth book in his writing about "Christian philosophy and transcendental medicine." He suggests that much self-healing can occur, and writes polemically against a materialism that ignores the spiritual depth of persons. He strongly affirms spiritual energies within individuals. This was intended to be a textbook on healing.

[1886] **512. Evans, Warren Felt.**
Esoteric Christianity and Mental Therapeutics. Boston: H. H. Carter & Karricks, 1886, 174 pp.

   Evans describes his work as Christian theosophy and phrenopathy, and relates it directly to the Hermetic tradition. The phrenopathic method involves "the transmission of a mental energy, and the action and reaction of one mind or spirit upon another." The energy involved has been described by the Hindus as Akasa, by Rosicrucians as astral light, by Plato as the *anima mundis* and by Christianity as the Holy Spirit. Because the basis of phrenopathy lies in the action of the Holy Spirit, the phrenopathic method involves convincing the world of sin, righteousness, and judgment. Evans asserts that we must ourselves be healthy and happy in order to apply the phrenopathic method of instruction. The patient must be educated to maintain an obstinate silence in regard to disease and symptoms, and encouraged to talk about the possible cure. The patient must also maintain a correct idea of the self in mind. Both suggestion (or positive affirmation) and silent or mental suggestion are tools of healing. Basic to the healing process is mental sympathy, the operations of one mind transmitted to another through mental induction. Evans wrote a number of other works on healing, including *Soul and Body; or, the Spiritual Science of Health and Disease; Mental Medicine: A Theoretical and Practical Treatise on Medical Psychology;* the *Divine Law of Cure; The Primitive Mind-Cure* (*see* entry 511); and *The Nature and Power of Faith; or, Elementary Lessons in Christian Philosophy and Transcendental Medicine*.

[1908] **513. *Dresser, Horatio Willis.***

A Physician to the Soul. New York and London: G. P. Putnam's Sons, 1908, v+171 pp.

Includes chapters on mental healing and the Emmanuel Movement.

[1908] **514. *Worcester, Elwood, McComb, Samuel, and Coriat, Isador Henry.***

Religion and Medicine: The Moral Control of Nervous Disorders. New York: Moffat, Yard, and Company, 1908, vii+427 pp. London: Kegan Paul, Trench & Trubner, 1908, x+427 pp. +illus.

This is the official history and teaching of the Emmanuel Movement, one of the earliest efforts in the twentieth century to integrate spiritual and psychological approaches to healing. Based on the initial effort of James Bissett Pratt with tuberculosis patients (Pratt was the founder of group therapy), Emmanuel Church, Boston, began work with the emotionally disturbed in 1906. The movement perceived itself as part of the demand for a functional faith similar to Christian Science. Most of the book details theories of personality and healing. Worcester's work was continued by the Craigie Foundation.

[1909] **515. *Dearmer, Percy.***

Body and Soul: An Inquiry into the Effects of Religion upon Health, with a Description of Christian Works of Healing from the New Testament to the Present Day. London: Sir Isaac Pitman & Sons, 1909, x+405 pp. New York: E. P. Dutton & Company, 1909, x+426 pp. +adv.

Dearmer cofounded the Guild of Health in 1905 with W. Harold Anson and Conrad Noel. All three founders were priests in the Church of England. Dearmer provides a thorough history of healing in the Christian church, including the text of the Resolutions of the Lambeth Conference of 1908 which reintroduced Apostolic Unction to the Anglican Church.

[1909] **516. *Huckel, Oliver.***

Mental Medicine: Some Practical Suggestions from a Spiritual Standpoint; Five Conferences with Students at the Johns Hopkins Medical School. New York: T. Y. Crowell & Co., 1909, xxxii+219 pp.

These five YMCA conferences demonstrate how Huckel, a pastor, helps troubled persons. Using a psycho-physical parallelistic model, Huckel presents to the medical students means for dealing with the moral and intellectual problems of their patients. Calls for a rapprochement between religion and medicine but does not advocate that clergymen become therapists. Presents fundamentals of mental science (health). Introduction by Leivelly Barker.

[1909] **517. *Münsterberg, Hugo.***

Psychotherapy. New York: Moffat, Yard and Company, 1909, xi+401pp.

In this book, Münsterberg takes on the task of convincing the medical establishment that all physicians should be trained in psychology for the purpose of learning psychotherapeutics. In the chapter on psychotherapy and the church, he reviews the history of physical and mental healing in primitive cultures and in Christianity, ending with the Emmanuel Movement. Although he is convinced that no fraud was involved in these movements, he questions whether the church should enter into psychotherapeutics. He asserts that the psychologist's task tends to be analytic while that of the minister tends to be synthetic. He also asserts that not every mind can be cured with religious emotion. He fears that the church may be tempted to substitute religious explanations for psychological ones, questions those movements which only apply healing to psychological problems and not to physical ones, and wonders if the leaders of the Emmanuel Movement have examined critically enough the relationship among body, mind, and soul.

[1909] **518. *Podmore, Frank.***

Mesmerism and Christian Science: A Short History of Mental Healing. London: Methuen, 1909, 306 pp. Philadelphia: G. W. Jacobs. Reprint. *From Mesmer to Christian Science: A Short History of Mental Healing.* New Hyde Park, N.Y.: University Books, 1963, xi+306 pp.

As described on the flyleaf, Podmore gives "the story of the progress from the idea that fluids, rays and emanations from the operator are effecting the cure to the final understanding that the curative agent is the power of imagination when stimulated by the Mesmerist." Podmore, who was active in the British Society for Psychical Research, begins his history with the work of Franz Anton Mesmer and includes overviews of Mesmerism in both France and Britain, and the work of the French investigatory commissions. He analyzes clairvoyance, including the theory that clairvoyance demonstrated the action of the soul apart from the body. His

147

overview of spiritualism in France and Germany includes the work of the Exegetical Society of Stockholm, Alphonse Cahagnet, and the famed Seeress of Prevorst. Later chapters discuss in detail Andrew Jackson Davis, Thomas Lake Harris, Phineas Parkhurst Quimby, Warren Felt Evans, Horatio W. Dresser, Mary Baker Eddy, and the New Thought and mental healing movements.

[1911] **519. *Flournoy, Theodore.***

Esprits et médiums; mélanges de métapsychique et de psychologie. Geneva: Librairie Kündig, 1911, viii+561 pp. ENGLISH: *Spiritism and Psychology.* Translated by Hereward Carrington. New York: Harper & Brothers, 1911, x+2+354 pp.

A critical study of supernatural psychology, including the following topics: (1) the study of the supernormal, (2) F.W.H. Meyers and subliminal psychology, (3) deceiving spirits, (4) beneficent spirits, (5) spirits and mediums, (6) the case of Eusapia Palladino, and (8) spiritism and spiritualism. A German translation appeared in 1921.

[1912] **520. *Boyd, Thomas Parker.***

The Voice Eternal: A Spiritual Philosophy of the Fine Art of Being Well. Berkeley,Calif.: Emmanuel Press, 1912, 173 pp.

Written by one of the founders of the Emmanuel Movement, an early twentieth-century effort in behalf of positive thinking and spiritual healing. This volume details methods and rationales for self-help based on religious faith.

[1913] **521. *Weaver, Edward Ebenezer.***

Mind and Health, with an Examination of Some Systems of Divine Healing. New York: Macmillan Co., 1913, xv+500 pp.

An elaboration of Weaver's doctoral dissertation at Clark University under G. Stanley Hall. An overview of religious healing movements with excellent indices and bibliography.

[1914] **522. *Geikje-Cobb, William Frederick.***

Spiritual Healing. London: G. Bell and Sons, 1914, xii+312 pp.

Written amidst the growing popularity of Christian Science and the wide acceptance of hypnotism. Cobb pleads for an appreciation of the healing powers embedded in the human spirit. This was one of the earlier calls for a model of the human being which included spiritual powers of healing. The book includes an historical survey of healing from ancient to modern times.

[1919] **523. *Janet, Pierre.***

Les médications psychologiques. Études historiques, psychologiques et cliniques, sur les méthodes de la psychothérapie. Vol. 1: *L'action morale, l'utilization de l'automatisme.* Vol. 2: *Les économies psychologiques.* Vol. 3: *Les acquisitions psychologiques,* Paris: Félix Alcan, 1919, 346 pp.,

308 pp., 494 pp. ENGLISH: *Psychological Healing*. 2 vols. Translated by Eden Paul and Cedar Paul. London: George Allen & Unwin, 1925; New York: Macmillan Co., 1925, 1265 pp. Reprint. New York: Arno Press, 1976, 1265 pp.

Volume One contains a history of healing movements including miraculous healings (religious, magic, and magnetism), the philosophical method of Christian Science, and the medical moralization of Paul Dubois. Volume Two ends with a discussion of moral guidance, focusing on the influence of the spiritual director and psychotherapist on the person.

[1920] **524. *Johnston, Donald K.***

Religious Aspects of Scientific Healing: A Psychoanalytic Guide Written from the Patient's Point of View. Boston: Richard G. Badger, 1920, 94 pp.

A rare application of psychoanalytic theory to religious psychotherapy.

[1921] **525. *Dresser, Horatio Willis, ed.***

The Quimby Manuscript, Showing the Discovery of Spiritual Healing and the Origin of Christian Science. New York: T. Y. Crowell Company, 1921, 474 pp.

An important book for the history of religious psychotherapy, including Phineas Parkhurst Quimby's correspondence with Mary Baker Eddy.

[1922] **526. *Bellwald, Augustine Matthias.***

Christian Science and the Catholic Faith, Including a Brief Account of New Thought and Other Modern Mental Healing Movements. New York: Macmillan Co., 1922, xvi+269 pp.

Bellwald reveals a broad background in the history of thought and of human psychology. His analysis does not include an understanding of the unconscious, but he does attempt a psychohistory of Mary Baker Eddy.

[1923] **527. *Brooks, Cyrus Harry, and Charles, Ernest.***

Christianity and Autosuggestion. London: George Allen & Unwin, 1923, 142 pp. New York: Dodd, Mead and Company, 1923, 158 pp.

The authors examine the theory and practice of Coué in the light of Christ's teaching and healing, finding them to be essentially in harmony. They discuss the question of how far the discovery of powers of autosuggestion affects Christian thought and practice and how far the teaching and principles of Christ deepen and enhance autosuggestion so that it can be applied to strengthening and developing the Christian life.

[1923] **528. *Coué, Emile.***

My Method, Including American Impressions. Garden City, Doubleday, Page & Co., 1923, xx+201 pp.

This is an account of Coué's approach to autosuggestion, a method distinct from hypnotism in that the person induced change in him- or herself while conscious. Coué clearly distinguishes himself and his method from religious healing, saying that he did not perform miracles but applies age-old principles.

[1924] **529. Rivers, William Halse.**

Medicine, Magic, and Religion. The Fitz Patrick Lectures Delivered before the Royal College of Physicians of London in 1915 and 1916. London: Kegan Paul, Trench, Trubner & Co.; New York: Harcourt, Brace & Co., 1924, viii+146 pp.

Rivers presents the ethnological approach to understanding the relations of religion to healing which were divined by the author over years of work in Melanesia. One of the earliest attempts to relate these ideas to cultural diffusion. He also includes a 1919 lecture on mind and medicine. Rivers studied under Ewald Hering and Emil Kraepelin and later directed the psychological laboratory at Cambridge.

[1927] **530. Crookshank, Francis Graham.**

Diagnosis and Spiritual Healing. London: Kegan Paul, 1927, 101 pp.

These were the Bradshaw Lectures given before the Royal College of Physicians in London in 1926. The author, an English physician, surveys the history and theory of diagnosis. The volume also includes a paper read at the meeting of the Hunterian Society in 1925 in a debate with the Bishop of Kensington. This paper is entitled "Spiritual healing and medical history." The author criticizes the materialistic dualism of many physicians which considers physical and spiritual experience to be unreal. He suggests that most physicians have unexamined metaphysical assumptions. Crookshank concludes that ministers should be open to any sober account of healing by spiritual methods.

[1931] **531. Worcester, Elwood, and McComb, Samuel.**

Body, Mind and Spirit. Boston: Marshall Jones Co., 1931, xix+367 pp.

Asserts that psychotherapy is mere patchwork without "the renewal of life at its source and its regulation by spiritual principles and laws." Spiritual modes of healing must accompany the scientific in order to be effective. The unconscious mind is the nexus between man and God. Worcester authored this book shortly after he resigned as pastor of Emmanuel Church, Boston, and emphasizes the importance of "in word transfer," his unique extension of Sigmund Freud's negative and positive transference.

[1931] **532. Zweig, Stefan.**

Die Heilung durch den Geist. Mesmer. Mary Baker-Eddy. Freud. Leipzig: Insel-verlag, 1931, 446 pp. ENGLISH: *Mental Healers: Franz Anton Mesmer, Mary Baker Eddy, Sigmund Freud.* Translated by Eden Paul and Cedar Paul. New York: Viking Press, 1932, xxvi+363 pp. London: Cassell, 1933, xxiv+363 pp.

Presents Mesmer, Eddy, and Freud as representatives of those who defy the materialistic tendencies of medicine to reduce illness to physical reality and the patient to a passive role in healing. Although Zweig denies he is taking more than an historical interest in these three, he implicitly espouses through his survey a sympathy for their ideas.

[1932] **533. *Embree, Edwin Rogers.***
Prospecting for Heaven; Some Conversations about Science and the Good Life. New York: Viking Press, 1932, 185 pp.
  Hypothetical conversations among a psychiatrist, a psychoanalyst, a psychologist, a sociologist, and a Chinese philosopher. Includes a discussion of the Mental Hygiene movement.

[1933] **534. *Worcester, Elwood.***
Making Life Better; An Application of Religion and Psychology to Human Problems. New York and London: Charles Scribner's Sons, 1933, x+244 pp.
  Worcester draws on a wealth of psychological experience, but is primarily spiritual in his approach to healing. The reviewer in the *Journal of Religion* chides him for giving too much credibility to the notions of spiritism and demoniacal possession.

[1935] **535. *Humble, Emil.***
The Gods in Plain Garb: A Study in Psychology. New York and London: G. P. Putnam's Sons, 1935, ix+314 pp.
  A Swiss psychologist shows that the gods of the ancient religions were symbolic representations of different phases of the all-governing mind. In his assertion that "right thinking would cure man-kind's physical ills," he reflects the influence of Emile Coué and the Christian Science movement. Extensive citations and bibliography.

[1936] **536. *Haushalter, Walter Milton.***
Mrs. Eddy Purloins from Hegel: Newly Discovered Source Reveals Amazing Plagiarism in "Science and Health." Boston: A. A. Beauchamp, 1936, viii+126 pp.
  Haushalter, minister of Christian Temple Church in Baltimore, makes public the Lieber-Hegel-Eddy Source Document and accuses Eddy of plagiarism of Georg Wilhelm Friedrich Hegel, John Ruskin, Emmanuel Swedenborg, Thomas Carlyle, Amiel, and others.

[1937] **537. *Ikin, Alice Graham.***
The Background of Spiritual Healing, Psychological and Religious. London: George Allen & Unwin, 1937, 224 pp.
  Ikin, a psychologist working under the Archbishop of York's committee of doctors and clergy, presented this lecture series at a conference held to consider the relation between psychotherapy and the church's ministry of healing. He recognizes very frankly the emergence and value of the spiritual factor in healing and includes chapters on suggestion and faith, and psychoanalysis and confession. A valuable contribution to this area of integration.

4. THE PRACTICAL DIMENSION

[1943] **538.** *Stolz, Karl Ruf.*

The Church and Psychotherapy. New York and Nashville: Abingdon-Cokesbury Press, 1943, 312 pp.

Reviewing the healing ministry of Jesus and how the Church anticipated psychiatry, Stolz claims that the Church has an almost unlimited therapeutic value of which multitudes stand in need. Therapies of the Church include prayer, confession, forgiveness, occupational therapy, suggestion, assurance, and clarification. Of special interest is a chapter on vocational neuroses of the minister.

[1946] **539.** *Brown, William.*

Personality and Religion. London: University of London Press, 1946, 195 pp.

Differentiating the study of the mind from the study of the soul (which is not the domain of psychology), Brown asserts that the source of healing is the process of arousing faith: suggestion is ultimately always dependent upon some form or other of faith, and not conversely. This book includes an overview of Christian Science, New Thought, the Emmanuel Movement, and the Guild of Health. Brown was Wilde Reader in Mental Philosophy at Oxford and consulting psychologist at Bethlehem Royal Hospital. He writes in the tradition of F. H. Bradley.

[1948] **540.** *Bonnell, John Sutherland.*

Psychology for Pastor and People: A Book on Spiritual Counseling. New York: Harper, 1948, xii+225 pp.

Originally the James Sprunt Lectures at Virginia's Union Theological Seminary. Psychiatry and spiritual counseling have in common the fact that faith in the counselor is a necessary element and that they seek to provide the consultant with a rational foundation for a new life.

[1948] **541.** *Cadbury, Henry Joel, ed.*

George Fox's "Book of Miracles." Cambridge: Cambridge University Press, 1948, xv+161 pp. +illus.

Cadbury has reconstructed Fox's book, which was destroyed before publication, from the index and his journals. Many mental cures are included.

[1950] **542.** *Peale, Normal Vincent, and Blanton, Smiley.*

The Art of Real Happiness. New York: Prentice-Hall, 1950, vi+247 pp.

An overview of problems in individual psychology and religion, with an emphasis on religious resources (scripture, prayer, exhortation).

[1950] **543.** *Roberts, David Everett.*

Psychotherapy and a Christian View of Man. New York: Charles Scribner's Sons, 1950, xiv+161 pp.

An early, and still superior, analysis of how the task of restoring a human to emotional "wholeness" and "holiness" is shared by the healing function of psychotherapy and the healing function of the church. Roberts blends psychoanalytic, existential, and classic theological concepts into an integrated view of persons.

[1950] **544. *Scherzer, Carl J.***

The Church and Healing. Philadelphia: Westminster Press, 1950, 272 pp.

Scherzer was the chaplain of the Protestant Deaconess Hospital in Evansville, Indiana. Here he presents a chronological account of the various manifestations of the healing ministry from pre-Christian times to the present day. He makes no attempt at criticism or evaluation.

[1951] **545. *Bergsten, Gote.***

Pastoral Psychology: A Study in the Care of Souls. London: George Allen & Unwin; New York: Macmillan Co., 1951, 227 pp.

In 1944, Bergsten became superintendent of the Institute for Spiritual Counsel and Psychological Treatment of the St. Luke's Foundation in Stockholm. His remarks are directed primarily to the spiritual director-advisor, sensitizing the reader to the psychology of confession, the psychology of unbelief, the role of guilt and the fear of punishment, symptomatic religiosity in neurosis and insanity, and the psychology of conversion and growth in grace. A sophisticated synthesis.

[1951] **546. *McNeill, John T.***

A History of the Cure of Souls. New York: Harper & Brothers, 1951, xii+371 pp.

This volume unites an understanding of the care and concern of religion for the spiritual direction of the individual with modern psychiatry. McNeill notes that a scientific psychiatry indifferent to religion and philosophy is a strange and new phenomenon. The book traces the aims and methods of religionists from the time of ancient Judaism, through the philosophers to Catholicism and the various branches of Protestantism.

[1951] **547. *Weatherhead, Leslie Dixon.***

Psychology, Religion and Healing: A Critical Study of all the Non-Physical Methods of Healing, with an Examination of the Principles Underlying Them and the Techniques Employed to Express Them, Together with Some Conclusions Regarding Further Investigation and Action in This Field. London: Hodder & Stoughton, 1951, 544 pp.; New York: Abingdon-Cokesbury Press, 1951, 543 pp.

Portions of this work were presented as the Lyman Beecher Lectures at Yale in 1949. Weatherhead calls for attention to the role of spiritual and psychological factors in physical illness, reviews "modern" psychological theories, and urges an integrated approach to healing in a context where ministers and doctors can cooperate.

[1954] **548. Outler, Albert Cook.**

Psychotherapy and the Christian Message. New York: Harper, 1954, 286 pp.

An exploration of many of the fundamental issues that seem to divide psychology and biblical Christianity. The author contrasts secular and Christian approaches to man in terms of the human quandary, man's freedom and potential, the basis for morality, and the potential for an alliance between the two approaches.

[1955] **549. Ikin, Alice Graham.**

New Concepts of Healing: Medical, Psychological, and Religious. London: Hodder & Stoughton, 1955, 186 pp. Rev. American ed. New York: Association Press, 1956, xxiii+262 pp.

Ikin espouses cooperation between pastors and psychotherapists, and sees the goal of healing as living from a spiritual center. Most valuable for historical purposes are the appendices provided by Wayne E. Oates. These include the American Standards for Clinical Pastoral Education; opportunities for study, training, and experience in pastoral psychology; seminaries offering courses in related areas, with or without a clinical practicum; centers for clinical pastoral training, description of the Texas Medical Center Institute of Religion; the Report of the Commission on Ministry, the New York Academy of Sciences; the pastor as counselor (Paul E. Johnson) religious and moral issues in psychotherapy and counseling (Noel Mailloux); study of spiritual healing in the churches (Charles S. Braden); Oral Roberts, Oklahoma evangelist and faith healer; official statement of the Christian Science approach to healing seminar; medical statement on science and religion by J. B. Rhine; an outline of the transactions of the Conference on the Ministry and Medicine in Human Relationships (Iago Galdston, Frank Fremont-Smith, Otis Rice, Erich Lindeman, Edwin S. Sunderland, George S. Stevenson, Sandor Rado, William R. Andrew, and Alice Graham Ikin).

[1957] **550. Doniger, Simon, ed.**

Healing: Human and Divine. Man's Search for Health and Wholeness through Science, Faith, and Prayer. New York: Association Press, 1957, xix+254 pp.

Consisting primarily of articles published in *Pastoral Psychology* from 1950 to 1957 with an introduction by Earl A. Loomis, Jr., this work offers essays by psychiatrists and psychologists "interested in man's search for wholeness" and by theologians "interested in and influenced by psychology." The articles are organized into four categories: body, mind, and spirit; religion and psychiatry; prayer; and spiritual healing. Contributors include John A. P. Millet, Gotthard Booth, Carl Rogers, Seward Hiltner, Walter Marshall Horton, Ernest E. Bruder, Walter G. Mulder,

L. Harold DeWolf, Paul E. Johnson, George Albert Coe, Paul Tillich, Cyril C. Richardson, and Wayne E. Oates.

[1957]   **551. *Oursler, William Charles.***
The Healing Power of Faith. New York: Hawthorn, 1957, 366 pp.
An overview of the contemporary scene by a popular writer.

[1959]   **552. *Moore, Thomas Verner.***
Heroic Sanctity and Insanity: An Introduction to the Spiritual Life and Mental Hygiene. New York: Grune & Stratton, 1959, 243 pp.
   With St. Thérèse of Lisieux as a model, Moore identifies heroic sanctity as the Christian goal of life. Moore, a Benedictine monk, was a leader in Catholic psychology of religion: he became the second psychology department head at Catholic University of America, and earned his Ph.D. there in 1903 under Edward Aloysius Pace, who was himself a student of Wilhelm Wundt. In 1909 he added teaching responsibilities at Paulist House of Studies. He earned an M.D. at Johns Hopkins in 1915, and in 1926 founded St. Gertrude's School of Arts and Crafts for the mentally retarded. He also served as an editor and contributed to several volumes of the series, Studies in Psychology and Psychiatry (entry number 1003).

[1961]   **553. *Frank, Jerome David.***
Persuasion and Healing: A Comparative Study of Psychotherapy. Baltimore: Johns Hopkins University Press, 1961, xiv+282 pp.+illus.
   Relevant chapters are those on religious healing and religious revivalism and thought reform. Elements common to all therapies examined are (1) a trained, socially sanctioned healer; (2) a sufferer who seeks relief from the healer; and (3) a circumscribed, more or less structured series of contacts between the healer and sufferer, through which the healer tries to produce certain changes in the sufferer's emotional state, attitudes, and behavior.

[1962]   **554. *Weatherhead, Leslie D.***
Wounded Spirits. London: Hodder & Stoughton, 1962, 124 pp. New York: Abingdon Press, 1963, 173 pp.
   A book of case studies written to stimulate research into spiritual healing and to encourage the continued cooperation of medicine, psychology, and religion.

[1965]   **555. *Meyer, Donald B.***
The Positive Thinkers: A Study of the American Quest for Health, Wealth, and Personal Power from Mary Baker Eddy to Norman Vincent Peale. Garden City, N. Y.: Doubleday, 1965, 358 pp.

4. THE PRACTICAL DIMENSION

Three major sections explore theology as psychology, sociology as psychology, and psychology as psychology. These are examined, respectively, in the exploration of mind cure as a distinguishable ideology entailing a distinguishable way of life, in ideas about industry and businessmen which describe the erosion of the Protestant ethic, and the preoccupation with therapeutic psychology among old-line protestant churches after World War II. Includes ideas of Phineas Parkhurst Quimby, Harry Emerson Fosdick, Reinhold Niebuhr, Joshua Loth Liebman, Fulton Sheen, James Keller, and the Jewish Science Movement.

Pastoral Counseling

In this section are included major works in the pastoral counseling tradition whose authors make an explicit effort to apply psychological principles to the pastoral task. Some of these, like the West and Skinner text, are general psychologies written with the ministerial audience in mind. Others focus more specifically on practical counseling skills.

[1880] **556. *Heuch, Johan Christian.***

> *Sjelesorgen hos de syge. En pastoral theologisk afhandling.* Drammen: C. Jensen, 1880, 135 pp. ENGLISH: *Pastoral Care of the Sick.* Translated by J. Melvin Moe. Minneapolis: Augsburg, 1949, ix+148 pp.
>
> Heuch was a pastor in the Lutheran Church of Norway.

[1896] **557. *Watson, John D.***

> *The Cure of Souls. The Lyman Beecher Lecture on Preaching at Yale University.* New York: Dodd & Mead, 1896, x+301 pp. Also under the title *The Cure of Souls. Yale Lectures on Practical Theology.* London: Hodder & Stoughton, 1896, x+244 pp.
>
> Watson was a Congregationalist preacher who used the pseudonym "Ian Maclaren."

[1924] **558. *Lachapelle, Paul.***

> *Quinze lecons de psychiatrie pastorale, préface du docteur Emile Legrand.* Montreal: Éditions Beauchemin, 1924, 294 pp. ENGLISH: *Psychiatry for the Priest.* Translated by G. J. Brady and rev. Pascal Translation Bureau. Westminister, Md.: The Newman Book Shop, 1945, 333 pp.
>
> Father Lachapelle was Professor of Psychopathology at the School of

Social Service and of Child Psychology at the Superior School of Pedagogy, Montreal University. Since Lachapelle was trained in France, his textbook of psychiatry reflects the influence of the French psychiatrists and scholastic psychology. He discusses the lesional psychopathies, the toxi-infectious psychopathies, and constitutional psychoses. Among the latter are included the psychasthenic constitution, the cyclothymic constitution, the paranoic constitution, the schizoid constitution, the hysteric constitution, and the perverted constitution. Psychotherapy is based on sympathy, the absolution of blame and shame, and persuasion/suggestion leading the attention outward.

[1928] **559. McKenzie, John G.**

Souls in the Making: An Introduction to Pastoral Psychology. London: George Allen & Unwin, 1928, 249 pp. New York: Macmillan Co., 1929, 259 pp.

Based on a series of lectures on pastoral psychology presented to graduating students of Paton College, Northampton (where McKenzie served on the faculty) and ministers of the city. McKenzie examines the basis of human nature in instincts, and its transmutation into a moral and spiritual self, including the realm of moral and spiritual conflict, its development and resolution. He asserts that religion alone can unify the once divided life. This is apparently the first text coupling the words "pastoral" and "psychology."

[1929] **560. Weatherhead, Leslie Dixon.**

Psychology in Service of the Soul. London: Epworth Press, J. Alfred Sharp, 1929, xxiii+226 pp. New York: Macmillan Co., 1930, xix+219 pp. London ed. reprint. 1958, 127 pp.

Written by the psychologist/minister of City Temple, London. This volume includes addresses on psychoreligious healing, dreams, hypnosis, and self help. Weatherhead was a pioneer in the practical integration of psychology and religion.

[1930] **561 West, Paul Vining, and Skinner, Charles Edward.**

Psychology for Religious and Social Workers. New York: Century Co., 1930, iii+528 pp. +illus.

Apparently the first psychology text written specifically for theology and social work students.

[1932] **562. Dewar, Lindsay, and Hudson, Cyril Edward.**

Psychology for Religious Workers. New York: R. Long & R. R. Smith, 1932, x+238 pp. Also under the title *A Manual of Pastoral Psychology.* London: P. Allan, 1932, x+238 pp. London: Society for Promoting Christian Knowledge, 1941, x+238 pp.

The authors provide a discussion of the application of modern-day psychology to everyday problems of ministers and religious workers. Offers the integration of a "high-church" theology with psychoanalysis and the work of William McDougall.

[1932] **563. *Stolz, Karl Ruf.***
Pastoral Psychology. Nashville: Cokesbury Press, 1932, 259 pp.
Stolz, dean at the Hartford School of Religious Education, here develops implications of mental hygiene and clinical psychology for the service of pastors to individuals. The Christian religion is defined as a "progressive integration of personality with a dynamic sense of ultimate reality." An overview of dynamic psychology for counseling with personality problems of a nonpathological nature.

[1936] **564. *Cabot, Richard Clarke, and Dicks, Russell Leslie.***
The Art of Ministering to the Sick. New York: Macmillan Co., 1936, viii+384 pp.
One of the earliest volumes in contemporary pastoral care written for ministers by a physician and a minister. The authors attempt to detail their best understanding of the psychology of illness and of the role of the minister. They include many seminal ideas which have subsequently influenced pastoral counseling.

[1937] **565. *Dewar, Lindsay, Balmforth, Henry, Hudson, Cyril E., and Sara, Edmund W.***
An Introduction to Pastoral Theology. London: Hodder & Stoughton, 1937, 306 pp.
Focuses on the priestly duties, especially the hearing of confession. The authors caution against allowing inexperienced clergy to hear confessions.

[1938] **566. *Zahniser, Charles Reed.***
The Soul Doctor. New York: Roundtable Press, 1938, viii+209 pp.
The psychologies of Sigmund Freud and Alfred Adler are applied to a set of actual case studies.

[1942] **567. *Holman, Charles Thomas.***
Getting Down to Cases. New York: Macmillan Co., 1942, 207 pp.
A casebook in pastoral counseling. Holman was affiliated with the University of Chicago.

[1943] **568. *Hiltner, Seward.***
Religion and Health. New York: Macmillan Co., 1943, xiii+292 pp.
Hiltner summarizes the mental hygiene movement, the history of medical missions and pastoral counseling, and other aspects of healing ministry as a prelude for discussing the relationship between religion and mental health.

[1945] **569. *Hiltner, Seward, ed.***
Clinical Pastoral Training. Federal Council of the Churches of Christ in America. New York: Commission on Religion and Health, 1945, xv+176 pp.

Proceedings of the Pittsburgh Conference of 1944. Contributors include Robert E. Brinkman, Joseph F. Fletcher, Henry Lewis, and John K. Benton.

[1946] **570. Boisen, Anton Theophilus.**

Problems in Religion and Life, A Manual for Pastors, with Outlines for the Cooperative Study of Personal Experience in Social Situations. New York and Nashville: Abingdon-Cokesbury Press, 1946, 159 pp.

A "primer" for pastoral counselors, with an emphasis on community and other social aspects of religious life.

[1946] **571 Thurneysen, Eduard.**

Die Lehre von der Seelsorge. Zollikon-Zürich: Evangelische Verlag, 1946, 327 pp. ENGLISH: *A Theology of Pastoral Care.* Translated by Jack A. Worthington and Thomas Wieser. Richmond: John Knox Press, 1962, 343 pp.

This Swiss pastor emphasizes the theological side of the religion-psychology dialogue. Counseling is characterized as a conversation that makes possible the forgiveness of sins under the mystery of grace.

[1946] **572. Zahniser, Charles Reed.**

Techniques of Counseling in Christian Service; A Handbook for Pastors and Other Christian Workers. Pittsburgh: Gibson Press, 1946, 29 pp.

[1949] **573. Demal, Willibald.**

Praktische Pastoralpsychologie: Beiträge zu einer Seelenkunde für Seelsorger und Erzieher. Vienna: Herder, 1949, 319 pp. ENGLISH: *Pastoral Psychiatry in Practice.* New York: P. J. Kenedy & Sons, 1955, 249 pp.

The major emphasis of this European Catholic priest is that pastoral duties should be carried out in the knowledge of the character structure of individuals. He includes sections on pathology and development. An Italian translation appeared in 1956.

[1949] **574. Dewar, Lindsay.**

Psychology and the Parish Priest. London: A. R. Mowbray; New York: Morehouse-Gorham Co., 1949, 122 pp.

A practical theology written by the Principal of Bishop's College, Cheshunt.

[1949] **575. Guntrip, Henry James Samuel.**

Psychology for Ministers and Social Workers. London: Independent Press, 1949, 298 pp. 2 ed. Chicago: Allensen, 1953, 356 pp.

Guntrip offers this text as an introduction to pastoral and social psychology, having previously presented his ideas at Yorkshire United Independent College. He cites the 1947 Annual Report of the British

Medical Association, which called for fuller cooperation between doctors and clergy in "healing." Individuation and personal relationships are seen as the inner and outer aspects of the whole life space.

[1949]   **576. Hiltner, Seward.**
Pastoral Counseling. New York: Abingdon-Cokesbury Press, 1949, 291 pp.
Focuses on principles of pastoral counseling, and resources and training for pastoral counseling.

[1950]   **577. Goulooze, William.**
Pastoral Psychology: Applied Psychology in Pastoral Theology in America. Grand Rapids: Baker Book House, 1950, 266 pp.
Goulooze taught at Western Theological Seminary in Holland, Michigan, which is affiliated with the Reformed Church in America. He covers the history of pastoral theology prior to 1850, from 1850 to 1900, and applications since 1900. His discussion and critique include a research analysis, a constructive analysis, and a technique analysis. Includes a selected bibliography.

[1951]   **578. Tournier, Paul.**
Bible et medecine. Neuchatel and Paris: Delachaux & Niestlé, 1951, 238 pp. ENGLISH: *A Doctor's Casebook in the Light of the Bible*. Translated by Edwin Hudson. New York: Harper & Row, 1954, 256 pp.
Besides the scientific or medical diagnosis, every illness requires a spiritual diagnosis of its meaning and purpose. The patient must make this diagnosis through the impulse of her inmost conscience.

[1951]   **579. Wise, Carroll Alonzo.**
Pastoral Counseling: Its Theory and Practice. New York: Harper, 1951, xi+231 pp.
An informal guidebook for ministers and theological students.

[1952]   **580. Cryer, Newman S., Jr., and Vayhinger, John Monroe, eds.**
Casebook in Pastoral Counseling. London: Pierce & Smith, 1952; New York: Abingdon Press, 1962, 320 pp.
A collection of fifty-six cases published between 1945 and 1952 in *The Pastor, The New Christian Advocate,* and *Christian Advocate*. Contributors are Jack Anderson, Oren H. Baker, Russell Becker, Roy Abram Burkhart, James H. Burns, J. Lennart Cedarleaf, John Dixon Copp, Russell Leslie Dicks, David D. Eitzen, Robert E. Elliott, O. Floyd Feely, Jr., Earl H. Ferguson, C. Newman Hogle, Homer L. Jernigan, Paul E. Jonson, Thomas W. Klink, Robert C. Leslie, Paul B. Maves, Wayne E. Oates, Charles W. Stewart, George A. Warmer, and Carroll A. Wise. Each case is followed by comments.

[1952]   **581. Curran, Charles Arthur.**
Counseling in Catholic Life and Education. New York: Macmillan Co., 1952, 486 pp.

Curran, on the faculty at Chicago's Loyola University, offers an overview of counseling theory and technique enriched with an awareness of the Catholic spiritual tradition.

[1952]   **582. Dobbelstein, Hermann.**
Psychiatrie und Seelsorge: eine praktische Anleitung für Seelsorger und ihre Hilfskräfte. Freiburg: Herder, 1952, v+165 pp. ENGLISH: *Psychiatry for Priests.* Translated by Meyrick Booth. Cork: Mercier Press, 1953, 118 pp. New York: P. J. Kenedy & Sons, 1954, 148 pp.

A physician provides a general introduction to psychiatry for the use of Catholic clergy.

[1952]   **583. Knubel, Frederick R.**
Pastoral Counseling. Philadelphia: Muhlenberg Press, 1952, 102 pp.

Knubel was recent president of the United Lutheran Synod of New York and New England, and presented these ideas as the Knubel–Miller Lectures in 1952. He offers an overview of the field from the perspective of a novice, and therefore offers little insight.

[1952]   **584. Murphy, Carol R.**
The Ministry of Counseling. Wallingford, Pa.: Pendle Hill Pamphlets, 1952, 32 pp.

A pamphlet for the lay person written by a student of Carroll A. Wise.

[1953]   **585. Johnson, Paul Emmanuel.**
Psychology of Pastoral Care. Nashville: Abingdon-Cokesbury Press, 1953, 362 pp.

A practical theology written in layman's language which includes little of the technical and academic but a great deal of wisdom (as described by the *Expository Times* reviewer).

[1953]   **586. Maves, Paul B., ed.**
The Church and Mental Health. New York: Charles Scribner's Sons, 1953, xiv+303 pp.

A symposium which covers the many areas and activities where the church can foster mental health. The theological basis for this area of church concern is well presented, along with very practical and specific examples of how a local church can both nurture healthy growth of its members and help those in crisis and distress. Contributors include Gene E. Bartlett, Daniel Blain, Gotthard Booth, Ernest E. Bruder, Seward Hiltner, Reuel L. Howe, Paul B. Maves, John T. McNeill, Florence Powdermaker, Dallas Pratt, Cyril C. Richardson, David E. Roberts, Howard C. Schade, and Luther E. Woodward.

[1953] **587. Ringel, Erwin, and Van Lun, Wenzel.**
Die Tiefenpsychologie hilft dem Seelsorger. Vienna: Seelsorger Verlag/
Herder, 1953, 145 pp. ENGLISH: *The Priest and the Unconscious.* Translated by Meyrick Booth. Westminster, Md.: Newman Press, 1954,
118 pp. Cork, Ireland: Mercier Press, 1954, 155 pp.

    Ringel, a doctor and psychologist, collaborates with Van Lun, a
theologian, "to provide a scientific and empirically well-founded introduction to the psychology of the unconscious and its practical application." In addition to a general discussion of pastoral medicine, the authors
discuss the psychology of the unconscious, the attitude of the priest, the
psychology of faith, a case of acute hysteria, and the problems of obsessional neurosis.

[1953] **588. Van Steenberghen, Fernand, ed.**
Psychologie et pastorale. Louvain: Nauwelaerts, 1953, 190 pp. ENGLISH:
Psychology, Morality and Education. Translated by Ruth Mary Bethell.
Springfield, Ill.: Templegate, 1958, ix+128 pp. London: Burns &
Oates, 1958, 128 pp.

    Six papers read at a conference of Belgian priests in the diocese of
Liege on the theme "the bearing of contemporary psychology on pastoral
work." Includes a chapter by Joseph Nuttin on "Psychology for Priests."

[1954] **589. Doniger, Simon, ed.**
Religion and Human Behavior. New York: Association Press, 1954,
xxiii+233 pp.

    This volume in the Pastoral Psychology Series includes chapters by
Karl Menninger, Lloyd E. Foster, Carl Binger, Paul E. Johnson, Frederick C. Grant, Bonaro W. Overstreet, Wayne E. Oates, O. Spurgeon
English, John Sutherland Bonnell, Willard R. Sperry, Fritz Kunkel,
Wesner Fallow, Seward Hiltner, and Randolph Crump Miller.

[1955] **590. Murphy, Carol.**
Religion and Mental Illness. Wallingford, Pa.: Pendle Hill Pamphlets,
1955, 31 pp.

    Pendle Hill was a Quaker retreat center.

[1956] **591. Belgum, David Rudolf.**
Clinical Training for Pastoral Care. Philadelphia: Westminster Press,
1956, 136 pp. +illus.

    A summary of some of the insights gained through clinical pastoral
education.

[1956] **592. Clinebell, Howard John.**
*Understanding and Counseling the Alcoholic through Religion and
Psychology.* New York and Cincinnati: Abingdon Press, 1956, 252 pp.

    Clinebell provides an extensive definition of alcoholism. It may be rooted in neurotic, historic, or existential anxiety. He regards religion as the one sure solution, and examines the approaches of the Rescue Mission, the Emmanuel Movement, and Alcoholics Anonymous. He ends with a discussion of prevention and ethical problems.

[1957] **593. *Carrington, William Langley.***

Psychology, Religion, and Human Need: A Guide for Ministers, Doctors, Teachers, and Social Workers. Great Neck, N.Y.: Channel Press, 1957, 315 pp. London: Epworth Press, 1957, xi+315 pp.

A general guide to pastoral counseling based on lectures presented at Ridley College, the Anglican Theological College of Melbourne.

[1957] **594. *Thilo, Hans Joachim.***

Der ungespaltene Mensch: ein Stück Pastoral Psychologie. Göttingen: Vandenhoek & Ruprecht, 1957, 190 pp. ENGLISH: *Unfragmented Man: A Study in Pastoral Psychology*. Translated by Arthur J. Seegers. Minneapolis: Augsburg, 1964, 208 pp.

Thilo's anthropology is trichotomic after the manner of Martin Luther, whom he quotes: "Scriptures divide man into three parts . . . and comparable to these three the whole man is also, in another way, divided into two parts. . . . This other, the soul, is exactly the same as spirit in nature, but in another function." In Thilo's terms, "The spirit is 'the house in which faith and God's Word dwell'; the soul is that which 'gives life to the body.'" While applauding the dialogue between psychotherapy and pastoral care, he asserts their independence: "We cannot countenance a mixing of psychology and pastoral counsel. And we must warn against juggling with such concepts as priestly physician and the pastor's office of healing. . . . We still walk on separate paths though they be parallel paths." At its core, Thilo regards the task of pastoral care as the proclamation of the Incarnation, and organizes his text around this proclamation. He regards the object of our proclamation as the human person: the child, the youth, the (sexual) adult—male and female, the aging and those in ill health. His view of the nature and method of proclamation is rooted in counseling and confession, assisted by play and ritual, the unconscious, the Image, and liturgy. The place of proclamation is discussed in relation to worship, congregational meetings, and counseling and confession. Finally, Thilo discusses the time of proclamation in relation to the liturgical year and the hours of the liturgical day.

[1959] **595. *Gross, Leonard.***

God and Freud. New York: D. McKay Co., 1959, 215 pp.

A journalist's perspective on the cooperation between the clergy and mental health professions, including the pastoral counseling movement, testing for ministry, and Christian education. An excellent overview directed at the layperson.

[1959] **596. *Hiltner, Seward.***

The Christian Shepherd. Nashville and New York: Abingdon Press, 1959, 190 pp.

A helpful blend of pastoral situations with sound psychological and theological insights.

[1959] **597. *Oates,Wayne Edward, ed.***

An Introduction to Pastoral Counseling. Nashville: Broadman Press, 1959, ix+331 pp.

Essays on pastoral counseling by faculty of the seminaries of the Southern Baptist Convention. Contributors are Albert L. Meiburg, James Lyn Elder, Samuel Southard, Wayne E. Oates, John W. Drakeford, Richard K. Young, A. Donald Bell, D. Allen Brabham, John M. Price, and Harold L. Rutledge.

[1960] **598. *Hofmann, Hans, ed.***

The Ministry and Mental Health. New York: Association Press, 1960, xi+251 pp.

Essays by Paul Tillich, Talcott Parsons, David C. McLelland, Frederick C. Reuther, William Douglas, Gotthard Booth, Robert C. Leslie, James E. Dittes, Granger E. Westberg, Earl A. Loomis, and Hans Hofmann. Resulted from the Harvard University Project on Religion and Mental Health, funded by National Institute of Mental Health.

[1960] **599. *Walker, Daniel D.***

The Human Problems of the Minister. New York: Harper, 1960, 203 pp.

Walker's book is directed toward the minister's denial of his own personal problems and conflict of interest.

[1960] **600. *Young, Richard K., and Meiburg, Albert L.***

Spiritual Therapy: How the Physician, Psychiatrist and Minister Collaborate in Healing. London: Hodder & Stoughton; New York: Harper, 1960, 184 pp.

This book stresses the importance of personality in the treatment of hospital cases. The focus is on the method of the chaplain.

[1961] **601. *Evans, Erastus.***

Pastoral Care in a Changing World. London: Epworth Press, 1961, 104 pp.

Evans asserts that when the depth psychologist has laid bare the person's inner conflict, the gospel must come in for total healing.

[1961] **602. *Hiltner, Seward, and Colston, Lowell G.***

The Context of Pastoral Counseling. New York: Abingdon Press, 1961, 272 pp.

Hiltner and Colston address the question of context in studying the impact of two settings on pastoral counseling, thus addressing the issue of whether one is actually teaching pastoral counseling when the setting is a mental health clinic. Context, method, representative cases and the use of test materials are presented for the uninitiated reader.

[1961] **603. Kean, Charles Duell.**
Christian Faith and Pastoral Care. Greenwich, Conn.: Seabury Press, 1961, 139 pp.
Kean, rector of the Church of the Epiphany in Washington, first presented these ideas at Union Theological Seminary in New York, under the auspices of their religion and psychiatry program.

[1961] **604. Oates, Wayne Edward, ed.**
The Minister's Own Mental Health. Developed from the articles . . . in two special issues of Pastoral Psychology magazine, with many contributions. Great Neck, N.Y.: Channel Press, 1961, 335 pp.
A collection of articles previously published in *Pastoral Psychology*. Contributors are George Christian Anderson, Donald Blain, Samuel W. Blizzard, Anton Theophilus Boisen, Gotthard Booth, Carl W. Christensen, Wallace Denton, Russell L. Dicks, James E. Dittes, Earl W. Furgeson, Seward Hiltner, Reuel L. Howe, Dean E. Johnson, John P. Kildahl, Charles F. Kemp, Frederick R. Kling, John G. Kohler, Robert C. Leslie, Jules Hyman Masserman, Albert L. Meiburg, John A. P. Millet, Wayne E. Oates, Ralph T. Palmer, James G. Ranck, William Rickel, Harry B. Scholefield, Leonard Small, Samuel Southard, Edward E. Thornton, Paul Tillich, Hazen G. Werner, Daniel Day Williams, Carroll A. Wise, and Richard K. Young.

[1961] **605. Williams, Daniel Day.**
The Minister and the Care of Souls. New York: Harper, 1961, iii + 157 pp.
The Sprunt Lectures delivered at Union Theological Seminary in Richmond in 1959. Williams provides a theological basis for pastoral care in the context of the church.

[1962] **606. Brillenburg Wurth, Gerritt.**
Christelijke Zielszorg in het licht der modern psychologie. ENGLISH: *Christian Counseling in the Light of Modern Psychology*. Translated by H. de Jongste. Philadelphia: Presbyterian and Reformed Publishing Company, 1962, 307 pp.
The author, a well-known Continental scholar, sees great evidence of spiritual distress in both the psychotherapy movement and mass spiritual movements. He asserts that "true spiritual care cannot look to modern psychology for support, nor to most revivals." He states that the church has not given pastoral care the attention it deserves; he suggests that theology should be more pastorally oriented and that every minister should be given training in pastoral care. Addressing these needs, Bril-

lenburg Wurth offers first a historical overview of pastoral care in the pre-Christian period, by Christ, the Apostles, in Roman Catholicism, and after the Reformation. Providing a context for contemporary pastoral care, he reviews modern psychology and psychotherapy, and discusses the central problems of recent psychology represented by the unconscious, the appetitive life, moods, corporality, cohumanity, and suggestion. His principles of pastoral care include not only basic pastoral counseling skills, but also a theology of pastoral care. Finally, he discusses practical aspects, addressing pastoral care in connection with general religious development, doubt, sin, suffering, sickness, death, and the difficulties of everyday life, and ends with some suggestions concerning pastoral care for the pastoral counselor.

[1962]   **607.** *Cavanagh, John R.*

Fundamental Pastoral Counseling: Technique and Psychology. Milwaukee: Bruce Publishing Co., 1962, 326 pp.

Cavanagh was a Special Lecturer in the School of Sacred Theology at the Catholic University of America. Pastoral counseling is defined as God-centered, focusing on what the pastor of souls feels the client needs. It is eclectic in its approach, religious in its orientation. Cavanagh offers a review of pastoral counseling, secular counseling, client-centered therapy, the counseling situation and the counseling interview in the first section. He regards pastoral counseling as complementary to spiritual direction. Client-centered therapy is critiqued as not being theocentric in its orientation, and holding to a situationist, personalist ethic. In the section on the pastor and mental health, Cavanagh summarizes the following list of basic needs: to be loved and love others; to feel secure; to be creative and procreative; to accept authority and be free; to achieve; to have new experiences and adventures; companionship and consideration for others; self-understanding leading to action; and God, or religion. Next, Cavanagh summarizes personality development in childhood and adolescence; he emphasizes the importance of healthy sexuality. Finally, he looks at the pastor's role in mental illness, which is not equivalent to the role of the psychiatrist. He concludes with a critique of contemporary schools of psychology, focusing on the analytic theories of Josef Breuer, Sigmund Freud, Alfred Adler, and Carl Gustav Jung; the existentialist psychologists Ludwig Binswanger, Viktor Frankl, and Rollo May; the behaviorism of John Broadus Watson; the constitutional psychology of George Draper; and the psychologies of Karen Horney and Adolf Meyer.

[1962]   **608.** *Faber, Heije, and Van der Schoot, Ebel.*

Het pastorale Gesprek; een Pastoraal-psychologische Studie. Utrecht: Erven J. Bijeveld, 1962, 247 pp. ENGLISH: *The Art of Pastoral Conversation.* New York and Nashville: Abingdon Press, 1965, 223 pp.

Both authors are pastors of the Dutch Reformed Church and Professors of Pastoral Psychology (at Leyden and Utrecht respectively). In addition to traditional topics, the authors discuss the unique dimensions of the pastoral conversation and its distinctive resources. Especially valuable are the discussions on prayers and confessions.

[1962] **609.** *Greeves, Frederick.*

Theology and the Cure of Souls; An Introduction to Pastoral Theology. Manhasset, N.Y.: Channel Press, 1962, 177 pp.

The Cato Lectures delivered by the principal of Didsbury College. Greeves, a Methodist, addresses particular needs related to beliefs about suffering, sin and sickness, and health and dying. He regards the distinction between revealed and natural theology as misleading. H. D. Miller's review in *Theology and Life* indicates that Greeves is helpful for dealing with the relationship between Christian doctrine and pastoral care, but he does not provide any practical advice for the counselor.

[1962] **610.** *Moser, Leslie E.*

Counseling: A Modern Emphasis in Religion. Englewood Cliffs, N.J.: Prentice-Hall, 1962, xi+354 pp.

Moser, a psychologist at Baylor University, wrote this book for all religious workers who have a counseling task. Eclectic in his theory, he encourages the counselor to maintain an earnest respect for the time-honored methods of pastoral counseling and the spiritual disciplines.

[1962] **611.** *Oates, Wayne Edward.*

Protestant Pastoral Counseling. Philadelphia: Westminster Press, 1962, 256 pp.

Oates, who was on the faculty in the Department of Psychology of Religion and Pastoral Care at Southern Baptist Theological Seminary, here draws on formulations from "the basic genius of protestantism." Pastoral counseling is examined as spiritual conversation, self-encounter, and religious history. Oates relies heavily on the work of Carl Rogers, Harry Stack Sullivan, Martin Buber, David E. Roberts, and Albert Cook Outler. His introduction includes an excellent review of major books in the field.

[1962] **612.** *O'Doherty, Eamonn Feichen, and McGrath, Sean Desmond, eds.*

The Priest and Mental Health. Dublin: Clonmore and Reynolds, 1962, xiii+249 pp.

A collection of papers by priests and psychiatrists originally read at the Stillorgan Conference in Dublin, 1960.

[1963] **613.** *Autton, Norman.*

The Pastoral Care of the Mentally Ill. London: Society for the Propagation of Christian Knowledge, 1963, 223 pp.

Autton, the Anglican chaplain at St. George's Hospital in London, made an extensive study tour to learn the history of clinical pastoral training in the United States. Obviously familiar with this material, he includes a history of this training movement as well as a full bibliography.

[1963] **614.** *Godin, André.*
La relation humaine dans le dialogue pastoral. Brussels: Desclée De Brouwer, 1963, 196 pp. ENGLISH: *The Pastor as Counselor.* Translated by Bernard Phillips. New York: Holt, Rinehart & Winston, 1965, vi+182 pp. Also published as *The Priest as Counselor.* Techny, Illinois: Divine Word Publications, 1968, vi+182 pp.
   A Belgian Jesuit writes for a Roman Catholic audience, analyzing pastoral conversations and emphasizing the importance of counseling in small groups.

[1963] **615.** *Jackson, Edgar Newman.*
The Pastor and His People: A Psychology for Parish Work. Manhasset: Channel Press, 1963, 224 pp.
   Jackson prefaces this pastoral psychology with a short pastoral theology focused on right relationships with the self, the community, and God. Covering the range of traditional topics in pastoral care, Jackson begins with the pastor's care of himself and ends with a focus on the social dimension.

[1964] **616.** *Brister, C. W.*
Pastoral Care in the Church. New York: Harper & Row, 1964, xxiv+262 pp.
   A pastoral theology in the tradition of Wayne Coulston and Seward Hiltner, adopting Edward Thurneysen's position that the care of souls involves pastoral conversation—person-to-person proclamation.

[1964] **617.** *Clebsch, William A., and Jaekle, Charles R.*
Pastoral Care in Historical Perspective: An Essay with Exhibits. Englewood Cliffs, N.J.: Prentice-Hall, 1964, x+344 pp.
   An historical overview, with a supplement of selections from the following authors and works: Clement of Alexandria, Tertullian, *DiDascalia Apostolorum*, Cyprian, John Chrysostom, John Cassian, Halitgar, Bernard of Clairvaux, John Keble, Francis of Assisi, *Ars Moriendi*, Heinrich Kramer and Jakob Sprenger, Martin Luther, Ignatius Loyola, John Knox, Jeremy Taylor, John Bunyan, John Walsh, Jean Joseph Gaume, and William James.

[1964] **618.** *Koch, Kurt E.*
Seelsorge und Okkultismus: Die seelsorgerliche Behandlung der Menschen, die durch die Beschäftigung mit okkulten Dingen seelisch angefochten oder erkrankt sind. Eine praktische-theologische und systematische Untersuchung unter Berücksichtigung der medizinischen und psychologischen Grenzwissenschaften. 7 ed. Berghausen: Evangelistionsverlag, 1964, 351 pp. ENGLISH: *Christian Counseling and Occultism: The Christian Counseling of Persons Who are Psychically Vexed or Ailing Because of Involvement in Occultism. A Practical Theological and Syste-*

matic Investigation in Consultation with Medical and Psychological Bordering Sciences. Translated by Andrew Petter. Grand Rapids: Kregel Publishers, 1965, 299 pp.

A Lutheran theologian here examines 120 cases of occult phenomena from the perspectives of parapsychology, medicine, pastoring, and pastoral counseling. Possible contributions of psychology (as the science of the mind), depth psychology (primarily psychoanalysis), psychotherapy, and pastoral counseling are explored. The latter are differentiated on the basis of their anthropocentrism versus theocentrism. Koch asserts that ". . . occult subjection is a theological problem with a medical external. To use a metaphor, it is a spiritual center of ailment with a medical metastasis. . . ." Pastoral treatment of possession involves differential diagnosis, confession, renunciation of the devil, absolution, and spiritual warfare characterized by prayer and fasting, intercession by a band of Christians, the imposition of hands, and exorcism. This process must be followed by active resistance on the part of the liberated person. The book constitutes an excellent guide to German-language sources in pastoral care.

[1964] **619. *Thornton, Edward E.***

Theology and Pastoral Counseling. Englewood Cliffs, N.J.: Prentice-Hall, 1964, 144 pp.

The proper approach to theology is inductive from psychology to theology rather than deductive from theology to psychology. Thus Thornton opposes the position of Thurneysen. Counseling contributes to our understanding of the faith. The book is primarily a theology of the church based on the shepherding function.

[1965] **620. *Draper, Edgar.***

Psychiatry and Pastoral Care. Englewood Cliffs, N.J.: Prentice-Hall, 1965, 138 pp.

This is one of a series edited by Russell L. Dicks in which problems and topics in ministry were considered. Draper was trained both as minister and psychiatrist. Here he presents a modified Freudian understanding of personal dynamics and relates them to pastoral diagnosis and pastoral treatment.

[1965] **621. *Klink, Thomas W.***

Depth Perspectives in Pastoral Work. Englewood Cliffs, N.J.: Prentice-Hall, 1965, 144 pp.

Klink, a Methodist pastor, emphasizes the importance of conflict (dynamic tension) and discusses the human significance of typical situations and requests in pastoral care.

Christian Psychotherapies

Here are included those books which offer a specifically Christian theory of psychotherapy. Many related ideas may be found in the sections on Christian personality theories, pastoral counseling, spiritual healing, morality, and in the Christian critiques of secular psychologies.

[1931] **622. Lichliter, McIlyar Hamilton.**
The Healing of Souls. New York and Cincinnati: Abingdon Press, 1931, 175 pp.
    Lichliter presents his views on spiritual healing with a focus on the normal personality and such basis human issues as youth, age and death, sex, mental tension, and nervous fears.

[1933] **623. Jahn, Ernst, and Adler, Alfred.**
Religion und Individualpsychologie. Eine prinzipielle Auseinandersetzung über Menschenführung. Vienna and Leipzig: R. Passer, 1933, 98 pp. ENGLISH: *Religion and Individual Psychology.* In *Alfred Adler: Superiority and Social Interest, A Collection of Later Writings.* Translated by Heinz Ansbacher and Rowena Ansbacher. Evanston, Ill.: Northwestern University Press, 1964, 274–308 pp.
    The original volume consisted of an essay by Jahn entitled "The Psychotherapy of Christianity," Adler's reply to it, and some closing statements by Jahn. The publication was promptly seized by the Nazis and destroyed. In the Ansbacher's volume, only the essay by Adler is included, with a new introduction by Jahn.

[1938] **624. *Murray, James Alan Cameron.***

An Introduction to a Christian Psycho-therapy. New York: Charles Scribner's Sons; Edinburgh: T & T Clark, 1938, xii+279 pp.

Based on the early psychoanalytic tradition, this work suggests that the task of Christian psychotherapy is twofold: to "tidy up" the mind and to make health and salvation synonymous. Religious faith is seen as the path along which we respond to suggestions from God. The psychologist and the church are both involved in redemptive tasks involving three steps: the location of errors, a rationale for liberation from the erroneous life-style, and the strengthening and pruning of the religious life.

[1939] **625. *Gregory, Marcus.***

Psychotherapy Scientific and Religious. London: Macmillan & Co., 1939, 495 pp.

This is one of the early attempts to integrate mental and spiritual healing in a theoretical manner. Written by a priest and pastoral psychologist, the volume includes historical and theoretical presentations of religious and psychological counseling. Forewords by William Brown and L. W. Grensted, experimental psychologist and theologian respectively, attest to the legitimacy of the content from both scientific and religious points of view.

[1944] **626. *Tournier, Paul.***

Technique et foi. Neuchatel: Delachaux & Niestlé, 1944, 269 pp. ENGLISH: *The Person Reborn.* Translated by Edwin Hudson. New York: Harper & Row, 1966, vi+248 pp.

Tournier here addresses the secret he has discovered deep in every heart that, as persons, we are becoming more lost and confused. He shows the way out of this confusion through case histories and the depth of his experience.

[1945] **627. *Maeder, Alphonse.***

Wege zur seelischen Heilung, kurze Psychotherapie aus der Praxis eines Nervenarztes. Zurich: Rascher, 1945, 288 pp. ENGLISH: *Ways to Psychic Health: Brief Therapy from the Practice of a Psychiatrist.* Translated by Theodor Lit. New York: Charles Scribner's Sons; London: Hodder & Stoughton, 1953, 200 pp.

In this book, Maeder writes as a committed Christian and claims that most patients require not only "psychagogik" (reeducation) but also "pastoral care," which may mean "leading the lonely, suffering, and searching human being to God." His format includes fifteen case histories. Maeder's theological background reflects primarily the influence of the Oxford Movement.

[1945] **628. *Outler, Albert Cook.***

A Christian Context for Counseling. New Haven: Edward W. Hazen Foundation, 1945, 18 pp. Hazen Pamphlet 18.

Based on the conference at Zwannanoa, N.C. in August 1945. The Christian context must include five areas: the human person as focus, the person's inner estrangement, the ideal of human fellowship, the Christian perspective on social issues, and a Christian context for higher education.

[1949] **629. *Hudson, Robert Lofton.***
The Religion of a Sound Mind. Nashville: Broadman Press, 1949, 117 pp.
   Hudson, a Baptist minister and theological instructor, presented these ten sermons to his congregation in Shawnee, Oklahoma. He offers a simplistic application of faith to everyday problems.

[1954] **630. *Daim, Wilfried.***
Tiefenpsychologie und Erlösung. Vienna: Herold, 1954, 360 pp.
ENGLISH: *Depth Psychology and Salvation.* Translated by Kurt F. Reinhardt. New York: Frederick Ungar, 1963, 315 pp.
   Considering the "psychological side of a theological problem," Daim examined the need for salvation, the place of the psychoanalytic process as part of the process of salvation, and the place of this only "partial salvation" within the frame of the total salvation brought about by Christ. He discussed those fixations which block growth, the seemingly innate desire to be free of them, the ways in which we frustrate this desire, and possible resolutions. Daim relies on Edmund Husserl, Martin Heidegger, Wilhelm Dilthey, Eduard Spranger, and Karl Jaspers as well as Sigmund Freud.

[1956] **631. *Hulme, William Edward.***
Counseling and Theology. Philadelphia: Muhlenberg Press, 1956, 249 pp.
   Hulme focuses his theology on (1) the concept of man, (2) the Universal Priesthood, (3) the concept of freedom, (4) the means of discipline, (5) the means of growth, and (6) the means of grace (scripture and the sacraments). Counseling is approached in spiritual terms.

[1956] **632. *Muedeking, George H.***
Emotional Problems and the Bible. Philadelphia: Muhlenberg Press, 1956, xi+188 pp.
   Muedeking asserts that "the Bible cannot be used to solve an emotional problem, the origins of which is beyond the recall of memory." He deals with the problems of anxiety, guilt, hatred, freedom, creativity, and inferiority.

[1959] **633. *Neill, Stephen Charles.***
A Genuinely Human Existence: Towards a Christian Psychology. Garden City, N.Y.: Doubleday & Co., 1959, 312 pp.
   An excellent model of integration. Neill, an Anglican Bishop serving in India, presents a provocative and lucid explanation of modern psychiatric principles and their importance within the Christian framework. He

discusses various problems which may conflict with the genuinely human existence. The greatest enemies are fear, frustration, and resentment, and these can be met through forgiveness and grace.

[1960] **634. Feinsilver, Alexander.**
In Search of Religious Maturity. Yellow Springs, Ohio: Antioch Press, 1960, 124 pp.
While psychology seeks to free the individual, religion seeks to transform him. Love is regarded as the key to both processes.

[1960] **635. Narramore, Clyde Maurice.**
The Psychology of Counseling: Professional Techniques for Pastors, Teachers, Youth Leaders, and All Who are Engaged in the Incomparable Art of Counseling. Grand Rapids, Mich.: Zondervan Publishing House, 1960, 303 pp.
Writing for a conservative Christian audience, the author emphasizes the importance of a conscious conversion experience and relies on a highly literalistic interpretation of the Bible. The emphasis is on spiritual backsliding, sexual problems, and the use of Scripture in counseling.

[1961] **636. Ducker, E. N.**
A Christian Therapy for a Neurotic World. London: George Allen & Unwin, 1961; New York: Taplinger Publishing Co., 1963, 225 pp.
This Anglican Canon reminds us that our aim in counseling and therapy must be the remaking of the sick soul (rebirth, regeneration, salvation, conversion). Although it is God who heals, psychology has been helpful in clarifying the role of the unconscious and the harm of spiritual misdirection. Ducker compares and contrasts sin and moral disease in their major characteristics.

[1964] **637. Ducker, E. N.**
Psychotherapy: a Christian Approach. London: George Allen & Unwin, 1964, 126 pp.
The author's second contribution in the tradition of Victor White.

[1965] **638. Lloyd-Jones, David Martyn.**
Spiritual Depression: Its Causes and Cure. London: Pickering & Inglis, 1965, 300 pp. Grand Rapids, Mich.: Eerdman's, 1965, 304 pp.
The author, a British minister and physician, examines the biblical teachings on depression via sermons on how to deal with discouragement.

Christian Education and
Character Research

Books in this section are primarily aimed at Christian educators. Many of these are focused on stages of spiritual development as a basis for educational theory. Others are focused more specifically on character development as a goal of Christian education. Some focus more specifically on personality development as it relates to the spiritual direction of adults. All are included because they apply the principles of contemporary psychology to Christian education, and many works on Christian education are not included here for that reason.

[1867] **639. Hecker, John.**

The Scientific Basis of Education Demonstrated. By an Analysis of the Temperaments and of Phrenological Facts, in Connection with Mental Phenomena and the Office of the Holy Spirit in the Processes of the Mind: in a Series of Letters to the Department of Public Instruction in the City of New York. New York: the author, 1867, xx + 167 + xxiv pp.

Hecker's series of letters offers essentially a textbook in phrenology, with an emphasis on the function and training of the spiritual faculties (Godliness, brotherly-kindness, steadfastness, righteousness, hopefulness, spiritual insight, aptitude), comparing his own classification of the latter faculties with those of Franz Joseph Gall, G. Spurzheim, and George Combe. These faculties are divided into a meditative group, characterized by susceptibility, and an intuitive group, characterized by impressibility. Conversion involves surrendering all the faculties to God, so that the propensities and intellectual faculties become subject to the spiritual faculties. Sectarianism, animal magnetism, and spiritualism are all perversions of the spiritual faculties. The final standard of truth lies not in ecclesiastical authority or private judgment or Scriptures, but in the

Triune godhead: Christ is the living standard, the Scriptures offer an outward or objective standard of God's action, and the Holy Spirit provides a subjective standard.

[1897] **640. Baldwin, James Mark.**
Social & Ethical Interpretations in Mental Development. A Study in Social Psychology. New York: Macmillan Co.; London: Macmillan & Co., 1897, xiv+574 pp. Reprint. New York: Arno Press, 1973, xx+580 pp.

Baldwin's views rely in important aspects on those of Josiah Royce and F. H. Bradley. Relevant sections of the book include those on the person as ethical self (pp. 34−56), the religious sentiment (pp. 327−357), and ethical and religious sanctions (pp. 434−446). Baldwin outlines three ethical stages which later influenced the theories of Jean Piaget and Lawrence Kohlberg. During the objective or adualistic stage, value is "syntelic" (failing to indicate the source of the evaluation) and projective. Duty is thought to be based on external, objective necessities. During the dualistic, prudential, or intellectual stage, value is relativistic and instrumental, and duty is perceived as a hypothetical command. During the ethical or ideal stage, value is public or synnomic (similar to Emmanuel Kant's "categorical imperative"), ideal and objective.

[1902] **641. Coe, George Albert.**
The Religion of a Mature Mind. Chicago, New York, Toronto, London and Edinburgh: Fleming H. Revell Co., 1902, 442 pp.

Examining the state of Christianity at the turn of the century, Coe notes that the Christian life is being simplified, its ideals are being socialized, and its motives are being intensified—all as part of its increasing maturity. Deals with the individual and institutional transformation of religion and calls for a revival of Christian experience and commitment.

[1904] **642. Hall, G. Stanley.**
Adolescence: its Psychology and its Relations to Physiology, Anthropology, Sociology, Sex, Crime, Religion, & Education. 2 vols. New York: D. Appleton & Co., 1904, xx+589 pp.; vi+784 pp.

Hall, who was the founder of the *Pedagogical Seminary* (later *The Journal of Genetic Psychology*), here combines his interest in developmental psychology with his interest in questions of a social and religious nature. Here, Hall presented evidence that most religious conversion occurs during adolescence and concluded that the coincidence of religious maturation and sexual maturity was no accident. Hall felt that deep religious experience was virtually impossible before adolescence, and that adolescent conversion was a normal, essential process if the person's life were to turn from an autocentric to a heterocentric basis.

[1909] **643. Dawson, George Ellsworth.**
The Child and His Religion. Chicago: University of Chicago Press, 1909, ix+124 pp.

Here are reprinted a series of articles and addresses. Topics discussed include interest as a measure of values, the natural religion of childhood, children's interest in the Bible, and the problem of religious education.

[1915] **644. Grose, George Richmond.**
Religion and the Mind. New York: Abingdon Press, 1915, 112 pp.
Grose, who was President of De Pauw University, first presented these ideas in a series on "Christ in the Intellectual Life" for the *Adult Bible Class Monthly* of the Methodist Episcopal Church. His topics include the failure of intellectual culture, the growing mind and the Christian ideal, intellectual honesty, the religion of the mind, education and vision, the limitations of knowledge, and the goal of Christian culture. He also addresses the question "Does education endanger faith?"

[1915] **645. Mumford, Edith Emily Read.**
The Dawn of Religion in the Mind of the Child; A Study of Child Life. London and New York: Longmans, Green and Co., 1915, xi+111 pp.
A well-known expert in childrearing, Mumford expands on a thesis in an earlier book, *The Dawn of Character.* Asserting that complete development of the child occurs only when character and will are dedicated to the highest ends, namely, when life is inspired by religious purpose, she shows how this develops and can be nurtured. Spiritual development, in her view, is as orderly as physical and mental development.

[1917] **646. Coe, George Albert.**
A Social Theory of Religious Education. New York: Charles Scribner's Sons, 1917, xiii+361 pp. Reprint. New York: Arno Press, 1969, xiii+361 pp.
Coe describes the aim of religious education as the "growth of the young toward and into mature and efficient devotion to the democracy of God, and happy self-realization therein." The social standpoint requires reconstruction in religious education, for which he describes the psychological background and organization. Existing trends in Christian Education within Roman Catholicism, Dogmatic Protestantism, Ritualistic Protestantism, Evangelicism, and Liberalism are examined.

[1919] **647. Hartshorne, Hugh.**
Childhood and Character: An Introduction to the Study of the Religious Life of Children. Boston and Chicago: Pilgrim Press, 1919, viii+282 pp.
Stimulated by the writings of George Albert Coe, this is Hartshorne's first book. It incorporates developmental theory and empirical observation. The development of religious experience (defined here as the moral life) is related to the socialization of the child into culture. It was the prelude to the Hartshorne and Mark A. May *Studies in the Nature of Character.*

[1919] **648. Lindworsky, Johannes.**
The Will, Its Manifestations and Control According to the Results of Experimental Research. Leipzig: Barth, 1919. 4 rev. ed. published as *The Training of the Will.* Translated by Arpad Steiner and Edward A. Fitzpatrick, 1929, 226 pp.

Based on lectures delivered at educational conferences at Arnsberg, Dortmund, and elsewhere, Lindworsky's book deals with the psychology of will, the pedagogy of will, the specific tasks involved in training the will, the complete task, and practice suggestions. In his psychological discussion, Lindworsky includes the researches of Narcissus (Narziss) Ach and Albert Edouard Michotte. Will power and the motive power of the will also are included. His discussion of the pedagogy of will includes a heavy emphasis on the reasons for the success of Couéism. For training the will, Lindworsky relies on the Spiritual Exercises of St. Ignatius of Loyola. He ends with questions for thought and discussion. The volume was Number 4 in the Marquette Monographs on Education.

[1920] **649. Kretzmann, Paul Edward.**
Psychology and the Christian Day-School. St. Louis: Concordia Publishing House, 1920, 139 pp. +illus.

A basic text, in the Lutheran tradition, by a writer very active in Christian education.

[1925] **650. Annett, Edward Aldridge.**
Psychology for Bible Teachers. New York: Charles Scribner's Sons, 1925, xii+241 pp.

A suggestive guide for religious education.

[1925] **651. O'Toole, George Barry.**
Psychology and the Catholic Teacher. New York: Paulist Press, 1925, 24 pp.

O'Toole, who served on the Catholic University of America faculty, here discusses principles of psychology in the context of Catholic education.

[1927] **652. Waterhouse, Eric Strickland.**
An ABC of Psychology for Sunday-School Teachers and Bible Students. London: J. A. Sharp, 1927, 127 pp. New and rev. ed. London: Epworth Press, 1950, 122 pp. Reprint. New York: Pastoral Psychology Book Club, 1953, 122 pp.

Waterhouse defines psychology as "the science of behavior studies as a manifestation of mental process," and claims that speculation on the nature of the soul is the task of philosophy and theology. Most interesting is his chapter on "Jesus as Teacher," emphasizing the use of interest, repetition, curiosity, simplicity, and positiveness in Christ's method. The Book Club edition is the sixth reprinting.

[1928] **653. Cock, William Hendy.**

Religious Psychology of the Child, The Drift from Organized Religion. London: The Faith Press, 1928, x+113 pp.

Cock, who served as Director of Religious Education for the York Diocese of the Church of England, here reports on the results of a questionnaire administered to more than 1,200 children between the ages of seven and fourteen. Results deal with the following topics: the child's understanding of why he or she is taught scripture; the child's thoughts on the use of Bible lessons; the child's conceptions of human beings, Spirit, the meaning of God, and the Holy Ghost; the child's learning concerning Jesus; the child's picture of heaven and imagination of hell; the significance of duty; and the child's view of Sunday School. Cock noted that "practically throughout the whole investigation, as the children passed from standard to standard, or increased in mental ability, there was no corresponding increase in spiritual insight or condition, but only in a wider range of so-called knowledge and in ability to express their thoughts." He ends with a summary and recommendations for those involved in Christian education.

[1928] **654. Hartshorne, Hugh, and May, Mark Arthur.**

Studies in Deceit. 2 vols. in 1, New York: Macmillan Co., 1928, xxi+414 pp.+illus. *Studies in Deceit*; Book 1. *General Methods and Results*; Book 2. *Statistical Methods and Results*. New York: Macmillan Co., 1930, 306 pp.+illus.

The first volume in the series, Studies in the Nature of Character, arising out of the Character Education Inquiry of 1924−1927 conducted at Teachers College, Columbia University, in cooperation with The Institute of Social and Religious Research. The most controversial finding in the first of these classic studies was that moral behavior appeared to be specific to the situation, so that a trait of honesty or morality cannot be presupposed.

[1928] **655. Howells, Thomas Henry.**

A Comparative Study of Those Who Accept as against Those Who Reject Religious Authority. Iowa City: The University of Iowa, 1928, 80 pp. University of Iowa Studies in Character, Vol. 2, Number 2.

This volume was based on Howells' Ph.D. dissertation. From a subject pool of 542 college students enrolled in an elementary psychology course, fifty conservatives and fifty liberal radicals were selected on the basis of extreme scores on the Point-Scale Self-Rating Test developed in conjunction with Daniel Sinclair and Edwin Diller Starbuck. Twelve critical items were embedded in a 160-item semantic-differential-type test; the items measured attitudes towards religious mores and institutional demands. Independent variables were the same sensorimotor, volitional, and intellectual characteristics used in Sinclair's study. Howells found that differences in religious attitude could not be accounted for on the basis of different "elemental equipment" (i.e., sensorimotor characteristics). Conservatives were found to be more suggestible, and they found encouragement more helpful. Howells concluded they had less "will power." Conservatives also had the poorest scores on intellectual measures. Catholics and women were concentrated in the conservative group. Reproductions of the tests and a display of the testing apparatus are included in the appendices.

[1929] **656. *Betts, George Herbert, ed.***

Conference on Religion as a Factor in Shaping Conduct and Character, Northwestern University, 1929. Religion and Conduct; the Report of a Conference Held at Northwestern University, November 15–16, 1929. Editorial committee: George H. Betts, Frederick C. Eiselen, George A. Coe. New York and Cincinnati: Abingdon Press, 1929, 288 pp.

Betts authored a number of books on religious education. This is included in the Abingdon Religious Education Monographs.

[1929] **657. *Hartshorne, Hugh, May, Mark Arthur, and Maller, Julius B.***

Studies in Service and Self-Control. New York: Macmillan Co., 1929, xxiii+559 pp.

The second volume in the series, Studies in the Nature of Character, arising out of the Character Education Inquiry of 1924–1927.

[1930] **658. *Beiswanger, George Wilhelm.***

The Character Value of the Old Testament Stories. Iowa City: The University of Iowa, 1930, 63 pp. University of Iowa Studies, First Series, Number 187.

This is Beiswanger's Ph.D. thesis. Old Testament stories were rated by a number of trained staff members at the Institute of Character Research. The readers independently judged the stories on the following dimensions: (1) a classification of the type of story or book; (2) an estimate of the most suitable grade level for reading; (3) a rank of literary excellence; (4) a statement of situations and attitudes; and (5) comments on aspects that influenced the reader, including classifications of the moral situations and attitudes. Of the sixty-three stories included, only six were judged worthwhile enough to be included in a bibliography of choice reading material for children. Most of them were placed in the later grade levels, and seventeen could not be placed at all. Readers found no character value in twenty-five of the stories. The author suggests that the time devoted to the teaching of these stories could more fruitfully be used teaching other material. Appendices include the standards used for judging the stories, individual ratings of the seven judges, grade placements of each story, reliability estimates for the judges.

[1930] **659. *Charters, Jessie Blount (Allen).***

College Student Thinking it Through. New York and Cincinnati: Abingdon Press, 1930, 166 pp.

A volume in the Abingdon Religious Education Monographs series. Charters' book includes a bibliography on religious problems, learning problems, and personality problems. She was associated with the Columbus, Ohio, Division of Charities.

[1930] **660. Hartshorne, Hugh, May, Mark Arthur, and Shuttleworth, Frank K.**
Studies in the Organization of Character. New York: Macmillan Co., 1930, xvi+503 pp.
The third volume in the series, Studies in the Nature of Character, arising out of the Character Education Inquiry of 1924–1927.

[1930] **661. Hightower, Pleasant Roscoe.**
Biblical Information in Relation to Character and Conduct. Iowa City: The University of Iowa, 1930, 72 pp. University of Iowa Studies, First Series, Number 186.
This represents Hightower's Ph.D. thesis. Aided by Edwin Diller Starbuck, Hightower used materials developed by Hugh Hartshorne and Mark A. May for this study, which originated at the Institute of Character Research. A multiple-choice Bible content exam was given to 485 students in grades 7 through 12. This exam consisted of five subtests embedded in a larger battery. Specific information included biblical characters, geography of the Bible, biblical sequencing/chronology, the discrimination of biblical quotations from standard literary quotations, and general biblical information. Other tests in the battery measured cheating, lying, class loyalty, and altruism. No relation of any consequence was found between the amount of biblical information and these aspects of character and conduct. All tests and measures are reproduced in the appendices.

[1930] **662. MacLean, Angus Hector.**
The Idea of God in Protestant Religious Education. New York: Teachers College, Columbia University, 1930, vi+150 pp. Columbia University Contributions to Education, No. 410.
This study was based on MacLean's Ph.D. dissertation and was included in the series *Columbia University Contributions to Education* (Volume 410). MacLean tested 575 children of elementary-school age, and found that the teaching of God is seldom done systematically, that there is a confusion of incompatible and contradictory ideas, that the method of presentation presumes a definite knowledge of God, and that scientific facts are used selectively. Explicitly expressing a liberal bias, MacLean recommends that teaching must include both more known facts about the Bible and more facts about nature. About one-half of the work is devoted to an examination of representative materials, including the following Sunday School series: The Abingdon Press Publications; The International Graded Lesson (Berean Version); The Beacon Press Publications; Chicago University Press Publications; The Christian Nurture Series (Episcopalian); The Pilgrim Press Week-Day Series; and The Scribner's Publications.

[1930] **663. Sinclair, Robert Daniel.**

A Comparative Study of Those Who Report the Experience of the Divine Presence and Those Who Do Not. Iowa City: The University of Iowa, 1930, 63 pp. University of Iowa Studies, Vol. 2, Number 3.

This report was based on Sinclair's Ph.D. dissertation. Five hundred and fifty subjects were asked to rate themselves on 110 pairs of contrasting qualities, using a Point-Scale Self-Rating developed by Sinclair and Edwin Diller Starbuck. Fifty subjects, representing the mystics and the nonmystics, were selected from each extreme of scale scores, and were tested for differences on sensory discrimination, motor abilities, intellectual traits, and suggestibility. The mystics performed less well on motor tasks involving intellectual components and in the general realm of intellectual functioning, and they were more suggestible. They were also more conservative in their religious beliefs. Catholics and women were more dominant among the mystics. Nonmystics felt estranged from or indifferent to organized religion. The appendices include all written research materials and a visual display of the apparatus used.

[1931] **664. Donnelly, Harold Irvin.**

Measuring Certain Aspects of Faith in God as Found in Boys and Girls. Also published as *Measuring Certain Aspects of Faith in God as Found in Boys and Girls Fifteen, Sixteen, and Seventeen Years of Age.* Philadelphia: The Westminster Press, 1931, 118 pp.

This volume, based on Donnelly's Ph.D. dissertation at the University of Pennsylvania, describes a research project performed under the auspices of the Department of Educational Research of the Presbyterian Board of Christian Education of the Presbyterian Church in the United States of America. Its essence is a reliability and validity study of the Religious Discovery Test, which was piloted on 566 subjects, with a revised version administered to an additional 639 subjects between fifteen and seventeen years of age. Faith was defined so as to include a belief in God, trust or confidence in God, and an actual influence upon conduct (intellectual, emotional, and behavioral dimensions). The test measured vocabulary relevant to God, whether faith was effective in conduct, the degree of trust or confidence in God, and the content of beliefs regarding God. All test items and statistical data relevant to reliability, norms, and validity are presented.

[1931] **665. Künkel, Fritz.**

Charakter, Wachstum und Erziehung. Leipzig: S. Hirzel, 1931, viii+223 pp. ENGLISH: *Character Growth Education.* Translated by Barbara Keppel-Compton and Basil Druitt. Philadelphia and New York: J. B. Lippincott Company, 1938, xii+348 pp. +illus.

The flyleaf on the cover identifies Künkel as "the most famous man in the field of child religious therapy today." Here, Künkel focuses on the characteristics of early childhood, the school period, and adolescence and adds his ideas on child guidance as it can incorporate the ideas of the We-Psychology.

[1931] **666. Künkel, Fritz.**

God Helps Those . . . Psychology and the Development of Character.
New York: I. Washburn, 1931, x+279 pp.

Here, Künkel provides "rules" for self-education and self-analysis,
along with rules for helping others. He predicts that at some time there
may be a differentiation among medical, spiritual, and pedagogic psychotherapy. While theology is regarded as the "doctrine of light," psychotherapeutic characterology is the "doctrine of the unwholesomeness of
darkness." Künkel warns against trying to force progress, spiritual healing, or convalescence.

[1932] **667. Nathan, Marvin.**

*The attitude of the Jewish Student in the Colleges and Universities
towards His Religion: A Social Study of Religious Changes.* Philadelphia
and New York: Bloch Publishing Co., 1932, 264 pp.

Nathan's Ph.D. dissertation completed at Pennsylvania University.
Fifteen hundred questionnaires and one hundred interviews from students representing fifty-seven colleges and universities indicated that
only one-third had retained their belief in a personal concept of God; nearly three-fifths had an attitude of doubt and confusion or indifference. The
author is dissatisfied with organized religion.

[1933] **668. Hickman, Franklin Simpson.**

The Possible Self; A Study in Religious Education as Adaptation. Cincinnati and New York: Abingdon Press, 1933, 128 pp.

Hickman was professor of Psychology and Religion at Duke University. This volume in the Abingdon Religious Education Monographs series
deals with adaptation (levels; active vs. passive), the functional self (self as
person, as changing, as having a hereditary foundation), dynamic selfhood
(hormic psychology), habitual self (religious habit), and the associational
structure of the self.

[1934] **669. Franzblau, Abraham Norman.**

Religious Belief and Character among Jewish Adolescents. New
York: Bureau of Publications of Teachers College, Columbia University,
1934, viii+80 pp. Columbia University Contributions to Education, No.
634.

In a study involving 701 adolescents between the ages of twelve and
sixteen, Franzblau concluded that there was no evidence that length of
attendance at a religious school, or knowledge of Jewish history or cere-
monials, or intensity of Jewish feeling had any significant relationship to
character or personality as tested.

[1934] **670. Russell, William Henry.**

The Bible and Character. Philadelphia: Dolphin Press, 1934, v+
294 pp.

This book was originally presented as a Ph.D. dissertation at the
Catholic University of America entitled "The Function of the New Testa-

ment in the Formation of the Catholic High School Teacher." S. J. Case, reviewing it in the *Journal of Religion*, considers it most valuable for its "scholarly and extensively annotated account of the views on the formative function of scripture in Christian education from earliest times down to the present day in the Catholic church."

[1935]   **671. *Burkhart, Roy Abram.***
Guiding Individual Growth: A Discussion of Personal Counseling in Religious Education. New York and Cincinnati: Abingdon Press, 1935, 205 pp. + illus.
A volume in the Abingdon Religious Education Monographs series. Burkhart outlines a proposed program for elementary religious education.

[1936]   **672. *Braham, Ernest Goodall.***
Psychology and the Child. London: Epworth Press, 1936, 104 pp.
In this work, Braham, who wrote extensively in the area of philosophical theology and on immortality, rejects the notion of religious instinct.

[1936]   **673. *Smith, James Walter Dickson.***
Psychology and Religion in Early Childhood. London: Student Christian Movement Press, 1936, 91 pp.
Smith asserts that religious education for young children should be indirect, helping them with an attitude of courage and security rather than teaching religious-theological content. Direct teaching may actually be harmful. Children at this age are not ready to look beyond their parents (to God) as a source of explanation.

[1937]   **674. *Anonymous.***
Child Psychology and Religion. New York: P. J. Kenedy & Sons, 1937, 138 pp.
Religious education from a Catholic perspective. The author is given as "A teacher of those who teach religion."

[1938]   **675. *Murray, Alfred Lefurgy.***
Psychology for Christian Teachers. New York: Round Table Press, 1938, ix+245 pp. Grand Rapids, Mich.: Zondervan Publishing House, 1943, 192 pp.
A developmental overview, with special advice for calling on the sick. Includes no references.

[1939]   **676. *Chave, Ernest John.***
Measure Religion: Fifty-two Experimental Forms. Chicago: University of Chicago, 1939, iv+142 pp.
The "state of the art" of measurement in the field of religious education by one of the leaders in the field.

[1939] **677. Ligon, Ernest Mayfield.**

Their Future is Now; The Growth and Development of Christian Personality. New York: Macmillan Co., 1939, xv+369 pp.

Ligon's personality theory outlined eight traits and utilized a developmental perspective. Based on what was then the Union–Westminster Character Research Project.

[1939] **678. Yeaxlee, Basil Alfred.**

Religion and the Growing Mind. London: Nisbet & Co., 1939, x+224 pp.

An overview of psychology and religion focusing on religious development, with chapters for parents and teachers.

[1940] **679. Künkel, Fritz, and Dickerson, Roy E.**

How Character Develops: A Psychological Interpretation. New York and London: Charles Scribner's Sons, xiii+274 pp.

An object-relational psychology based in the We-experience and The-Breach-of-the-We as the source of isolation. Strongly committed to the Christian perspective.

[1942] **680. Pothier, G. Edward.**

Practical Psychology and Catholic Education. Alfred, Maine: Brothers of Christian Instruction, Notre Dame Institute, 1942, 213 pp.

[1943] **681. Künkel, Fritz.**

In Search of Maturity: An Inquiry into Psychology, Religion, and Self-Education. New York: Charles Scribner's Sons, 1943, xii+292 pp.

A later version of Künkel's ego psychology applies to religious psychology.

[1943] **682. Mathias, Willis D.**

Ideas of God and Conduct. New York: Bureau of Publications, Teachers College, Columbia University, 1943, vi+134 pp. Columbia University Contributions to Education, No. 874.

In cooperation with the Character Education Inquiry directed by Hugh Hartshorne and Mark A. May, Mathias administered the Idea of God Test to fifth, sixth, seventh, and eighth graders in order to throw light on the relationship between ideas of God and conduct. Mathias's results and discussion focus on the composite idea of God, background factors, behavior patterns, and some in-depth studies of individuals.

[1944] **683. McKenzie, John Grant.**

Nervous Disorders and Character; A Study in Pastoral Psychology and Psychotherapy. London: George Allen & Unwin, 1944, ix+94 pp. New York: Harper, 1947, 126 pp.

The Tate Lectures of 1944.

[1947] **684. Chave, Ernest John.**
A Functional Approach to Religious Education. Chicago: University of Chicago Press, 1947, ix+168 pp.
Outlines a Unified Functional Curriculum with a "dynamic" foundation.

[1948] **685. Ligon, Ernest Mayfield.**
A Greater Generation. New York: Macmillan Co., 1948, xii+157 pp.
Outlines the methods and principles adopted by the Union College Character Research Project.

[1950] **686. Ross, Murray George.**
Religious Beliefs of Youth; A Study and Analysis of the Structure and Function of the Religious Beliefs of Young Adults, Based on a Questionnaire Sample of 1,935 Youth and Intensive Interviews with 100 Young People. New York: Association Press, 1950, xviii+251 pp.

[1952] **687. McDowell, John Bernard.**
The Development of the Idea of God in the Catholic Child. Washington, D.C.: Catholic University of America Press, 1952, xiv+146 pp.
Results are based on a test administered to 2,263 boys and girls in grades 4 through 12.

[1953] **688. Bowley, Agatha Hilliam, and Townroe, Michael.**
The Spiritual Development of the Child. Edinburgh: Livingstone, 1953, 84 pp.
Practical advice for parents and teachers.

[1955] **689. Hudson, Robert Lofton.**
Growing a Christian Personality. Nashville: Sunday School Board, Southern Baptist Convention, 1955, 117 pp.
Advice on the teaching of adolescents by a Baptist minister.

[1956] **690. Gutzke, Manford George.**
John Dewey's Thought and Its Implications for Christian Education. New York: King's Crown Press, Columbia University, 1956, xv+270 pp.
In this doctoral dissertation for Columbia University, Gutzke suggests that "the method of experimental science can be properly and profitably employed in the propagation of the Christian gospel." Providing an evangelical perspective, the author places special emphasis on John Dewey's distinction between final and instrumental elements and on the relational aspects of the things under consideration.

[1956] **691. Ligon, Ernest Mayfield.**
Dimensions of Character. New York: Macmillan Co., 1956, 497 pp.
Outlines further findings and research methodology of the Character Research Project, focusing especially on religious faith and human potential, and on the Christian concept of Agape in personality and society.

[1956] **692. Simoneaux, Henry J.**
Spiritual Guidance and the Varieties of Character. New York: Pageant Press, 1956, 248 pp.

Simoneaux, who was with the De Mazenod Scholasticate of San Antonio, Texas, here reports the results of a questionnaire study conducted with 563 seminarians in spiritual direction. Following the work of René LeSenne (which in turn was based on the works of G. Heymans and Wiersma of the University of Groningen, the Netherlands), he examines eight types of character (passionate, choleric, sentimental, nervous, phlegmatic, sanguine, apathetic, and amorphic) based on three traits: emotionality, activity, and retention of impressions. Persons can be said to be emotional or nonemotional, active or nonactive, and secondary or primary (depending on their manner of retaining impressions). Each character type is described, with a historical example. Simoneaux concludes that "the eight characters are not at all alike in their approach to spiritual direction," and offers suggestions to the spiritual director.

[1957] **693. McCann, Richard Vincent.**
Delinquency: Sickness or Sin? New York: Harper, 1957, 179 pp.

Reports on a Harvard Divinity School clinical study of the greater role religion might play in preventing delinquency. Delinquency is regarded as a deficiency disease, symptomatic of an illness of the personality, mind, and spirit. McCann emphasizes the importance of acceptance and nurturance as prerequisites to the imparting of sanctions and principles.

[1958] **694. Meadows, Thomas Burton.**
Psychology of Learning and Teaching Christian Education: Psychology for Christian Workers (with teacher's manual supplement). New York: Pageant Press, 1958, 393 pp. +illus.

Christian psychology is defined as a study of Christlike behavior. Meadows offers a broadranging psychology of education with a section on Jesus' methods in teaching and evangelism.

[1959] **695. Oraison, Marc.**
Amour ou Contrainte? Paris: Spes, 1959? ENGLISH: *Love or Constraint? Some Psychological Aspects of Religious Education.* Translated by Una Morrissy. New York: P. J. Kenedy & Sons, 1959, 172 pp.

According to Oraison, the most important insights that modern psychology has contributed to Christian education are that the human being is a collection of dynamisms and that the emotional life is of primordial importance in the progressive integration of the child. He states that "the emotional evolution of the human being consists in a progressive passage through successive stages, from an *instinctual*, primitive attitude, primarily of the narcissistic type where everything is turned in upon the subject, to an *instinctual* giving and serving attitude harmoniously adjusted to others." Oraison reminds parents that children are not their "personal property" and that the child's interests, not those of the adult, should guide the efforts of education. He also points out that the development of morality and free choice come much later than the basic ability to reason. Faith must be objective, based on an *a priori* existence of someone to whom we consent in relationship that has historical reality. Because the religious commitment of faith conditions the moral, we can speak only of moral education, and not really of religious or Christian education. In his discussion of the development of the religious sentiment, Oraison emphasizes the importance of the child's view of the mother and father in conditioning the views of God and the Blessed Virgin. Religious content is important in religious education, because the history of the people of God shows us the drama of our own destiny.

[1960]   **696.** *Babin, Pierre.*

Les jeunes et la foi. Lyon: Editions du Chalet, 1960, 279 pp. ENGLISH: *Crisis of Faith: The Religious Psychology of Adolescence.* New York: Herder and Herder, 1963, 251 pp.

Babin, a Catholic scholar and priest, was affiliated with the Center for Research in Religious Adolescent Psychology. He first reviews the psychological data relevant to adolescent faith, including the experience of conversion and stages in the growth of faith. He then discusses conditions for Christian education, which must take into account the adolescent need for understanding, which can be met through having a deeper vision of the adolescent's potentialities, through confirming the potentialities of the adolescent through the genuineness of friendship and the weight of the teacher's prestige, and through confirming the adolescent through teaching, which must always include witness. Finally, Babin offers some pedagogical and pastoral reflections. Christian education must aim first of all at communicating a sense of dependence, of spiritual poverty and spiritual childhood. Then, the idea of vocation or mission must replace the idea of "aiming for the stars." Third, the Christian educator must help adolescents overcome their anxiety and fears. He concludes by outlining the main lines of catechesis and the aims of Christian education. The book has abundant footnotes.

[1962]   **697.** *Cook, Stuart Wellford, ed.*

Research Plans Formulated at the Research Planning Workshop on Religious and Character Education, Cornell University, August 18–29, 1961. New York: Auspices of the Religious Research Education Association, 1962, vii+310 pp.

This volume details plans for forty-five research projects, sponsored by the Religious Research Education Association, on religion, values, and morality and their bearing on religious character education.

[1962]   **698.** *Lewis, Eve.*

Children and Their Religion. New York: Sheed and Ward, 1962, 316 pp.

A Jungian perspective on child development and Christian Education.

[1962] **699. Cook, Stuart W., ed.**
Review of Recent Research Bearing on Religious and Character Formation. Research Supplement to *Religious Education*, Vol. 57, Number 4, July-August, 1962, 172 pp.

This supplement includes an introduction by Stuart W. Cook and featured articles by Urie Bronfenbrenner, Martin L. Hoffman, Stephen P. Withey, Allen Barton, Charles Y. Glock, John M. Schlien, Seward Hiltner, William R. Rogers, James E. Dittes, and André Godin. The supplement includes sixty-two references. A more extensive bibliography, including 554 items, was edited by Rogers and Hiltner and published in *Research on Religion and Personality Dynamics*, published by the Menninger Foundation Department of Education in July 1961.

[1962] **700. Ziegler, Jesse H.**
Psychology and the Teaching Church. New York and Nashville: Abingdon Press, 1962, 125 pp. +illus.

A theory of Christian education incorporating the findings of personality and learning theories, group process, and development as it relates to religious readiness.

[1963] **701. Bier, William Christian, ed.**
The Adolescent: His Search for Understanding. New York: Fordham University Press, 1963, x+246 pp.

The 1961 Fordham University Institute of Pastoral Psychology. Includes contributions by Paul H. Furfey, Edgar Z. Friedenberg, Francis Bauer, Pius Riffel, Robert J. Campbell, Brother Augustine, Graham B. Blaine, Alfred R. Joyce, Alexander A. Schneiders, and James J. Cribbin.

[1963] **702. Evoy, John J., and Christoph, Van F.**
Personality Development in the Religious Life. New York: Sheed and Ward, 1963, 247 pp.

A book on the rare topic of the psychology of Sisterhood, which emphasizes that religious life must be lived in terms of what is rather that what might have been. Personality development is traced from birth, with an Adlerian emphasis.

[1964] **703. Goldman, Ronald J.**
Religious Thinking from Childhood to Adolescence. London: Routledge & Kegan Paul, 1964, xii+276 pp. +illus.

Here, the author explores the form and level of religious understanding of children and adolescents, offering a critique of current Christian education programs which fail to take these limitations into account.

[1965] **704. Goldman, Ronald J.**
Readiness for Religion: A Basis for Developmental Religious Education. London: Routledge & Kegan Paul, 1965, xii+238 pp. +illus.

Goldman was principal-president of Didsbury College of Education in Manchester. In this book, he reviews the psychological basis for religious development, exploring the natural limitations as well as the basic needs of the child, and explains how religious education should be affected by current educational theory and practice. In the second part of the book, he examines the content and methods of teaching consistent with the healthy development of children and adolescents.

PART FIVE

Theological Perspectives on Personality Theory and Psychology

Christian Personality Theories, Critiques, and Apologetics

Included here are works which go beyond the Christian anthropologies and Biblical psychologies to speculate on the nature of a personality theory reflecting both a biblical perspective and the understandings of contemporary psychology. Most common among these efforts are those of Catholic writers relying on a Scholastic psychology which is integrated with the psychologies of the nineteenth and twentieth century. Also included here are books which offer a defense of traditional theological perspectives based on the findings of the "new psychology." Finally, we have included those books which critique secular psychology from a Christian perspective.

[1829] **705. Epps, John.**
Horae Phrenologicae Being Three Phrenological Essays. London: 1829.
Epps, a physician, here writes "on morality," "on the best means of obtaining happiness," and "on veneration."

[1831] **706. Beecher, Catherine Ester.**
The Elements of Mental and Moral Philosophy, Founded upon Experience, Reason, and the Bible. Hartford: n.p., 1831, 452 pp.
Beecher, who served on the faculty at Hartford Female Seminary, was a prolific writer whose other interests included slavery and abolitionism, women's suffrage, and the history of the Beecher family.

[1836] **707. Reese, David Meredith.**
Phrenology Known by Its Fruits, Being a Brief Review of Doctor Brigham's Late Work, Entitled, "Observations on the Influence of Reli-

gion Upon the Health and Physical Welfare of Mankind." New York: Howe & Bates, 1836, 195 pp.

Reese, a physician, here combines a review of Amariah Brigham's book with a more general critique of phrenology, which he had earlier supported. In reference to Brigham, Reese felt a need "for a prompt attempt to repel this assault upon both medical and theological truth, and to refute the heresies it contains against science, as well as religion." Specifically, Reese denounces as foolish *(ignis fatuus)* Brigham's postulation of a "religious sentiment," examines theologically Brigham's denunciation of revivals, and criticizes Brigham's theory of insanity, trusting "that he has fully succeeded in vindicating religion from the charge of being the cause of insanity." Reese regards Brigham's work as further evidence for his general feeling that the cultivation of phrenology "leads to coarse infidelity and irreligion."

[1837] **708. Fowler, Orson Squire, and Fowler, Lorenzo Niles.**

Phrenology Proved, Illustrated, and Applied, Accompanied by a Chart . . . Together With a View of the Moral and Theological Bearing of the Science. New York: W. H. Colyer, 1837.

An apologetic by the Fowler Brothers, who led the popular phrenological movement in America.

[1839] **709. Ingalls, William.**

A Lecture on the Subject of Phrenology not Opposed to the Principles of Religion; Nor the Precepts of Christianity. Boston: Dutton and Wentworth, Printers, 1839, 50 pp.

[1843] **710. Fowler, Orson Squire.**

The Christian Phrenologist: Or, the Natural Theology and Moral Bearings of Phrenology; Its Aspect on, and Harmony With Revelation; Including Answers to the Objection That Phrenology Leads to Fatalism and Materialism, and is Incompatible With A Change of Heart, &. Cazenovia, New York: n.p., 1843, 32 pp.

An apologetic by the leader of the popular phrenology movement in America.

[1843] **711. Kierkegaard, Søren.**

Gjentaglesen; et Forsog i experimenterende Psychologi, af Constantin Constantius. Copenhagen: Reitzel, 1843, 157 pp. ENGLISH: *Repetition: an Essay in Experimental Psychology.* Translated by Walter Lowrie. Princeton: Princeton University Press, 1941, xlii+212 pp. New York: Harper & Row, 1964, pp. 1–178.

Here, Kierkegaard explores the problem of unity of personhood and of identity within change: continuity is gained by the continual recommitment of the new self to the ideals of the former self. Anticipates Freud's view of the intimate relationship between religion and the repetition compulsion. The ultimate significance of repetition is that God must be

194

born anew in the hearts of men, and that personhood involves becoming rather than mere being. Authored under the pseudonym Constantine Constantius.

[1848] **712. *Edgerton, Walter.***

A Brief Review of Certain Phrenological Works of O. S. Fowler. Newport, Iowa: B. Stanton, 1848, 40 pp.

Fowler's work is here reviewed from a Quaker perspective.

[1849] **713. *Rice, Nathan Lewis.***

Phrenology Examined, and Shown to be Inconsistent with the Principles of Phisiology (sic), Mental and Moral Science, and the Doctrines of Christianity. Also an Examination of the Claims of Mesmerism. New York: Robert Carter & Bros.; Cincinnati: J. D. Thorpe, 1849, viii+318 pp.

This book, by a minister, inspired several lengthy defenses of "neurology."

[1850] **714. *Pierpont, John.***

Phrenology and the Scriptures. New York: Fowler and Wells, 1850, iv+44 pp.

An analysis of phrenology by a minister and popular author.

[1887] **715. *Johnson, Franklin.***

The New Psychic Studies in Their Relation to Christian Thought. New York: Funk & Wagnall's, 1887, iv+5+91 pp.+illus.

Reviews the work of the British Society for Psychical Research.

[1890] **716. *Maher, Michael.***

Psychology: Empirical and Rational. London, New York, and Bombay: Longmans, Green & Co., 1890, xiv+569 pp.

Maher, a Jesuit, was Professor of Mental Philosophy at Stonyhurst College and Examiner for the Diploma in Teaching of the Royal University of Ireland. He brings together an overview of the principles of general psychology with an apologetic for classical psychology and the neo-Scholastic tradition. The book is listed as part of the Stonyhurst Philosophical Series, as well as the series of Manuals of Catholic Philosophy. At least nine editions were printed during the next two decades.

[1902] **717. *Mercier, Desiré Felicien François Joseph.***

ENGLISH: *The Relation of Experimental Psychology to Philosophy. Lecture Delivered Before the Royal Belgian Academy.* Translated by Edmund J. Wirth. New York, Cincinnati, and Chicago: Benziger Brothers, 1902, 62 pp.

A lecture delivered to the Royal Belgian Society. The reviewer in *The Ecclesiastical Review* describes the book as a "brief but lucid sketch of the rise and progress of the 'new psychology' and a clear presentation of its points of contact with spiritualistic philosophy and of the manner in which experimental research gives on the one hand a concrete setting and extension to that philosophy whilst receiving therefrom on the other hand its rational or metaphysical foundations."

[1910] **718. *Coit, Stanton.***

The Spiritual Nature of Man. London: West London Ethical Society, 1910, 112 pp.

Coit discusses the reality of the mental life, the mystery of spirit communications, the power of the group spirit, and the spiritual environment as the origin of moral life.

[1911] **719. *Barrett, Edward John Boyd.***

Motive-Force and Motivation Tracks, A Research in Will Psychology. London, New York: Longmans, Green and Co., 1911, xiv+225 pp.

[1913] **720. *Riddell, Newton N.***

Methods; The Riddell Lectures on Applied Psychology and Vital Christianity. Chicago: Riddell Publishers, 1913, 305 pp.

In these sermon-like lectures, Riddell emphasizes the need to combine psychology with religion, brainbuilding with regeneration.

[1914] **721. *Rashdall, Hastings.***

Is Conscience an Emotion? Three Lectures on Recent Ethical Theories. Boston and New York: Houghton Mifflin Company; London: T. F. Unwin, 1914, x+199 pp.

Rashdall opposes the view that conscience is an act of emotion or feeling, and claims moral judgment as an act of reason. These ideas were originally presented at the Leland Stanford junior university "West Lectures on Immortality, Human Conduct, and Human Destiny." The lecture titles are (1) moral reason or moral sense? (2) the morality of savages; and (3) value or satisfaction?

[1916] **722. *Snowden, James Henry.***

The Psychology of Religion and Its Application in Preaching and Teaching. New York and Chicago: Fleming H. Revell Co., 1916, 390 pp. +adv.

These are popular lectures to general audiences, based on faculty psychology. They reflect little appreciation for the science-religion controversies of the times and benignly apply psychology to practicalities and religious practice. Evangelical and persuasive.

[1920] **723. *Dunlap, Knight.***

Mysticism, Freudianism and Scientific Psychology. St. Louis: C. V. Mosby Company, 1920, 173 pp.

Dunlap actually treats his three topics separately. Psychoanalysis is denounced as having mystical appeal and committing the fallacies of

secundum quid and of the *ambiguous middle*. Neuroses as described by
Sigmund Freud and his followers are often iatrogenic or induced by actual
pathological sex activity.

[1921] **724. Barrett, Edward John Boyd.**
Psychoanalysis and Christian Morality. N.p.: Catholic Theological
Society, 1921.
    Barrett, who later became an apostate priest, here evaluates psycho-
analysis for the Catholic layperson, explaining where it may be valuable
and where it is not.

[1921] **725. Hill, Owen Aloysius.**
Psychology and Natural Theology. New York: Macmillan Co., 1921,
xiii+351 pp.
    Hill was Lecturer on Psychology, Natural Theology, and Ethics at
Fordham University. Psychology and natural theology are here treated
together as the two divisions of special metaphysics. Hill distinguishes
between empirical-phenomenal psychology, or "effect-psychology," and
rational psychology, or "cause-psychology." Effect-psychology employs
the subjective method of introspection and the objective method of
experimentation. Hill also distinguishes between inferior and superior
psychology, the former dealing with plant and animal psychology, the
latter with human psychology. Hill's psychology is grounded in the Scholastic philosophy of St. Thomas Aquinas.

[1921] **726. Raupert, John Godfrey Ferdinand.**
Human Destiny and the New Psychology. Philadelphia: Peter Reilly,
1921, 138 pp.
    Raupert, formerly a member of the British Society for Psychical
Research, undertakes "to show to what extent modern research when
rightly interpreted, confirms the teachings of the Catholic church respect-
ing the Last Things." He offers an overview of the science of the subconscious, or subliminal self.

[1922] **727. Buber, Martin.**
Ich und Du. Berlin: Schocken, 1922, 137+3 pp. ENGLISH: *I and Thou*.
Translated by Ronald Gregor Smith. Edinburgh: T & T Clark, 1937,
xiii+119 pp. New York: Charles Scribner's Sons, 1958, xii+137 pp.
    Buber, well-known for his revival of Hasidism, here presents an
answer to the question "how may I understand my experience of a relation
with God?" The "I–Thou" and "I–it" are two aspects of one world in
which we move, in an interweaving of the personal and impersonal which
affects all our relationships. God's otherness is emphasized, such that man
and God cannot be regarded as equal partners in dialogue.

[1922] **728.** *Ellis, Charles Calvert.*
The Religion of Religious Psychology. Philadelphia: S. S. Times, Co.,
1922, 46 pp. Rev. ed. Los Angeles: Biola Book Room, Bible Institute of
Los Angeles, 1928, 60 pp.
    Leander Sylvester Keyser evaluates this work from his Christian
perspective as follows: "This brochure is an acute study of the religion of a
number of leading psychologists, showing which are truly Christian and
which are not. Authors like James Starbuck, Coe, and Pratt are here
analyzed."

[1923] **729.** *Balmforth, Henry.*
*Is Christian Experience an Illusion? An Essay in the Philosophy of
Religion.* London: Student Christian Movement Press, 1923, xvi+139 pp.
    Based on a lecture series read in 1922 to the joint conference of the
Anglican and Free Church Fellowships. While the critique focuses on
Carl G. Jung, Balmforth points out that "many psychologists have cast out
the notion of 'soul' altogether" and "some have turned their back on
consciousness." He asserts that psychology cannot show that religion is an
illusion, and that psychologists who attempt to do so make "a leap from
origin to validity."

[1923] **730.** *Barry, Frank Russell.*
Christianity and Psychology: Lectures toward an Introduction.
London: Student Christian Movement Press, 1923, 195 pp. New York:
George H. Doran, 1923, vii+195 pp.
    Aspects of psychology which are enriching to theology are the focus
on the individual and the therapeutic power of suggestion. But psychol-
ogy must look to theology for a description of the healthy person.

[1923] **731.** *Crabb, Cecil Van Meter.*
Psychology's Challenge to Christianity. Richmond: Presbyterian Committee of Publication, 1923, 210 pp.
    Leander Sylvester Keyser, in his Christian psychology text, com-
ments on Crabb's book as follows: "Thoroughly evangelical. Deals with
monistic views. Indicates how Christianity may use all the valid results of
psychological research."

[1923] **732.** *Hopkinson, Arthur Wells.*
*Hope. Reflections of an Optimist on the Psychology of Holiness,
Happiness, and Health.* London: Constable & Company; Boston: Small,
Maynard & Co., 1923, xv+226 pp.
    Hopkinson, the Vicar of Banstead, presents chapters on the conquest
of various illnesses and on evil, the cure of which is intimately connected
with being right with God.

[1923] **733. Hudson, Cyril Edward.**
Recent Psychology and the Christian Religion; Some Points of Contact and Divergence. New York: George H. Doran, 1923, 124 pp. London: George Allen & Unwin, 1923, 121 pp.

A mild apologetic for Christianity and the validity of the religious instinct. Hudson makes clear distinctions between the scope of theology and psychology, and responds to William H. R. Rivers, William McDougall, Wilfred Trotter, Ernest Jones, Sigmund Freud, James Bissett Pratt, Frank Podmore, Arthur George Tansley, and James Henry Leuba.

[1925] **734. Barrett, Edward John Boyd.**
Man: His Making and Unmaking. New York: T. Seltzer, 1925, ix+269 pp.

A Catholic perspective on abnormal psychology. Barrett was professor of Psychology at Georgetown University.

[1925] **735. Barrett, Edward John Boyd.**
The New Psychology: How It Aids and Interests. New York: P. J. Kenedy & Sons; London: Harding and Moore, 1925, ix+358 pp.

Barrett, who was professor of Psychology at Georgetown University, emphasizes human nature from the perspective of dynamic psychology, for an audience of priests, spiritual guides, and teachers. Of special interest are Barrett's descriptions of the work of Antonin Eymieu and Dr. Vittoz of Lausanne, who worked especially with the treatment of scruples. He also describes the major methods of mind-healing and critiques those psychologies of religion which are designed to explain religion away in terms of mental processes or primitive intincts.

[1925] **736. Brennan, Robert Edward.**
Theory of Abnormal Cognitive Processes According to St. Thomas Aquinas. Washington, D.C.: Catholic University of America, 1925, 76 pp.

This is Brennan's doctoral dissertation at the Catholic University of America, where he studied under Thomas Verner Moore and Edward Aloysius Pace. Brennan asserts that "the principles of the traditional psychology, when employed in their proper capacity, that is, as norms of interpretation, may render invaluable assistance to the empiricist by giving him a solid foundation upon which to construct an orderly system out of the phenomena that he observes." His goal is "to analyze the *nature* of abnormal products of cognition in accordance with the principles of St. Thomas; and, with the knowledge thus gained, to establish the groundwork for a philosophical interpretation of the prominent phenomena of insanity." Thus, he focuses on the metaphysical understanding of abnormality rather than the biological understanding. Brennan distinguishes between empirical and philosophical psychology. He also distinguishes between the traditional, rational psychology and the modern, empirical one, the latter not dealing with "the nature or destiny of the soul." In the area of normal cognitive processes, Brennan discusses the psychosensory fundaments of mental processes (sensation, memory, imagination), and the functions of mind in the order of knowledge (perception, judging, reasoning, consciousness). In the area of abnormal cognitive processes, his focus is on illusions, hallucinations, delusions, disturbances in the train of thought, and the psychological meaning of these. He then explores the relationship of insanity to the cognitive faculties (sensation, idea formation, judgment formation, the reasoning processes, imagination, memory) and to mental associations. He arrives at six conclusions: (1) there can be no primary disorder of the rational faculty; (2) a close psychological relationship is observed to exist between mental unsoundness and disorders of affectivity; (3) the root of insanity lies in the sphere of fantasy; (4) all conditions of insanity are referable either to excess or defect in the formal modes of rational mental exercise; (5) there are as many degrees of mental as of physical unsoundness; (6) absence of free volitional activity is an effect of mental unsoundness.

[1925] **737.** *Spurr, Frederic Chambers.*
The New Psychology and the Christian Faith. Chicago: Fleming H. Revell Co., 1925, 190 pp.
Leander Sylvester Keyser, in his textbook of Christian psychology, evaluates this work as follows: "This is a welcome addition to psychological literature. One might differ from several individual statements, but on the whole, it is a successful effort to correlate supernatural experience and the attained results of scientific research. The errors of the New Psychology are clearly pointed out; the truths preserved and applied. The work is not a system, but a discussion of some of the vital topics pertaining to this discipline."

[1926] **738.** *Squires, Walter Albion.*
Psychological Foundations of Religious Education. New York: George H. Doran, 1926, xvii+153 pp. Philadelphia: Westminster Press, 1926, 153 pp.
In the introduction to Squire's book, A. Duncan Yocum states that "the chief concern of a psychology of religion and of the science of education to which it contributes is to build up cumulative complexes for faith, love, responsibility and strength as great key ideals." Squires is critical of mechanistic psychology and regards purposive psychology as upholding Christianity in its major claims.

[1927] **739.** *Berman, Louis.*
The Religion called Behaviorism. New York: Boni & Liveright, 1927, 153 pp.
According to Berman, "a religion consists of a self-conscious attitude toward life. It consists of gestures toward the universe. It appeals to invisible powers, to intangible forces, to impalpable sources of inspirations and strengths. All of which are simply homage to the Unknown."

Berman adds that a religion is always mystic. He stresses that "the word God may or may not be an ingredient. A form of worship may or may not be implicit. The ultimate test of every religion is its effect upon conduct as well as feeling, its reaction upon behavior. And it always has a history." While much of Berman's critique rests upon Gestalt Psychology, he asserts that Behaviorism has had a bad effect, and that "Worst of all has been the effect upon those scientists of the whole personality, the physicians, who should be diagnosticians of the soul in order to be therapists of the body."

[1928] **740. Wickham, Harvey.**
The Misbehaviorists: Pseudo-Science and the Modern Temper. New York: Dial Press, MacVeagh, 1928, 294 pp. Toronto: Longmans, Green & Co., 294 pp.

Wickham proposes a counter to the then emerging psychoanalytic and behavioristic ethos, grounded in materialist reductionism. Wickham argues for an alternative, namely, the return to a belief that reality can be found not in science but in faith.

[1930] **741. Runestam, Arvid.**
Psychoanalyse und Christentum. Gütersloh: L. Bertelsman, 1930. ENGLISH: *Psychoanalysis and Christianity*. Translated by Oscar Winfield. Rock Island, Ill.: Augustana Press, 1958, ix+194 pp.

Runestam's thesis is that of Mowrer and Glasser in Christian form: the root of neurotic illness lies in the fact that the moral force has been too weak, and the psychiatrist must deal with issues that are moral or religio-moral in nature. The critique is directed at Sigmund Freud, Oskar Pfister, Alfred Adler, and Carl G. Jung.

[1930] **742. Yellowlees, David.**
Psychology's Defence of the Faith. London: Student Christian Movement Press, 1930, 190 pp.

This book considers the analyses of religion proposed by psychoanalysis as conceived by Sigmund Freud and Carl G. Jung. Yellowlees suggests that the science of psychology can examine mental life and emotional reactions in religion but cannot invalidate the object of that experience— God. He perceives faith as not threatened, but instead informed, by psychology.

[1931] **743. Cameron, William A.**
The Clinic of a Cleric. New York: R. Long & R. R. Smith, 1931, 249 pp.

A Toronto minister tells the layperson how to deal with fear, worry, temptation, anger, cynicism, and other common problems. The book evidences a mystical strain.

[1931] **744.** *Horton, Walter Marshall.*

A Psychological Approach to Theology. New York and London: Harper & Brothers, 1931, xii+279 pp. Reprint. In *Theology in Transition.* New York and London: Harper & Brothers, 1943, xxix+186 pp.

Horton's book was written just as Karl Barth was reacting to the liberal movement in theology and at the "close of the age of psychology." Horton suggests that theology should take account of psychology and reinterpret itself in light of its findings while reasserting itself as "the custodian of the general body of human wisdom." He discusses the impact of psychology on theology at the individual, social, and cosmic levels. Horton was taught by George Albert Coe and indebted to James Bissett Pratt, William James, and Edward Scribner Ames.

[1931] **745.** *Main, Arthur Elwin.*

New Psychology, Behaviorism, and Christian Experience. Alfred, New York: The Compiler, 1931, 9+43 pp.

Main, a member of the Seventh Day Baptist Church, was the president of Alfred University from 1893 to 1895, and the dean of Alfred Theological Seminary. He also founded the periodical *Helping Hand.*

[1932] **746.** *Leys, Wayne Albert Risser.*

The Religious Control of Emotion. New York: R. Long & R. R. Smith, 1932, x+229 pp.

Advocates organizing the religious endeavor of the world to attain higher levels of emotional maturity and health. Religion must be made ethically defensible, logically valid, economically stable, aesthetically appealing, and metaphysically sound.

[1932] **747.** *Morgan, James.*

The Psychological Teaching of St. Augustine. London: E. Stock, 1932, 264 pp.

Morgan regards Augustine's writings as a synthesis of ontology, psychology, deontology, and theology. From a historical perspective, he examines the influence of the ancient (classical) writers and St. Paul on Augustine, as well as the motivation inspired by Manichaeism. From a theological perspective, he examines Augustine's teaching on the human soul (its origin, nature, relation to the body, and immortality) and the belief in the existence of God. Morgan describes Augustine as a "virtuoso in the art of self-observation and self-analysis," and supports the assertion that Augustine may be regarded as "the founder of the introspective method." In Augustine's writings on freedom of the will, Morgan discerns four different uses of the concept of freedom: (1) in a general sense it was the power that distinguished persons from machines, referring to spontaneity or self-activity; (2) more specifically it was a freedom enjoyed by Adam alone *("posse non peccare"),* the freedom to will the right *or* the wrong; (3) more generally it referred to the freedom enjoyed by persons since the fall, a freedom to sin; (4) finally, it referred to the highest form of freedom, the free decision of self-determination of the will towards the good and holy, to be exercised in the next life by the righteous. Of greatest relevance for general psychology is the chapter on Augustine's epistemology, which includes discussions of the following topics: soul and human faculties; knowledge through the senses; the nature of sense perception; the external senses (vision, sound, smell); impressions to the inner man; self-examination; memory and understanding; instincts; intellectual desires; admiration; weeping (psychophysiology); crowd psychology; child psychology; internal sense; observation; interior illumination; affective tone, (pain, pleasure, conation-desire, and will); certitude; perception and cognition; memory; imagination; phantasia; hallucination, mental aberration and the mystery of dreams; the subconscious and memory; the subconscious; dreams; the rational faculties; the disciplinae. While Morgan asserts that little had previously been written on Augustine's psychology, he cites *La Psychologie de Saint Augustine* published in Paris in 1862 by M. Ferraz.

[1933] **748. *Murphy, Edward Francis.***
New Psychology and Old Religion. New York and Cincinnati: Benziger Brothers, 1933, xiii+265 pp.
   Murphy, who was on the faculty at Xavier College in New Orleans, demonstrates that many of the discoveries of modern psychology are nothing more than the natural attainment of truths long known through other means. The book is written in colorful language saturated with paradoxes and is permeated with awareness of Catholic theology.

[1934] **749. *Clark, Robert Edward David.***
Conscious and Unconscious Sin; A Study in Practical Christianity. London: Williams & Norgate, 1934, ix+186 pp.
   Clark adopts Francis William Newman's distinction between provoked and unprovoked sins. The provoked sins, of which we are consciously aware, are accompanied by the possibility of repentance. The unprovoked sins, the secret and unaware sins of the heart, do not lead to the possibility of repentance, and are therefore the more serious.

[1934] **750. *McDougall, William.***
Religion and the Sciences of Life, with Other Essays on Allied Topics. London: Methuen & Co., 1934, xiii+263 pp.+adv. Durham, N. C.: Duke University Press, 1935, xiii+263 pp.
   A collection of fifteen essays by the well-known social psychologist and Fellow of the Royal Society. In the title essay McDougall supports the two affirmations of religion which science denies: (1) spiritual potency and (2) spiritual participation. He critiques Freud's *Future of an Illusion* and argues for purposive activity in humankind.

[1935] **751. Ligon, Ernest Mayfield.**

The Psychology of Christian Personality. New York: Macmillan Co., 1935, x+393 pp.

Ligon derives a definition of the religious life from a study of the Sermon on the Mount. This work became the foundation of the Character Research Project at Union College, and was inspired by the psychology of Jean Piaget.

[1936] **752. Glenn, Paul Joseph.**

Psychology: A Class Manual in the Philosophy of Organic and Rational Life. St. Louis: B. Herder Book Co., 1936, viii+391 pp.

An entirely philosophical consideration of the life of the mind, with an emphasis on the scholastic tradition.

[1936] **753. Hughes, Thomas Hywel.**

Psychology and Religious Origins. London: Duckworth, 1936; New York: Charles Scribner's Sons, 1937, 242 pp.

An apologetic for Christianity and a critique of much of the new psychology. The lectures presented in this volume of the Studies in Theology series were first presented at Edinburgh in 1933–34. Hughes offers both an excellent overview of issues in the psychology of religion (origins of religion, religious consciousness and experience) and an excellent bibliography of philosophers and psychologists of religion.

[1937] **754. Brennan, Robert Edward.**

General Psychology; an Interpretation of the Science of Mind Based on Thomas Aquinas. New York: The Macmillan Company, 1937, xxxvii+509 pp.

Brennan was Professor of Psychology and Director of the Thomistic Institute of Providence College. In his preface to this textbook, Rudolf Allers defines psychology as the science of inner experience, determined by nonmental laws. Brennan roots his system in the following aspects of Thomistic psychology: (1) a fundamental reverence for fact, wed to an attitude of critical doubt; (2) a method involving the synthetic principle as a point of departure for particular inferences, using the technique of introspection, and combining observed fact with metaphysical inference; (3) a content knit together by the single unifying principle of the antithesis of potency and act. The textbook deals with the following topics: the psychology of Thomas Aquinas; the notion of general psychology; the notion, nature, and origin of organic life; the theory of matter and form; mental life; the organic basis of consciousness; reflex activity; sensation; somesthetic processes; the chemical senses; hearing; vision; perception; imagination; instinct; memory; emotional life; the nature of sensory life; the origin of animal life; the human mind; the conceptual process; the judicial process; the inferential process; motivation, volition; determining tendencies; attention; association; action; habit; character; the ego; the faculty theory; the nature of intellectual knowledge; the nature of volition; the nature of the human mind.

[1936] **755. *Link, Henry Charles.***

The Return to Religion. New York, London and Toronto: Macmillan Co., 1936, 181 pp.

Link advocates a return to Christianity as embracing principles of positive mental health, especially the virtue of extroversion, or other-centeredness. His observations are based largely on results of psychological testing applied to more than 10 thousand subjects. Similar themes are pursued in his *The Rediscovery of Man*, (1938).

[1937] **756. *Norborg, Christopher Sverre.***

Varieties of Christian Experience. Minneapolis: Augsburg, 1937, x+289 pp. +illus.

Relying heavily on the categories supplied by William James, Norborg demonstrates that there is a psychological uniqueness in Christian experience and that psychology of religion must be rewritten in light of this uniqueness. Christian faith is differentiated from Christian experience. An excellent bibliography is included.

[1937] **757. *O'Donnell, Clement Maria.***

The Psychology of St. Bonaventura and St. Thomas Aquinas. Washington, D.C.: Catholic University of America Press, 1937, 111 pp.

A doctoral thesis for the Catholic University of America.

[1938] **758. *Menninger, Karl.***

Man Against Himself. New York: Harcourt, Brace & Co., 1938, xii+485 pp.

This is Menninger's first book on suicidal tendencies in the human being. He suggests that only by intelligence and love can human inclinations toward self-destruction be overcome. He calls this a spiritual malignancy. This volume was followed by *Love Against Hate*.

[1938] **759. *Stuart, Grace Croll.***

The Achievement of Personality in the Light of Psychology and Religion. London: Student Christian Movement Press, 1938, 192 pp.

Stuart, in her assertion that "all personality is the result of relationship," makes one of the earliest statements of the British object-relational perspective. In dealing with the struggles among human beings, she asserts that "psychology . . . points the way, through and beyond these terrible death struggles of our old individualism, to a love of man for man such as the world has not yet known." In her basic psychology of sentiments, Stuart relies on the works of William McDougall and A. F. Shand, but she also reflects a strong grounding in the personalist tradition. Based on the psychologies of Sigmund Freud, Alfred Adler, and Carl Gustav Jung, respectively, she describes the three basic needs for love, significance, and security which are articulated independently in the concurrent work of Ian Suttie. Stuart asserts that psychology "affirms a morality of a more absolute and essential kind than the moral code," and discusses the doctrine of sacrifice which involves a giving of the whole self. Moving beyond other psychologies, she also asserts a need for God which is met by the God of Christianity: "And further—if there be a God whose nature it is to express himself in active, self-giving love, then it must be that we have not only found an object for the most effective master-sentiment possible, but also a hitherto neglected way to the strengthening of that sentiment in the outward-going activity of recognition we call worship."

[1939] **760. Conn, J.C.M.**
The Menace of the New Psychology. London: Inter-Varsity Fellowship, 1939, 76 pp.
Conn's focus is on the effort of psychologists to rule out God and all that is basic in biblical teaching and fundamental theology. His primary psychological source is Donald Maclean of Edinburgh.

[1939] **761. Hoban, James Henry.**
The Thomistic Concept of Person and Some of Its Social Implications. Washington, D.C.: Catholic University of America Press, 1939, viii+ 97 pp.
Focuses especially on the Thomistic distinction between the person and the individual and its implications for a Christian personality theory.

[1939] **762. Holman, Charles Thomas.**
The Religion of a Healthy Mind. New York: Round Table Press, 1939, xi+210 pp.
Fruits of religion and marks of the healthy life are love, faith, hope, social interest, a lofty goal in life, a sense of belonging, a sureness of direction, and a conviction of life's meaning and worth. The church must administer such healthy religion, and encourage its members to think on these positive qualities. Relies on Sigmund Freud, Carl G. Jung, Alfred Adler, and Wilfred Trotter.

[1940] **763. McKenzie, John Grant.**
Psychology, Psychotherapy and Evangelicism. George Allen & Unwin, 1940, xiii+239 pp. New York: Macmillan Co., 1940, 239 pp.
Motivated by the need to study a type of religious experience not previously studied, the author offers psychological insights into British "Evangelical" experience and doctrine. After defining "evangelicalism," McKenzie considers such specific topics as salvation, conversion, guilt, forgiveness, and atonement and discusses more broadly evangelical experience and doctrine, the spiritual life of an evangelical, and applications of psychology to church work.

[1940] **764. Sherrington, Sir Charles Scott.**
Man on His Nature. The Gifford Lectures, Edinburgh, 1937–8. Cambridge: Cambridge University Press, 1940, 5+413 pp.
The Gifford Lectures 1937–1938. Sherrington focuses on the works of Jean Fernel, the sixteenth-century physician.

[1941]   **765. Brennan, Robert Edward.**
Thomistic Psychology: A Philosophic Analysis of the Nature of Man. New York: Macmillan Co., 1941, xxvi+40 pp.
   An excellent review of Aristotelian and Thomistic psychology. Brennan, a Dominican teaching at the University of Montreal, reunites the scientific and philosophical studies of man by defining psychology as "the study of the acts, powers, habits and nature of man."

[1941]   **766. Rank, Otto.**
Beyond Psychology. New York: Dover, 1941, 290 pp.+adv. Camden, N.J.: Haddon Craftsmen, 1941, 291 pp.
   In this, his first English book, Rank pleads for the recognition and acceptance of the irrational element as the most vital part of human life, searching for a balance between the rational and the irrational. He states that "Man is born beyond psychology and he dies beyond it but he can *live* beyond it only through vital experience of his own—in religious terms, through revelation, conversion or rebirth."

[1942]   **767. Gaffney, Mark Aloysius.**
The Psychology of the Interior Senses. St. Louis and London: B. Herder Book Company, 1942, 260 pp.
   Gaffney was Professor of Psychology at Mount St. Michael's Graduate School, Gonzaga University, Spokane, Washington. He differentiates the interior senses (instinct, memory, imagination, the common sense) from the traditional exterior senses (vision, smell, touch, hearing, taste). He also asserts that these interior senses are distinct from the higher intellectual power and that they are distinct from each other. In his discussion of the common sense, he emphasizes its centripetal nature, which counteracts the centrifugal nature of the exterior sensations through the processes of both object and subject union. In his overviews of instinct, memory, and imagination, he relies heavily on the earlier Thomistic works of Robert Brennan, Michael Maher, and Jules De La Vaissière.

[1942]   **768. Menninger, Karl.**
Love against Hate. New York: Harcourt, Brace & Co., 1942, ix+311 pp.
   This volume includes original material presented at the Menninger School of Psychiatry on the theme of the dialectial relationship between love and hate in the human being and in society. He developed the theme of love as that which can overcome hate, and sees Jesus as the prime example of this power. The volume includes chapters on faith and hope as well as love. Menninger sees values in all three.

[1943]   **769. Tournier, Paul.**
De la solitude à la communauté. Neuchatel: Delachaux & Niestlé, 1943, 225 pp. ENGLISH: *Escape from Loneliness.* Translated by John S. Gilmour. Philadelphia: Westminster Press, 1962, 192 pp.

Deals with the problem of true fellowship or "community" as an antidote to loneliness.

[1943] **770. *Witcutt, William Purcell.***

Catholic Thought and Modern Psychology. London: Burns, Oates and Washbourne, 1943, 57 pp.

Rejecting the psychologies of Sigmund Freud and Alfred Adler as incompatible with Catholic teaching, Witcutt reviews the compatibilities between Jungian psychology and Catholicism. He traces the concept of libido to the Thomistic theory of amor, or love. The Jungian idea of the Unconscious supplements the Aristotelian/Thomistic maxim that nothing can be in the mind which was not formerly in the senses. In relating Jung's types and functions to the Thomist "soul," Witcutt asserts that "they are functions of the psyche, the soul including its relation to the body, not of the soul by itself, considered as separable." Jungian dream interpretation is considered highly consistent with the psychology of St. Thomas, who asserted that it was lawful for "doctors to study dreams with intent to gather therefrom evidence as to man's interior dispositions." Witcutt relates the major archetypes of the Unconscious to the symbolism of Catholicism, and asserts that Christ was aware of the importance of these archetypes: ". . . and it will be observed how closely His system appears to fit in with the symbols. He used them for His parables. . . . When He spoke of a treasure hidden in a field, there was a dream-image used pat. When He gave us, in the person of St. John, His mother to be ours, then a whole set of mythological dream images was crystallized for us. His cross, pointing four ways, is another such image. And the sacraments are the primordial images concretised. Nay, in becoming our Savior, He took on Himself the deepest and best-loved symbol of all."

[1944] **771. *Moore, Thomas Verner.***

Personal Mental Hygiene. New York: Grune & Stratton, 1944, vii+331 pp.

Moore, who was Professor of Psychology and Psychiatry at the Catholic University of America, provides a nontechnical discussion of depression, anxiety and scrupulosity, hatred and race prejudice (discussing the contemporary problem of Nazi Germany as an example of an unbalanced nation), defects of guidance and control (asserting that "constitutional psychopathic inferiority" may be due to a defect of training), the interplay of intellect and emotion, the sense of values in balanced and unbalanced persons, the mental hygiene of the home (overprotected children, rejected children, home organization and problems of dating, the ideal of family life), mental hygiene and the school, religious values and mental hygiene, unwholesome drives (fame, feminine charm, the lure of pleasure), religious sublimation, and religious ideals. Written in a popular style, richly illustrated with examples from literature and history, the book went into ten printings in the two decades following its first publication.

[1947]   **772. *Duffey, Felix D.***

Testing the Spirit. St. Louis and London: B. Herder Book Company, 1947, 174 pp.

Duffey argues that mental hygiene (as opposed to physical hygiene) has been relatively neglected in the screening of applicants for religious vocation. He elaborates on twenty-one questions the spiritual director can keep in mind in assessing the psychological well-being of the novitiate, emphasizing the biological, moral and ascetical aspects of the sexual life. These questions are followed by a section guiding the novitiate in the process of examining his or her own spirit. This particular "testing of the spirit" is "a religious exercise having as its aim the systematic control of the predominant tendency of pride by eradication of the faults that spring from this tendency. This aim is pursued by proposing good motives of virtuous action in the light of the vocational ideal." He further discusses the predominant tendencies of pride: sensuality, timidity, sensitivity, complacency, and authority. He ends with a short theology of vocation.

[1947]   **773. *Tournier, Paul.***

Desharmonie de la vie moderne. Neuchatel and Paris: Delachaux & Niestlé, 1947, 203 pp. ENGLISH: *The Whole Person in a Broken World*. Translated by John Doberstein and Helen Doberstein. New York: Harper & Row, 1964; London: Collins, 1965, 180 pp. + illus.

Tournier, writing after World War II, views the "sick" world as analogous to a neurotic person. He delineates modern society's neurosis as a repression of the Spirit and all things spiritual; he outlines his view of the human "person," whose essence is spirit, which manifests itself in man's physical, psychic, and mental envelope and then draws parallels from this view of human nature to the nature of the world as a whole. His final chapters focus critically on such philosophical notions and scientific theories as the dogma of objectivity, evolution, and the myth of power, especially as it dominates secular psychology. He concludes by addressing the task of the church in subsequent decades which he sees as promotion of the spiritual unity of the church at large and in the reconciliation of science and religion, or matter and spirit.

[1948]   **774. *Bonthius, Robert Harold.***

Christian Paths to Self-Acceptance. New York: King's Crown Press, 1948, xi+254 pp.

Explores three classic paths to self-acceptance: (1) rejectionism (self-rejection), (2) forensic (self-regulation), and (3) meliorist (self-affirmation). Each is critiqued from a therapeutic perspective. The common elements in Christian and therapeutic paths to self-acceptance are expression (vs. repression), responsibility, appreciation of self, benevolent relationships, and freedom to choose goals.

[1948]   **775. *Frankl, Viktor Emil.***

Der unbewusste Gott. Vienna: Amandus-Verlag, 1948, 119 pp. ENGLISH: *The Unconscious God: Psychotherapy and Theology*. New York: Simon and Schuster, 1975, 161 pp.

In this illuminating book, Frankl rediscovers the truth that so many of today's philosophers and psychologists ignore: essential to man's humanity is his awareness, conscious or unconscious, of a God within him that distinguishes him from other animals. Claiming that the repression of religiosity in a patient does not belie a belief within, he contends that an intense denial frequently reflects an equally intense acknowledgment of God.

[1948] **776. Moore, Thomas Verner.**
The Driving Forces of Human Nature and Their Adjustment; an Introduction to the Psychology and Psychopathology of Emotional Behavior and Volitional Control. New York: Grune & Stratton, 1948, 461 pp. + illus.

Undergirded by a Thomistic philosophy and psychology, Moore presents a Roman Catholic point of view on motivation. He defends "will" and "responsibility."

[1948] **777. Tournier, Paul.**
Les forts et les faibles. Neuchatel: Delachaux & Niestlé, 1948, 219 pp. ENGLISH: *The Strong and the Weak.* Translated by Edwin Hudson. Philadelphia: Westminster Press; London: Student Christian Movement Press, 1963, 254 pp.

Spiritual strength is offered as an alternative to the politics of strength and the politics of weakness.

[1949] **778. Holman, Charles Thomas.**
Psychology and Religion for Everyday Living. New York: Macmillan Co., 1949, x+178 pp.

Faith, hope, and love are the emotions of the healthy mind as fear, anxiety, and guilt are those of the sick mind. The Christian doctrine of the forgiveness of sins is seen as curative. Both clear theology and vital experience of religion are necessary.

[1949] **779. Sanders, Benjamin Gilbert.**
Christianity after Freud: An Interpretation of the Christian Experience in the Light of Psychoanalytic Theory. London: Bles, 1949; New York: Macmillan Co., 1950, 157 pp.

Sanders begins with the question of what happens to the body of psychiatric belief when God is presupposed as its scientific starting point. His analysis and critique of Freud are from a philosophical and anthropological perspective. His three sections deal with the belief in God and the psychoanalytic method; the sense of shame and origin of sin; and the universal neurosis and the divine psychiatry.

[1949] **780. Terruwe, Anna Alberdina Antoinette.**
De Neurose in het Licht van der Rationale Psychologie. Roermond-Maaseik: J. J. Romen & Zonen, 1949? ENGLISH: *The Neurosis in the*

Light of Rational Psychology. Translated from the 3 ed. (1954) by Conrad W. Baars, edited by Jordan Aumann. New York: P. J. Kenedy & Sons, 1960, xxii+200 pp.

Inspired by the work of W.J.A.J. Duynstee, Terruwe wrote this book as her doctoral dissertation at the University of Leiden. She begins with a discussion of the psychology of the sensory and intellectual life, followed with a discussion of repression and conflict, which is generally focused on the sensory appetites and the will. She asserts that moral norms are rational rules appealing to intellect and will, thus opposing Sigmund Freud's moral theory. In addition to the hysterical, obsessive-compulsive and pseudoneurotic reactions, Terruwe describes four kinds of neuroses: the fear neurosis, the energy neurosis, the energy neurosis camouflaging the fear neurosis, and the frustration neurosis. Terruwe then discusses the origins, development and therapy of neurosis and the prevention of repression, illustrating these with case histories. Finally, she examines the issue of freedom of the will in neurotics, asserting that "the will's lack of control over repressed emotions is a proven fact," so that repressing emotions must be eliminated before freedom of the will can be restored.

[1950] **781. *Dempsey, Peter J. R.***

The Psychology of Sartre. Westminster, Md.: Newman Press; Cork: Cork University Press, 1950, 174 pp.

A summary of Jean-Paul Sartre's psychology with an honest critique based on Thomistic psychology.

[1951] **782. *Hiltner, Seward.***

Self-Understanding through Psychology and Religion. New York: Charles Scribner's Sons; New York: Abingdon Press, 1951, xii+224 pp.

The importance of self-understanding gained through scientific psychology and a liberal Christian theology is here discussed by Hiltner.

[1952] **783. *Barta, Frank R.***

The Moral Theory of Behavior. Springfield, Ill.: Charles C. Thomas, 1952, 35 pp. +illus.

The causes of mental illness are rooted in religious principles involving the moral theories of Aristotle and Aquinas in a Thomistic synthesis.

[1952] **784. *Vander Veldt, James Herman, and Odenwald, Robert P.***

Psychiatry and Catholicism. New York, Toronto, and London: McGraw-Hill Book Company, 1952, ix+433 pp.

A careful evaluation of the principles of psychiatry from the perspective of traditional morality. Vander Veldt, trained at Louvain, combines his psychological-philosophical insights with those of Odenwald, a psychiatrist. Both are on the faculty at the Catholic University of America.

[1953] **785.** *Gemelli, Agostino.*
La psicoanalisi, oggi. Milan: Vita e pensiero, 1953, 99 pp. ENGLISH: *Psychoanalysis Today*. Translated by John S. Chapin and Salvator Attanasio. New York: P. J. Kenedy & Sons, 1955, 153 pp.
Gemelli was Rector of the Catholic University of the Sacred Heart in Milan and President of the Papal Academy of Sciences. His critique of Freud and Jung relies heavily on the address of Pope Pius XII to the Fifth International Congress of Psychotherapy and Clinical Psychology in April 1953.

[1953] **786.** *Howe, Reuel L.*
Man's Need and God's Action. New York and Greenwich, Conn.: Seabury Press, 1953, xiii+159 pp.
Lectures presented to the College of Preachers of the Protestant Episcopal Church. Howe emphasizes the need for relationships and the Christian affirmation of the same.

[1953] **787.** *Magner, James Aloysius.*
Mental Health in a Mad World. Milwaukee: Bruce Publishing Company, 1953, vii+303 pp.
Answers the question, "How does the Catholic religion look at mental hygiene?"

[1953] **788.** *Nolan, Paul.*
St. Thomas and the Unconscious Mind. Washington, D.C.: Catholic University of America Press, 1953, v+30 pp.
An abstract of the author's doctoral dissertation.

[1953] **789.** *Snoeck, André.*
L'hygiène mentale et les principes Chrétiens. Paris: P. Lethielleux, 1953, 192 pp. ENGLISH: *Mental Hygiene and Christian Principles*. Translated by Malacy Gerard Carroll. Cork: Mercier Press, 1954, 67 pp.
The first of several integrationist books by this Jesuit priest.

[1954] **790.** *Evans, Erastus.*
An Assessment of Jung's "Answer to Job." Delivered on November 13th, 1953. London: Guild of Pastoral Psychology, 1954, 26 pp. Guild Lecture no. 78.
A critique of Carl G. Jung's well-known statement on the problem of evil (see entry number 985).

[1954] **791.** *Hudson, Robert Lofton.*
Taproots for Tall Souls. Nashville: Broadman Press, 1954, 148 pp.
Examines modern psychology in the perspective of New Testament theology. A conservative point of view is presented in a readable style with a devotional emphasis.

[1955] **792. *Davies, John Dunn.***

Phrenology: Fad and Science: A 19th-Century American Crusade. New Haven: Yale University Press; London: Oxford University Press, 1955, xiii+203 pp. +adv.

Davies assumes that phrenology was a serious, inductive discipline, scientific in its determination to study the mind objectively, without metaphysical presuppositions. Of special interest are the Christian critiques of phrenology and the ensuing defenses.

[1955] **793. *Donceel, Joseph F.***

Philosophical Psychology. New York: Sheed and Ward, 1955, xiii+363 pp. 2 ed., New York: Sheed and Ward, 1961, xv+492 pp.

Donceel received his doctorate at the University of Louvain and joined the faculties at Loyola College in Baltimore and later at Fordham University. Guided by the Aristotelianism of St. Thomas Aquinas, Donceel discusses the popular, scientific, philosophical, and metaphysical conceptions of life, and its mechanistic and vitalistic interpretations. Plant and animal life and human sense life are discussed, with a focus on the affective and appetitive functions, and the cognitive and appetitive faculties. The human intellect and will, and the freedom of the latter, also receive extensive discussion. Donceel defends the human soul as spiritual, simple, and immortal, and discusses the major theories of the body/soul relationship. A summary of major personality theories and characterology studies is followed by a discussion of man as a person in the philosophical tradition. Donceel's appendix on "theology and psychology" focuses primarily on the Catholic response to evolutionary theory.

[1955] **794. *Jaspers, Karl.***

Wesen und Kritik der Therapie. Munich: R. Piper, 1955, 63 pp. ENGLISH: *The Nature of Psychotherapy: A Critical Approach*. Translated by J. Hoenigh and Marian W. Hamilton. Chicago: Phoenix Books, 1965, 52 pp.

This book is an excerpt from the well-known volume *General Psychopathology* originally published in 1913. Jaspers was well versed in clinical psychiatry as well as philosophy. He suggests that the human being can only be understood by a combination of the study of the body through the methods of science and the study of the person through the methods of intuition. In the latter these are two aspects: the subjective understanding of the meaning in the moment, and an existential understanding of the self which includes unpredictable glimpses of transcendence.

[1955] **795. *Royce, James E.***

Personality and Mental Health. Milwaukee: Bruce Publishing Company, 1955, xiv+352 pp.

An elementary Christian textbook from a Catholic perspective. Normal personality functioning implies living in accordance with the design of nature.

5. THEOLOGICAL PERSPECTIVES

[1955] **796. *Terruwe, Anna Alberdina Antoinette.***
Psychopathie en Neurose; ten Gerieve van Zielzorgers. Roermond-Massaik, Holland: J. J. Romen & Zonen, 1955, 153 pp. ENGLISH: *Psycho-pathic Personality and Neurosis.* Translated by Conrad W. Baars and Jordan Aumann. New York: P. J. Kenedy & Sons, 1959, 123 pp. Also under the title *The Priest and the Sick in Mind.* London: Burns & Oates, 1959, vi+123 pp.

A Catholic psychiatrist, Terruwe offers guidance for the spiritual direction of psychopathic personalities and neurotics. Thoroughly ground-ed in Thomistic psychology, she assumes that much pathological behavior may be attributed to spiritual unrest. The English translation follows the European nosological system.

[1955] **797. *Tournier, Paul.***
Le personnage et la personne. Neuchatel and Paris: Delachaux & Niestlé, 1955, 191 pp. ENGLISH: *The Meaning of Persons.* Translated by Edwin Hudson. New York: Harper; London: Student Christian Movement Press, 1957, 238 pp.

Makes the critical distinction between person and "personage," and emphasizes the spiritual component of the person which is as real as the mental or psychological.

[1955] **798. *White, Ernest.***
Christian Life and the Unconscious. New York: Harper & Broth-ers; London: Hodder & Stoughton, 1955, 190 pp.

A serious attempt to demonstrate that religion and psychology, far from being mutually antagonistic, are both of immense value in the attainment of the integration of the mind and the health of the soul. White explores traditional Christian ideas about sin, evil, guilt, conversion, baptism, and sanctification in relation to Freudian and Jungian psycho-analytic concepts such as unconscious motivation, emotional conflict, archetypes, and complexes.

[1956] **799. *Little, L. Gilbert.***
Nervous Christians. Lincoln: Back to the Bible Publishing Co., 1956.

[1956] **800. *Mairet, Philip, ed.***
Christian Essays in Psychiatry. New York: Philosophical Library; London: SCM Press, 1956, 187 pp.

This is a collection of essays written by English psychiatrists, theolo-gians, and educators collected by Mairet, editor of *The Frontier.* It is largely concerned with comparing the approaches of psychiatry and reli-gion to personality, development, treatment, guilt, and symptoms. Con-tributions by D. Stafford-Clark, Desmond Pond, Anthony Storr, Eve Lewis, Erastus Evans, Gilbert Russell, E. B. Strauss, Victor White, and Denis V. Martin are included.

[1956] **801. Wise, Carroll Alonzo.**
Psychiatry and the Bible. New York: Harper, 1956, 169 pp.
From the Methodist perspective in pastoral psychology, Wise relates the insights of modern medicine and psychiatry to those of religious faith as expressed in the Bible. He includes such topics as health and wholism, fear, anxiety, guilt, forgiveness, love, hate, and the healing power of Christian fellowship.

[1957] **802. Anderson, Camilla May.**
Beyond Freud: A Creative Approach to Mental Health. New York: Harper, 1957; London: Owen, 1958, 282 pp.
Writing in the tradition of interpersonal psychiatry and ego psychology, Anderson explores the role of private religion in the determination of behavior, symptoms, and one's style of life. She asserts that psychiatric illnesses are illnesses of the soul.

[1957] **803. Crane, Edward Villeroy.**
My Minds and I; A Development of Spiritual Psychology Essential to Physical and Mental Well-Being. Boston: Christopher Publishing House, 1957, 269 pp.
This popular work deals with the mind and body relationship while also developing a spiritual psychology.

[1957] **804. Leach, Max.**
Christianity and Mental Health. Dubuque, Iowa: Wm. C. Brown, 1957, 135 pp.
Leach offers excellent insights into factors which aid in the maintenance of emotional balance. He asserts that Christianity is the best food for the person.

[1957] **805. Oates, Wayne Edward.**
The Religious Dimensions of Personality. New York: Association Press, 1957, xiii+320 pp.
A scholarly treatment of religion and personality grounded deeply in both psychology and theology while maintaining a well-articulated expression of the Christian gospel.

[1958] **806. Jaspers, Karl.**
Die Atombombe und die Zukunft des Menschen; politisches Bewusstsein in unserer Zeit. Munich: R. Piper, 1958, 506 pp. ENGLISH: *The Future of Mankind.* Translated by E. B. Ashton. Chicago: University of Chicago Press, 1961, v+ix+342 pp.
In this volume Jaspers philosophizes about the future of mankind in the face of the reality of the atomic bomb. He suggests in platonic fashion that only high reason can save mankind from technology and survival ethics. As in his other volumes he suggests that the symbols by which persons live are inherently religious.

[1958]   **807. Meehl, Paul Everett, Klann, Richard,**
Schmieding, Alfred, Breimeier, Kenneth H., and
Schroeder-Slomann, Sophie.
What, Then, is Man? A Symposium of Theology, Psychology, and Psychiatry. Saint Louis: Concordia Publishing House, 1958, ix+356 pp.

One in a series of 'graduate studies' prepared under the direction of the School for Graduate Studies at Concordia Theological Seminary, and commissioned by the Committee for Scholarly Research of the Lutheran Church—Missouri Synod. The symposium constitutes "an examination of the *concepts* employed by the psychological sciences in relation to the Christian doctrine of man as received within confessional Lutheranism."

[1959]   **808. Maves, Paul B.**
Understanding Ourselves as Adults. Nashville: Published for the Cooperative Publication Association by Abingdon Press, 1959, 217 pp.

An examination of the nature of personality development, education, and change in the adult years. Social factors, family influences, developmental tasks of adulthood, and concepts of maturity are related to a Christian view of man.

[1959]   **809. Stinnette, Charles Roy.**
Faith, Freedom, and Selfhood: A Study in Personal Dynamics. Greenwich, Conn.: Seabury Press, 1959, xiii+239 pp.

Explores a response to Erich Fromm's *Escape From Freedom* in the context of Christian community, focusing on the psychological and motivational conditions necessary for the experience of freedom and selfhood.

[1960]   **810. Bowie, Walter Russell.**
Jesus and the Trinity. New York: Abingdon Press, 1960, 160 pp.

Bowie critiques psychoanalysis as insufficient for the process of healing: it cannot put an integrating purpose in the place of the "old complexes." The key to healing is faith in the triune God, and the key to deeper religious experience is a personal relationship with Christ, the embodiment of the Trinity.

[1960]   **811. Dicks, Russell Leslie.**
Toward Health and Wholeness. New York: Macmillan Co., 1960, xi+158 pp.

For five years Dicks edited *Religion and Health,* a journal no longer published. Here he describes the "healing force" and how it operates and discusses the dynamic operation of eight pairs of destructive and healing emotions: anxiety/faith, hostility/joy, guilt/self-awareness, despair/hope, loneliness/love, pain/courage, boredom/creative work, and rejection/acceptance.

[1960] **812. Henry, Paul.**
Saint Augustine on Personality. New York: Macmillan Co., 1960, 44 pp.

Henry, affiliated with the Augustinian University of Villanova, here demonstrates the Aristotelian and Christian influences in Augustine.

[1960] **813. Loomis, Earl A., Jr.**
The Self in Pilgrimage. New York: Harper, 1960, xvii+109 pp.

Loomis was the Director of the Religion and Psychiatry program at Union Theological Seminary. Parts of the book were delivered as the 1958 Auburn Lectures. Titled "On coming to ourselves in Christ," they combine the insights of psychology and religion into selfhood.

[1960] **814. Nelson, Marion H.**
Why Christians Crack Up. The Causes and Remedies for Nervous Trouble in Christians. Chicago: Moody Press, 1960, 125 pp.

The author, a physician, assumes that distress of body, soul, and mind results from a lack of submission to God's laws. He offers ten rules for good mental health based on scriptual principles.

[1961] **815. Narramore, Clyde M.**
Christian Psychology Series. Grand Rapids: Zondervan's, 1961.

A series of twelve pamphlets for the lay reader.

[1961] **816. Tournier, Paul.**
Les saisons de la vie. Geneva: Editions Labor et Fides, 1961. ENGLISH: *The Seasons of Life.* Translated by John S. Gilmour, Richmond: John Knox Press, 1963, 63 pp.

Explores the turning points, crises, and changes which mark man's life, in the context of God's plan to harmonize the natural and the spiritual.

[1961] **817. Tweedie, Donald F., Jr.**
Logotherapy and the Christian Faith: An Evaluation of Frankl's Existential Approach to Psychotherapy from a Christian Viewpoint. Grand Rapids, Mich.: Baker Book House, 1961, 183 pp.

Viktor Emil Frankl's logotherapy, which recognizes a truly spiritual dimension in man, is taken as a significant contribution in the dialogue between theology and psychology. However, the logotherapeutic world view is not a valid substitute for the Christian one. The preface is by Frankl.

[1961] **818. Ungersma, Aaron J.**
The Search for Meaning: A New Approach in Psychotherapy and Pastoral Psychology. Philadelphia: Westminster Press, 1961, 188 pp.

A Presbyterian scholar sensitively explores Frankl's existential analysis, logotherapy, psychotherapy, and pastoral counseling. He seriously confronts the question of man's basic nature in naturalistic psychology and existential logotherapy. The latter regards man as somatic, psychic, and spiritual, with the spirit denoting the care or nucleus of personality.

[1962] **819. *Doniger, Simon, ed.***

The Nature of Man in Theological and Psychological Perspective. New York: Harper & Brothers, 1962, xxi+264 pp.

Doniger, the first editor of *Pastoral Psychology*, presents a collection of essays by noted theologians, psychologists, and psychiatrists covering man's nature, good and evil, problems and potentialities. Contributors are Franz Alexander, Valerie Saiving Goldstein, William Hamilton, Seward Hiltner, Hans Hofman, Elmer G. Homrighausen, Karen Horney, Walter M. Horton, Harold Kelman, Bernard M. Loomer, Noel Mailloux, James I. McCord, Margaret Mead, Karl Menninger, Randolph Crump Miller, Howard L. Parsons, Paul W. Pruyser, Carl Rogers, Elliott Dunlap Smith, Willard L. Sperry, Paul Tillich, Edith Weigert, and Frederick A. Weiss.

[1962] **820. *Ritey, Hector J.***

The Human Kingdom: A Study of the Nature and Destiny of Man in the Light of Today's Knowledge. New York: University Publishers, 1962, 498 pp.

This is a physician's literate attempt to find a common ground for psychiatry and religion. He relates the concept of "One God" to the intrapsychic sense of security and groundedness which he perceives to be so necessary for the full realization of human potential. He defines God as the "concept limit of every synthesis" and perceives God as the unifying principle of the human spirit.

[1962] **821. *Siegmund, Georg.***

Gottesglaube und seelische Gesundheit. Wurzburg: Echter-Verlag, 1962, 231 pp. ENGLISH: *Belief in God and Mental Health.* Translated by Isabel McHugh and Florence McHugh. New York: Declee, 1965, 210 pp.

Siegmund taught at the Episcopalian University at Fulda. In this volume the author presents anew the contention that both the analysts and the existentialists are in error in reducing religion to wants and choice to compulsions. The search for truth and admitting of one's need to find God are the essence of mental health. Siegmund discusses Henri Bergson and gives several biographical illustrations via essays.

[1962] **822. *Tournier, Paul.***

Tenir tête ou céder. Geneva: Labor et Fides, 1962, ENGLISH: *To Resist or to Surrender?* Translated by John S. Gilmour. Richmond: John Knox Press, 1964, 63 pp.

A logical answer to the "why?" of resistance or surrender will never be found. When we seek the will of God he leads us more wisely than our wisest thoughts.

[1963] **823.** *Howe, Reuel L.*
The Miracle of Dialogue. Greenwich, Conn.: Seabury Press, 1963, 154 pp.

Howe first presented these ideas as the Kellogg Lectures at the Episcopal Theological School in Cambridge in 1961. He outlines various barriers to dialogue and how these might be overcome, and describes the elements in dialogical crisis. Courage to resume real dialogue lies in the gospel truth that "He who loses his life for my sake and the Gospel shall find it." Dialogue is prerequisite to the formulation of a doctrine of man as well as to church renewal.

[1963] **824.** *Robinson, Marie Dolores.*
Creative Personality in Religious Life. New York: Sheed and Ward, 1963, viii+179 pp.

Robinson focuses on the importance of "psychism," as it functions in religious life, to clarify, to counsel, to awaken a desire to learn more from competent persons.

[1963] **825.** *Rosenberg, Stuart E.*
More Loves than One: The Bible Confronts Psychiatry. Edinburgh and New York: Nelson; Toronto: Longmans, Green & Co., 1963. 190 pp.

Rosenberg calls us back to biblical principles of relationship (as opposed to egocentrism) by studying the concepts of love in the Old Testament and relating these to basic principles of health.

[1963] **826.** *St. Clair, Robert James.*
Neurotics in the Church. Westwood, N.J.: Fleming H. Revell Co., 1963, 251 pp.

Thomas W. Klink, reviewing this book in the *Journal of Pastoral Care*, describes St. Clair's work as "unsystematic exegeses of pastoral observations and haphazard allusion to randomly chosen psychological concepts." St. Clair equates neurosis with idolatry, and regards the church as suffering from problems of secularization.

[1963] **827.** *Tournier, Paul.*
Le secret. D'après une conférence donnée à Athènes en la Salle de la Société d'archéologie le 12 mai 1963. Geneva: Éditions Labor et Fides, 1963, 83 pp. ENGLISH: *Secrets*. Translated by Joe Embry. Richmond: John Knox Press, 1965, 63 pp.

Describes the double action of withdrawing and giving as essential to human dialogue and parallels this with refusal and surrender in relation to God.

[1963] **828.** *Tweedie, Donald F., Jr.*
The Christian and the Couch: An Introduction to Christian Logotherapy. Grand Rapids, Mich.: Baker Book House, 1963, 240 pp.

A broadranging book on psychotherapy. From a basically Christian,

critical viewpoint, Tweedie approaches such problems as anxiety, alternative models for understanding human behavior, Freudian theory, types of
mental disorder, and treatment.

[1964] **829. Van Kaam, Adrian L.**
Religion and Personality. Englewood Cliffs, N.J.: Prentice-Hall,
1964, viii+170 pp.
Van Kaam discusses the structure, perfection, development, and
deviations of the religious personality. He develops the concepts of
"modes of existence" and "existential project" involved in the personal
realization of meaning.

[1965] **830. Devlin, William Joseph.**
Psychodynamics of Personality Development. Staten Island, N.Y.: Alba
House, 1965, 324 pp.
Devlin was coordinator of the Loyola Mental Health Project. Here
he offers a basic guidebook to assist in the "cure of souls" for those in the
Catholic tradition. The bibliography is edited by Vincent V. Herr.

[1965] **831. Lynch, William F.**
Images of Hope: Imagination as Healer of the Hopeless. Baltimore:
Helicon Press, 1965, 319 pp. +illus.
Lynch explores the tension between hope and hopelessness in the
life of the psyche, and the relationship between hope and help. Maturity
involves the capacity for decisive wishing and acting as well as the capacity
to wait. It is the ability to tolerate ambivalence. Because hope is an
interior sense that there is help on the outside of us, it is grounded in a
relationship of mutuality.

[1965] **832. McCurdy, Harold Grier.**
Personality and Science: A Search for Self-Awareness. Princeton, N.J.:
Van Nostrand, 1965, viii+151 pp. +illus.
This volume includes lectures at Beloit College in 1962 and extends
the author's ideas as presented in his volume *The Personal World: An
Introduction to the Study of Personality.* McCurdy emphasizs those parts
of the person which are qualitative and cannot be measured and encour-
ages psychology not to "ape" physics or chemistry.

[1965] **833. O'Brien, Michael, J., and Steimel, Raymond J., eds.**
*Psychological Aspects of Spiritual Development. Proceedings of the
Institute of Catholic Pastoral Counseling and of the Conferences for
Religious Superiors of Men under the Auspices of the Director of Summer
Sessions and Workshops, the Catholic University of America.* Washing-
ton D.C.: Catholic University of America Press, 1965, vii+234 pp.
A book in the series by the Institute of Catholic Pastoral Counseling,
this volume treats the selection and formation of religious and pastoral
counseling. Contributions are by Timothy J. Gannon, Eugene C. Ken-

nedy, James F. Moynihan, Dunstan J. Wack, Paul F. D'Arcy, John W. Stafford, Carroll F. Tageson, Charles Arthur Curran, Robert S. Waldrop, Marvin M. Freihage, and George Hagmaier.

[1965.] **834. *Ronaldson, Agnes Sutherland.***

The Spiritual Dimension of Personality. Philadelphia: Westminster Press, 1965, 156 pp.

Affirms those psychologies which reassert the view of man as a psychophysical-spiritual unity. Ronaldson reviews the philosophical views on spirit of Martin Buber, John Macmurray, Alois Guggenburger, Philip H. Phenix, and Jacques Maritain, and the psychological views of Joseph Donceel, Josef Goldbrunner, Ira Progoff, Viktor E. Frankl, Donald F. Tweedie, Jr., Clark E. Moustakas, Erich Fromm, Carl Rogers, and Joseph Nuttin. Implications for childhood development, family life, and education are also discussed.

Anxiety and Guilt

Beginning with the work of Sigmund Freud, psychologists have attempted to reinterpret the meaning of guilt and to internalize its source. Even earlier, Kierkegaard explored new depths in the theological understanding of anxiety and despair. Included here are works which attempt to integrate psychological insights with Christian theology in the understanding of both guilt and anxiety. Integrative efforts in both of these areas evidence a depth and sophistication evident in few other attempts.

[1844]   **835. Kierkegaard, Søren.**
Begrebet angst. En simpel psychologisk-paapegende overveielse i retning af det dogmatise problem om arvesynden af Vigilius Haufniensis. Copenhagen: Reitzel, 1844, 8+184 pp. ENGLISH: *The Concept of Dread: a Simple Deliberation on Psychological Lines in the Direction of the Dogmatic Problem of Original Sin.* Translated by Walter Lowrie. Princeton: Princeton University Press, 1944, xiii+154 pp.

Published under the pen-name of Vigilius Haufniensis, this treatise describes the nature and forms of anxiety, placing the domain of anxiety within the mental-emotional states of human existence that precede the qualitative leap of faith to the spiritual state of Christianity. It is through anxiety that the self becomes aware of its dialectical relation between the finite and infinite, the temporal and eternal. Kierkegaard's ontological view of the self as a synthesis of body, soul, and spirit has influenced such theologians as Jaspers and Tillich and such psychologists as Rollo May.

[1849] **836. Kierkegaard, Søren.**

Sygdommen til doden: en christelig psychologisk udvikling til opbyggelse og opvaekkelse, af Anti-Climacus. Copenhagen: Reitzel, 1849, 4+136 pp. ENGLISH: *The Sickness unto Death: A Christian Psychological Exposition for Edification and Awakening.* Translated by Walter Lowrie. Princeton: Princeton University Press, 1941, xix+231 pp.

Following the train of thought begun in *The Concept of Dread*, Kierkegaard regards despair as a deeper expression for anxiety and a mark of the eternal, which is intended to penetrate temporal existence. The varieties of inner despair are viewed as doorways to spiritual recovery and faith. Despair is the dreadful sickness which befalls spirit through its wrong use of freedom, and constitutes any life attitude other than Christian faith. The nature of spirit is responsible freedom, allowing the choosing of oneself. The "sickness unto death" involves the loss of that which reflects the will of God.

[1927] **837. Oliver, John Rathbone.**

Fear, the Autobiography of James Edwards. New York: Macmillan Co., 1927, viii+366 pp.

Oliver's book is reviewed by Ralph T. Flewelling in *The Personalist*. Religion is regarded as basic to the conquest of fear.

[1938] **838. Roche, Aloysius.**

Fear and Religion. New York: P. J. Kenedy & Sons, 1938, 128 pp. Rochester, Kent: The Stanhope Press, Ltd., 1938, 128 pp.

The author, writing from a Catholic perspective, discusses fear and its objects: God, the Church, the dead, death, purgatory, hell, and old age. He also discusses the inappropriate use of fear as a religious motive, the use of fear as a factor in education, and the fear of God. In relation to the latter, he states that "God has planted the fear of Himself in us as a protection, as a weapon against every other form of fear." Thus, Roche explains that fear of God is more similar to respect that it is to dread, which is the core of the other fears. In combating these various forms of dread, Roche employs the biblical dictum that "perfect love casteth out fear."

[1944] **839. Pfister, Oskar.**

Das Christentum und die Angst: religions-psychologische, historische und religions hygienische Untersuchung. Zurich: Artemis, 1944, xix+ 530 pp. ENGLISH: *Christianity and Fear: A Study in History and in the Psychology and Hygiene of Religion.* Translated by W.H. Johnston. London: George Allen & Unwin, 1948.

Pfister asserts that "all fear results from a damning of love in the widest sense." The crowd becomes a medium whereby the individual may resolve the fear compulsion, thus resulting in mass religion and ceremonial religion as examples of neurotic religion. He attempts to demonstrate that religious truths are accepted in terms of an individual's attitude rather than on the basis of logic or epistemology. Pfister, a pastor, uses the Bible and Christian truth as diagnostic instruments.

[1948] **840. *Bergler, Edmund.***
The Battle of the Conscience: A Psychiatric Study of the Inner Working of the Conscience. Washington, D.C.: Washington Institute of Medicine, 1948, x+296 pp.
In the author's preface, he states that "Psychiatric—psychoanalytic investigations confirm the consoling intuitive belief of humanity that *everyone has an inner conscience and is constantly under the influence of that inner department of the personality.* A feeling of guilt follows every person like his shadow, whether or not he knows it." Bergler examines the development of conscience and the neurotic appeasement techniques of the *unconscious* part of the conscience. The psychology is primarily Freudian, but the author relies on a rich tradition of literature and intellectual history as well.

[1950] **841. *May, Rollo.***
The Meaning of Anxiety. New York: Ronald Press, 1950, xv+376 pp. Rev. ed. New York: Norton, 1977, 376 pp.
A comprehensive study of the nature of anxiety, assessing the theories of Baruch Spinoza, Blaise Pascal, Søren Kierkegaard, Sigmund Freud, Carl G. Jung, Alfred Adler, Otto Rank, Karen Horney, Harry Stack Sullivan, O. Hobart Mowrer, and Abram Kardiner. Extensive bibliography and case studies.

[1950] **842. *Thomas, George Ernest.***
Faith Can Master Fear. New York: Fleming H. Revell Co., 1950, 160 pp.
Thomas presented most of the ideas in this book in a series of lectures before the Learning for Life School of the Haddonfield (N.J.) Methodist Church. He addresses fear in a variety of guises, including fear of the future and past, fear of the unexpected, fear of a crisis, fear of being one's self, fear of insecurity, fear of people, fear of failure, fear of loneliness, fear of life, fear of being young or of growing old, fear of facing God, fear of sickness and death, and fear as potentially either a servant or a tyrant.

[1951] **843. *Houselander, Frances Caryll.***
Guilt. London and New York: Sheed and Ward, 1951, 179 pp. +illus. London: Sheed and Ward, 1952, xiii+268 pp.
A sophisticated treatment of guilt by a Catholic theologian. Guilt is seen as an ego-neurosis: a disease of the soul, or a spiritual ailment. Examines "religions of escape" and offers examples from literature.

[1951] **844. *Scherzer, Carl J.***
Springs of Living Water. Philadelphia: The Westminster Press, 1951, 93 pp.
Here, Scherzer deals with apprehension, anxiety, pain, and loneliness as they are encountered in hospital ministry.

5. THEOLOGICAL PERSPECTIVES

[1952] **845. Tillich, Paul.**

The Courage to Be. New Haven and London: Yale University Press, 1952, 197 pp. London: Nisbet, 1955, 185 pp.

Originally presented as the Terry Lectures at Yale, Tillich's book has become a "classic" on the topic of anxiety. Linking existential anxiety to the meaning of nonbeing, he distinguishes among the anxiety of fate and death, the anxiety of emptiness and meaninglessness, and the anxiety of guilt and condemnation. These differ from pathological-neurotic anxieties, to which courage is an antidote in the form of participation, individualization, and transcendence.

[1953] **846. Pike, James Albert.**

Beyond Anxiety: The Christian Answer to Fear, Frustration, Guilt, Indecision, Inhibition, Loneliness, Despair. New York and London: Charles Scribner's Sons, 1953, 149 pp.

In the Anglican–Episcopal tradition, Pike asserts that Christian faith supplies answers to most basic human questions. The appropriate methodology for such integration involves understanding the real nature of problems and restating relevant portions of the faith.

[1955] **847. Oates, Wayne Edward.**

Anxiety in Christian Experience. Philadelphia: Westminster Press, 1955, 156 pp.

"Materials are drawn from the Bible, contemporary psychotherapy, and clinical pastoral experience to define, clarify, and illustrate different types of anxiety and their interlocking relationship to each other as anxiety moves from one depth of meaning to another in Christian experience." A sensitive, highly integrative account.

[1955] **848. Stinnette, Charles Roy.**

Anxiety and Faith: Toward Resolving Anxiety in Christian Community. Greenwich, Conn.: Seabury Press, 1955, 209 pp.

Stinnette first distinguishes among three types of anxiety: primary (or existential), sinful (based in guilt), and neurotic. Anxiety is ineradicable, and sin is man's desperate effort to secure himself against the anxiety he feels in isolation and apart from faith in God. Reconciliation is mediated through the Christian community, the eucharist, and pastoral care. Psychotherapy should *not* be attempting to answer religious questions.

[1956] **849. Weatherhead, Leslie Dixon.**

Prescription for Anxiety. London: Hodder & Stoughton, 1956, 153 pp. New York: Abingdon Press, 1956, 157 pp.

A Christian prescription for anxiety which includes the importance of an accurate view of ourselves and God, a clear definition and focus for our concerns, the power of confession and the comfort of the spiritual.

[1957] **850. *Miller, Randolph Crump.***
Be Not Anxious. Greenwich, Conn.: Seabury Press, 1957, 237 pp.
　　Sermons based on the work of Paul Tillich, Martin Buber, Rollo May, and Charles Stinnette.

[1957] **851. *Reik, Theodor.***
Myth and Guilt: The Crime and Punishment of Mankind. New York: George Braziller, 1957, iii+432 pp. London: Hutchinson, 1958, 335 pp.
　　An inquiry into the origin of the sense of guilt to uncover the secret meaning of the Fall story and its continuation in the myth of Christ's passion.

[1958] **852. *Bertocci, Peter Anthony.***
Religion as Creative Insecurity. New York: Association Press, 1958, 128 pp.
　　A succinct, psycho-theological appraisal of the role of anxiety in human life and religion. Attacking the peace-of-mind cult in religion, Bertocci asserts that to flee from insecurity is to miss the whole point of being human, religious, or Christian. Mature religion emerges as creative insecurity that brings not happiness but blessedness.

[1958] **853. *Bonnell, John Sutherland.***
No Escape from Life. New York: Harper & Brothers, 1958, 215 pp. Evesham and Worcestershire: Arthur James, 1958, 190 pp.
　　Bonnell deals with problems of anxiety, suicide, alcoholism, and spiritual healing.

[1958] **854. *Michalson, Carl.***
Faith for Personal Crises. New York: Charles Scribner's Sons, 1958, 184 pp.
　　Michalson's ideas were first presented as the Wilson Lectures at Southwestern University in 1957. Crises are regarded as crucial situations which are inescapable and require decisiveness. They determine whether we will live or die, and confront us with the dimension of ultimate significance. In this "poimenical theology" Michalson explores the crises of anxiety, guilt, doubt, vocation, marriage, suffering, and death.

[1958] **855. *Oraison, Marc.***
Devant L'illusion et L'angoisse. Paris: A. Fayard, 1958, 187 pp. ENGLISH: *Illusion and Anxiety.* Translated by Bernard Murchland. New York: Macmillan Co., 1963, 153 pp.
　　Offering an integration of Freudian psychology with Catholic theology, Oraison regards Christian morality as a drama of fall and redemption.

[1958] 856. *Tournier, Paul.*
Vraie ou fausse culpabilité. Neuchatel: Delachaux & Niestlé, 1958, 236 pp. ENGLISH: *Guilt and Grace: A Psychological Study.* Translated by Arthur W. Heathcote, J. J. Henry, and P. J. Allcock. New York: Harper & Row; London: Hodder & Stoughton, 1962, 224 pp.

Shows how to handle the inevitable guilt that arises in human relationships so that it leads to the experience of grace.

[1959] 857. *Berthold, Fred.*
The Fear of God: The Role Of Anxiety in Contemporary Thought. New York: Harper, 1959, 158 pp.

Synthesizing the theories of anxiety of Teresa of Avila, Martin Luther, Sigmund Freud, Søren Kierkegaard, and Martin Heidegger, Berthold concludes that "religious anxiety is the mark of the struggle between our created end of fellowship with God and the many threats to its fulfillment." Anxiety witnesses to our desires for God.

[1959] 858. *Schanberger, William J.*
A Factorial Investigation of Some Theoretical Distinctions between Anxiety and Guilt Feelings. Washington, D.C.: Catholic University of America Press, 1959, 65 pp.

A dissertation applying factor analysis, the methodology which became a hallmark of the Catholic University under Thomas V. Moore.

[1962] 859. *McKenzie, John Grant.*
Guilt, Its Meaning and Significance. London: George Allen & Unwin, 1962; New York and Nashville: Abingdon Press, 1963, 192 pp.

McKenzie presents a study of man's conscience in terms of both depth psychology and contemporary theology. He examines the legal, ethical, and religious concepts of guilt and shows how each must take into account the findings of the others. He accents the role of Christian faith in relation to forgiveness while psychological methods of treatment address themselves to neurotic aspects of guilt.

[1963] 860. *Belgum, David Rudolph.*
Guilt: Where Psychology and Religion Meet. Englewood Cliffs, N.J.: Prentice-Hall, 1963, ix+148 pp.

In the tradition of O. Hobart Mowrer, Belgum examines the ministry to sin and guilt in the following religious traditions: Eastern Orthodox, Roman Catholic, Anglican (Episcopal), Lutheran, Presbyterian, Methodist, and Baptist. An historical survey and questionnaire data are included.

[1963] 861. *Hiltner, Seward, and Menninger, Karl A., eds.*
Constructive Aspects of Anxiety. Work Papers. Nashville: Abingdon Press, 1963, 173 pp.

Contributions to the Sixth Gallahue Conference at the Menninger Foundation by Ishak Ramzy, Seward Hiltner, Paul W. Pruyser, Fred Berthold, Jr., Albert C. Outler, and Charles Curran. Hiltner and Pruyser conclude that existential anxiety is a misused phrase.

Morals, Responsibility, and Sexuality

Psychology has been regarded as posing some degree of threat to Judeo-Christian morality almost from its inception, especially since the advent of psychoanalysis. In this section are included books responding in some way to these issues. The founding of both Mowrer's responsibility therapy and Glasser's reality therapy constituted a response to the amoral position of psychology and psychiatry, launching an era of increasing concern for the issue of therapist values in psychotherapy.

[1909] **862. Davies, Arthur Ernest.**
    Library of Genetic Science and Philosophy. Vol. I. *The Moral Life: A Study in Genetic Ethics.* Baltimore: Williams & Wilkins, 1909, xi+187 pp.
    Davies asserts "that the mental and the moral are seen to be interrelated and inseparable factors in the organization and growth of human societies, that moral soundness is based in mental development, and that mental integrity is impossible apart from moral growth." Influenced strongly by the work of James Mark Baldwin, Davies considers the nature and method of genetic ethics, social and ethical phenomena, the moral ideal and the moral self, motive and its relationship to morality and moral judgment, and moral freedom.

[1923] **863. Hadfield, James Arthur.**
    Psychology and Morals: an Analysis of Character. London: Methuen & Co.; New York: R. M. McBride, 1923, vii+186 pp.
    Hadfield first presented these ideas in the 1920 Dale Lectures, Mansfield College. The English version went into at least fifteen editions

and was translated into Swedish. Writing at a time when psychology was considered opposed to religion and morals, the author attempts to show that this is not necessarily true.

As a physician, he draws heavily on case material and shows how morals are necessary but developed through experience. Coins the term "psycho-physician."

[1925] **864. *Howard, Clifford.***
Sex and Religion. A Study of Their Relationship and Its Bearing Upon Civilization. London: Williams & Norgate, 1925, xi+201 pp.

A sexualized interpretation of the religious impulse which takes the Freudian theory to its extreme. In 1897, Howard authored *Sex Worship: An Exposition of the Phallic Origin of Religion*, thus authoring a pre-Freudian theory which went through six editions by 1917.

[1930] **865. *Barbour, Clifford Edward.***
Sin and the New Psychology. New York: Abingdon Press, 1930, 269 pp. London: George Allen & Unwin, 1931, 224 pp.

Barbour counters the view that sin can be explained as complexes. He reacts to the psychologizing of human failings and examines the teachings of Sigmund Freud, Alfred Adler, and William McDougall as well as the teachings of Christianity. He calls for a renewed understanding of sin as willfull wrongdoing.

[1931] **866. *Weatherhead, Leslie Dixon, and Greaves, Marion.***
The Mastery of Sex through Psychology and Religion. London: Student Christian Movement Press, 1931, xxv+253 pp. New York: Macmillan Co., 1932, xxv+246 pp.

This popular work went through at least sixteen editions.

[1937] **867. *Cabot, Richard Clarke.***
Christianity and Sex. New York, London and Toronto: Macmillan & Co., 1937, vii+78 pp.

Cabot approaches the problem of chastity by advocating a consecration of the affections. He regards sexual immorality not as a matter of social disorder or inconvenience, nor one of personal misfortune or disease, but as a rupture of the relationship between the Soul and God. He decries approaches based on sexual hygiene or simple sex education, since they are out of tune with the relational-affectional components of sexuality.

[1937] **868. *La Vaissière, Jules de.***
Modesty, A Psychological Study of Its Instinctive Character. Translated by Sidney A. Raemers. St. Louis and London: B. Herder Book Co., 1937, v+163 pp.

La Vaissière discusses sex modesty as an instinct having both secondary and primary manifestations. The primary individuation of sex modesty is displayed in the hesitancy of the sex instinct, the "sensitive principle of almost instinctive fear which usually centers around the sexual process-es." The secondary individuation is manifest in standards for dress and other guidelines which assume different forms in different individuals or culture. Education for sexual self-control should be indirect, as direct discussion simply suggests the very behavior and thoughts we want to avoid. From his Catholic perspective, the author singles out several false theories relating to sexual morality: the individualism of Alfred Adler; the assumption that intellectual approaches will guarantee the supremacy of mind over body/instinct; free-mindedness and nudism; and the sexual theory of Sigmund Freud. Particular education should be based on imita-tion, play (into which the child itself introduces appropriate restraints), the training of the aesthetic sense, and the perfection of modesty. The book includes an excellent bibliography of French-language sources.

[1939] **869. *Waterhouse, Eric Strickland.***
Psychology and Pastoral Work. London: University of London Press, 1939, vii+293 pp. Nashville: Cokesbury Press, 1940, 316 pp.

Divides psychology into four schools: behaviorism, general psychol-ogy, hormic psychology, and psychoanalysis. Waterhouse predicts that the Church will have to rethink her definition of sin, proposing it be regarded as "those things which cause harm to others."

[1948] **870. *Casey, Dermot M.***
The Nature and Treatment of Scruples: A Guide for Director of Souls. Dublin: Clonmore & Reynolds, 1948, 66 pp.

A guide for the spiritual director originating at the Catholic Univer-sity of America.

[1949] **871. *Hollingworth, Harry L.***
Psychology and Ethics: A Study of the Sense of Obligation. New York: Ronald Press Company, 1949, ix+247 pp.

Hollingworth asserts that "the contemporary schools of psychology have in common a scant respect for the fundamental human experiences known as conscience, the sense of obligation, the feeling expressed by 'ought.'" He explores the various meanings of the sense of obligation and the rudiments of moral doctrine and moral instruction. Also included is an appendix presenting an outline for a course on the meaning of ought, and the Revised Ethical Insight Test.

[1950] **872. *O'Brien, Virgil Patrick.***
Emotions and Morals: Their Place and Purpose in Harmonious Living. New York: Grune & Stratton, 1950, xii+241 pp.

O'Brien takes the Thomistic assumption that Fundamental Moral Theology and Psychology are complementary and applies modern psy-chology to refine the classical categories of advertence and moral re-sponsibility.

[1952] 873. *De Grazia, Sebastian.*

Errors of Psychotherapy. Garden City, N.Y.: Doubleday, 1952, 288 pp.

De Grazia boldly asserts that "The problems of the wayward and sinful are political and religious, nothing more." He challenges social scientists, especially psychotherapists, to recall that the problem of mental health was originally "entrusted to them by a conditional delegation of religious and political authority." Mental illness is so prominent a disorder in contemporary society that it must be regarded as a problem for the commonwealth rather than an issue of "curing a few sick." He asserts that "when the community is cracked with dissidence, then its morals and laws are bad, and the theologian and political scientist bear a heavy share of the blame." The problem can be solved "through the creation of an ideal man for all therapists to work toward and the recognition that the exemplary man must live not alone but in a community with other men."

[1952] 874. *Hiltner, Seward.*

Psychotherapy and Christian Ethics: An Evaluation of the Ethical Thought of A. E. Taylor and Paul Tillich in the Light of Psychotherapeutic Contributions to Ethics by J.C. Flugel and Erich Fromm. Chicago: University of Chicago, 1952, vii+490 pp.

Hiltner's doctoral dissertation.

[1953] 875. *Doniger, Simon.*

Sex and Religion Today. New York: Association Press, 1953, xii+238 pp.

A collection of articles from *Pastoral Psychology* by Seward Hiltner, Roland H. Bainton, Reuel L. Howe, Gotthard Booth, John A. P. Millet, Carroll A. Wise, Peter A. Bertocci, Joseph Fletcher, Luther E. Woodward, and Thomas J. Bigham.

[1955] 876. *Cole, William Graham.*

Sex in Christianity and Psychoanalysis. New York: Oxford University Press, 1955, xiv+329 pp.

The historical survey includes the views of Jesus and Paul, Augustine, Aquinas, Martin Luther and John Calvin, contemporary Catholicism, and contemporary Protestantism. After examining the views of Sigmund Freud and contemporary psychoanalysis, the author offers a critical reconstruction. The original version was a Ph.D. dissertation at Columbia.

[1956] 877. *Moberly, Sir Walter Hamilton.*

Responsibility; The Concept in Psychology, in the Law, and in the Christian Faith. Greenwich, Conn.: Seabury Press, 1956, 62 pp.

Christianity is seen as bridging the paradox of legal responsibility and psychological determinism, in that it assumes guilt and responsibility while also holding out the possibility of regeneration.

[1957] **878. *Bertocci, Peter Anthony.***
Free Will, Responsibility and Grace. New York and Nashville: Abingdon Press, 1957, 110 pp.
Four lectures delivered in 1956 to the Montreat joint faculty conference of the Board of Christian Education of the Presbyterian Church in the United States and the Board of Education of the Methodist Church.

[1957] **879. *Meyer, Arthur Ernest.***
Mind, Matter and Morals: The Impact of the Revolutionary New Findings in Neurophysiology and Psychology Upon the Problems of Religion, Ethics, and Human Behavior. New York: American Press, 1957, 192 pp.
Meyer, a specialist in endocrinology, physiology, and pharmacology, uses his special areas of expertise to reexamine the classic issues of freedom and determinism and the mind-body relationship. He summarizes his religious-ethical contribution in the following words: "In recognizing the identity of the individual with the world principle and other beings, a religious ethical belief that is in accord with the intimate needs of the human organism and with the natural laws is visualized. The resulting world conception is essentially optimistic, affirming the individual's right to happiness and self-assertion and reconciling it with the interests of society. It acknowledges his inborn need to love and be loved as a base of ethics, using the word "love" in the widest sense and including all ramifications." Religious systems and symbols are regarded by Meyer as vestiges of primitive culture.

[1959] **880. *Hagmaier, George, and Gleason, Robert W.***
Counseling the Catholic: Modern Techniques and Emotional Conflicts. New York: Sheed and Ward, 1959, xiv+301 pp. Also under the title *Moral Problems Now; Modern Techniques and Emotional Conflicts.* London: Sheed and Ward, 1960, xiv+290 pp.
An introduction to pastoral counseling with a special emphasis on the moral aspects of masturbation, homosexuality, and alcoholism.

[1959] **881. *Oraison, Marc, Coudreau, François, Niel, Henry, de Baciocchi, J., and Siewerth, Gustav.***
Le Peche, études de Marc Oraison, François Coudreau, Henry Niel, J. de Baciocchi, Gustav Siewerth. Paris: Desclée de Brouwer, 1959, 248 pp. ENGLISH: *Sin: A Symposium.* Translated by Bernard Murchland and Raymond Meyerpeter. New York: Macmillan Co., 1962, 177 pp.
A symposium addressed to the relationship between responsibility and culpability and sin, doing justice to both theological and psychological concepts. French Roman Catholic theologians contributing to the volume are Bernard Murchland, Marc Oraison, Henri Niel, François Coudreau, J. de Baciocchi, and Gustav Siewerth.

5. THEOLOGICAL PERSPECTIVES

[1959] **882. Rieff, Philip.**

Freud: The Mind of the Moralist. New York: Viking, 1959, xvi+397 pp.

Rieff demonstrates that Freud handed down no final answers and no ethical imperatives, though he worked ceaselessly on the problem of morality. Rieff concludes that moral implications run throughout the whole of Freud's work, which he summarizes carefully.

[1960] **883. Hartmann, Heinz.**

Psychoanalysis and Moral Values. New York: International Universities Press, 1960, 121 pp.

The Freud anniversary lecture delivered at the New York Psychoanalytic Institute in 1959 by the founder of ego psychology. Hartmann presents psychoanalysis as deeply involved with moral issues but as uninvested in any given set of morals or values. He provides a study of Freud's morality and discusses the scientific objectivity necessary for analytic work. The book concludes with a bibliography of Hartmann's writings.

[1961] **884. Mowrer, O. Hobart.**

The Crisis in Psychiatry and Religion. Princeton: Van Nostrand Insight Books, 1961, vii+264 pp.

Includes material previously presented as the 1960 E. T. Earl Lectures at the Pacific School of Religion, the North Park College Seminary David Nyvall Lectures, and the Geehns Lectures at Southern Baptist Theological Seminary. The major thesis running throughout these essays is that disingenuous amorality may be a cause of personality disorder and deviation, thus challenging the Freudian position that all guilt feelings are neurotic in origin. Mowrer's work reintroduced the notion of responsibility into psychotherapy.

[1962] **885. Zavalloni, Roberto.**

La Libertà Personale: nel quadro della psicologia della condotta umana. Milan: Vita e Pensiero. ENGLISH: *Self Determination: the Psychology of Personal Freedom.* Translated by Virgilio Biasiol and Carroll Tageson. Chicago: Forum Books/Franciscan Herald Press, 1962, xvi+341 pp.

In the first part of this book, Zavalloni outlines the history of the problem of personal freedom as approached by different disciplines. He analyzes various factors influencing human behavior, and elaborates theoretically on psychological observations. In the second part, he discusses these observations as they have been understood by philosophers.

[1963] **886. Lepp, Ignace.**

La morale nouvelle. Psychosynthèse de la vie morale. Paris: Editions Bernard Grasset, 1963, 308 pp. ENGLISH: *The Authentic Morality.* Translated by Bernard Murchland. New York: Macmillan Co.; Toronto: Collier-Macmillan Canada, Ltd., 1965, xix+203 pp.

Lepp, a Roman Catholic priest, relies heavily on Henri Bergson's distinction between open and closed morality: the closed morality is super-ego based and manifested in legalism; the open morality acts out of charity and generosity. Psychological morality is regarded as an inadequate substitute for religious morality. Christian morality, whose emotional sources are love and generosity, transforms natural morality in a qualitative way. Lepp discusses submorality and supermorality as maladies of morality. Concrete applications include the family, truth and falsehood, the just estimation of self, sexual morality (which must be inspired by the mutual love of partners), conjugal morality (based on regarding marriage as a vocation), the moral value of asceticism, and moral education, as well as several political issues.

[1964] **887. Bier, William Christian, ed.**
Personality and Sexual Problems in Pastoral Psychology. New York: Fordham University Press, 1964, xiii+256 pp.

Papers first presented at the 1955 and 1957 Pastoral Psychology Institutes at Fordham University and dealing with anxiety, guilt, scrupulosity, homosexuality, autosexuality, sexual development, and education. Contributors are William Joseph Devlin, Richard D'Isernia, Gregory Zilboorg, William C. Bier, Gustave A. Weigel, Joseph S. Duhamel, James F. Cox, Walter J. Coville, Noel Mailloux, Alexander A. Schneiders, Thomas L. Doyle, Joseph J. Reidy, John J. Nurnberger, James E. Hayden, Robert J. Campbell, Paul J. Ecker, John C. Ford, Robert W. Gleason, J. Franklin Ewing, and John J. McCarthy.

[1964] **888. Birmingham, William, and Cunneen, Joseph E., eds.**
Cross Currents of Psychiatry and Catholic Morality. New York: Pantheon Books, 1964, xvi+396 pp.

A collection of eighteen essays originally published in *Cross Currents* and all written by Roman Catholics. Contributors include Louis Beirnaert, Piet Fransen, Maryse Choisy, Albert Ple, Jean Rimaud, Jacques Leclercq, Gerald Vann, Marc Oraison, Bruno de Jesus-Marie, George Mora, L. J. Lebret, T. Suavet, Marcel More, Louis Van Haecht, Jaques Maritain, and Igor A. Caruso. Essentially a psychoanalytic perspective.

[1964] **889. Mowrer, O. Hobart.**
The New Group Therapy. Princeton: Van Nostrand, 1964, ix+262 pp.

Mowrer asserts that "it is only as the alienated, lonely, 'sinful' individual becomes reconciled and reintegrated in the interpersonal sense that he finds his own soul and experiences a sense of peace as he looks out into the Universe and Eternity." Mowrer emphasizes the similarity in the new self-help group movement and Apostolic Christianity as reinforcers of moral sanctions. In this collection of essays Mowrer also reexamines several psychoanalytic concepts and their meanings.

[1965] **890. *Glasser, William.***

Reality Therapy: A New Approach to Psychiatry. New York: Harper & Row, 1965, xxii+167 pp.

Glasser's major thesis follows that of O. Hobart Mowrer: human beings find themselves in emotional difficulty, not because their standards are too high, but because their performance is too low. Responsible living is the key to meeting our basic human needs for relatedness and respect, and follows upon a realistic assessment of our situation. This reintroduction of morality into therapy is supported in the foreword by O. Hobart Mowrer.

PART SIX

Psychiatric and Psychoanalytic Perspectives

Religion and Psychiatry

The cooperation between mental health professionals and religious workers in many ways followed a developmental path parallel to that of the pastoral counseling movement and the several movements in psychology and religion. In this section are books focusing specifically on psychiatry and religion, and the various stages in the development of their cooperative efforts.

[1932] **891. Oliver, John Rathbone.**
> *Pastoral Psychiatry and Mental Health*. Also under the title *Psychiatry and Mental Health*. New York and London: Charles Scribner's Sons, 1932, xiv+330 pp.
>
> The 1932 Hale Lectures at Western Theological Seminary in Evanston. Oliver was associate in the history of medicine at Johns Hopkins University, and his lectures include an emphasis on putting basic principles of Catholicism into practice. Most valuable are the appendices, which include a bibliography on pastoral psychiatry and a descriptive list of books on morals, moral theology, and psychiatry, including classical references. This is apparently the first title coupling the terms "pastoral" and "psychiatry."

[1938] **892. Bonnell, John Sutherland.**
> *Pastoral Psychiatry*. New York: Harper & Brothers, 1938, xii+237 pp.
>
> Psychiatry is defined here as "the healing of the soul of man." Bonnell's writing is in the warm, informal style of Paul Tournier.

[1940] **893. Blanton, Smiley, and Peale, Norman Vincent.**
> *Faith is the Answer; A Psychiatrist and a Pastor Discuss your Problems*. New York and Nashville: Abingdon-Cokesbury, 1940, 223 pp.

Here, the founders of the Church Clinic introduce cooperation of pastor and psychiatrist in addressing basic psychological problems.

[1946] **894. *Frankl, Viktor Emil.***

Ein Psychologe erlebt das Konzentrationlager. Vienna: Verlag für Jugend und Volk, 1946, 130 pp. ENGLISH: *From Death-Camp to Existentialism: A Psychiatrist's Path to a New Therapy.* Translated by Ilse Lasch. Boston: Beacon Press, 1959, 111 pp. Also under the title *Man's Search for Meaning: An Introduction to Logotherapy.* Boston: Beacon Press, 1962, 142 pp. New York: Washington Square Press, 1963, xv+214 pp. +adv.

Frankl's exposition of the principles and founding of logotherapy, the "Third Viennese School of Psychotherapy." Logotherapy focuses on the meaning of human existence as well as the search for meaning, which is regarded as man's primary motivational force.

[1948] **895. *Ginsburg, Solomon Wiener.***

Man's Place in God's World, a Psychiatrist's Evaluation. Cincinnati: Hebrew Union College, Jewish Institute of Religion, 1948, 30 pp.

Originally addressing the Institutes of Psychiatry and Religion, Ginsberg encourages cooperation in the furtherance of constructive resources for psychic health.

[1948] **896. *Liebman, Joshua Loth.***

Psychiatry and Religion. Boston: Beacon Press, 1948, xix+202 pp.

Includes presentations at the 1947 Temple Israel Institute on Religion and Psychiatry, Boston, led by Liebman, author of *Peace of Mind* and an early supporter of psychoanalysis. Contributions affirm the need for religion to encourage health, defined as the ability to stand conflict. Authors include Seward Hiltner, Otis F. Kelly, Harry Salomon, Albert Deutsch, George Gardner, Martin A. Berezin, Lydia G. Dawes, Paul E. Johnson, F. Alexander Magnun, Joseph J. Michaels, Eric F. McKenzie, Henry H. Wiesbauer, and Suzanne T. Van Amerungen.

[1950] **897. *Anderson, Camilla May.***

Saints, Sinners and Psychiatry. Philadelphia: Lippincott, 1950, ix+206 pp. A popular work intended for the lay reader.

[1950] **898. *Duffey, Felix D.***

Psychiatry and Asceticism. St. Louis: Herder, 1950, 132 pp.

From a Catholic perspective, Duffey critiques the psychiatric understanding of the conative—-trends, drives, instincts, urges. He asserts that "Philosophically those who subscribe to the theory of psychic necessity are guilty of psychological and environmental determinism to which we, as Catholics, cannot adhere." He offers an apologetic for asceticism, asserting that it "sets up barriers against the formation of complexes in the inner man by intelligent and volitional control aided by the grace of God. Ascetical effort keeps the mind free from elements calculated to disrupt mental poise and balance, by determining what shall enter the mind's storehouse and what shall not. . . . It does not deny or ignore the warring factions on the battle ground of spirit . . . its aim is to conquer and subdue them, to purify and canalize their energy to the pursuit of the good in accordance with the true dignity of man." Specific topics treated by Duffey include the psychology of asceticism, the psychology of mental prayer, the psychology of self-knowledge, and the psychology of mortification.

[1954] **899. *Stern, Karl.***

The Third Revolution: A Study of Psychiatry and Religion. New York: Harcourt, Brace & Co., 1954, xii+306 pp. London: M. Joseph, 1955, 256 pp.

The psychological revolution has the potential for moral nihilism. Stern makes a clear distinction between objective and neurotic guilt and between the roots and fruits of religious experience. He takes the Jungian position that psychoanalytic work inevitably confronts us with ultimate questions, and emphasizes the serious "neurosis of unbelief." In order to go "beyond psychology" we must follow the movement toward personalism which is inherent in psychoanalysis: the goal is the unity of the person, which cannot be found apart from Christ.

[1955] **900. *Biddle, William Earl.***

Integration of Religion and Psychiatry. New York: Macmillan Co., 1955, xii+171 pp.

Asserts that the basic tenets of Christianity are sound principles of mental health, and that "each individual can best further social integration by appointing himself as a 'committee of one' to investigate and review his personal relationship with the Supreme Being. Psychotherapy restores both faith and hope—Christianity provides the concept of charity in its pristine significance. This is apparently the first use of the term "integration" in this context.

[1955] **901. *Braceland, Francis James.***

Faith, Reason, and Modern Psychiatry: Sources for a Synthesis. New York: P. J. Kenedy & Sons, 1955, xv+31 pp.

A Catholic perspective is offered by the following authors: F. J. Braceland, Rudolph Allers, Juan J. Lopez Ibor, Gregory Zilboorg, Karl Stern, Vincent Edward Smith, Dorothy Donnelly, Pedro Lain Entralgo, Noel Mailloux, and Jordan Aumann.

[1955] **902. *Galdston, Iago, ed.***

Ministry and Medicine in Human Relations. New York: International Universities Press, 1955, 173 pp.

Proceedings of two conferences at the New York Academy of Medicine. Contributors include Sandor Rado, George Stevenson, Gregory Zilboorg, Ashley Montague, and Paul Tillich. General topics are "ministry and medicine in human relations" and "morals and moralism."

[1955]   **903.** *Helweg, Hjalmar.*
Soul Sorrow: The Psychiatrist Speaks to the Minister. Translated by Jens Grano. New York: Pageant Press, 1955, 151 pp.
   Lectures delivered in 1932 to the theological branch of the universities of Copenhagen and Uppsala. Helweg's psychology follows that of Kretschmer, and mental problems as well as the religious views of Luther, Calvin, and Loyola are attributed to inherited constitution. The section on religious development includes a discussion of theologies of predestination and the hysterical element in religious movements.

[1955]   **904.** *Marti-Ibanez, Felix.*
Psychiatry and Religion: International Symposia. New York: MD Publications, 1955, 62 pp.
   A special issue of the *International Record of Medicine and General Practice Clinic*, this symposium features thirteen authors who are primarily Jungian in their orientation.

[1956]   **905.** *Noveck, Simon, ed.*
Judaism and Psychiatry: Two Approaches to the Personal Problems and Needs of Modern Man. New York: Basic Books, 1956, xi+ 197 pp. New York: National Academy for Adult Jewish Studies of the United Synagogue of America, 1956, xiii+197 pp.
   Sponsored by the National Academy for Adult Jewish Studies of the United Synagogue of America, this book presents teachings of the Jewish tradition regarding basic emotional problems, with responses by psychiatrists. Contributors are David Kairys, Edward T. Sandrow, Rollo May, Henry Enoch Kagan, Mortimer Ostow, Alexander Alan Steinbach, Abram Blau, Louis I. Newman, Simon Noveck, Milton R. Sapirstein, Louis Linn, Milton Malev, Hector J. Ritey, Paul Friedman, Henry Raphael Gold, and Abraham M. Franzblau.

[1956]   **906.** *Silverstone, Harry.*
Religion and Psychiatry. New York: Twayne Publishers, 1956, 214 pp.
   Silverstone lectured at the All Soul's School in Washington. He was a scholar in Old Testament Literature (the prophets and the apocrypha), Judaism, and comparative religions. In this book he discusses the partnership of religion and psychiatry in dealing with mental illness.

[1956]   **907.** *Wolff, Werner, ed.*
Psychiatry and Religion. New York: MD Publications, 1956, 62 pp. +illus.

[1958]   **908.** *Group for the Advancement of Psychiatry.*
Some Considerations of Early Attempts in Cooperation Between Religion and Psychiatry. New York: Group for the Advancement of Psychiatry, 1958, pp. 307–351. Symposium no. 5.
   This group met at the Berkeley-Carteret Hotel in Asbury Park, New Jersey, on 7 April 1957. Dana L. Farnsworth presided over the meeting.

Participants whose reports are printed here included Rabbi I. Fred Hollander, Earl A. Loomis, Hans Hofmann, Royden Astley, and William C. Bier.

[1958] **909. *Linn, Louis, and Schwarz, Leo Walder.***

Psychiatry and Religious Experience. New York: Random House, 1958, xii+307 pp.

The authors provide a broad overview of the many overlapping situations where mental health professionals and church professionals collaborate in the treatment of the mentally ill. They summarize the domains of psychiatry and religion, religious development, principles of religious counseling, methods of psychiatric treatment, and the practical ways in which religion may help people face inevitable stresses and crises throughout life.

[1959] **910. *Cushing, Richard James.***

A Look at Psychiatry. Boston: Daughters of St. Paul, 1959, 14 pp. New York: Issued by Academy of Religion and Mental Health, 1959, 11 pp.

Cardinal Cushing argues that psychiatry and religion are complementary when the imitation of Christ is regarded as the ego-ideal.

[1959] **911. *Olsen, Peder.***

Sjelesorg og Psykoterapi—Samarbeid mellom lege og prest. Oslo: Luther-stiftelsen, 1959, 155 pp. ENGLISH: *Pastoral Care and Psychotherapy: a Study in Cooperation Between Physician and Pastor.* Translated by Herman E. Jorgensen. Minneapolis: Augsburg, 1961, xii+144 pp.

Olsen, the chaplain at Lovisenberg Deaconess Hospital in Oslo, Norway, states that "a person in distress is in need not only of medical and psychiatric, physiological and social help, but also of sound assistance in solving his ethico-religious problems." He summarizes positions on integration of Poul Bjerre, H. I. Schou, and Gote Bergsten, and reviews other Scandinavian approaches. The bibliography includes English, German, Swedish, Norwegian, and Danish sources.

[1960] **912. *Group for the Advancement of Psychiatry.***

Psychiatry and Religion: Some Steps Toward Mutual Understanding and Usefulness. Formulated by the Committee on Psychiatry and Religion. New York: Group for the Advancement of Psychiatry, 1960, pp. 317–373. Report no. 48.

The Group for the Advancement of Psychiatry formed a committee in the spring of 1956 with the "charge that it consider the psychiatric aspects of an important dimension of life—religion." The group suggested to psychiatrists that religion might be used as a source of greater knowledge of the contents of the id, of the structure of the psychic apparatus, and to study the application of psychologic principles to the influencing of behavior. Recommendations were also made concerning further collaboration on moral issues, public policy, and issues in religion.

[1961] **913. *Hofmann, Hans.***

Religion and Mental Health: A Casebook with Commentary and an Essay on Pertinent Literature. New York: Harper & Brothers, 1961, 333 pp.

This was a casebook derived from the Harvard University Project on Religion and Mental Health. It was intended to provide a basis for discussion of the relation of mental health to religion for theological and psychiatric training. Hofmann includes a survey of the literature, a wealth of cases from real life and literature, and questions for discussion.

[1961] **914. *Rodriguez, Luis J.***

God Bless the Devil: The Key to Liberation of Psychiatry. New York: Bookman Associates, 1961, 256 pp.

In his preface, Rodriguez states that "this book emphasizes that the abundance of phenomena with which the psychiatrist is, by choice, in daily contact, contain within their etiology the enlightening answer of what man is. In expounding this thesis, I have been led at times to use harsh words. These are not meant to offend anybody, but only to emphasize the damaging consequences flowing from the ignorance of what we are." The author also acknowledges his obligation "to cooperate with ethical, determined and resolute research workers in the field of psychiatry, with the purpose of exposing the facts to the light, where they may be evaluated fearlessly and constructively." He explores the relationship between psychiatry and the priesthood in the search for answers to questions relating to the nature of humanity in light of the threat of nuclear war and other contemporary issues epitomizing the role of the devil.

[1962] **915. *Dominian, Jacob.***

Psychiatry and the Christian. London: Burns and Oates, 1962, 141 pp. New York: Hawthorn Books, 1962, 138 pp.

This Catholic psychiatrist briefly summarizes the psychologies of Carl G. Jung, Alfred Adler, and Ivan Pavlov as well as the major mental disorders and their treatment, with some reflections on psychiatry and Christianity.

[1962] **916. *McKann, Richard Vincent.***

The Churches and Mental Health: A Report to the Staff Director, Jack R. Ewalt. New York: Basic Books, 1962, x+278 pp.

A theologically impartial look at the churches and the clergy and their role in the national problem of mental health. This is one of ten monographs published by the Joint Commission on Mental Health as part of a national study.

[1963] **917. *Menninger, Karl Augustus, Mayman, Martin, and Pruyser, Paul W.***

The Vital Balance: The Life Process in Mental Health and Illness. New York: Viking Press, 1963, 531 pp.

A textbook of psychiatry with extensive appendices relating to the history of nosology. Menninger advocates a unitary, holistic approach to mental illness and health. Of religious interest is the chapter on the "intangibles" of love, faith, and hope as crucial determinants of effective healing. Sustained by hope we can move beyond endurance to transcendence.

[1964] **918.** *Gassert, Robert G., and Hall, Bernard H.*

Psychiatry and Religious Faith. New York: Viking Press, 1964, xx+171 pp. Also under the title *Mental Health and Religious Faith.* London: Darton, Longman & Todd, 1966, xviii+171 pp.

Writing from a Catholic perspective, the authors demonstrate that there is no conflict between psychiatry and faith.

[1964] **919.** *Klausner, Samuel Z.*

Psychiatry and Religion: A Sociological Study of the New Alliance of Ministers and Psychiatrists. New York: Free Press of Glencoe, 1964, xvi+299 pp.

The first half of the book is a description of the pioneering Religio-Psychiatric Clinic at the Marble Collegiate Church. The second half examines the roles and goals of psychiatrically-oriented ministers and religiously-oriented psychiatrists. They have a joint endeavor, yet frame their work in competitive ideologies.

[1965] **920.** *Clinebell, Howard John, Jr.*

Mental Health through Christian Community: The Local Church's Ministry of Growth and Healing. New York: Abingdon Press, 1965, 300 pp.

This is the second book by Clinebell, one of the foremost contemporary theorists in pastoral counseling. It relates the goal of mental health to the several functions of the pastor and to the various settings of the local church. Clinebell sees the mission of the local church as integrally related to the goals of mental health.

Psychoanalysis and Religion

Featured here are books which focus on the integration of traditional theological perspectives with those of psychoanalytic theory. In this section are included the more general works, while those focused on Freudian and Jungian psychology are featured in subsequent sections.

[1909] **921. Rank, Otto.**

Der Mythus von der Geburt des Helden: Versuch einer mythologischen Mythendeutung. Leipzig, Vienna: Franz Deuticke, 1909, 93 pp. ENGLISH: *The Myth of the Birth of the Hero: A Psychological Interpretation of Mythology.* Translated by F. Robbins and Smith Ely Jeliffe. New York: Nervous and Mental Diseases Publishing Co., 1914, iii+100 pp. Nervous and Mental Disease Monograph 18. Reprint. In *The Myth of the Birth of the Hero and Other Writings.* New York: Vintage Books, 1964, pp. xvi+100.

This archetypal myth theme is abstracted from thirty-four myths from the Mediterranean basin and western Asia.

[1913] **922. Pfister, Oskar Robert.**

Die psychoanalytische Methode, eine erfahrungswissenschaftlich-systematische Darstellung. Leipzig and Berlin: Klinkhardt, 1913, viii+512 pp. ENGLISH: *The Psychoanalytic Method.* Translated by Charles Rockwell Payne. London: Kegan Paul, Trench, Trubner & Co., 1915, xvii+588 pp. New York: Moffat, Yard & Company, 1917, xviii+588 pp.

Pfister's survey of the theory and practice of psychoanalysis was written in order to make analysis available for educators. Introductory statements are written by both Sigmund Freud and G. Stanley Hall.

Pfister suggests that the book be used as an introduction for theologians and psychologists as well as educators. He asserts a position later restated in his response to Freud's *The Future of an Illusion* ("The Illusion of the Future"), that love, not sex, is the essence of life.

[1920] **923. *Pfister, Oskar Robert.***

Zum Kampf um die Psychoanalyse. Leipzig: Internationaler psychoanalytischer Verlag, 1920, 462 pp. ENGLISH: *Some Applications of Psychoanalysis.* London: George Allen & Unwin, 1923, 352 pp. New York: Dodd, Mead & Co., 1923.

This is a sequel to Pfister's earlier book *The Psychoanalytic Method.* It relates psychoanalysis to art, philosophy, war, missionary work, and religion. Of special interest are Pfister's suggestions concerning how psychoanalysis can relate to functioning on the mission field and to personal and social ethics. This is a seminal volume by the first Protestant pastor to embrace psychoanalysis.

[1920] **924. *Swisher, Walter Samuel.***

Religion and the New Psychology: A Psycho-analytic Study of Religion. Boston: Marshall Jones Company, 1920, xv+261 pp.

A limited and uncritical synthesis based on early works by Sigmund Freud, Alfred Adler, Carl G. Jung, Isadore H. Coriat, Wilfred Lay, Albert Mordell, Oskar Pfister, F. B. Prescott, Morton Prince, Joseph Jastrow, Rudolf Eucken, William James, Joseph Grasset, and Henri Bergson.

[1920] **925. *Tansley, Arthur George.***

The New Psychology and Its Relation to Life. London: George Allen & Unwin, 1920, 283 pp. +illus.; New York: Dodd, Mead, & Co., 1921, 283 pp.

Offering little integrative material, Tansley provides an overview of dynamic psychology, drawing on the works of William McDougall, Sigmund Freud, Carl Gustav Jung, Charles Baudouin, Emile Coué, Wilfred Trotter, and Julien Varendonck. God and the Devil are the focus of the discussion on projection and idealism.

[1927] **926. *Reik, Theodor.***

Dogma und Zwangsidee, eine psychoanalytische Studie zur Entwicklung der Religion. Leipzig: Internationaler psychoanalytischer Verlag, 1927, 141 pp. ENGLISH: *Dogma and Compulsion: Psychoanalytic Studies of Myths and Religions.* Translated by Bernard Miall. New York: International Universities Press, 1951, 332 pp.

In Part One Reik carefully defends the assertion that "religious beliefs correspond to obsessional conceptions, dogmas to obsessional ideas, and the considerations, proofs and conclusions furnished by rational theology to the deliria of humanity in its religious evolution." In the final phase of religion and neurosis, forbidden impulses erupt. Reik further analyzes the meaning of prayer shawls and phylacteries, presents psychoanalytically-oriented exegesis of several Old Testament passages and the Oedipus myth.

[1934] **927. *Weatherhead, Leslie Dixon.***

Psychology and Life. London: Hodder & Stoughton, 1934, xix+320 pp. New York: Abingdon Press, 1935, xix+280 pp.

An overview of dynamic psychology, with an introduction on the relationship between psychology and religion in the healing process.

[1935] **928. *Forsyth, David.***

Psychology and Religion; A Study by a Medical Psychologist. London: Watts and Co., 1935, ix+221 pp.

Forsyth, a psychiatrist, regards science and religion as in perpetual conflict. Psychoanalysis proves that Christianity is riddled with archaic and pathological characteristics.

[1940] **929. *May, Rollo.***

The Springs of Creative Living: A Study of Human Nature and God. New York and Nashville: Abingdon-Cokesbury Press, 1940, 271 pp.

An attack upon twentieth-century egocentrism and its failure to quench man's thirst for meaning. May subscribes to Fritz Künkel's "subject-object" interplay, in which subject and object are experienced simultaneously in a balance of freedom and determinism. Healthy religion involves an affirmation of God without demanding that God affirm the self. Happiness lies in self-transcendence and the acceptance of God's grace. May also relies on the psychological theories of Sigmund Freud, Carl G. Jung, Otto Rank, and Alfred Adler.

[1950] **930. *Fromm, Erich.***

Psychoanalysis and Religion. New Haven: Yale University Press, 1950, vi+119 pp. London: Gollancz, 1951, 126 pp.

Originally presented as the Dwight H. Terry Lectures at Yale. Fromm challenges psychoanalysis and religion to unite in a search for the person's highest good, and warns against the perils of technology and production, which are modern forms of idolatry.

[1950] **931. *Nuttin, Jozef.***

Psychoanalyse et conception spiritualiste de l'homme. Une théorie dynamique de la personnalite normale. Louvain: Publications Universitaires de Louvain, 1950, 436 pp. ENGLISH: *Psychoanalysis and Personality: A Dynamic Theory of Normal Personality.* Translated by George Lamb. New York: New American Library, 1962, xvi+332 pp.

Nuttin, a Belgian priest and Louvain psychologist, addresses the question, "how can the presence of unconscious drives be reconciled with freedom of the will?" His ideas are based primarily on the psychologies of Sigmund Freud and Alfred Adler.

[1951] **932. Fromm, Erich.**
The Forgotten Language: An Introduction to the Understanding of Dreams, Fairy Tales and Myths. New York: Rinehart, 1951, vii+263 pp. Reprint. New York: Grove Press, 1957, 263 pp.

Includes a history of dream interpretation and an overview of the Oedipus myth. Interprets the latter as concerned with the political conflict between matriarchal and patriarchal societies.

[1951] **933. Jones, Ernest.**
Essays in Applied Psychoanalysis. Vol. 2. *Essays in Folklore, Anthropology and Religion.* London: Hogarth Press, 1951, 383 pp.

The four essays included here are "The God Complex" (1913), "A Psychoanalytic Study of the Holy Ghost Concept" (1922), "The Psychology of Religion" (1926), and "Psychoanalysis and the Christian Religion" (1930). As described by Paul W. Pruyser, in his review, "Jones traces psychodynamic implications of the shift from a single father-god to the Christian conception of the Trinity, the idea of the Holy Ghost, and Mariology. Jones' major contribution is to trace the origins of the Holy Ghost concept to feminine roots in the Great Mother religions."

[1952] **934. Mollegen, Albert Theodore.**
Christianity and Psychoanalysis: Four Lectures and Panel Discussion Delivered at Satterlee Hall, St. Alban's, in the Washington Cathedral Grounds, April–May, 1952. Washington, D.C.: Organizing Committee, Christianity and Modern Man, 1952, 86 pp.

Essays include "A Christian view of psychoanalysis" (A. T. Mollegen), "The psychoanalytic view of human personality" (Edith Weigert), "Psychoanalysis and modern views on human existence and religious experience" (Hans W. Loewald), and "The Christian roots of psychoanalysis" (Don Shaw).

[1953] **935. May, Rollo.**
Man's Search for Himself. New York: W. W. Norton; London: George Allen & Unwin, 1953, 281 pp.

Addresses the dilemmas and possibilities of the self in the modern world. Includes chapters on anxiety and loneliness, becoming a person, freedom and inner strength, the creative conscience, courage as the virtue of maturity, and man as the transcender of time.

[1956] **936. Guntrip, Harry (Henry James Samuel).**
Mental Pain and the Cure of Souls. London: Independent Press, 1956, 206 pp. Also under the title *Psychotherapy and Religion: The Constructive Use of Inner Conflict.* New York: Harper, 1957, 206 pp.

Guntrip offers an excellent review of object relations theory and psychotherapy, drawing on the works of John Bowlby, Melanie Klein, W.R.D. Fairbairn, Phyllis Greenacre, and others. Religion is defined as "experiencing a relationship with the ultimate all-embracing reality re-

garded as personal." Although religion may be involved in psychopatholo-
gizing, it also offers "the most comprehensive and invulnerable security,
and the largest scope of self-realization possible to man." Psychotherapy
and Christian experience both involve a quest for salvation and the
experience of communion.

[1956] **937. *Progoff, Ira.***
*The Death and Rebirth of Psychology: An Integrative Evaluation of
Freud, Adler, Jung and Rank and the Impact of Their Culminating
Insights on Modern Man.* New York: Julian Press, 1956, 275 pp.

   The four psychoanalysts considered in his book are regarded by
Progoff as having made the most fundamental and continuous contribution to depth psychology. Ultimately, each of them discovered that to find
the meaning of life man must be guided to an experience beyond theology. Though concerned with the transcendent, Progoff takes no particular
theological orientation.

[1958] **938. *Erikson, Erik Homburger.***
Young Man Luther: A Study in Psychoanalysis and History. New York:
Norton, 1958, 288 pp. London: Faber & Faber, 1959, 280 pp.

   Erikson's "classic" in psychoanalytic psychohistory, examining Martin Luther in terms of the developmental crises of adolescence and young
adulthood.

[1959] **939. *Brown, Norman Oliver.***
Life against Death: The Psychoanalytical Meaning of History. Middle-
town, Conn.: Wesleyan University Press, 1959, 366 pp. London: Routledge & Kegan Paul, 1959, xii+366 pp.

   Brown offers a "systematic statement, critique, and reinterpretation
of the crucial concepts in psychoanalytic theory." History is regarded as
the general neurosis of mankind which must be conquered to prevent the
specific neuroses. Pointing out the methodological affinity of psychoanalytic theory with dialectic logic, and its doctrinal affinity with the
heretical mysticism of Jacob Boehme, Brown regards psychoanalysis as
the missing link between various movements critical of the inhuman
character of human civilization. A classic in the field.

[1959] **940. *Campbell, Joseph.***
The Masks of God. Vol. 1, *Primitive Mythology.* Vol. 2, *Oriental
Mythology.* New York: Viking Press, 1959–1962. Also under the titles
The Masks of God: Primitive Mythology. London: Secker & Warburg,
1960, 504 pp. +illus. and *The Masks of God: Oriental Mythology.* Lon-
don: Secker & Warburg, 1962, 561 pp.

   In his section on the psychology of myth, Campbell states that "a
functional mythology can be defined as a corpus of culturally maintained
sign stimuli fostering the development and activation of a specific type, or
constellation of types, of human life." Volume 1 focuses on the paleolithic
and neolithic eras. Volume 2 extends these insights to oriental mythology.

[1959] **941.** *Lepp, Ignace.*

Psychoanalyse de l'Amour. Paris: Editions Bernard Grasset, 1959. ENG-LISH: *The Psychology of Loving.* Translated by Bernard B. Gilligan. Montreal: Palm Publishers; Baltimore and Dublin: Helicon Press, 1963, ix+223 pp.

From a Catholic perspective, Lepp provides what he claims may best be described as a "psychosynthesis of love." His goal in the writing of the book, which is aimed at the layperson, "is to help people to love, to help them to love in a better way, and to show them how to face up to the suffering that comes from the absence of love." He feels that *eros* is present to some degree in every form of love. He begins with a discussion of psychophysical symbiosis which is actually a critique of the androgyny myth and an affirmation of the creation of male and female. Then he discusses the choice of partner as a search for the ego's ideal, based on one's complexes. He regards platonic love as an impossible goal, often motivated by neurotic fears. The Oedipal myth is examined and discarded as a product of Freud's imagination, and a distortion of the normal parenting process. Lepp discusses the death of love and the special love of friendships, and ends with a discussion of the sublimation of love as manifested by the great religious mystics.

[1959] **942.** *Progoff, Ira.*

Depth Psychology and Modern Man: A New View of the Magnitude of Human Personality, Its Dimensions and Resources. New York: Julian Press, 1959, 277 pp.

Integrates depth psychology, the biological perspective of Edmund W. Sinnott, and observations on art by Herbert Read and Jacob Bronowski.

[1960] **943.** *Muensterberger, Warner, and Axelrad, Sidney, eds.*

The Psychoanalytic Study of Society. Vol. 1. New York: International Universities Press, 1960, 384 pp.

Two relevant chapters are "The role of the mother in the development of Hebraic monotheism: as exemplified in the life of Abraham," by Dorothy F. Zeligs, and "The development of early ethical monotheism," by Andrew Peto.

[1960] **944.** *Peseguer, Pedro.*

El secreto do los Suenos. Madrid: Editorial Fax, 1960. ENGLISH: *The Secret of Dreams.* Translated by Paul Burns. London: Burns and Oates, 1960, 232 pp.

Father Peseguer, Jesuit theologian, psychologist and international authority in the field of dream theory here explores the significance of dreams from the Old Testament to Freud and Jung. In a section on "telepathic, prophetic and mystic dreams" he includes a discussion of "history, scripture, and the Catholic tradition." His unique contribution is the incorporation of dreams into spiritual directions, focusing on the following topics: dreams as a source of temptation; the question of moral responsibility in dreams; dreams as a source of information about the state of the soul; dreams as a source of instruction and guidance; dreams as a source of energy; conditions and limitations; and the basis of a practical method of utilizing dreams in spiritual direction.

[1961] **945. *Lepp, Ignace.***

Psychoanalyse de l'atheisme moderne. Paris: Editions Bernard Grasset, 1961, 260 pp. ENGLISH: *Atheism in Our Time*. Translated by Bernard Murchland. New York: The Macmillan Company; Galt, Ontario: Collier-Macmillan Canada, Ltd., 1963, 195 pp.

Beginning with an examination of his own atheism, Lepp offers a taxonomy of atheism based on the dynamics of the individuals involved, and providing examples for each group. He discusses neurotic atheism, Marxist atheism (subdivided into the Christian apostates, intellectuals, and those who have always been atheists), rationalist atheism (Jean Rostand), existentialist atheism (Jean-Paul Sartre), atheism in the name of value (Friedrich Nietzsche, André Malraux, Albert Camus), and the unbelief of believers, who emphasize the secondary rather than primary aspects of their faith.

[1961] **946. *Schaar, John H.***

Escape from Authority: The Perspectives of Erich Fromm. New York: Basic Books, 1961, 349 pp.

This is a series of essays evaluating the contribution of Fromm to our present understanding of human conditions, noting that Fromm's basic position is that civilization crushes our deepest needs and noblest powers. Schaar notes Fromm's conviction that while society has provoked an expression of our sordid potential, there is also hope that persons can live in freedom with justice and love. He suggests that Fromm calls for freedom without loneliness, reason without rationalism, self-love without selfishness, authority without question, and religion without theology.

[1962] **947. *LaBarre, Weston.***

They Shall Take up Serpents, Psychology of the Southern Snake-Handling Cult. Minneapolis: University of Minnesota Press, 1962, 208 pp. +illus.

A detailed description of a curious example of cultic religion. LaBarre explores the symbolism involved, explaining it in psychoanalytic terms, and describes the sociology of culturally determined religion.

[1962] **948. *Zilboorg, Gregory.***

Psychoanalysis and Religion. Edited by M. S. Zilboorg. New York: Farrar, Strauss and Cudahy, 1962, 243 pp.; London: George Allen & Unwin, 1967, xi+243 pp.

Eleven essays by the well-known Catholic psychoanalyst. Zilboorg examines the relationship between psychoanalysis and religion with depth and sympathy, and sees no need for hostility between the disciplines. He asserts that "man cannot be cured of those ethicomoral and religious demands of his personality which live in him and make him what he is" and that healthy religious belief cannot be touched by psychoanalysis.

[1963] **949. *Fingarette, Herbert.***
The Self in Transformation: Psychoanalysis, Philosophy, and the Life of the Spirit. New York: Basic Books, 1963, viii+356 pp.

Psychoanalytic theory is examined in the context of the spiritual life, outlining stages in the transformation of the self to selflessness as advocated in Eastern mysticism.

[1964] **950. *Becker, Ernest.***
The Revolution in Psychiatry: The New Understanding of Man. New York: Free Press of Glencoe, 1964, xi+276 pp.

Becker presents a systematic analysis of two major psychiatric syndromes, schizophrenia and depression, within a behavioral framework. His starting point is John Dewey's transactional philosophy. He challenges Freudian thinking but incorporates certain Freudian views along with concepts from sociology, anthropology, social psychology, and psychology, as well as existentialism and phenomenology, as he develops his basic pragmatist thesis: mind subserves total organismic striving; in this universe, action is primary. Becker sees identity as resulting from the full reach of culture into the human personality, understood as both a symbolic self and behaving organism.

[1964] **951. *McLaughlin, Barry.***
Nature, Grace, and Religious Development. Westminster, Md.: Newman Press, 1964, ix+164 pp.

This Jesuit psychologist presents applications of Erikson's thought to religious life in general and to the life of the professional religious in particular.

[1964] **952. *Stern, Paul J.***
The Abnormal Person and His World: An Introduction to Psychopathology. Princeton, N.J.: Van Nostrand, 1964, xi+239 pp.

A text based on a course in abnormal psychology which the author taught for many years at Harvard Divinity School. Stern discounts laboratory research and emphasizes psychoanalytic and existential understanding, and the continuity between normality and abnormality.

[1965] **953. *Hammond, Guyton B.***
Man in Estrangement: A Comparison of the thought of Paul Tillich and Erich Fromm. Nashville: Vanderbilt University Press, 1965, xii+194 pp.

Hammond, Professor of Philosophy and Religion at Virginia Polytechnic Institute, traces the development of the idea of alienation from its inception with Friedrich Hegel through its various transformations in L. Feuerbach, Karl Marx, Sigmund Freud, and the modern existentialists. He demonstrates that the same general concept is treated by Erich Fromm in terms of psychological and social thought and by Paul Tillich in terms of a theologically oriented ontology. Foreword by Langdon Gilkey.

[1965]   **954. *Wolf, Arnold Jacob, ed.***
Rediscovering Judaism: Reflections on a New Theology. Chicago: Quadrangle Books, 1965, 288 pp.

Wolf, a rabbi at Congregation Solel in Highland Park, Illinois, describes this book as providing neoclassical answers to theological questions. Of interest is Wolf's chapter entitled "Psychoanalysis and the temperaments of man."

The Freudian Perspective

Included here are both expositions and critiques of the Freudian position.

[1913] **955. Freud, Sigmund.**
> *Totem und Tabu. Eine Ubereinstimmungen im Seelenleben der Wilden und der Neurotiker.* Leipzig and Vienna: H. Heller & Cie, 1913, 149 pp. ENGLISH: *Totem and Taboo; Resemblances between the Psychic Lives of Savages and Neurotics.* Translated by Abraham Arden Brill. New York: Moffat, Yard & Company, 1918, x+265 pp. London: G. Routledge & Sons, 1919, xii+268 pp. Also under the title *Totem and Taboo; Some Points of Agreement Between the Mental Lives of Savages and Neurotics.* Translated by James Strachey. London: Routledge & Kegan Paul, 1950, xi+172 pp. New York: Norton, 1952.
>
> These essays were first published in *Imago.* The topics discussed include the horror of incest; taboo and emotional ambivalence (parallel between taboo and obsessional neurosis, the treatment of enemies, the taboo upon rulers, the taboo upon the dead, taboo and conscience); animism, magic and omnipotence of thought; and the return of totemism in childhood (the nature of totemism, the origin of totemism, the origin of exogamy and its relation to totemism, animal phobias, sacrificial feasts, relation of totem meals to father and God, Oedipus complex and society).

[1915] **956. Freud, Sigmund.**
> *Zeitgemässes über Krieg und Tod.* Leipzig: Internationaler psychoanaly-tischer Verlag, 1915, 34 pp. ENGLISH: *Reflections on War and Death.* Translated by Abraham Arden Brill and Alfred B. Kuttner. New York: Moffat, Yard & Company, 1918, 72 pp.

In these essays Freud addresses the instinctual impulses that lie at the root of war and the attitudes toward death that impoverish life, thus giving his perspective on the problem of suffering.

[1926]   **957. Malinowski, Bronislaw.**
Myth in Primitive Psychology. London: Kegan Paul, Trench, Trubner & Co., 1926, 128 pp. New York: W. W. Norton, 1926, 94 pp. Reprint. Westport, Conn.: Negro Universities Press, 1971, 94 pp.
Critiques Freud's Oedipal theory of myth on the basis of anthropological evidence.

[1926]   **958. Moxon, Cavendish.**
Freudian Essays on Religion and Science. Boston: R. A. Badger, Gorman Press, 1926, 133 pp.
These are reprints of articles previously printed in various psychoanalytic journals, only four of which are directly related to the questions of religion. They reflect the traditional Freudian view that religion is a creation of projection by the mind.

[1927]   **959. Freud, Sigmund.**
Die Zukunft einer Illusion. Leipzig, Vienna, and Zurich: Internationaler psychoanalytischer Verlag, 1927, 91 pp. ENGLISH: The Future of an Illusion. Translated by W. D. Robson-Scott. London: L. & Virginia Woolf at the Hogarth Press and the Institute of Psychoanalysis, 1928, v+98 pp. New York: Liveright Publishing Corp., 1928, 98 pp.
Religious ideas are born of the need to make tolerable man's helplessness in his environment and are conceived in man's memories of his own personal childhood and that of the human race. They owe their vitality to mankind's hostility to culture and the instinctual renunciation it demands.

[1930]   **960. Money-Kyrle, Roger Ernie.**
The Meaning of Sacrifice. London: L. & Virginia Woolf and the Institute of Psychoanalysis, 1930, 273 pp.
A Ph.D. dissertation for the University of London. Money-Kyrle analyzes religious sacrifice according to Freudian theory, with a special emphasis on the Oedipus Complex.

[1939]   **961. Freud, Sigmund.**
Der Mann Moses und die monotheistische Religion: drei Abhandlungen. Amsterdam: A. DeLange, 1939, 241 pp. ENGLISH: Moses and Monotheism. Translated by Katherine Jones. New York: Alfred A. Knopf, 1939, v+218+vi pp.
The developmental model of the neuroses is: early trauma, defense, latency, outbreak of the neurosis, partial return of the repressed. This model, Freud held, is applicable to the phylogenetic development of religion. Totem and Taboo documents the aboriginal phases, Moses and Monotheism the later, more highly developed and refined phases of this

ever-repeated sequence, from the rise of a Hebrew monotheistic father-religion to the modification introduced by the Christian father-and-son religion. Parts 1 and 2 were published in Germany in *Imago* in 1937.

[1945] **962. *Flugel, John Carl.***

Man, Morals and Society: A Psychoanalytical Study. London: Duckworth; New York: International Universities Press, 1945, 328 pp.

Discusses the origins and vagaries of the ego-ideal, nemesism and asceticism, sadomasochism, the super-ego, the taboo, punishment (the Polycrates complex and "hubris"), and guilt.

[1949] **963. *Blanco White, Amber Reeves.***

Ethics for Unbelievers. London: Routledge & Kegan Paul, 1949, vi+222 pp.

An exposition of the Freudian view of conscience and guilt.

[1949] **964. *Lee, Roy Stuart.***

Freud and Christianity. New York: A. A. Wyn, 1949, 204 pp.

Lee examines maldevelopments leading to fixation and repression, and their expression in Christian belief and conduct. Themes explored include the dynamic tension between life and death, the role of the church as mother and God as father (in both their healthy and unhealthy aspects), the development of conscience and moral obligation.

[1956] **965. *Dempsey, Peter J. R.***

Freud, Psychoanalysis, Catholicism. Cork, Ireland: The Mercier Press, 1956, x+209 pp. Chicago: H. Regnery Co., 1956, 209 pp.

Dempsey was Lecturer in Psychology at University College, Cork, Ireland. Acknowledging his indebtedness to the works of Roland Dalbiez, Rudolf Allers, Josef Nuttin, and Maryse Choisy, Dempsey wrote this volume to be a supplement to their earlier works. He states that he is "convinced, absolutely, of the truth of Catholicism, convinced too that between faith and reason, between Revelation, rightly interpreted and authentic science, no real ultimate conflict is possible. . . . " Furthermore, Dempsey writes that he "believes that the Catholic mind can benefit from any facts or truths that have been unearthed by analysis and that analysis can draw profit from the age-old wisdom of the Catholic Church." Dempsey's overview of psychoanalytic theory follows a section on "integration and perspective in psychology" and "Freud and religion," and is applied to psychology and literature.

[1956] **966. *Philp, Howard Littleton.***

Freud and Religious Belief. London: Rockliff; New York: Pitman, 1956, 140 pp.

Philp claims that Freud's case against religion in general was unsound, and reflected his own opinions rather than the findings of psychoanalysis. This assertion is supported in an analysis and critique of Freud's writings on religion.

[1958] **967. Bakan, David.**
Sigmund Freud and the Jewish Mystical Tradition. Princeton, N.J.: Van Nostrand, 1958, 326 pp.

Freud's works are interpreted as rooted in the medieval Kabbala, the Zohar, and Hasidism, and as borrowing the Moses theme and that of the Devil from the mystical tradition.

[1958] **968. Zilboorg, Gregory.**
Freud and Religion: A Restatement of an Old Controversy. Westminster, Md.: Newman Press, 1958, 65 pp. London: Geoffrey Chapman, 1958, v+65 pp.

Zilboorg was Professor of Pastoral Psychopathology at Woodstock College. In contrast with Freud, Zilboorg was himself religious (more so toward the end of his life) and affirmed the cultural value of religion even though he felt religion lacked "scholarship." These essays in Woodstock's *Occasional Essays in Theology* were previously published articles detailing his contention that psychoanalysis' chief conflict with religion is its threat (through the unconscious) to free will and immortality. Here he calls for keeping analytic and theological concepts separate.

[1959] **969. Guirdham, Arthur.**
Christ and Freud: A Study of Religious Experience and Observance. London: George Allen & Unwin, 1959, 193 pp.+adv.

Freud's theory of religion as neurosis is rejected because it is based on the limited, patriarchal Judeo-Christian theology, which is especially conducive to the induction of neurosis. The exclusivist orientation of Christianity is also rejected. Individualism must be replaced by self-surrender. Cooperation between doctor and priest is encouraged.

[1963] **970. Clouzet, Maryse (Choisy).**
Sigmund Freud: A New Appraisal. New York: Citadel Press; London: P. Owen, 1963, 141 pp.

Clouzet asserts that Freud cut himself off from the Hasidic tradition and that this rejection is responsible for his unbalanced view of man.

[1963] **971. Freud, Sigmund, and Pfister, Oskar.**
Psychoanalysis and Faith: The Letters of Sigmund Freud and Oskar Pfister. Translated by Eric Mosbacher. Edited by Heinrich Meng and Ernst L. Freud. London: Hogarth Press; New York: Basic Books, 1963, 152 pp.

The record of a long, cooperative, and stimulating friendship (1909–1937) between Freud and Pfister, a Reformed Church pastor in Zurich who was also a leader in the Swiss Analytic Society. Pfister to a large extent regarded psychoanalysis as a rediscovery of the traditional "cure of souls," and regarded his practice as part of his pastoral work. In contrast to Freud, Pfister felt that the Judeo-Christian religious experience offered freedom from neuroses, that the need for trust was not confined to the realm of religion, and asserted that ". . . the world of spiritual order . . . stands more securely . . . than the whole deceptive world of the senses."

[1964] **972. *Masih, Y.***

Freudianism and Religion. Calcutta: Thacker Spink, 1964, x+356 pp.

An overview of Freudian psychology and metapsychology, with a critique of Freud's analysis of religion.

[1965] **973. *Grollman, Earl A.***

Judaism in Sigmund Freud's World. New York: Appleton-Century, 1965; New York: Block Publishing Co., 1966, xxv+173 pp.

This volume attempts to summarize the teachings of Freud in the Jewish setting of this time. Freud was a Jewish "unbeliever" who suffered from anti-Semitism all his life. Grollman explores the extent to which psychoanalysis was a Jewish product. Freud's Jewishness freed him from many prejudices and prepared him to enter a world of opposition. The foreword is by Nathan W. Ackerman.

The Jungian Perspective

Included here are both expositions and critiques of the Jungian position as well as later works in the neo-Jungian tradition.

[1931] **974. Jung, Carl Gustav.**
Seelenprobleme der Gegenwart. (Psychologische Abhandlungen Vol. 3.) Zurich: Rascher & Cie, 1931, vii+435 pp. ENGLISH: *Modern Man in Search of a Soul.* Translated by W. S. Dell and Cary F. Baynes. New York: Harcourt, Brace & Co., 1933, ix+282 pp. London: Kegan Paul, Trench, Trubner & Co., 1933, ix+282 pp.

In the English edition is contained Jung's essay on "Psychotherapists or the clergy—a dilemma" in which is made the oft-quoted assertion that "Among all my patients in the second half of life . . . there has not been one whose problem in the last resort was not that of finding a religious outlook on life." Other essays deal more broadly with the spiritual implications of man's journey into the unconscious.

[1938] **975. Jung, Carl Gustav.**
Psychology and Religion. London: Oxford University Press, H. Milford; New Haven: Yale University Press, 1938, 131 pp. Revised and augmented edition. *Psychologie und Religion. Die Terry Lectures 1937 gehalten an der Yale University.* Zurich and Leipzig: Rascher Verlag, 1940, 192 pp. Translated from revised, augmented edition by R.F.C. Hull.

The Terry lectures for 1937, including "The autonomy of the unconscious mind," "Dogma and natural symbols," and "The history and psychology of a natural symbol." With a focus on one lengthy dream series,

Jung illustrates the concepts of the archetype, quaternity, mandala, and related ideas. Jung states that his observations are not proof of the existence of God, "they prove only the existence of an archetypal image of the Deity, which to my mind is the most we can assert psychologically about God."

[1940] **976. *Baynes, Helton Godwin.***

Mythology of the Soul: A Research into the Unconscious from Schizo-phrenic Dreams and Drawings. Baltimore: Williams & Wilkins, 1940, xii+939 pp. London: Balliere, Tindall and Cox, 1940, xii+939 pp. +illus.

Baynes utilizes the "introverted technique" of Carl Gustav Jung and depicts schizophrenics as those who have lost touch with their origins, as did the Prodigal son in the Bible. He sees healing as the regaining of one's myth and presents case material to illustrate his theory of religion, i.e., tying together the conscious and the unconscious.

[1946] **977. *Goldbrunner, Josef.***

Heiligkeit und Gesundheit, ein Vortrag. Freiburg: Herder, 1946, 61+ 3 pp. ENGLISH: *Holiness is Wholeness.* Translated by Stanley Goodman. New York: Pantheon Books, 1955, 63 pp.

Here, Goldbrunner deals with the issues of health and illness, body and psyche.

[1946] **978. *Schaer, Hans.***

Religion und Seele in der Psychologie C. G. Jungs. Zurich: Rascher Verlag, 1946, 273 pp. *Religion and the Cure of Souls in Jung's Psychology.* Translated by R.F.C. Hull. New York: Pantheon Books, 1950, 222 pp. Bollingen Series Vol. 21.

An overview of Jung's psychology of religion. Schaer notes his affinity with Hermann Ludemann, Friedrich Schleiermacher, and Kurt Leese in his emphasis on the problem of nature and the experience of God. He also notes Jung's affinities with the "life-philosophers" Friedrich Schelling, Jakob Boehme, Max Ferdinand Scheler, Ludwig Klages, and Carl Gustav Carus. Similarities with Albert Schweitzer and Hans Overbeck are also noted. Schaer emphasizes the Jungian hermeneutic principle that all dogma and religious attitudes are psychic realities that can be understood psychologically.

[1946] **979. *Witcutt, William Purcell.***

Blake, A Psychological Study. London: Hollis & Carter, 1946, 127 pp.

Witcutt subjects the works of William Blake to a Jungian analysis, asserting that "in exploring the mythological world of Blake, we are really exploring our own minds." Of Blake's descent into the unconscious, he states, that "Many others . . . have descended into the unconscious as far as Blake, but they have not returned. The asylums are full of them; . . . Blake is the only one who has ventured as far as they and yet remained sane." Applying the Jungian typology, he describes Blake as an intuitive (or bigoted) introvert: "He regarded Nature as having no real existence, as but a reflection of the eternal symbols of the imagination." Blake fell prey to the heresy of identifying religion with the imagination, or the collective unconscious—a temptation common to all Jungians. The four Jungian functions are reflected in Blake's Four Zoas, each of which was accompanied by a Spectre (shadow) and an Emanation (anima). Thus, Blake's epics "deal with nothing less than the story of the soul, its disintegration through sin and ultimate reintegration." In examining Blake's theory of disintegration, Witcutt asserts that "Sin causes the disorientation of all the powers of the soul; they shift and turn the wrong way about like a group of iron filings when the magnet is moved from its former position." From the Catholic perspective, Blake is regarded as a material heretic, whose position was inspired primarily by Emanuel Swedenborg, and constituted a revolt against the Old Testament emphasis of eighteenth-century Calvinism. Comparing Blake's work to that of the other Romantic poets in terms of Jung's typology, Witcutt classifies Blake and Percy Bysshe Shelly as "introverted intuition," William Wordsworth as "introverted sensation," and John Keats as "extraverted sensation."

[1949] **980. Campbell, Joseph.**

The Hero with a Thousand Faces. New York: Pantheon Books, 1949, xxiii+416 pp.+illus. Reprint. Princeton: Princeton University Press, 1968, xxiii+416 pp.+illus. Bollingen Series Vol. 17.

Campbell analyzes the adventure of the hero in the Jungian style, drawing from many religious and folkloric traditions, and considering the "cosmogonic cycle" using the life histories of deities and demigods as a type for man's psychological development. He states in the preface, "It is the purpose of the present book to uncover some of the truths disguised for us under the figures of religion and mythology by bringing together a multitude of not-too-difficult examples and letting the ancient meaning become apparent of itself."

[1949] **981. Goldbrunner, Josef.**

Individuation: Die Tiefenpsychologie von Carl Gustav Jung. Munich: E. Wewel, 1949, 212 pp. ENGLISH: *Individuation: A Study of the Depth Psychology of Carl Gustav Jung.* Translated by Stanley Godman. London: Hollis and Carter, 1955, viii+204 pp.+illus. Notre Dame, Ind.: University of Notre Dame Press, 1964, xii+204 pp.

Jungian psychology examined in its continuity with personality development and theological conceptions of the healthy personality. The Jungian concepts can give the priest a psychological revival in himself, a first-hand knowledge of spiritual process and of the relationships between the various powers within the soul and their polarities. Psychology is an important adjunct to spiritual direction because most modern men and women must make religious decisions in the solitude of self-discovery.

[1949] **982. Neumann, Erich.**

Ursprungsgeschichte des Bewusstseins. Zurich: Rascher Verlag, 1949, xii+546 pp. ENGLISH: *The Origins and History of Consciousness.* Translated by R.F.C. Hull. New York: Pantheon Books, 1954, xxiv+ 493 pp. Princeton: Princeton University Press, 1954, xxiv+495 pp. Bollingen Series Volume 42.

Through the interpretation of mythologems, Neumann describes the passage of individual consciousness through the archetypal stages that have marked the history of human consciousness. An excellent work in the Jungian tradition. Foreword by Carl Gustav Jung.

[1949] **983. Neumann, Erich.**

Tiefenpsychologie und neue Ethik. Zurich: Rascher Verlag, 1949, 128 pp. ENGLISH: *Depth Psychology and a New Ethic.* Translated by Eugene Rolfe. London: Hodder & Stoughton, 1969, 158 pp. New York: G. P. Putnam's Sons, for the C. G. Jung Foundation for Analytical Psychology, 1969, 158 pp.

In reaction to the Holocaust, Neumann argues that the old Judeo-Christian ethic is inadequate for contemporary culture. The problem of evil is analyzed from a Jungian perspective, focusing on the compensatory significance of the shadow in light of ethical responsibility and the need for both individual and collective to come to terms with the shadow side. Foreword by Carl Gustav Jung.

[1952] **984. Corbin, Harry Henry.**

Avicenne et le récit visionnaire. 2 vols. Teheran: Département d'iranologie de l'Institut Franco-iranien, 1952. ENGLISH: *Avicenna and the Visionary Recital.* Translated by William R. Trask. New York: Pantheon Books, 1954, xiii+423 pp. Bollingen Series Vol. 66.

Corbin's book takes the reader into the borderlands of symbolism, depth psychology, agnosticism, and the history of religion. Included are translations of three parables by Avicenna, the 11th-century Arabian physician—scholar, along with commentary and explanatory chapters.

[1952] **985. Jung, Carl Gustav.**

Antwort auf Hiob. Zurich: Rascher, 1952, 169 pp. ENGLISH: *Answer to Job.* Translated by R.F.C. Hull. London: Routledge & Paul, 1954, xviii+194 pp. New York: Pastoral Psychology Book Club, 1955, xviii+ 194 pp. New York: Meridian Books, 1960, 223 pp. Also included in *Psychology and Religion: West and East (see* entry number 993), Vol. 11 of the *Collected Works of C. G. Jung.* New York: Pantheon Books, 1958. Bollingen Series, Vol. 20. Reprint. Princeton: Princeton University Press, 1969, xv+121 pp.

Gerhard Adler, in his introduction to the Princeton edition, states that *Answer to Job* was Jung's attempt "from intense personal experience, to make his peace with this ambivalent God who could allow his faithful servant Job to become the object of a wager with Satan and permit the untold sufferings of millions in Jung's own time." Jung's basic assertion is that every good is balanced by a corresponding evil. Thus, the Old Testament God encounters the evil within himself in the book of Job; and the New Testament Christ faces the anti-Christ in himself in the book of Revelation. The book comprises Jung's theory of the psychological and theological origins of evil, and is probably the most controversial of all Jung's writings.

[1952] **986. Neumann, Erich.**

Apuleius Madaurensis: Amor und Psyche. Mit einem Kommentar von Erich Neumann. Ein Beitrag zur seelischen Entwicklung des Weiblichen. Zurich: Rascher Verlag, 1952, 217 pp. +illus. ENGLISH: *Amor and Psyche: The Psychic Development of the Feminine. A Commentary on the Tale by Apuleius.* Translated by Ralph Manheim. London: Routledge & Kegan Paul, 1956, 181 pp. New York: Pantheon Books, 1956, 181 pp. + illus. Bollingen Series Vol. 54.

Neumann's book includes translation of the myth and a Jungian interpretation of the archetypal themes.

[1952] **987. White, Victor Francis.**

God and the Unconscious. Cleveland: World, 1952, 287 pp. London: Harvill Press, 1952, 277 pp. Chicago: H. Regnery Co., 1953, xxv + 277 pp.

A collection of essays by a Jungian Catholic theologian, with a foreword by Carl Gustav Jung. White regarded his work as complementary to that of Hans Schaer and Josef Goldbrunner. The book includes translation of an essay by Gebhart Frei, "The method and teaching of C. G. Jung."

[1953] **988. Progoff, Ira.**

Jung's Psychology and Its Social Meaning: An Introductory Statement of C. G. Jung's Psychological Theories and a First Interpretation of Their Significance for the Social Sciences. London: Routledge & Kegan Paul, 1953, 295 pp. New York: Julian Press, 1953, 299 pp. New York: Grove Press, 1953, xviii + 299 pp. + adv.

An overview of Jung's work, with a summary of the contributions of Heinrich Zimmer and Carl Kerenyi, applying Jungian analysis to the myths of Greece and pre-Christian western Europe.

[1954] **989. Goldbrunner, Josef.**

Personale Seelsorge; Tiefenpsychologie und Seelsorge. Freiburg: Herder, 1954, vi + 135 pp. ENGLISH: *Cure of Mind and Cure of Soul.* Translated by Stanley Godmann. New York: Pantheon Books; London: Burns & Oates, 1958, 127 pp.

A broad synthesis of Jungian psychology and existentialism applied to the priestly task.

[1954] **990.** *Hostie, Raymond.*

Analytische psychologie en Godsdienst. Utrecht: Het Spectrum, 1954, 260 pp. ENGLISH: *Religion and the Psychology of Jung.* Translated by G. R. Lamb. London and New York: Sheed and Ward, 1957, vi+249 pp.

A Louvain scholar's expository and critical discussion of Jung's work on religious attitudes, individuation, and dogma. Hostie's major criticism of Jung is that while his theory is limited to the structure of the psyche, his practice is related to the whole man, forcing him to deal with the bonds that connect man with everything above and beyond the psyche.

[1957] **991.** *Jacobi, Jolande.*

Komplex, Archetypus, Symbol in der Psychologie C. G. Jungs. Zurich and Stuttgart: Rascher Verlag, 1957, xi+223 pp. +illus. ENGLISH: *Complex, Archetype, Symbol in the Psychology of C. G. Jung.* Translated by Ralph Manheim. New York: Pantheon Books, 1959, xii+ 236 pp. +illus. London: Routledge & Kegan Paul, 1959, xii+236 pp. Bollingen Series Vol. 57.

Jacobi here illuminates these three constructs in the hope of clearing up misunderstandings and misrepresentations.

[1958] **992.** *Jung, Carl Gustav.*

Ein moderner Mythus: von Dingen, die am Himmel gesehen werden. Zurich: Rascher Verlag, 1958, 122 pp. +illus. ENGLISH: *Flying Saucers. A Modern Myth of Things Seen in the Skies.* Translated by R.F.C. Hull. New York: Harcourt, Brace & Co., 1959, 186 pp. +illus. London: Routledge & Kegan Paul, 1959, 184 pp. +illus.

In his understanding of the psychological meaning of flying saucers, Jung concentrates on collective fantasies of hope for deliverance from a terror-ridden terrestrial epoch by a power or powers from "beyond."

[1958] **993.** *Jung, Carl Gustav.*

Zur Psychologie westlicher und hostlicher Religion, 1958. ENGLISH: *Psychology and Religion: West and East.* Translated by R.F.C. Hull. New York: Pantheon Books, 1958, xiii+699 pp. +adv. London: Routledge & Kegan Paul, 1959, xiii+699 pp.

Sixteen studies in religious phenomena, including "Psychology and Religion," and "Answer to Job."

[1958] **994.** *Philp, Howard Littleton.*

Jung and the Problem of Evil. London: Rockliff, 1958, xiii+271 pp. New York: Robert M. McBride, 1959, 271 pp.

This volume grew out of Jung's answers to five questions on religion and psychology posed by Philp. A critique of Jung's understanding of evil as seen in *Answer to Job,* the book is a sequel to Philp's earlier *Freud and Religious Belief.* He concludes that the Freudian and Jungian critiques of religion are not as convincing as they once were.

[1960] **995. *Rudin, Josef.***

Psychotherapie und Religion; Seele-Person-Gott. Olten and Freiburg;
Walter Verlag, 1960, 230 pp. ENGLISH: *Psychotherapy and Religion.*
Translated by Elisabeth Reinecke and Paul C. Bailey. Notre Dame and
London: University of Notre Dame Press, 1968, xiii+244 pp.

Rudin describes forms of soul anxiety manifested in the fear of
psychology, resistance, fixation, and various kinds of escape. He also
develops a typology of neuroticized God-images and discusses religious
and psychotherapeutic experiences from a theological perspective. Although his orientation is essentially Jungian, Rudin includes a critique of
Answer to Job.

[1962] **996. *Jung, Carl Gustav.***

*Erinnerungen Träume Gedanken. Aufgezeichnet und hrsg. von Aniela
Jaffé.* Zurich: Rascher, 1962, 422 pp.+illus. ENGLISH: *Memories,
Dreams, Reflections. Recorded and edited by Aniela Jaffé.* Translated by
Richard Winston and Clara Winston. New York: Pantheon Books, 1963,
398 pp. London: Collins and Routledge & Kegan Paul, 1963, 383 pp.+
illus.

Jung's autobiographical reflections. According to Jaffé, "this book is
the only place in his extensive writings that Jung speaks of God and his
personal experience of God."

[1963] **997. *Progoff, Ira.***

*The Symbolic and the Real: A New Psychological Approach to the
Fuller Experience of Personal Existence.* New York: Julian Press, 1963,
234 pp.

The symbolic here refers to the elemental symbols which reflect in
the person the primary processes of the universe. For Jung's unconscious,
Progoff substitutes the *psyche:* the principle which guides the development of the individual in unfolding a meaningful life from the seed of
potentiality. He insists that we must expect new breakthroughs in the
form and content of the life of the spirit.

[1964] **998. *Campbell, Joseph, ed.***

Man and Transformation. Translated by R. Manheim. New York: Pantheon Books, 1964, xviii+413 pp.

Papers from the *Eranos* yearbooks, resulting from roundtable dis-
cussions sponsored by Olga-Kapteyn and C. G. Jung. Contributors are
Mircea Eliade, Fritz Meier, Henry Corbin, Paul Tillich, Daisetz Suzuki,
Ernst Benz, Lancelot Whyte, Jean Danielou, Adolf Portmann, Heinrich
Zimmer, and Gerardus van der Leeuw. Topics include comparative
religion, mysticism, theology, history of ideas, and animal biology.

[1964] **999. Hillman, James.**

Suicide and the Soul. New York: Harper & Row, 1964, 191 pp.

From the perspective of depth psychology and analysis, suicide constitutes an attempt to move from one realm of the psyche to another through the force of death. Such an urge for hasty transformation involves confusion of the inner and outer worlds. Hillman discusses implications for therapeutic intervention with suicidal patients.

[1965] **1000. Jacobi, Jolande.**

Der Weg zur Individuation. Zurich: Rascher & Cie, 1965, 160 pp.
ENGLISH: *The Way of Individuation.* Translated by R.F.C. Hull. New York: Harcourt, Brace & World, 1967, xi+167 pp.

A deeply moving personal account by a psychotherapist, including an extensive and sensitive discussion of the function of religion. The book is richly documented with footnotes and includes a biography of the author by David Holt.

PART SEVEN

The Professionalization
of Psychotheology

Special Book Series

Listed here are book series devoted especially to integrative topics as well as those which contain a large number of relevant titles. Individual titles are not annotated in this section.

[1888] **1001. *The Gifford Lectures.***

Adam Gifford, Lord Gifford, a jurist with literary and philosophical interests, left £80,000 for a lectureship in natural theology which was begun in 1888; £25,000 went to Edinburgh, £20,000 each to Glasgow and Aberdeen, and £15,000 to St. Andrews, with the lectureships rotating through the four universities. The lecturers might be of any, or no, religion, with complete freedom, as long as they dealt with natural theology as a strictly natural science. Karl Barth, who was an avowed opponent of natural theology, at first declined the invitation to the lectureship. Eventually he accepted the invitation, resolving his conflict by attacking natural theology and offering in its place a theology of revelation. This latter tension, as well as much of the other material in the lecture series, is highly relevant to the integration of theology and psychology. Furthermore, the list of lecturers in this series includes nearly every prominent theologian of the late nineteenth and twentieth centuries. The titles are presented here in order of publication; the place and date of the original lecture are bracketed following the bibliographic information.

1001.01 *Müller, Friedrich Max.*

[1889] *Natural Religion*. London and New York: Longmans, Green & Co., 1889, xix+608 pp. [Glasgow, 1888.]

7. PROFESSIONALIZATION

1001.02 Stirling, James Hutchison.

[1890] *Philosophy and Theology*. Edinburgh: T & T Clark, 1890, xvi+407 pp. [Edinburgh, 1888–1889.]

1001.03 Müller, Friedrich Max.

[1891] *Physical Religion*. London and New York: Longmans, Green & Co., 1891, xii+410 pp. Reprint. New York: AMS Press, 1975, xii+410 pp. [Glasgow, 1890.]

1001.04 Stokes, Sir George Gabriel.

[1891] *Natural Theology*. London and Edinburgh: A. and C. Black, 1891, viii+272 pp. [Edinburgh, 1891.]

1001.05 Müller, Friedrich Max.

[1892] *Anthropological Religion*. London and New York: Longmans, Green & Co., 1892, xxvii+464 pp. [Glasgow, 1891.]

1001.06 Caird, Edward.

[1893] *The Evolution of Religion*. 2 vols. Glasgow: J. MacLehose and Sons, 1893, xv+400 pp., vii+325 pp. New York: Macmillan Co., 1893. [St. Andrews, 1890–1891.]

1001.07 Müller, Friedrich Max.

[1893] *Theosophy; or, Psychological Religion*. London and New York: Longman's Green & Co., 1893, xxiii+585 pp. [Glasgow, 1892.]

1001.08 Pfleiderer, Otto.

[1894] *Philosophy and Development of Religion*. 2 vols. Edinburgh and London: Blackwood & Sons, 1894, 333 pp., 356 pp. [Edinburgh, 1894.]

1001.09 Fraser, Alexander Campbell.

[1895] *Philosophy of Theism*. 2 vols. Edinburgh: W. Blackwood, 1895–1896, 303 pp. [Edinburgh, 1895–1896.]

1001.10 Bruce, Alexander Balmain.

[1897] *The Providential Order of the World*. London: Hodder & Stoughton, 1897, viii+391 pp. New York: C. Scribner's Sons, 1897, viii+346 pp. [Glasgow, 1897.]

1001.11 Bruce, Alexander Balmain.

[1899] *The Moral Order of the World in Ancient and Modern Thought*. London: Hodder & Stoughton, 1899, viii+431 pp. New York: Charles Scribner's Sons, 1899, viii+431 pp. [Glasgow, 1898.]

1001.12 Caird, John.

[1899] *The Fundamental Ideas of Christianity*. 2 vols. Glasgow: J. MacLehose, 1899, xcli+232 pp., vii+297 pp. [St. Andrews, 1892–1893.]

1001.13 Royce, Josiah.

[1900] *The World and the Individual*. 2 vols. New York: Macmillan Co., 1900–1901. [Aberdeen, 1899.]

1001.14 Fairbairn, Andrew Martin.

[1902] Unpublished. Incorporated into: *The Philosophy of the Christian Religion*. New York: Macmillan Co.; London: Macmillan & Co., 1902, xxviii+583 pp. [Aberdeen, 1891–1892.]

Special Book Series

1001.15 James, William.

[1902] *The Varieties of Religious Experience; A Study in Human Nature.* New York and London: Longmans, Green & Co., 1902, xii+534 pp. *See* entry number 400. [Edinburgh, 1901–1902.]

1001.16 Sayce, Archibald Henry.

[1902] *The Religions of Ancient Egypt and Babylonia.* Edinburgh: T & T Clark, 1902, vii+509 pp. [Aberdeen, 1902.]

1001.17 Caird, Edward.

[1904] *The Evolution of Theology in the Greek Philosophers.* 2 vols. Glasgow: J. MacLehose and Sons, 1904, xvii+382 pp., xi+377 pp. [Glasgow, 1900–1902.]

1001.18 Gwatkin, Henry Melvill.

[1906] *The Knowledge of God and Its Historical Development.* 2 vols. Edinburgh: T & T Clark, 1906, xi+308 pp., 334 pp. [Edinburgh, 1905.]

1001.19 Adam, James.

[1908] *The Religious Teachers of Greece.* Edited by Adele Marion Adam. Aberdeen: Printed for the University, 1908, xix+iv+467 pp. Edinburgh: T & T Clark, 1908, xix+iv+467 pp. [Aberdeen, 1904–1906.]

1001.20 Fowler, William Ward.

[1911] *The Religious Experience of the Roman People from the Earliest Times to the Age of Augustus.* London: Macmillan & Co., 1911, xviii+504 pp. [Edinburgh, 1909–1910.]

1001.21 Ward, James.

[1911] *The Realm of Ends; Or, Pluralism and Theism.* Cambridge: Cambridge University Press, 1911, xv+490 pp. New York: Putnam, 1911, xv+490 pp. [St. Andrews, 1907–1910.]

1001.22 Bosanquet, Bernard.

[1912] *The Principle of Individuality and Value.* London: Macmillan & Co., 1912, xxxvii+409 pp. [Edinburgh, 1911.] *See* entry number 86.

1001.23 Bosanquet, Bernard.

[1913] *The Value and Destiny of the Individual.* London: Macmillan & Co., 1913, xxxii+331 pp. [Edinburgh, 1912.] *See* entry number 87.

1001.24 Balfour, Arthur James Balfour.

[1915] *Theism and Humanism.* London: Hodder & Stoughton; New York: G. H. Doran, 1915, xv+274 pp. George H. Doran, 1915, xv+274 pp. [Glasgow, 1914.]

1001.25 Seth Pringle-Pattison, Andrew.

[1917] *The Idea of God in the Light of Recent Philosophy.* Aberdeen: For the University, 1917, xvi+423 pp. London and New York: Oxford University Press, H. Milford, 1917, xvi+443 pp. Oxford: Clarendon Press, 1917, xvi+423 pp. [Aberdeen, 1912–1913.]

1001.26 Inge, William Ralph.

[1918] *The Philosophy of Plotinus.* 2 vols. London and New York: Longmans, Green & Co., 1918. [St. Andrews, 1917–1918.]

7. PROFESSIONALIZATION

1001.27 Sorley, William Ritchie.

[1918] *Moral Values and the Idea of God.* Cambridge: Cambridge University Press, 1918, xix+534 pp. [Aberdeen, 1914−1915.]

1001.28 Webb, Clement Charles Julius.

[1918] *God and Personality.* London: George Allen & Unwin; New York: Macmillan Co., 1918, 281 pp. [Aberdeen, 1918−1919.]

1001.29 Thomson, Sir John Arthur.

[1920] *The System of Animate Nature.* 2 vols. London: Williams & Norgate, 1920; New York: Holt & Co., 1920, xi+347 pp., v+353 pp. [St. Andrews, 1915−1916.]

1001.30 Webb, Clement Charles Julius.

[1920] *Divine Personality and Human Life.* London: George Allen & Unwin; New York: Macmillan Co., 1920, 291 pp. [Aberdeen, 1918−1919.]

1001.31 Farnell, Lewis Richard.

[1921] *Greek Hero Cults and Ideas of Immortality.* Oxford: Clarendon Press, 1921, xv+434 pp. [St. Andrews, 1920.]

1001.32 Jones, Henry.

[1922] *A Faith that Enquires.* London: Macmillan & Co., 1922, 361 pp. New York: Macmillan Co., 1922, x+278 pp. [Glasgow, 1920−1921.]

1001.33 Seth Pringle-Pattison, Andrew.

[1922] *The Idea of Immortality.* Oxford: Clarendon Press, 1922, xii+210 pp. [Edinburgh, 1922.]

1001.34 Balfour, Arthur James Balfour.

[1923] *Theism and Thought: A Study in Familiar Beliefs.* London: Hodder & Stoughton, 1923, xii+270 pp. New York: George H. Doran, 1924, xii+15+283 pp. [Glasgow, 1922−1923.]

1001.35 Hobson, Ernest William.

[1923] *The Domain of Natural Science.* Aberdeen: University; Cambridge, England: University Press, 1923, xvi+510 pp. [Aberdeen, 1921−1922.]

1001.36 Morgan, Conway Lloyd.

[1923] *Emergent Evolution.* London: Williams & Norgate, New York: H. Holt & Co., 1923, xii+313 pp. [St. Andrews, 1922.]

1001.37 Farnell, Lewis Richard.

[1925] *The Attributes of God.* Oxford: Clarendon Press, 1925, x+283 pp. [St. Andrews, 1924−1925.]

1001.38 Morgan, Conway Lloyd.

[1926] *Life, Mind and Spirit.* London: Williams & Norgate, 1926; New York: H. Holt and Co., 1925, xix+316 pp. [St. Andrews, 1923.] *See* entry number 65.

1001.39 Paterson, William Paterson.

[1926] *The Nature of Religion.* New York: George H. Doran 1926, 508 pp. London: Hodder & Stoughton, 1925?, xii+508 pp. [Glasgow, 1924−1925.]

1001.40 Frazer, Sir James George.

[1926] *The Worship of Nature.* Vol. 1. London: Macmillan & Co.; New York: Macmillan Co., 1926, xxvi+672 pp. [Edinburgh, 1924–1925.]

1001.41 Ramsey, Sir William Mitchell.

[1927] *Asianic Elements in Greek Civilization.* London: J. Murray, 1927, xi+303 pp. [Edinburgh, 1915–1916.]

1001.42 Eddington, Sir Arthur Stanley.

[1928] *The Nature of the Physical World.* Cambridge, England: University Press, 1928, xix+361 pp. New York: Macmillan Co., 1928, xvii+361 pp. [Edinburgh, 1927.]

1001.43 Haldane, John Scott.

[1928] *The Sciences and Philosophy.* London: Hodder & Stoughton, 1928, ix+334 pp. Garden City, N.Y.: Doubleday, Doran and Company, Inc., 1929, x+330 pp. [Glasgow, 1927.]

1001.44 Dewey, John.

[1929] *The Quest for Certainty: A Study of the Relation of Knowledge and Action.* New York: Minton, Balch, and Co., 1929, 4+318 pp. London: George Allen and Unwin, 1930, 302 pp. [Location uncertain, 1929.]

1001.45 Whitehead, Alfred North.

[1929] *Process and Reality: An Essay in Cosmology.* Cambridge, England: University Press; New York: Macmillan Co., 1929, xii+547 pp. [Edinburgh, 1927–1928.]

1001.46 Gore, Charles.

[1930] *The Philosophy of the Good Life.* London: J. Murray, 1930, xiii+346 pp. New York: Charles Scribner's Sons, 1930, 346 pp. [St. Andrews, 1929–1930.]

1001.47 Seth Pringle-Pattison, Andrew.

[1930] *Studies in the Philosophy of Religion.* Oxford: Clarendon Press, 1930, vi+256 pp. [Edinburgh, 1923.]

1001.48 Taylor, Alfred Edward.

[1930] *The Faith of a Moralist.* 2 vols. London: Macmillan & Co., 1930, xxii+437 pp., xx+437 pp. [St. Andrews, 1926–1928.]

1001.49 Stout, George Frederick.

[1931] *Mind and Matter.* Cambridge, England: University Press, 1931, xiv+325 pp. [Aberdeen, 1919–1921.] *See* entry number 72.

1001.50 Barnes, William Ernest.

[1933] *Scientific Theory and Religion: The World Described by Science and Its Spiritual Interpretation.* Cambridge: Cambridge University Press, 1933, xxiv+685 pp. New York: Macmillan Co., 1933, xxiv+685 pp. [Aberdeen, 1927–1929.]

1001.51 Soderblom, Nathan.

[1933] *The Living God: Basal Forms of Personal Religion.* London: Oxford Press, H. Milford, 1933, xxix+398 pp. Reprint. Boston: Beacon Press, 1962. [Edinburgh, 1931.]

7. PROFESSIONALIZATION

1001.52 Temple, William.
[1934.] *Nature, Man, and God.* London: Macmillan & Co., 1934, xxxii+ 530 pp. [Glasgow, 1932–1933.]

1001.53 Hanson, Herbert Hensley.
[1936] *Christian Morality: Natural, Developing, Final.* Oxford: Clarendon Press, 1936, xiv+340 pp. [St. Andrews, 1935–1936.]

1001.54 Dixon, William Macneile.
[1937] *The Human Situation.* London: E. Arnold & Co.; New York: Longmans, Green & Co., 1937, 438 pp. [Glasgow, 1935–1936.]

1001.55 Barth, Karl.
[1938] *Gotteserkenntnis und Gottesdienst nach reformatorischer Lehre: 20 Vorlesungen über das Schottische Bekenntnis von 1560.* Zollikon: Evangelische Buchhandlung Verlag, 1938, 226 pp. ENGLISH: *The Knowledge of God and the Service of God According to the Teaching of the Reformation, Recalling the Scottish Confession of 1560.* Translated by J.L.M. Haire and Ian Henderson. London: Hodder & Stoughton, 1938, xxix+ 255 pp. [Aberdeen, 1937–1938.]

1001.56 Bevan, Edwyn Robert.
[1938] *Symbolism and Belief.* London: George Allen & Unwin; New York: Macmillan & Co., 1938, 391 pp. [Edinburgh, 1933–1934.]

1001.57 De Burgh, William George.
[1938] *From Morality to Religion.* London: Macdonald & Evans, 1938, xxii+ 352 pp. [St. Andrews, 1938.]

1001.58 Ross, William David.
[1939] *Foundations of Ethics.* Oxford: Clarendon Press, 1939, xvi+328 pp. [Aberdeen, 1935–1936.]

1001.59 Bevan, Edwyn Robert.
[1940] *Holy Images: An Inquiry into Idolatry and Image-Worship in Ancient Paganism and in Christianity.* London: George Allen & Unwin, 1940, 184 pp. [Edinburgh, 1933.]

1001.60 Bradley, Andrew Cecil.
[1940] *Ideals of Religion.* London: Macmillan & Co., 1940, viii+286 pp. [Glasgow, 1907.]

1001.61 Sherrington, Sir Charles Scott.
[1940] *Man on His Nature.* Cambridge, England: University Press, 1940, 413 pp. [Edinburgh, 1937–1938.]

1001.62 Laird, John.
[1941] *Mind and Deity.* London: George Allen & Unwin, 1941, 322 pp. [Glasgow, 1940.]

1001.63 Niebuhr, Reinhold.
[1941] *The Nature and Destiny of Man: A Christian Interpretation.* 2 vols. London: Nisbet & Co., 1941–1943, New York: Charles Scribner's, 1941–1943, xii+306 pp., xii+329 pp. [Edinburgh, 1939–1940.]

Special Book Series

1001.64 Kroner, Richard.

[1943] *The Primacy of Faith*. New York: Macmillan & Co., 1943, ix+226 pp. [St. Andrews, 1939–1940.]

1001.65 Jaeger, Werner Wilhelm.

[1947] *The Theology of the Early Greek Philosophers*. Translated from manuscript by Edward S. Robinson. Oxford: Clarendon Press, 1947, vi+259 pp. [St. Andrews, 1936.]

1001.66 Dawson, Christopher Henry.

[1948] *Religion and Culture*. London and New York: Sheed and Ward, 1948, v+225 pp. [Edinburgh, 1947.]

1001.67 Brunner, Heinrich Emil.

[1948] *Christianity and Civilization*. 2 vols. London: Nisbet, 1948–1949, New York: Charles Scribner's Sons, 1948–1949, xi+167 pp., ix+143 pp. [St. Andrews, 1947–1948.]

1001.68 Dawson, Christopher Henry.

[1950] *Religion and the Rise of Western Culture*. London and New York: Sheed & Ward, 1950, xvi+286 pp.+illus. [Edinburgh, 1948–1949.]

1001.69 Marcel, Gabriel.

[1951] *Le mystère de l'être*. Paris: Aubier, 1951, 2 vols. ENGLISH: *The Mystery of Being*. 2 vols. Translated by René Hague. Chicago: Henry Regenery, 1950; London: Harvill Press, 1951, xiv+219 pp., viii+188 pp. [Aberdeen, 1949–1950.]

1001.70 Raven, Charles Earle.

[1953] *Natural Religion and Christian Theology*. 2 vols. Cambridge, England: University Press, 1953, vii+224 pp., vii+227 pp. [Edinburgh, 1951–1952.]

1001.71 Farmer, Herbert Henry.

[1954] *Revelation and Religion: Studies in the Theological Interpretation of Religious Types*. London: Nisbet, 1954, 244 pp. New York: Harper, 1954, xi+244 pp. [Glasgow, 1950.]

1001.72 Paton, Herbert James.

[1955] *The Modern Predicament: A Study in the Philosophy of Religion*. London: George Allen & Unwin; New York: Macmillan & Co., 1955, 405 pp. [St. Andrews, 1950–1951.]

1001.73 Toynbee, Arnold Joseph.

[1956] *An Historian's Approach to Religion*. London and New York: Oxford University Press, 1956, 316 pp. [Edinburgh, 1952–1953.]

1001.74 Hodgson, Leonard.

[1956] *For Faith and Freedom*. 2 vols. Oxford: Blackwell; New York: Charles Scribner's Sons, 1956–1957, xii+237 pp., vii+223 pp. [Glasgow, 1955–1957.]

1001.75 Bultmann, Rudolf Karl.

[1957] *History and Eschatology*. Edinburgh: Edinburgh University Press, 1957, ix+170 pp. Also under the title *The Presence of Eternity: History and Eschatology*. New York; Harper, 1957, ix+170 pp. [Edinburgh, 1955.]

1001.76 Campbell, Charles Arthur.

[1957] *On Selfhood and Godhood*. London: George Allen & Unwin, 1957, xxxvi+436 pp. New York: Macmillan & Co., 1957, xxxvii+436 pp. [St. Andrews, 1953−1954.]

1001.77 MacMurray, John.

[1957] *The Form of the Personal*. Vol. 1. *The Self as Agent*, Vol. 2. *Persons in Relation*, London: Faber & Faber, 1957−1961, 230 pp., 235 pp. [Glasgow, 1953−1954.]

1001.78 Farrer, Austin Marsden.

[1958] *The Freedom of the Will*. London: A. & C. Black, 1958, xi+315 pp. [Edinburgh, 1957.]

1001.79 Baillie, John.

[1962] *The Sense of the Presence of God*. New York: Scribner, 1962, 269 pp. [Edinburgh, 1961−1962.]

1001.80 Wright, Georg Henrik von.

[1963] *Norm and Action: A Logical Enquiry*. London: Routledge & Kegan Paul; New York: Humanities Press, 1963, xviii+214 pp. [St. Andrews, 1959.]

1001.81 Wright, Georg Henrik von.

[1963] *The Varieties of Goodness*. London: Routledge & Kegan Paul; New York: Humanities Press, 1963, 222 pp. [St. Andrews, 1960.]

1001.82 Weizsacker, Carl Friedrich von.

[1964] *The Relevance of Science: Creation and Cosmogeny*. London: Collins; New York: Harper & Row, 1964, 192 pp. [Glasgow, 1959−1960.]

[1924] **1002. *Dwight Harrington Terry Lectures—Yale University.***

The Dwight Harrington Terry Lectureship on Religion in the Light of Science and Philosophy was established in 1924. The terms of the lectureship include the following: "The object of this foundation is . . . the assimilation and interpretation of that which has been or shall be hereafter discovered, and its application to human welfare, especially by the building of the truths of science and philosophy into the structure of a broadened and purified religion." For a detailed examination of the lectureship see: Burwell, Ronald Joseph. "Religion and the Social Sciences: A Study of Their Relationships as set Forth in the Terry Lectures: 1924−1971," New York: New York University Ph.D. dissertation, 1976 (available through Xerox University Microfilms). The following volumes rising out of the lectureship are all also published by Yale University Press in New Haven and are of relevance to the integration of theology and psychology:

1002.01 Hocking, William Ernest.

[1928] *The Self, Its Body and Freedom*. 1928, 178 pp. London: Oxford University Press, H. Milford, 1938, 131 pp. *See* entry number 106.

1002.02 Brown, William.

[1929] *Science and Personality*. 1929, 258 pp. London: Oxford University Press, H. Milford, 1929, viii+258 pp.

1002.03 Dewey, John.

[1934] *A Common Faith*. 1934, 87 pp. London: Oxford University Press, H. Milford, 1934, 87 pp.

1002.04 MacMurray, John.

[1936] *The Structure of Religious Experience*. 1936, xi+77 pp. London: Faber & Faber Ltd., 1936, 114 pp.

1002.05 Jung, Carl G.

[1938] *Psychology and Religion*. 1938, 131 pp. London: Oxford University Press, H. Milford, 1938, 131 pp. *See* entry number 975.

1002.06 Fromm, Erich.

[1950] *Psychoanalysis and Religion*. 1950, vi+119 pp. *See* entry number 930.

1002.07 Tillich, Paul.

[1952] *The Courage to Be*. 1952, 197 pp. *See* entry number 845.

1002.08 Allport, Gordon Willard.

[1955] *Becoming: Basic Considerations for a Psychology of Personality*. 1955, 106 pp.

1003. Catholic University of America: Studies in Psychology and Psychiatry.

A series of publications devoted to the two fields of psychology and psychiatry, it contained the results of original research on individual topics (usually student dissertations), monographs of particular subjects, and critical reviews of the literature on special problems. The series was published irregularly. Edward Aloysius Pace edited the series from Volume 1, Number 1 (June 1926) through Volume 4, Number 3 (January 1938). Collaborating editors were Cornelius Joseph Connelly, John Albert Haldi, Thomas George Foran, Paul Hanly Furfy, Thomas Verner Moore, John William Rauth, and Francis Augustine Walsh. Thomas Verner Moore edited Volume 4, Number 4 (January 1939) through Volume 5, Number 3 and perhaps several issues beyond. No series editor is listed for Volume 5, Number 4 (June 1942) through Volume 6, Number 8 (June 1947). John W. Stafford edited Volume 7, Number 1 (January 1948) through Volume 10,

7. PROFESSIONALIZATION

Number 3 (June 1959). A list of authors, titles, volumes, and serial numbers is included here for volumes relevant to the task of integration:

1003.01 Mullen, Joseph John.

[1927] *Psychological Factors in the Pastoral Treatment of Scruples*. Vol. 1, no. 3. Baltimore: Williams and Wilkins Co., 1927, viii+165 pp.

1003.02 McGrath, Marie Cecelia, and Hughes, Margaret Mary.

[1936] *The Moral and Religious Development of the Preschool Child*. Vol. 4, no. 1. Baltimore: Williams and Wilkins Co., 1936, vii+51 pp.

1003.03 Barrett, Mary Constance.

[1941] *An Experimental Study of the Thomistic Concept of the Faculty of Imagination*. Vol. 5, no. 3. Washington, D.C.: Catholic University of America Press, 1941, vi+51 pp.

1003.04 McCarthy, Thomas John.

[1942] *Personality Traits of Seminarians*. Vol. 5, no. 4. Washington, D.C.: Catholic University of America Press, 1942, 46 pp.

1003.05 Peters, Richarda.

[1942] *A Study of the Intercorrelations of Personality Traits among a Group of Novices in Religious Communities*. Vol. 5, no. 7. Washington, D.C.: Catholic University of America Press, 1942, 38 pp.

1003.06 Betke, Mary Angela.

[1944] *Defective Moral Reasoning in Delinquency. A Psychological Study*. Vol. 6, no. 4. Washington, D.C.: Catholic University of America Press, 1944, 95 pp.

1003.07 Lorang, Mary Corde.

[1945] *The Effect of Reading on Moral Conduct and Emotional Experience*. Vol. 6, no. 5. Washington, D.C.: Catholic University of America Press, 1945, viii+122 pp.

1003.08 Keckeissen, Mary Gertrude.

[1945] *An Empirical Study of Moral Problems and Character Traits of High School Pupils*. Vol. 6, no. 6. Washington, D.C.: Catholic University of America Press, 1945, vii+31 pp.

1003.09 Lhota, Brian.

[1948] *Vocational Interests of Catholic Priests*. Vol. 7, no. 1. Washington, D.C.: Catholic University of America Press, 1948, vii+40 pp.

1003.10 Dowd, Mary Amadeus.

[1948] *Changes in Moral Reasoning Through the High School Years*. Vol. 7, no. 2. Washington, D.C.: Catholic University of America Press, 1948, ix+120 pp.

1003.11 Bier, William Christian.

[1948] *A Comparative Study of a Seminary Group and Four Other Groups on the Minnesota Multiphasic Personality Inventory*. Vol. 7, no. 3. Washington, D.C.: Catholic University of America Press, 1948, xi+107 pp.

1003.12 Wack, Dunstan John.

[1964] *Constancy of Interest Factor Patterns within the Specific Vocation of Foreign Missioner*. Vol. 9, no. 1. Washington, D.C.: Catholic University of America Press, 1964.

[1927] **1004.** *University of Iowa Studies: Studies in Character.*

Iowa City: University of Iowa 1927–1931.

The series was edited by Edwin Diller Starbuck from 1927 to 1930 and by James C. Manry in 1931, and included the following works relevant to the psychology of religion:

1004.01 Franklin, Samuel Petty.

[1928] *Measurement of the Comprehension Difficulty of the Precepts and Parables of Jesus*, 1928, 63 pp.

1004.02 Howells, Thomas Henry.

[1928] *A Comparative Study of Those Who Accept as Against Those Who Reject Religious Authority*, 1928, 80 pp. +illus. *See* entry number 655.

1004.03 Beiswanger, George Wilhelm.

[1930] *The Character Value of the Old Testament Stories*, 1930, 63 pp. *See* entry number 658.

1004.04 Case, Ralph Thomas.

[1930] *A Study of the Placement in the Curriculum of Selected Teachings of the Old Testament Prophets*, 1930, 72 pp.

1004.05 Hightower, Pleasant Roscoe.

[1930] *Biblical Information in Relation to Character and Conduct*, 1930, 72 pp. + illus. *See* entry number 661.

1004.06 Sinclair, Robert Daniel.

[1930] *A Comparative Study of Those Who Report the Experience of the Divine Presence and Those Who Do Not*, 1930, 63 pp. *See* entry number 663.

[1939] **1005.** *Guild of Pastoral Psychology, London. Lectures.*

London: Guild of Pastoral Psychology, 1939–1950+.

Featured authors up to 1950 included Gerhard Adler, Karl Abenheimer, Amy I. Allenby, Culver Barker, Carol Baumann, Eleanor Bertine, Canon F. Boyd, Alice E. Buck, Phyllis Collard, Howard E. Collier, R. F. Dosseter, L. A. Duncan-Johnstone, Michael Fordham, Rolf Gledhill, Barbara Hannah, Werner Heider, E. Graham Howe, Margaret E. Hone, Hector Hoppin, H. J. Jacoby, Carl Gustav Jung, James Kirsch, Kathleen F. Kitchin, Derek Kitchin, Wm. P. Kraemer, Kenneth Lambert, K. Forsaith Lander, John Layard, Peter D. Lucas, Adeline M. Matland, Philip Metman, Eva Metman, W. I. Moore, Stephen Neill, W. H. Peacy, Rivkah Schaerf, A. Segal, Peter Slade, M. Oswald Sumner, H. Westmann, Victor White, W. P. Witcutt, Charlotte E. Woods, Toni Wolff, and Henry R. Zimmer.

[1945] **1006.** *Bollingen Series—Bollingen Foundation.*

The Bollingen Foundation was founded in 1945 by Paul Mellon and Mary Conover Mellon. The initial motive for the Foundation's establishment was to assure a wider audience in the English-speaking world for Carl Jung's scientific works, and the collected works of Jung form the central core of the publication series.

The foundation also offered fellowships and grants-in-aid to scholars in a variety of humanistic and scientific fields. The Bollingen Series was published for the Bollingen Foundation by Pantheon Books from 1946 through 1960, when the Foundation assumed its publication, with Pantheon continuing its distribution. In 1967, Princeton University Press became publisher and distributor, and it assumed full responsibility for the series in 1969, with the Foundation becoming inactive. Relevant titles in the series include the following:

1006.01 *Campbell, Joseph.*

[1949] *The Hero With a Thousand Faces*. New York: Pantheon Books, 1949, xxiii+416 pp.+illus. [Vol. 17.] *See* entry number 980.

1006.02 *Jung, Carl J., and Kerenyi, C.*

[1949] *Essays on a Science of Mythology; The Myth of the Divine Child and the Mysteries of Eleusis*. Translated by R.F.C. Hull. New York: Pantheon Books, 1949, 299 pp.+illus. [Vol. 22.]

1006.03 *Schaer, Hans.*

[1950] *Religion and the Cure of Souls in Jung's Psychology*. Translated by R.F.C. Hull. New York: Pantheon Books, 1950, 221 pp. [Vol. 21.] *See* entry number 978.

1006.04 *Jacobi, Yolande Szekacs, ed.*

[1953] *Psychological Reflections: An Anthology of the Writings of C. G. Jung*. New York: Pantheon Books, 1953, xxvii+342 pp. [Vol. 31.]

1006.05 *Jung, Carl Gustav.*

[1953] *The Collected Works*. Edited by Herbert Read, Michael Fordham, and Gerhard Adler. 20 vols. in 21. New York: Pantheon Books, 1953–1979. [Vol. 20.]

1006.06 *Neumann, Erich.*

[1954] *The Origins and History of Consciousness*. Translated by R.F.C. Hull. New York: Pantheon Books, 1954, xxiv+493 pp.+illus. [Vol. 42.] *See* entry 982.

1006.07 *Campbell, Joseph, ed.*

[1955] *The Mysteries; Papers from the Eranos Yearbooks*. New York: Pantheon Books, 1955, xvi+476 pp. [Vol. 30.]

1006.08 *Jung, Carl Gustav, and Pauli, Wolfgang.*

[1955] *The Interpretation of Nature and the Psyche. Synchronicity: An Acausal Connecting Principle. The Influence of Archetypal Ideas on the Scientific Theories of Kepler*. New York: Pantheon Books, 1955, vii+247 pp.+illus. [Vol. 51.]

1006.09 Neumann, Erich.

[1955] *The Great Mother; An Analysis of the Archetype.* Translated by Pal Manheim. New York: Pantheon Books, 1955, xiii+380 pp. +illus. [Vol. 47.]

1006.10 Neumann, Erich.

[1956] *Amor and Psyche: The Psychic Development of the Feminine. A Commentary on the Tale by Apuleius.* Translated by Ralph Manheim. New York: Pantheon Books, 1956, 181 pp. +illus. [Vol. 54.] *See* entry number 986.

1006.11 Jacobi, Jolande Szekacs.

[1959] *Complex/Archetype/Symbol in the Psychology of C. G. Jung.* Translated by Ralph Manheim. New York: Pantheon Books, 1959, xii+236 pp. + illus. [Vol. 57.] *See* entry number 991.

1006.12 Neumann, Erich.

[1959] *Art and the Creative Unconscious; Four Essays.* Translated by Ralph Manheim. New York: Pantheon Books, 1959, 232 pp. +illus. [Vol. 61.]

[1957] **1007.** *Academy of Religion and Mental Health: Symposia.*
A limited series of published symposia proceedings dealing with the interrelationship between mental health, religion, science, and culture.

1007.01 Religion, Science, and Mental Health: Proceedings of the First Academy of Inter-Disciplinary Responsibility for Mental Health—A Religious and Scientific Concern.

[1959] New York: New York University Press, 1959, xvi+107 pp. [1957 Symposium]

1007.02 Religion, Culture, and Mental Health. Proceedings of the Third Academy Symposium, 1959.

[1961] New York: New York University Press, 1961, 157 pp. [1959 Symposium]

1007.03 The Place of Value Systems in Medical Education.

[1961] New York: [no publisher indicated, other than the Academy], 1961, 11+218 pp. [1960 Symposium]

1007.04 Research in Religion and Health: Selected Projects and Methods.

[1963] New York: Fordham University Press, 1963, x+165 pp+illus. [1961 Symposium]

[1959] **1008.** *Lumen Vitae Studies in Religious Psychology.*
These studies "are intended to contribute to the development of positive research in religious psychology and to make the results available for the advancement of Christian education." Preference is given to theoretical studies which provide new working hypotheses along with practical attempts to build and validate tests suitable for the evaluation of religious dimensions. The studies also include an international bibliographical survey of recent works.

1008.01 Research: Speculative and Positive.

[1959] Brussels: Lumen Vitae Press, 1959, 200 pp. Lumen Vitae Studies, Vol. 1. Reprinted from *Lumen Vitae*, 1957, Vol. 12, Number 2, pp. 301–376.

Contributions to this volume included Pierre Fransen, Augustin Léonard, Werner D. Gruehn, Killiam McDonnell, André Godin, Anne Coupez, Edward H. Nowlan, Alois Grüber, Vera Denty, Charles Sandron, Leonhard Gilen, Miriam de Lourdes McMahon, and Henry Loves.

1008.02 Child and Adult Before God.

[1961] Brussels: Lumen Vitae Press, 1961, 164 pp. Lumen Vitae Studies, Vol. 2. Chicago: Loyola University Press, 1965, 160 pp. 164 pp. Reprinted from *Lumen Vitae*, 1960, Vol. 15, Number 1, pp. 7–120.

Contributors to this volume included Jonas Gutauskas, Hilda Laible, Klemens Tilmann, Mother Albert, Pierre Ranwez, C. Ferrière, M. Missone and Henri Bisonnier.

1008.03 From Religious Experience to a Religious Attitude.

[1964] Brussels: Lumen Vitae Press, 1964, 248 pp. Lumen Vitae Studies, Vol. 3. Chicago: Loyola University Press, 1965, viii+210 pp. Reprinted from *Lumen Vitae*, 1964, Vol. 19, Number 2, pp. 191–348.

Contributors to this volume included André Godin, Antoine Vergote, Walter Houston Clark, Pierre Ranwez, Monique Hallez, Jean-Pierre Deconchy, Robert H. Thouless, L. B. Brown, Ronald J. Goldman, Christian Van Bunnen, and Joan Brothers.

[1964] **1009. *Faith Learning Studies: A Series Examining the Academic Disciplines.***

Edited by William B. Rogers, the Faith Learning Studies series "seeks to do three things: (1) to raise the critical questions of the faith-particular discipline relation, (2) to suggest some directions in which answers are being sought, and (3) to annotate a bibliography which would be helpful in the further pursuit of the issues raised.

1009.01 Havens, Joseph D.

[1964] *Psychology*. Faith Learning Studies Number 3. New York: Faculty Christian Fellowship, 1964. 12 pp.

Havens' study includes the following topics: (1) Reacting organism vs. Imago Dei, (2) Genuine freedom or a feeling of freedom? (3) Can psychology deal with subjective experience? (4) Is religion, then, simply a datum of psychology? (5) Are "transcendental experiences" mystical or psychotic? (6) Salvation or mental health? (7) Bibliography of sixty items. Havens was affiliated with the University Health Service, University of Massachusetts, Amherst.

Institutions

Here are listed various institutions, professional societies, and organizations devoted to psychology and religion, the integration of psychology and theology, and the area of mental or spiritual healing.

[1901] **1010. *American Academy of Religion.***

The American Academy of Religion was founded in 1901 as the National Association of Biblical Instructors. The name was changed in 1964. The academy is a professional society of college and university professors and others engaged in teaching and research in the field of religious studies. Its purpose is to stimulate scholarship, foster research, and promote learning in the complex of subdisciplines that constitutes religion as a field of academic inquiry. The academy maintains an extensive scholarly publishing program, holds regional and national meetings for the exchange of research, and keeps its membership informed of significant opportunities in the field.

[1905] **1011. *The Emmanuel Movement (Boston).***

The Emmanuel Movement arose in 1905 at Emmanuel Church in Boston under the direction of Elwood Worcester, Samuel McComb, and Isadore S. Coriat. When Worcester resigned from the pastorate at Emmanuel Church the work was continued under the leadership of The Craigie Foundation. The leaders were committed to the value of both science and religion as healing arts for mind, body, and spirit. The work is detailed in Worcester, McComb, and Coriat's *Religion and Medicine* (entry number 514) and in Worcester's *Body, Mind and Spirit* (entry number 531).

[1905] **1012.** *The Guild of Health (London).*

The Guild of Health was founded in 1905 by W. Harold Anson, Percy Dearmer, and Conrad Noel, priests in the Anglican Church. The Guild stated its objectives as: 1) The study of the interaction of the spiritual, mental and physical factors in well-being; 2) The cultivation of both individual and corporate health through spiritual means; 3) The exercise of healing by the readjustment of the whole personality in harmony with scientific methods; and 4) The practice of personal and united prayer in all efforts toward the fullness of health.

[1909?] **1013.** *The Divine Healing Mission (London).*

An Anglican association linked with the work of James Moore Hickson. Their goals were stated in part as follows: "From the outset we have been guided (we believe by the Holy Spirit) to seek the closest cooperation with all who are working on mental and material levels toward the same end, namely—the complete health of man's whole being; and we regard the effective working of members of the medical profession and of the psychologists as deriving all its power and efficiency from the same divine Source, God Himself."

[1910] **1014.** *Bethesda Hospital Association.*

As stated in the 1982 report of the Bethesda Heritage Task Force, "Bethesda Hospital is a private, church-related psychiatric facility with a history dating back to 1910 when it was founded by the Reformed Church in America and the Christian Reformed Church in North America as a sanitarium for tubercular patients. Along with the physical care of persons, there was also concern for the spiritual welfare of persons. This was evidenced in the work of the Reverend Idzerd Van Dellen who preached Sunday sermons and offered spiritual counsel to patients. The hospital has a strong heritage of Dutch culture and Reformed theology which continues to be expressed in our logo: 'Dedicated to Christian Mercy.'" The transition from tuberculosis sanitarium to private psychiatric facility began in 1948. Klaire Kuiper, who developed the psychiatric treatment program, believed that "many mental aberrations were due to sinful orientation or attitudes toward life," and his treatment philosophy addressed this through an attitude of Christian love. Franklin G. Ebaugh was also employed at this time as a consultant in psychiatry.

[1910] **1015.** *Pine Rest Christian Hospital and Rehabilitation Services.*

In December of 1910 an interested group purchased the Cutler Farm, south of Grand Rapids, Michigan, in order to begin a program of Christian services to the mentally ill. By 1912 both men and women were receiving care at what was then known as the Christian Psychopathic Hospital. By 1930 three hospital buildings had been constructed, and by 1962 an additional five centers, including the Children's Retreat, the Retreat Training School, the Sheltered Workshop, and the Mulder Therapy Center. Facilities and services continued to expand after 1965.

[1915] **1016.** *The Guild of St. Raphael.*

The Guild of St. Raphael was founded in 1915 "with the desire that in the revival of the use of spiritual means for the healing of the sick, there should be a society for this purpose belonging distinctively to the Anglican Church. Its object is to forward this form of ministry both by sacramental means and by intercessory prayer, until the Church, as a whole, accepts Divine Healing as part of its normal work." Two archbishops, thirty home diocesan bishops and a variety of other home and overseas bishops were involved in its patronage. Similar to the Guild of Health in its goals, it employed three methods, as summarized by Leslie Weatherhead: 1) To prepare the sick for all ministries of healing by teaching the need of repentance and faith; 2) To make use of the sacrament of Holy Unction and the rite of Laying on of Hands for healing; 3) To bring to the aid of the Ministry of Healing the power of intercession, individual and corporate, and also the other spiritual forces of Meditation and Silence.

[1924] **1017.** *Character Education Inquiry.*

Sponsored by the Religious Education Association and the Institute of Social and Religious Research (funded by John D. Rockefeller), this project was conducted by Mark A. May and Hugh Hartshorne from 1924 through 1927. Hartshorne announced the project in the journal *Religious Education* in 1924, and starting in 1926, he and May published a series of six articles on their experiences with the Inquiry (in vol. 21 and 22), with the collaboration of D. E. Sonquist, C. A. Kerr, and L. Stidley. (*See also* entries number 649, 652, and 655.)

[1935] **1018.** *Union College Character Research Project.*

The Union College Character Research Project was founded in 1935 by Professor Ernest Mayfield Ligon who served from 1944 through 1962 as the chairman of the Psychology Department. The project provides rationale for research into the development of attitudes and values and a direction for the development of parent-involving educational programs for schools, churches, and other community agencies. Accomplishments have been in the fields of curriculum development, cooperative work and program development with other agencies, publication, continuing basic and applied research, and the encouragement of cross-disciplinary international contacts. Annual workshops were begun in 1945, and from 1954 through 1965+ a series of Youth Conferences and Congresses were held. Significant publications growing out of the project are listed below. In addition, reviews of research compiled by Ligon and his colleagues were published in *Religious Education* from 1948 to 1965.

1018.01 *Ligon, Ernest M.*

[1935] *The Psychology of Christian Personality.* New York: Macmillan Co., 1935. *See* entry number 751.

1018.02 *Jones, Vernon.*

[1936] *Character and Citizenship Training in the Public School.* Chicago: University of Chicago Press, 1936.

1018.03 Ligon, Ernest Mayfield.

[1939] *Their Future is Now; The Growth and Development of Christian Personality*. New York: Macmillan Co., 1939, xv+369 pp. *See* entry number 677.

1018.04 Ligon, Ernest Mayfield.

[1948] *A Greater Generation*. New York: Macmillan Co., 1948, xii+157 pp. *See* entry number 685.

1018.05 Jones, Vernon.

[1950] *Character and Citizenship Education; A Syllabus for Use in Teacher Training*. Washington, D.C.: National Education Association, 1950, ix+149 pp.

[1937] **1019.** *Milton Abbey (Dorset and London).*

Milton Abbey, described as a "Home for the Spiritual Treatment of Nervous Suffering" was opened in 1937. Its first warden was John Maillard, whose book, *Healing in the Name of Jesus* led to a large following of "prayer helper" groups. Neurotic patients were the focus of its treatment regimen, which included occupational therapy. According to Leslie Weatherhead, "The promoters hope to make Milton Abbey a kind of research establishment where illnesses which are partly physical, partly mental and partly spiritual may be investigated, studied and treated by physical, psychological and spiritual methods in harmonious combination and in an atmosphere of healthy religion and of fellowship with others."

[1941] **1020.** *The American Scientific Affiliation.*

The American Scientific Affiliation describes itself as "a fellowship of men and women of science who share a common fidelity to the Word of God and to the Christian faith." It has grown from a handful in 1941 to a membership of over 2,400 in 1975. The stated purposes of the ASA are "to investigate any area relating to the Christian faith and science" and "to make known the results of such investigations for comment and criticism by the Christian community and by the scientific community."

[1944] **1021.** *The Churches Council on Healing.*

This council was begun in 1944 under the leadership of Archbishop William Temple. All Protestant denominations in England had membership in the council, which sought to coordinate various efforts and organizations focused on healing ministries.

[1945] **1022.** *Mennonite Mental Health Services.*

In June 1945, the Mennonite Central Committee appointed a study committee to address the possibility of establishing a mental hospital, at the direction of the General Conference Mennonite group. By 6 December 1947, the first patients were admitted to Brook Lane Psychiatric Center in Hagerstown, Maryland and the basic groundwork was laid for initiating Kings View Hospital in Reedley, California (1951) and Prairie View in Newton, Kansas (1954). Later facilities included Oaklawn Psychiatric Center in Elkhart, Indiana (1963) and Kern View Hospital in Bakersfield, California (1966).

Eventually the work of the Mental Health Committee was delegated to the Mennonite Mental Health Services, which was incorporated in 1952 and took over the work of the Homes for Mentally Ill Committee. A brief published history is available in: Neufeld, Vernon H. *After Twenty-Five Years: The Mennonite Mental Health Story*. Fresno, Calif.: Mennonite Mental Health Services, Inc., 1972, 16 pp.

[1946] **1023.** *The Methodist Society for Medical and Pastoral Practice.*
Founded in 1946 under the joint presidency of Leslie D. Weatherhead and Percy Backus. It emerged from the work of the Methodist Spiritual Healing Committee appointed in 1937 to examine the field of spiritual healing. The work of this group is described in detail in Weatherhead's *Psychology, Religion and Healing* (*see* entry number 547).

[1947] **1024.** *The American Catholic Psychological Association.*
The American Catholic Psychological Association (later known as Psychologists Interested in Religious Issues) began with a luncheon at the 1947 meeting of the American Psychological Association. Under the chairmanship of William C. Bier, S. J. (Fordham University), the organizing committee included Charles I. Doyle (Loyola University), Walter L. Wilkins (Notre Dame), Alexander A. Schneiders (University of Detroit), Sister Mary (Marygrove College), Brother Roger Philip (Queen's University), Lawrence T. Dayhaw (University of Ottawa), Joseph F. Kubis and Richard T. Zegers (Fordham University), and John W. Stafford and M. Gertrude Reiman (Catholic University).

A constitution and membership requirements were adopted in Boston at the 1948 APA Convention. It was desired to have an organization of professionally qualified psychologists rather than a mere interest group, thus the membership requirements adopted were those of the APA. The first president of the ACPA was Brother Roger Philip. There were 231 charter members. The aims of the Association at the time of its founding were twofold: (1) to bring psychology to Catholics; and (2) to bring a Catholic viewpoint into psychology.

In the early years, the ACPA would meet at the same time as the APA, but would hold its meetings at a nearby Catholic institution. In 1957, the ACPA offered a symposium at one of the convention hotels, jointly sponsored by the Association and by the Clinical Division of the APA. In the following years, other such symposia were presented at the APA conventions, all of them cosponsored by one of the APA divisions. Such topics as guilt, values in counseling, teaching psychology in church colleges, human nature, moral development, freedom and responsibility, ethical implications in sensitive training, and aging were considered.

The *ACPA Newsletter*, begun in 1950, continued publication until 1963, when it was reduced from a bimonthly to a biannual "journal." William C. Bier was the editor of the newsletter and Virginia S. Sexton, M. Irene Wightwick, Jean Mundy, and Donald J. Dillon were the book review editors.

From 1956 to 1959, the papers presented at the annual meeting were published in three separate volumes. This was discontinued in 1963, with the advent of the ACPA journal, the *Catholic Psychological Record*, which was published at the rate of two issues per year until 1968, under the editorship of Alexander A. Schneiders.

[1949] **1025.** *Society for the Scientific Study of Religion.*
In 1949 a Committee for the Scientific Study of Religion was created by J. Paul Williams of the Department of Religion, Mount Holyoke College; Walter H. Clark of the Department of Psychology, Middlebury College; and Prentice Pemberton of the Student Christian movement, who later became the first editor of the *Journal for the Scientific Study of Religion*.

A number of well-known scholars soon were persuaded to join the Committee for the Scientific Study of Religion. Among them were: Paul Tillich, Talcott Parsons, Gordon W. Allport, Pitirim Sorokin, Horace Kallen, James Luther Adams, Ralph Burhoe, Allan Eister, and Lauris Whitman.

The earliest stated goals were set forth in a letter sent by Clark and Williams to those people who were being invited to join the Committee for the Scientific Study of Religion. These included the intent to (1) bring together social scientists and religious persons; (2) pursue joint research; (3) stimulate students and scholars to work on religion as a research topic; and (4) create an audience who would read religious research. Later statements of goals were to place less emphasis on apologetic and more emphasis on scientific endeavors.

At the early meetings both business and academic sessions were conducted. In addition to academic papers, bibliographic lists of resources were often distributed. *The Journal for the Scientific Study of Religion*, which was founded in 1961, came out of these endeavors.

The Committee became the Society for the Scientific Study of Religion in November 1955. In the mid-1950s discussions arose as to how involved the group should be in approving research projects, how the group should be related to other organizations such as the American Academy of Religion and the American Psychological Association's section on religion, and whether there should be sectional meetings of the Society. These have been continuing issues in the Society's life.

Ralph Burhoe had suggested creating a journal in 1957. The prime concern was to find an outlet for the papers presented at the annual meetings. In an effort to keep the Society financially viable several relationships with extant journals were explored. A joint publication with the Religious Research Fellowship (later to become the Religious Research Association,) was considered. The establishment of the *Review of*

Religious Research by the Religious Research Association, and the hesitancy of the academics to become too closely associated with the churchmen, provoked the Society to establish the *Journal for the Scientific Study of Religion* in June 1960 with a grant from the Kaplan Foundation. A campaign for additional members and an increase in dues followed this venture.

[1951] **1026. *Menninger Foundation: Religion and Psychiatry.***

Interest in religion and in good working relations with clergy and churches has always been part of the personal stance of Karl and William Menninger, even during the pre-World War II era when those interests were not widely shared by their psychiatric colleagues. Karl Menninger taught for years a Sunday morning class to selected patients in the C. F. Menninger Memorial Hospital, which addressed religious and ethical topics and involved Bible study. William Menninger was on the editorial board of *Pastoral Psychology* since its inception in 1950. Both men were in close contact with Seward Hiltner, who had started a doctoral program in Religion and Personality within the Federated Theological Faculty of the University of Chicago and was in the forefront of relating pastoral-theological education to both the lore and the organizations of medicine and psychiatry. An elective seminar on religion and psychiatry was held by Karl Menninger in the Menninger School of Psychiatry.

Formal enterprises addressing both religion and psychiatry started at the Menninger Foundation in 1951, when William Menninger enticed Robert Foster, later joined by Dean Johnson, to undertake a training program in marriage counseling for clergymen—most of whom happened to be chaplains in the military. The program was a part of William Menninger's Department of Social Applications of Psychiatry which he launched upon his return from military service.

In the 1950s, a series of developments occurred. In 1954, with the help of the Methodist layman and insurance company executive Edward F. Gallahue, annual meetings were inaugurated for invited theologians and mental health professionals to discuss weighty topics on the borderland of the two groups of disciplines. These "Gallahue" conferences comprised such topics as freedom, suffering, healing, and anxiety, interspersed with meetings devoted to planning strategies for program development. Except for the conference on anxiety which resulted in a book *Constructive Aspects of Anxiety*, (*see* entry number 861), the meetings were held behind closed doors and were not publicized.

In 1957, the Marriage Counseling Training Program was shifted to the Department of Education, and Thomas W. Klink, hitherto chaplain at Topeka State Hospital, was appointed Director of a new Division of Religion and Psychiatry that was to develop various programs. Most important was a change in content from marriage counseling to general pastoral care and counseling for parish clergy, using a network of cooperating Topeka churches as practicum sites. The program was postgraduate and required one year in residence, full-time, accredited by the (then)

Council for Clinical Training. This program has continued uninterrupt-edly, but with changes in personnel, until today.

In 1960 Paul W. Pruyser obtained a grant from the Danforth Founda-tion to offer theological scholars a one-year period of study at the Men-ninger Foundation to systematically relate psychiatric theory to divinity studies. These "Theological Fellows" completed various projects, many of which eventually appeared in book form. The program (and the grant) ran for three years.

Under the sponsorship of the Faculty Christian Fellowship a small group of scholars in the theological and psychological disciplines held twice a year work-and-study sessions, in which one member took re-sponsibility for writing a paper that would elicit discussion. This fertile group comprised David Bakan, Walter H. Clark, Charles Arthur Curran, James Dittes, Joseph Havens, Keith Irwin, Robert Kimball, Paul W. Pruyser, William R. Rogers, Joseph Royce, Richard Rubinstein, and Phillip Woolcott. Many of the above later became involved in the Society for the Scientific Study of Religion and other organizations. One of their periodic meetings, in 1960, was held at the Menninger Foundation. As a group and as individuals these people have been very productive contrib-utors to the ongoing dialogue between religion and the personality sci-ences.

In addition, workshops in pastoral care were given to various groups, some quite sizeable. For several years theology students of the Jesuits' Saint Louis University who were then educated in St. Mary's College in Kansas spent a week at the Menninger Foundation for instruction and demonstration; conversely, Bernard H. Hall, Paul W. Pruyser, and Thomas Klink, were appointed to the St. Mary's faculty and gave addi-tional lectures at the seminary. A number of Foundation staff members led workshops for clergy elsewhere, under different auspices.

In 1957 Seward Hiltner was chosen for the Alfred P. Sloan Visiting Professorship in the Menninger School of Psychiatry. For many years afterward, due to the generosity of Edward Gallahue, he was a regular consultant to the Menninger Foundation as a whole and a frequent visiting lecturer in its education programs.

The foundation's various programs in religion and psychiatry re-ceived much encouragement and guidance from Margaret Mead, Leo Bartemeier, Howard P. Rome, and John D. Sutherland, all of whom were in their own way involved in relating psychiatry and theology to each other.

The 1960s were also an era of consultations with various theological schools interested in bringing the psychological disciplines into their curricula. Paul W. Pruyser consulted with Union Theological Seminary in New York and McCormick Theological Seminary in Chicago; in the latter seminary, he was for many years a regular visiting professor and helped organize its Weyerhaeuser Program in pastoral care and counseling, which included a number of annual national conferences. Other members of the Menninger Foundation Staff consulted to other seminaries. Karl

Menninger and Paul W. Pruyser served for several years on the Ecumenical Affairs Committee of the National Council of Churches, and Pruyser participated in a Task Force on Career Evaluation Centers for clergy.

[1951] **1027.** *The Religious Research Association.*

This is an association of over five hundred ecclesiastical researchers and academic social scientists which grew out of the Religious Research Fellowship, a group of church researchers who had been meeting together since 1944. Central to this early group of twenty-four participants was H. Paul Douglas, Chief Researcher for the Federal Council of Churches and director of the Institute of Social and Religious Research. The Religious Research Fellowship organized in 1951, became the Religious Research Association in the late 1950s and created the *Review of Religious Research* in 1959 to disseminate the Douglas lectures, which were presented at its annual meeting.

Originally organized to promote institutional and church-based religious research, the Religious Research Association increasingly encouraged the participation of academic social scientists. Although it retains an applied focus, its membership and its journal have included a high percentage of academics and scholarly articles.

The Religious Research Association meets annually with the Society for the Scientific Study of Religion and periodically engages in the publication of institution-sponsored surveys and research investigations on organized religious activity.

Increasingly the activities of the Religious Research Association and the Society for the Scientific Study of Religion began to be seen as competitive on the one hand and compatible on the other. Many persons belonged to and were officers in both. The Religious Research Association emphasized denominational research and included church persons while the Society for the Scientific Study of Religion was more academic. There were extended discussions over the role of each in a jointly sponsored conference on the Sociology of Religion in 1962. By this time the Society had grown to eight hundred members.

[1953] **1028.** *International Federation of the Catholic Institutions for Socio-Religious Research (FERES).*

This is a coordinating group aiming its efforts at the establishment of research centers, the improvement of research methods and the promotion of scientific studies. Membership is open to institutions and organizations. Based in Switzerland and Brussels, the group also publishes the *Social Compass* (1953+, published in The Hague) and organizes international congresses.

[1954] **1029.** *Academy of Religion and Mental Health.*

The Academy of Religion and Mental Health, founded in 1954 as the National Academy of Religion and Mental Health, is an information and

7. PROFESSIONALIZATION

research institution that publicizes and analyzes the results of various studies of human behavior, with the purpose of promoting spiritual well-being and mental health. The Academy integrates these studies with moral and religious values, and in particular emphasizes closer relations between members of the psychiatric profession and the clergy. The group includes representatives of Catholicism, Protestantism, and Judaism. In 1972, the Academy was incorporated into the Institutes of Religion and Health, which publishes the *Journal of Religion and Health*.

[1963] **1030.** *The Graduate School of Psychology, Fuller Theological Seminary.*

In the early 1960s a psychologist from Tacoma, Washington, John G. Finch, suggested to the Weyerhaeuser family that there was a need for a place to train Christian psychologists. Subsequent to lectures delivered by Finch at Fuller Theological Seminary the establishment of such a center for training was made possible by a grant of $1 million by C. Davis Weyerhaeuser, the chairman of Fuller's Board of Trustees.

Lee Edward Travis, a well-known clinical physiological psychologist from the University of Iowa and University of Southern California, was selected as the founding dean. A counseling center under the direction of Adrin Sylling was established in 1963 and the first class of students was admitted in the fall of 1964. The faculty included Donald F. Tweedie (an existential psychologist of some repute), Ted Cole (a Baptist minister turned psychologist), Paul F. Barkman (a Mennonite who formerly taught at Taylor University), Paul Fairweather (professor of pastoral care at the seminary), and Robert Bower (educational psychologist and professor of family counseling at the seminary).

The curriculum included doctoral training in clinical psychology with a required co-curriculum in theology. Among the requirements was a series of integration courses relating psychology and theology, jointly taught by theologians and psychologists.

The goal of the program has been to train psychologists who integrate the Christian faith with their clinical psychology in theory, practice, and research. This implies practical, personal, theoretical, and professional goals. The curriculum in clinical psychology has been based on the Boulder Conference scientist-professional model in which general psychology is seen as a basis for clinical psychology.

Journals

This chapter lists journals devoted specifically to the psychology of religion or the integration of psychology and theology as well as special issues of more general journals and some highly relevant religious-theological periodicals.

[1887] **1031.** *The American Journal of Psychology.*

Vol. 1–78; 1887–1965+.

Founded in 1887 and edited until 1921 by G. Stanley Hall, *The American Journal of Psychology* was America's first journal to publish psychological work of a scientific (experimental) nature. The Journal published articles relating to the psychology of religion for a period of thirty years (vol. 4–30) and continued to publish relevant book reviews even after E. B. Titchener assumed the editorship in 1921. Only three articles appeared in *The American Journal of Psychology* during the short period when Hall also edited and published the *American Journal of Religious Psychology and Education.* Authors on psychology of religion included (in chronological order) James Henry Leuba, Stephen S. Colvin, Samuel Perkins Haves, H. B. Woolston, L. D. Arnett, Arthur H. Daniels, Edwin Diller Starbuck, Henry H. Goddard, Charles W. Waddle, T. Okabe, G. Stanley Hall, Walter Franklin Prince, Ivy G. Campbell, Wesley Raymond Wells, Edmund S. Conklin, Frederick Goodrich Henke, Theodore Schroeder, Mark A. May, Pierce Butler, John M. Fletcher, Martha Warren Beckwith, Walter Marshall Horton, and Franklin Simpson Hickman. These articles reflected a broad definition of "psychology of religion," including not only such traditional psychological topics as conversion, mysticism, and religious growth, but also more theological interests like the history and views of the soul, examinations of episodes in church history, religion and literature, healing miracles, the fear of death (thanatophobia) and its relationship to immortality, and psychological questions relating to the authorship of the Book of Mormon. The journal also features many book notices in religion and theology. Most of the articles in this journal are *not* referenced in Capps, Rambo, and Ransohoff (*see* the Preface of this Bibliography, p. ix).

[1899] **1032.** *Journal of Psychosophy.*

Vol. 1, Numbers 1–5, February–June, 1899.

Volume 1, number 1 of this journal, published by the School of Practical Psychosophy and Psychosophical Society in Toronto, states: "Among the many occult and psychic questions that may be regarded within the scope of this journal are: Psychiatry, Psychography, Psychesthesia, Psychometry, Psycholysis, Hypnotism—its therapeutic and medico-legal aspects and attendant phenomena—Sleep, Somnambulism, Dream, Clairvoyance, Clairaudience, Levitation, Materialization, Astrology, Symbolism, Thought-transference, Mythology, and Mysticism." Editorial involvement came from William Newton Barnhardt, Professor of Theoretical Psychosophy and Richard S. J. DeNiord, Professor of Practical Psychosophy. The journal also features articles by Flora Macdonald Denison and John D. Boyle. The *Union List of Serials* and *British Union-Catalogue* indicate that copies of the journal are available only at the Toronto Public Library.

[1902] **1033.** *Hibbert Journal: A Quarterly Review of Religion, Theology, and Philosophy.*

Vol. 1–63+; 1902–1965+.

Early issues are especially valuable for their book and journal reviews and bibliographies, which include psychology as a division of philosophy.

[1904] **1034.** *The American Journal of Religious Psychology and Education.*

Vol. 1, Number 1–Vol. 4, Number 3; May 1904–July 1911.

Became The *Journal of Religious Psychology, (Including Its Anthropological and Sociological Aspects)* Vol. 5, Number 1–Vol. 7, Number 4; Jan. 1912–Dec. 1915.

Edited by G. Stanley Hall, the journal reflected a spectrum of topics in the psychology of religion and included articles by the following authors: Frank Orman Beck, Edward Carpenter, Alexander F. Chamberlain, George E. Dawson, Jean du Buy, R. S. Ellis, G. Stanley Hall, Percy Hughes, Jacob Hyman Kaplan, Karl Johan Karlson, L. W. Kline, Berthold Laufer, James Henry Leuba, J. A. Magni, F. T. Mayer-Oakes, Margaretta Morris, Josiah Morse, Howard W. Odum, A. Oosterheedt, James Bissett Pratt, S. Walter Ranson, Charles Frederick Robinson, V. P. Robinson, Clarence D. Royse, E. L. Schaub, Theodore Schroeder, W. T.

Shepherd, C. F. Sparkman, Edwin Diller Starbuck, Anna Louise Strong, Charles W. Super, J. S. van Teslaar, Wilson D. Wallis, Arthur E. Whatam. Complete references for articles may be found in Capps. Rambo, and Ransohoff (*see* the Preface of this Bibliography, p. ix).

[1908] **1035.** *Psychotherapy; a Course of Reading in Sound Psychology, Sound Medicine and Sound Religion.*
Vol. 1, Number 1–Vol. 3, Number 4; 1908–1909.

Editors of this short-lived journal were William Belmont Parker and H. J. Judson. As the term "psychotherapy" had been coined only two decades earlier, much of the first issues was devoted to an explication of its meaning and philosophy. Contributors to the first issue included Richard Clarke Cabot, a cardiologist and professor at Harvard Medical School who first established the clinical case conference at Massachusetts General Hospital and was influential in the early years of clinical pastoral education; Harvard's James Jackson Putnam, one of the first Americans to adopt Freud's psychoanalytic theories; the psychologist James Rowland Angell, who discussed the mind-body relationship; the Reverend Loring W. Batten, who provided a summary of healing in the Old Testament; the Reverend Lyman P. Powell, who gave a personal account of "religious therapeutics" at Northampton State Hospital; and Frederick T. Simpson, who discussed the structure and function of the nervous system.

[1920] **1036.** *The Personalist.*
Vol. 1–46+; 1920–1965+.

The Personalist was founded under the editorship of Ralph Tyler Flewelling as a voice for the philosophy of personalism. Its title was changed to *Pacific Philosophical Quarterly* in 1980. Issues into the early 1930s, at which time George D. Starbuck was one of its editors, are valuable for book reviews in the realm of psychology and religion. Also listed here are articles of psychological relevance published during these early years:

Flewelling, Ralph Tyler.
"The Pseudo-Science of Psychoanalysis." 2, no. 1 (1921): 25–34.

Grover, Delo C.
"The Psychological Approach to the Study of the Bible." 4, no. 1 (1923): 39–45.

Calkins, Mary Whiton.
"A Personal Idealist's Concern for Psychology." 5, no. 1 (1924): 5–11.

Beardslee, Claude G.
"Personalism and Behaviorism." 5, no. 1(1924): 12–17.

Long, Wilbur Harry.
"The Religious Philosophy of Bowne and James." 5, no. 4 (1924): 250–263.

Flewelling, Ralph Tyler.
"Using the Subconscious." 6, no. 1 (1925): 42–48.

Grover, Delo C.
"The Value of a Psychology of Religion." 6, no. 2 (1925): 108–113.

Flewelling, Ralph Tyler.
"Personality and Society." 7, no. 3 (1926): 157–163.

Marshall, John S.
"James Ward as Personal Idealist." 10, no. 3 (1929): 163–167.

Brown, Harold C.
"A Philosopher Looks at Psychology." 11, no. 2 (1930): 87–104.

Smith, Ethel Sabin.
"The Influence of Psychology upon Philosophy." 11, no. 2 (1930): 104–114.

Franz, Shepherd Ivory.
"Philosophies and Psychologies." 11, no. 2 (1930): 114–119

Carr, H. Wildon.
"Imagination and Reason." 12, no. 2 (1931): 81–91.

Adams, John.
"Herbart vs. Plato." 12, no. 3 (1931): 157–165.

[1933] **1037.** *Journal of Bible and Religion.*
Vol. 1–33; 1933–1965+.

 This journal includes scholarly articles on the full range of world religious traditions together with studies of the methodologies by which they are explored. Each issue contains major articles of general interest and importance and a lengthy book review section. Title changed to *Journal of the American Academy of Religion* in 1967.

[1937] **1038.** *Inward Light: Journal of the Friends Conference on Religion and Psychology.*
Vol. 1–68+; 1937–1965+.

 In September 1937, during the World Conference of Friends at Swarthmore, a small group met to exchange thoughts on meditation and worship, and agreed to keep in touch through an occasional bulletin, one of which was sent out by Howard Brinton. In July 1938, at the Pendle Hill summer session, a similar group met with Gerald Heard and Elined Kotschnig. The bulletin was revived, with a more definite plan and a quarterly publication schedule, edited by Erminie Huntress. The group proposed to cover the following ground: "the place of bodily training and health; the place of psychology and psycho-analysis; reviews of relevant books; questions about private meditation; questions about group worship; the economic form in which the 'beloved community' in our day might best express itself; the kind of service which such an integrated group would render the world in the present crisis of civilization." Erminie Huntress resigned as editor in 1944, and was replaced by Irene Pickard and Helen Buckler. Brinton, Heard, Kotschnig, and Fredrick J.

Tritton continued to serve on the editorial board. During the 1950s, the journal expressed its goal as follows: "Seeks to be an organ of expression and intercommunication among those concerned with cultivating the inner life and relating it to the problems of our time."

[1946] **1039.** *The Journal of Pastoral Care.*

Vol. 1–20+; 1946–1965+.

When the Institute of Pastoral Care merged with the Council for Clinical Training in 1950, *The Journal of Pastoral Care* absorbed *The Journal of Clinical Pastoral Work*, which had also begun publication in 1947. Publication was taken over by the Council for Clinical Training at that time. The original editorial board included Rollin J. Fairbanks, James H. Burns, Henry H. Wiesbauer (who was the original director of Boston's Pastoral Counseling Center in 1947), Charles M. Styron, Seward Hiltner, Vaughan Dabney, and David R. Hunter. The journal focuses on the application of psychology in ministry and features regular book reviews in the fields of personality theory and psychotherapy.

[1949] **1040.** *The American Scientific Affiliation Bulletin.*

Vol. 1–17+; 1949–1965+.

The bulletin became the *Journal of the American Affiliation* with Volume 2. The journal was dedicated to publishing articles dealing with a witness to the truth of the Scriptures and elucidating the relationship of both the ideology and fruits of science to that witness. Relevant articles include the following:

Beukema, M. J.
"Christian Treatment of the Mentally Ill." 2, no. 1 (1950): 28–37.

Marquart, Phillip B.
"Basic Anxiety and Academic Motivation." 2, no. 3 (1950): 1–6.

Howitt, John R.
"The Guilt Reaction (and Comments)." 3, no. 1 (1951): 10–19.

Marquart, Phillip B.
"More Than Five Senses." 5, no. 1 (1953): 12–14.

Peterson, Norvell L.
"The Psychological Implications of the New Birth." 6, no. 4 (1954): 10–12.

Marquart, Phillip B.
"The Biblical Psychology of Conviction." 7, no. 2 (1955): 13–16.

Rouch, Jon H.
"The Christian Physician and Faith Healing." 8, no. 2 (1956): 6–9.

Moberg, David O.
"Christian Sexual Mores and Contemporary Social Science." 8, no. 3 (1956): 5–10.

7. PROFESSIONALIZATION

Dilworth, R. P.
"Statistical Problems in Extrasensory Perception." 9, no. 2 (1957): 5—8.

Marquart, Phillip B.
"Extrasensory Perception." 9, no. 2 (1957): 8—10.

Moberg, David O.
"Christian Beliefs and Personal Adjustment to Old Age." 10, no. 1 (1958): 8—12.

Sullivan, Tandy.
"A Consideration of Sociological and Psychological Principles Used in Alcoholics Anonymous." 10, no. 4 (958): 4—7.

Sinclair, John C.
"Motivation." 10, no. 4 (1958): 4—7.

Sinclair, John C.
"The Mind/Brain Problem." 13, no. 3 (1961): 72—73.

Lindquist, Stanley, E.
"Psychology." 14, no. 2 (1962): 52—53.

Larson, F. Wilmer.
"Psychotherapy and the Patient's Ethical System." 14, no. 3 (1962): 82—83.

Fair, Donald C.
"Psychology and the Christian." 14, no. 4 (1962): 98—99.

Van Eyl, F. Phillip.
"Psychology as Science." 14, no. 4 (1962): 99—103.

Grounds, Vernon C.
"Christian Perspectives on Mental Illness." 14, no. 4 (1962): 108—113.

Busby, David F.
"Guilt." 14, no. 4 (1962): 113—116.

Walters, Orville S.
"The Dimensions of Psychiatry." 15, no. 1 (1963): 8.

Herje, Raymond R.
"Implications of Freudianism for American Social Work." 15, no. 1 (1963): 8—15.

Anderson, Clifford V.
"Group Effects on Value Change." 15, no. 1 (1963): 20—23.

Moberg, David O.
"Empirical Social Science and the Christian Faith." 16, no. 1 (1964): 20—26.

Finch, John.
"The Need for a New Approach in Psychology." 16, no. 4 (1964): 97—102.

Mecherikoff, Michael, and Walker, Eugene.
"The Need for a Better Understanding of Current Psychology: A Reply to Dr. Finch." 17, no. 2 (1965): 56—59.

[1950] **1041.** *Pastoral Psychology.*
Vol. 1−16+; 1950−1965+.

Pastoral Psychology focused especially on dynamic psychology and psychiatry and religion. Issues of the journal featured methods of pastoral counseling, personal advice for the minister as person, an integrative series exploring concretely the insights of pastoral psychology in relation to the offices of the church and its ministers, articles on major areas of pastoral counseling and special problem areas, an interprofessional series as well as a "consultation clinic," book reviews and notices of major events.

The original editorial board was headed by Simon Doniger, assisted by Oren Huling Baker, Daniel Blain, William Barnett Blakemore, John Sutherland Bonnell, Russell L. Dicks, Rollin J. Fairbanks, Lawrence K. Frank, Seward Hiltner, Molly Harrower, Paul E. Johnson, C. E. Crumholz, Halford E. Luccock, Rollo May, William C. Menninger, Wayne E. Oates, Carl R. Rogers, and Luther E. Woodward. The Pastoral Psychology Press took over publication in 1952, Meredith Publishing Company in 1966. Volume 12 in 1962 reprinted "A selected bibliography on Christian faith and health," compiled by Seward Hiltner for the 172nd General Assembly of the United Presbyterian Church. The January issues in 1954 and 1955 included a "Bibliography with reading course suggestions." January issues from 1956 through 1972 included an annual review of "Books in pastoral psychology." These articles were authored by Seward Hiltner, Wayne E. Oates, Samuel Southard, Thomas McDill, and Liston Mills. Issues from 1960 through 1972 also included listings of doctoral dissertations compiled by Helen Spaulding and later by Edward E. Thornton.

[1953] **1042.** *Christian Association for Psychological Studies: The Proceedings.*
Grand Rapids, Michigan, 1953−1974.

Topics of the Christian Association for Psychological Services conventions included the following: miscellaneous issues (1954, 32 pp.; 1955, 44 pp.; 1956, 69 pp.; 1957, 86 pp.); theories of personality (1958, 74 pp.); personality change (1959, 78 pp.); guilt in Christian perspective (1960, 71 pp.); the psychology of Christian conversion (1961, 112 pp.); the social-psychology of Christian nurture (1962, 70 pp.); understanding and helping teenagers and the married (1963, 106 pp.); the dynamics of forgiving (1964, 79 pp.); the dynamics of learning Christian concepts (1965, 107 pp.).

[1954] **1043.** *Journal of Psychotherapy as a Religious Process.*
Vol. 1−3; 1954−1956.

Published by the Institute for Rankian Psychoanalysis in Dayton, Ohio, the editor was William Rickel, with associate editor Doris Mode.

Prescott Vernon assisted in the editing of the first issue. Contributors to the three volumes were Fritz Künkel, Paul Tournier, Elizabeth Bowden Howes, Wilfried Daim, Aleck D. Dodd, Doris Mode, A. Aspiotis, William Rickel, Martha Jaeger, Igor A. Caruso, Alphonse Maeder, Beatrice Beebe, Charles Baudouin, Roberto Assagioli, Sheila Moon, and Beatrice Burch. The Articles of Incorporation of the Institute for Rankian Psychoanalysis, Inc. state that: "The basic point of view concerning human nature and the world, as understood by the Institute, is set forth *in part* in a book entitled "Beyond Psychology" and written by Otto Rank; and the Institute believes these insights to be in accord with the fundamental beliefs of the New Testament and particularly of the Letters of St. Paul."

[1961] **1044.** *Journal of Religion and Health.*
Vol. 1–5+; 1961–1965+.
Published in cooperation with the Institutes of Religion and Health, the *Journal of Religion and Health* is a quarterly for all who are interested in the indivisibility of human well-being: spiritual, physical, and emotional. The journal welcomes contributions from professional representatives of all religious faiths and all disciplines concerned with human health and well-being. Emphasis is on conceptual-theoretical and practical integration, with few empirical studies.

[1961] **1045.** *Journal for the Scientific Study of Religion.*
Vol. 1–21+; 1961–1965+.
This quarterly journal, the organ of the Society for the Scientific Study of Religion, features articles and research in the "psychology of religion" tradition. Includes sociological as well as psychological research with an empirical and experimental focus.

[1963] **1046.** *Insight: Quarterly Review of Religion and Mental Health.*
Vol. 1–3+; 1963–1965+.
Founded by Father Fintan McNamee, a Franciscan in the St. Louis Province, *Insight* focuses on the crossroads of psychology, phenomenology, psychiatry and theology, and features authors in the American Catholic tradition. Early contributors included Adrian Van Kaam, Carroll F. Tageson, Michael V. O'Brien, George Mora, John R. Cavanaugh, Alden Fischer, Robert P. Jacobs, E. Mark Stern, William Ellis, and Marygrace McCullough.

[1964] **1047.** *Envoy. Journal of Formative Reading.*
Vol. 1–19+; 1964–1982+.
Envoy is a monthly journal published by the Institute of Formative Spirituality at Duquesne University and edited by Adrian Van Kaam. It was founded at the motherhouse of the Franciscan Sisters in Millvale as a nonacademic, religious magazine dedicated to the spiritual renewal of

religious life. Each issue features articles on biblical and formative topics (most of them authored by Van Kaam), reader's pages including poetry, letters, and other reflections, and a "question of the month" section responding to questions asked at conferences and symposia and in letters. Responses to the latter are characterized by practical psychology-theology and are compiled by a team of religious consultants.

Indexes

Name Index

The Name Index lists all individuals mentioned in the Bibliography. This includes all authors, editors, and translators of the works cited, as well as individuals named in the annotations. The numbers in the Index refer to entry numbers, with the following exceptions: roman numerals refer to pages in the Preface and Acknowledgments, and arabic numerals preceded by "p." are page numbers referring to the Chapter introductions.

Cutten, George Barton, 20, 265, 278, 328, 405, 430
Cyprian, 617

d'Agnel, Arnaud, 37
D'Arcy, Paul F., 833
D'Isnernia, Richard, 887
Dabney, Vaughn, 1039
Daim, Wilfried, 630, 1043
Dalbiez, Roland, 37, 965
Danielou, Jean, 998
Daniels, Arthur H., 1031
Dare, Ernest, 137
Darwin, Charles, 45
Daub, Carl, 176
Davenport, Frederick Morgan, 403
Davies, Arthur Ernest, 862
Davies, John Dunn, 792
Davies, Sir John, 136
Davis, Andrew, 518
Davis, Ric., 122
Davis, Thomas Kirby, 152
Dawes, Lydia G., 896
Dawson, Christopher Henry, 1001.66, 1001.68
Dawson, George Ellsworth, 643, 1034
Day, Albert Edward, 243
Day, Clarence, 314
Dayhaw, Lawrence T., 1024
Dearmer, Percy, 515, 1012
de Baciocchi, J., 881
De Beauvoir, Simone, 118
De Burgh, William George, 1001.57
de Chardin, Pierre Teilhard, 362
Deconchy, Jean Pierre, 1008.03
De Corte, Marcel, 380
De Grazia, Sebastian, 873
De Greeff, Etiènne, 37, 380
De Jesus-Marie, Father Bruno, 380, 888
De Jongste, H., 606
De Kerlor, W., 280
De La Trinite, Philippe, 380
de la Vaissieré, Jules, 37, 767, 868
Delitzsch, Franz Julius, 178, 183, 187, 188
Dell, W. S., 974
Dellaert, Rene, 37
de Loosten, George, 235
Delp, Father Alfred, 362
Demal, Willibald, 573
Democritus, 157
De Montpellier, Bernard, 37

Dempsey, Peter J. R., 37, 781, 965
De Munnynck, Marc P., 37
De Niord, Richard S. J., 1032
Denison, Flora MacDonald, 1032
Denton, Wallace, 604
Denty, Vera, 1008.01
de Ste. Marie-Madeline, Pere Gabriel, 380
de Saint-Joseph, Lucien-Marie, 380
De Sanctis, Sante, 421
Descartes, René, 80, 136
Dessoir, Max, 21
De Tonquédec, J., 37
Deutsch, Albert, 29, 896
Devlin, William Joseph, 830, 887
Dewar, Lindsay, 224, 316, 440, 562, 565, 574
Dewey, John, 30, 35, 157, 950, 1001.44, 1002.03
De Wolf, L. Harold, 550
Dickerson, Roy E., 679
Dicks, G. H., 469
Dicks, Russell Leslie, 564, 580, 604, 620, 811, 1041
Dickson, James, 239
Digby, Kenelm, 136
Dillon, Donald J., 1024
Dilthey, Wilhelm, 110, 275, 630
Dilworth, R. P., 1040
Dimond, Sydney George, 315, 428
Dittes, James E., 9, 598, 604, 699, 1026
Dix, G. H., 469
Dixon, James Main, 239
Dixon, William MacNeile, 1001.54
Dobbelstein, Hermann, 582
Doberstein, Helen, 773
Doberstein, John, 773
Dodd, Aleck D., 1043
Dodds, Eric Robertson, 458
Dodwell, Henry, 136
Dolto, Francoise, 380
Dominian, Jacob, 915
Donceel, Joseph F., 793, 834
Doniger, Simon, 550, 589, 819, 875
Donnelly, Dorothy, 901
Donnelly, Harold Irwin, 664
Dosseter, R. F., 1005
Dougall, Lily, 95, 154
Douglas, Bryan, 283
Douglas, H. Paul, 1027
Douglas, William, 598
Dowd, Mary Amadeus, 1003.10
Dowie, John Alexander, 261

Name Index

Doyle, Charles L., 887, 1024
Doyle, Thomas L., 887
Drakeford, John W., 173, 597
Draper, Edgar, 620
Draper, George, 607
Dreissen, Josef, 510
Dresser, Horatio Willis, 140, 307, 513, 518, 525
Drew, Samuel, 124
Driesch, Hans Adolf Eduard, 58, 59, 158
Dring, Thomas, 122
Driscoll, John Thomas, 141
Druitt, Basil, 665
Du Buy, Jean, 1034
Dubois, Paul, 523
Ducker, E. N., 636, 637
Duffey, Felix D., 772, 898
Duhamel, Joseph S., 887
Duncan-Johnstone, L. A., 1005
Dunlap, Knight, 242, 336, 723
Durkheim, Emil, 357
Duynstee, W.J.A.J., 780
Dworak, Kazimierz, 37
Dybowski, Mieczyslaw, 37

Ebaugh, Franklin G., 1014
Ebbinghaus, Hermann, 110
Ecker, Paul J., 887
Eddington, Sir Arthur Stanley, 1001.42
Eddy, Mary Baker, 261, 518, 525, 526, 532, 555
Edgerton, Walter, 712
Edward, Kenneth, 429
Edwards, James, 837
Edwards, Jonathan, 30, 35, 362, 395, 403, 453
Edwards, Richard, 124
Ehrenfels, Christian von, 281, 343
Eiselen, Frederick C., 656
Eiselen-Lewis-Downey, 213
Eisenbud, J., 337
Eister, Allan, 1025
Eitzen, David D., 580
Elder, James Lyn, 597
Eliade, Mircea, 998
Elijah, 206
Ellenberger, Henri F., 15
Ellerbeck, J.P.W., 37
Ellicot, 187, 188
Elliott, Harrison, 295
Elliott, Robert E., 580

Ellis, Charles Calvert, 728
Ellis, Havelock, 398
Ellis, R. S., 1034
Ellis, William, 1046
Embree, Edwin Rogers, 533
Embry, Joe, 827
Emmet, C. W., 60, 95, 154
England, Frederick Ernest, 443
English, O. Spurgeon, 589
Entralgo, Pedro Lain, 34, 901
Epps, John, 705
Ericksen, Ephraim Edward, 287
Erickson, Erik Homburger, 23, 362, 938, 951
Eschenmayer, C. A. von, 176
Espinosa, Aurelia M., Jr., 34
Estabrooks, George Hoben, 337
Ettlinger, Max, 37
Eucken, Rudolf, 96, 105, 924; p. 27
Evans, Erastus, 601, 790, 800
Evans, Warren Felt, 512, 518
Eve, 225
Everett, Charles Carroll, 260
Ewalt, Jack, 916
Ewing, J. Franklin, 887
Ey, Henry, 23
Eymieu, Antonin, 37, 735
Ezekiel, 206, 228

Faber, Heije, 608
Fabre, Jean Henri, 37
Fair, Donald C., 1040
Fairbairn, Andrew Martin, 1001.14
Fairbairn, W.R.D., 936
Fairbanks, Rollin J., 1039
Fairweather, Paul, 1030
Fallow, Wesner, 589
Faraon, Michael J., 340
Farmer, Herbert Henry, 1001.71
Farnell, Lewis Richard, 1001.31, 1001.37
Farnsworth, Dana L., 908
Farrer, Austin Marsden, 1001.78
Faunce, Daniel Worchester, 396
Fauville, Arthur, 37
Fay, Jay Wharton, 30
Fechner, Gustav Theodor, 23, 125, 266, 343, 483
Federn, Paul, 23
Feely, O. Floyd, 580
Feinsilver, Alexander, 634
Felix, Richard W., 466

Name Index

Woodward, Luther E., 586, 875, 1041
Woodward, Thomas Best, 180
Woodworth, Robert Sessions, 35
Woolcott, Phillip, 1026
Woolf, L., 283, 958
Woolf, Virginia, 283, 958
Woolman, John, 362
Woolner, Henry, 136
Woolston, H. B., 1031
Worcester, Elwood, 266, 514, 531, 534, 1011
Wordsworth, William, 979
Worthington, Jack A., 571
Wright, Emily Dudley, 234
Wright, Georg Hendrik von, 1001.80, 1001.81
Wright, J. Stafford, 348
Wundt, Wilhelm, 61, 414, 552
Wurst, T., 124
Wyckoff, Albert Clarke, 491
Wythe, Joseph Henry, 55

Yahweh, 218
Yeaxlee, Basil Alfred, 678
Yellowlees, David, 742
Yocum, A. Duncan, 738
Young, Richard K., 597, 600, 604
Yountz, H. A., p. 27

Zaccheus, 203, 248
Zahniser, Charles Reed, 566, 572
Zavalloni, Roberto, 884
Zegers, Richard T., 1024
Zeligs, Dorothy F., 943
Ziegler, Jesse H., 700
Zilboorg, Gregory, 28, 30, 887, 901, 902, 948, 968
Zilboorg, M. S., 948
Zimmer, Heinrich, 998
Zimmer, Henry R., 1005
Zweig, Stefan, 532

Institution Index

This index gives access to the numerous institutions, organizations, and lecture-ships mentioned in this Bibliography. The numbers refer to entry numbers, with the following exceptions: roman numerals refer to pages in the Preface and Acknowledgments, and arabic numerals preceded by "p." are page numbers referring to the Chapter introductions.

Aberdeen, University of, 84, 117, 190, 1001
Academy of Religion and Mental Health, 6, 385, 1007, 1029
Alcoholics Anonymous, 592, 1040
Alfred Theological Seminary, 745
All Soul's Search, 906
American Academy of Religion, The, 1010, 1025
American Catholic Psychological Association, The, 359, 1024
American Jewish Committee, 377
American Philosophical Society, 331
American Psychological Association, 3, 93, 1024, 1025
American Scientific Affiliation, The, 1020
American Society for Psychical Research, 276
American Theological Library Association, 214
American Tract Society, 49
Anderson College, 347

Andover Newton Theological Seminary, 94, 182
Anglican Church, 1012
Anglican Evangelical Group Movement, 472
Anglican Fellowship, 729
Anglican Theological College of Melbourne, 593
Armstrong College, 322
Auburn Lectures, 813
Auburn Theological Seminary, 190
Augustinian University of Villanova, 812

Baird Lectures, 422
Bampton Divinity Lectures, 82, 809
Bangor Diocese, 200
Bangor University College, 212
Basel, University of, 177
Baylor University, 610
Belfast, University of, 458
Beloit College, 832

Title Index

The Title Index provides a single alphabetical listing of all books, monographs, psychological tests, and journals that are cited in this Bibliography. For foreign works, the titles of both the original edition and any published English translation are provided. Numbers in this Index refer to entry numbers, with the following exceptions: roman numerals refer to pages in the Preface and Acknowledgments, and arabic numerals preceded by "p." are page numbers referring to the Chapter introductions.

Title Index

Development of the Idea of God in the Catholic Child, The, 687
Diagnosis and Spiritual Healing, 530
Dictionary of Pastoral Psychology, A, 4
Dictionary of Philosophy, p. 27
Dictionary of Philosophy and Psychology, 1
Didascalia, 616
Die Atombombe und die Zukunft des Menschen, 896
Die Entwicklung des Christus Dogmas, 241
Die Gestalt des Satans im Alten Testament, 215
Die Hauptrichtungen der gegenwärtigen Psychologie, 25
Die Heilung durch den Geist, 532
Die Lehre von der Seelsorge, 571
Die psychiatrische Beurteilung Jesu, 235
Die psychoanalytische Methode, 922
Die Stellung des Menschen im Kosmos, 68
Die Tiefenpsychologie hilft dem Seelsorger, 587
Die tiefenpsychologischen Schulen, 23
Die Zukunft einer Illusion, 959
Dietetics of the Soul, The, 126
Differentiation of the Religious Consciousness, The, 263
Dimension of Future in Our Faith, The, 510
Dimensions of Character, 691
Discovery of the Unconscious, 15
Disease and Remedy of Sin, The, 371
Disorders of the Emotional and Spiritual Life, 387
Divine Law of Cure, 512
Divine Pedigree of Man, The, 257
Divine Personality and Human Life, 1001.30
Doctor and the Soul, The, 165
Doctor's Casebook in the Light of the Bible, 578
Dogma and Compulsion, 926
Dogma of Christ, The, 241
Dogma und Zwangsidee, 926
Domain of Natural Science, The, 1001.35
Dramatic Personality of Jesus, The, 242
Driving Forces of Human Nature, The, 776

Ecclesiastical Review, x
Effect of Reading on Moral Conduct and

Emotional Experience, The, 1003.08
Ein moderner Mythus, 992
Ein Psychologe erlebt des konzentration Lager, 894
Elementary Christian Psychology, An, 192
Elements of Mental and Moral Philosophy, The, 706
El Secreto do los Buenos, 944
Emergent Evolution, 1001.36
Emotional Plague of Mankind, The, 247
Emotional Problems and the Bible, 632
Emotions, 49
Emotions and Morals, 872
Empirical Argument for God in Late British Thought, The, 114
Empirical Psychology, 12
Empirical Study of Moral Problems and Character Traits of High School Pupils, An, 1003.08
Enquiry into the Nature of the Human Soul, An, 123
Envoy, Journal of Formative Reading, 1047
Epistle of James, 229
Eranos Yearbooks, 998, 1006.07
Erinnerungen Träume Gedanken, 996
Eros and Evil, 358
Errors of Psychotherapy, 873
Escape from Authority, 946
Escape from Freedom, 499, 809
Escape from Loneliness, 769
Essai sur les Fondements de la Connaissance Mystique, 397
Essay on the Bases of the Mystic Knowledge, 397
Essay on the Immateriality and Immortality of the Human Soul, An, 124
Essays in Applied Psychoanalysis, 933
Essays on a Science of Mythology, 1006.02
Esoteric Christianity and Mental Therapeutics, 512
Esprit, 112
Esprits et Mediums, 519
Esquisse d'une Philosophie de la Religion d'après la Psychologie et l'Historie, 256
Essentials in the Development of Religion, 109
Eternal Life, The, 147
Ethics for Unbelievers, 963
Études sur la Psychologie des Mystiques, 423
Evolution of Modern Psychology, The, 25

Title Index

Greek Hero Cults and Ideas of
    Immortality, 1001.31
Group Dynamics in the Religious Life,
    365
Growing a Christian Personality, 689
Growth of the Soul, The, 144
Grundprobleme der Psychologie, 158
Guiding Individual Growth, 671
Guild of Pastoral Psychology Lectures,
    790, 1005
Guilt, 843
Guilt and Grace, 856
Guilt, Its Meaning, and Significance, 859
Guilt: Where Psychology and Religion
    Meet, 860

Handbook of Christian Psychology, A, 193
Harvard College Books in Psychology, 275
Hazen Pamphlet, 628
Healing, 550
Healing in the Name of Jesus, 1019
Healing of Souls, The, 622
Healing Power of Faith, The, 551
Health for Mind and Spirit, 326
Heart and Spirit, 319
Heiligkeit und Gesundheit, 977
Helping Hand, 745
Heredity and Christian Problems, 230
Hero with a Thousand Faces, The,
    980, 1006.01
Heroic Sanctity and Insanity, 552
Het Pastorale Gesprek, 608
Het Zielsbegrip in de Metaphysische en in
    de Empirische Psychologie, 168
Hibbert Journal, x, 361, 1033
Hidden Face: A Study of St. Thérèse of
    Lisieux, The, 450
Historian's Approach to Religion, An,
    1001.73
Historie de la Philosophie, 17
History and Eschatology, 1001.75
History of American Psychology, 35, 127
History of Medical Psychology, A, 31
History of Psychology, A, 22
History of Psychology and Psychiatry, 39
History of Psychology from the Standpoint
    of a Thomist, 32
History of the Cure of Souls, A, 546
History of the Problems of Philosophy, A,
    17

History of the Warfare of Science with
    Theology in Christendom, A, 18
Holiness Is Wholeness, 977
Holy Images, 1001.59
Holy Spirit and Modern Thought, The, 224
Hope, Reflections of an Optimist, 732
Horae Phrenologicae, 705
How Character Develops: A Psychological
    Interpretation, 679
How Religion Arises, 253
How to Preach to People's Needs, 478
Human Destiny and the New Psychology,
    726
Human Immortality, 142
Human Intellect, The, 133
Human Kingdom, The, 820
Human Nature under God, 384
Human Problems of the Minister, The, 599
Human Situation, The, 1001.54

I and Thou, 727
Ich und Du, 727
Idea of God In Protestant Religious
    Education, The, 662
Idea of God in the Light of Recent
    Philosophy, The, 1001.25
Idea of God Test, 682, 687
Idea of Immortality, The, 1001.33
Idea of the Development of the Soul in
    Medieval Jewish Philosophy, The, 167
Idea of the Holy, The, 414
Idea of the Soul, The, 148, 157
Idealism as a Philosophical Doctrine, 100
Idealism as a Philosophy, 100
Ideals of Religion, 1001.60
Ideas of God and Conduct, 682
Illusion and Anxiety, 855
Illustrations of the Influence of the Mind
    upon the Body in Health and Disease, 50
Image and the Idol, The, 362
Images of Hope, 831
Imagination: Its Uses and Abuses, The, 49
Imagination and Religion, 316, 427
Imago, 955
Immortality, 60, 154
Imperialistic Religion and the Religion of
    Democracy, 418
In Search of a Soul, 140
In Search of Maturity, 681
In Search of Religious Maturity, 634
Indispensable Soul, The, 161

347

Title Index

Title Index

Lehrbuch der Storungen des
Seelenlebens, 10
Leib und Seele, 59
Le Mystere de l'Etre, 1001.69
Le Origines de la Psychologie
Contemporaine, 19
Le Peche, 881
Le Personnage et la Personne, 797
Le Secret, 827
Les Forts et les Faibles, 777
Les Juenes et la Foi, 696
Les Medications Psychologiques, 523
Les Religions d'Authorité et la Religion
de l'Esprit, 258
Les Saisons de la Vie, 816
L'Hygiène Mentale et les Principes
Chretiens, 789
Library of Genetic Science and
Philosophy, 862
Lichaam-Ziel-Geest:, 80
Life against Death, 939
Life, Faith, and Prayer, 345
Life in Christ, 182
Life, Mind, and Spirit, 65, 1001.38
Life of Man with God, The, 477
Literature of Theology, 183
Little Book of Life after Death, The, 125
Living God, The, 1001.51
Living Word, The, 266
Logotherapy and the Christian Faith, 817
Look at Psychiatry, A, 910
Love against Hate, 758, 768
Love or Constraint, 695
Lumen Vitae, 1008.03
Lumen Vitae Studies in Religious
Psychology, 1008, 1008.01, 1008.02

Magic and Religion, 352
Making Life Better, 534
Malleus Maleficorum, 28
Man above Humanity, 36
Man against Himself, 758
Man and God, 440
Man and His Relations, 47
Man and Transformation, 998
Man: Divine or Social, 355
Man: His Making and Unmaking, 734
Manifeste au Service du Personnalisme,
112
Man in Conflict, 229

Man in Estrangement, 953
Man in the Process of Time, 348
Man, Morals, and Society, 962
Man on His Nature, 764, 1001.61
Manual of Pastoral Psychology, A, 562
Man, Real, and Ideal, 331
Man's Need and God's Action, 786
Man's Right to Be Human, 385
Man's Place in God's World, 895
Man's Place in Nature, 68
Man's Search for Himself, 115, 935
Man's Search for Meaning, 894
Manuals of Catholic Philosophy, 716
Marquette Monographs on Educations,
648
Masculine in Religion, The, 264
Masks of God, The, 940
Masks of God: Primitive Mythology, The,
940
Masks of God: Oriental Mythology, The,
940
Mastery of Sex through Psychology and
Religion, The, 866
Matter and Spirit, 61
Matter, Life, Mind, and God, 98
Meaning of Anxiety, The, 841
Meaning of Persons, The, 797
Meaning of Sacrifice, The, 960
Measure Religion, 676
Measurements of Attitude, The, 308
Measurement of the Comprehension
Difficulty of the Precepts and Parables of
Jesus, 1004.01
Measuring Certain Aspects of Faith in
God, 664
Medical Man and the Witch during the
Renaissance, The, 28
Medicine, Magic, and Religion, 529
Memories, Dreams, Reflections, 996
Menace of the New Psychology, The, 760
Mental Healers, 532
Mental Health and Religious Faith, 918
Mental Health in a Mad World, 787
Mental Health through Christian
Community, 920
Mental Hygiene and Christian Principles,
789
Mental Illness and the Religious Life, 389
Mental Medicine, 512, 516
Mental Pain and the Cure of Souls, 936

349

Nature of the Physical World, The, 1001.42

Natural History of Religious Feeling, The, 407

Natural Order of Spirit, The, 276

Need to Believe, The, 504

Nervous Christians, 799

Nervous Disorders and Character, 683

Nervous Disorders and Religion, 117

Neurosis and Sacraments, 378

Neurosis in the Light of Rational Psychology, The, 780

Neurotics in the Church, 826

New Atavar and the Destiny of the Soul, 149

New Christian Advocate, The, 580

New Concepts of Healing, 549

New Group Therapy, The, 889

New Jerusalem Magazine, 249

New Psychic Studies in Their Relation to Christian Thought, The, 715

New Psychology and Its Relation to Life, The, 925

New Psychology and Old Religion, 748

New Psychology and Religious Experience, The, 439

New Psychology and the Bible, The, 204

New Psychology and the Christian Faith, The, 737

New Psychology and the Hebrew Prophets, The, 205

New Psychology and the Parent, The, 465

New Psychology and the Preacher, The, 465

New Psychology and the Teacher, The, 465

New Psychology, Behaviorism, and Christian Experience, 745

New Psychology: How It Aids and Interests, The, 735

New Republic, The, 374

New Studies in Mystical Religion, 431

Newman on the Psychology of Faith in the Individual, 494

Nineteenth Century Miracles, 15

No Escape from Life, 853

Norm and Action, 1001.80

Observations on the Influence of Religion upon the Health and Physical Welfare of Mankind, 366, 707

Occasional Essays in Theology, 968

Old Testament and Modern Problems in Psychology, The, 207

On Life after Death, 125

On Selfhood and Godhood, 120, 1001.76

Open Court, The, 146

Oriental Mythology, 940

Origins and History of Consciousness, The, 982, 1006.06

Origins of Contemporary Psychology, The, 19

Origins of European Thought about the Body, the Mind, the Soul, the World, Time and Fate, The, 78

Origins of Primitive Beliefs, The, 357

Our Minds and Their Bodies, 64

Out of the Depths, 386

Outlines of a Philosophy of Religion, 256

Outlines of Biblical Psychology, 177

Outlines of the History of Psychology, 21

Outlines of the Psychology of Religion, 307

Pacific Philosophical Quarterly, 1036

Pagan and Christian in an Age of Anxiety, 458

Pastor, The, 580

Pastor as Counselor, The 617

Pastor and His People, The, 615

Pastoral Care and Psychotherapy, 911

Pastoral Care in a Changing World, 601

Pastoral Care in Historical Perspective, 617

Pastoral Care in the Church, 616

Pastoral Care of the Mentally Ill, The, 613

Pastoral Care of the Sick, 556

Pastoral Counseling, 576, 579, 583

Pastoral Psychiatry, 573, 892

Pastoral Psychiatry and Mental Health, 891

Pastoral Psychology, xi, 545, 550, 563, 577, 604, 819, 875, 1026, 1041

Pastoral Psychology Series, 589

Pathological Aspects of Religions, 369

Peace of Mind, 896

Pedagogical Seminary, 642

Person Reborn, The, 626

Person or the Significance of Man, The, 119

Personal Mental Hygiene, 771

Personal Realism, 113

Personale Seelsorge, 989

Personalist Manifesto, A, 112

351

Psychology and Sacraments, 473
Psychology and the Catholic Teacher, 651
Psychology and the Child, 672
Psychology and the Christian Day-School, 649
Psychology and the Christian Life, 285
Psychology and the Church, 469
Psychology and the Cross, 222
Psychology and the Franciscan School, 26
Psychology and Theology, 251
Psychology and the Parish Priest, 574
Psychology and the Promethean Will, 164
Psychology and the Religious Quest, 324
Psychology and the Soul, 160
Psychology and the Teaching Church, 700
Psychology and Worship, 476
Psychology: Empirical and Rational, 716
Psychology. Faith Learning Series, 1009.01
Psychology for Bible Teachers, 650
Psychology for Christian Teachers, 675
Psychology for Ministers and Social Workers, 575
Psychology for Pastor and People, 540
Psychology for Preaching, A, 478
Psychology for Priests, 588
Psychology for Religious Workers, 562
Psychology for Religious and Social Workers, 561
Psychology in Search of a Soul, 173
Psychology in Service of the Soul, 560
Psychology, Morality, and Education, 588
Psychology of Alcoholism, 405
Psychology of Belief, The, 484, 497
Psychology of Character with a Survey of Temperament, The, 24
Psychology of Christ, The, 234
Psychology of Christian Faith, The, 301
Psychology of Christian Conversion, The, 455
Psychology of Christian Life and Behavior, The, 288
Psychology of Christian Personality, The, 751, 1018.01
Psychology of Conversion, The, 441, 451
Psychology of Conviction, The, 488
Psychology of Counseling, The, 635
Psychology of Inspiration, 199
Psychology of Jesus, The, 232
Psychology of Learning and Teaching Christian Education, 694

Psychology of Loving, The, 941
Psychology of Methodism, The, 315
Psychology of Pastoral Care, 585
Psychology of Prayer, The, 461, 462
Psychology of Preaching and Pastoral Work, The, 475
Psychology of Prophecy, 198
Psychology of Religion: A Guide to Information Sources, ix
Psychology of Religion, The, 196, 277, 291, 298, 321, 335, 341, 350, 398, 933
Psychology of Religion and Its Application in Preaching and Teaching, The, 722
Psychology of Religious Experience, 424
Psychology of Saint Teresa of the Child Jesus, 302
Psychology of the Moral Self, 83
Psychology of the Religious Life, 271
Psychology of Religious Adjustment, The, 306
Psychology of Religious Awakening, The, 434
Psychology of Religious Belief, The, 481
Psychology of Religious Certainty, The, 495
Psychology of Religious Experience, The, 406, 425, 459
Psychology of Religious Living, The, 323
Psychology of Religious Prophecy, The, 214
Psychology of Religious Sects, The, 273
Psychology of Saint Albert the Great Compared with That of St. Thomas, The, 27
Psychology of St. Bonaventure and St. Thomas Aquinas, The, 757
Psychology of St. Thomas Aquinas and Divine Revelation, The, 496
Psychology of Sartre, The, 781
Psychology of the Christian Life, The, 185, 274
Psychology of the Christian Soul, The, 150
Psychology of the Future, The, 280
Psychology of the Interior Senses, The, 767
Psychology of the Methodist Revivals, The, 428
Psychology of the New Testament, The, 187
Psychology of the Suffering Mind, The, 216
Psychology of Unbelief, The, 501
Psychology of Worship, The, 472

Title Index

Subject Index

The Subject Index provides a more detailed means of access to the individual entries, acting as an alternative classification system to the thematic organization used in the Bibliography itself. Major theological and psychological theories and movements are included, as are specific topics and concepts. The numbers in the Index refer to entry numbers, with the following exceptions: roman numerals refer to pages in the Preface and Acknowledgments, and arabic numerals preceded by "p." are page numbers referring to the Chapter introductions.